CW01370715

THE ROYAL CHARTERS
OF JERSEY, 1341–1687

THE ROYAL CHARTERS
OF JERSEY, 1341–1687

Tim Thornton

THE BOYDELL PRESS

© Tim Thornton and the Jersey Legal Information Board 2024

All Rights Reserved. Except as permitted under current legislation no part of this work may be photocopied, stored in a retrieval system, published, performed in public, adapted, broadcast, transmitted, recorded or reproduced in any form or by any means, without the prior permission of the copyright owner

The right of Tim Thornton and the Jersey Legal Information Board to be identified as the authors of this work has been asserted in accordance with sections 77 and 78 of the Copyright, Designs and Patents Act 1988

First published 2024
The Boydell Press, Woodbridge

ISBN 978 1 83765 121 4

The Boydell Press is an imprint of Boydell & Brewer Ltd
PO Box 9, Woodbridge, Suffolk IP12 3DF, UK
and of Boydell & Brewer Inc.
668 Mt Hope Avenue, Rochester, NY 14620–2731, USA
website: www.boydellandbrewer.com

A CIP catalogue record for this book is available
from the British Library

The publisher has no responsibility for the continued existence or accuracy of URLs for external or third-party internet websites referred to in this book, and does not guarantee that any content on such websites is, or will remain, accurate or appropriate

CONTENTS

List of Plates   vi
Acknowledgements   vii
Abbreviations   ix
Timeline   x
Glossary   xii
Foreword by Sir Timothy Le Cocq KC, Bailiff of Jersey   xiii

Introduction   1
Edward III: 1341   5
Richard II: 1378 and 1394   13
Henry IV: 1400   23
Henry V: 1414   31
Henry VI: 1442   37
Edward IV: 1469   47
Richard III: 1483   59
Henry VII: 1486   67
Henry VIII: 1510   77
Edward VI: 1548   85
Elizabeth I: 1562   101
James I: 1604   117
Charles I: 1627   139
Charles II: 1662   159
James II: 1687   187

Postscript   215
Bibliography   219
Index   233

PLATES

1.	The Royal Charter of Edward III, 1341	4
2.	The Royal Charter of Richard II, 1378	13
3.	The Royal Charter of Richard II, 1394	13
4.	The Royal Charter of Henry IV, 1400	23
5.	The Royal Charter of Henry V, 1414	30
6.	The Royal Charter of Henry VI, 1442	36
7.	The Royal Charter of Edward IV, 1469	46
8.	The Royal Charter of Richard III, 1483	58
9.	The Royal Charter of Henry VII, 1486	66
10.	The Royal Charter of Henry VIII, 1510	76
11 (i–ii).	The Royal Charter of Edward VI, 1548	86–7
12 (i–ii).	The Royal Charter of Elizabeth I, 1562	102–3
13 (i–vi).	The Royal Charter of James I, 1604	118–23
14 (i–v).	The Royal Charter of Charles I, 1627	139–43
15 (i–v).	The Royal Charter of Charles II, 1662	160–67
16 (i–v).	The Royal Charter of James II, 1687	188–96

ACKNOWLEDGEMENTS

A particular pleasure of the project to produce this work has been the extent of the positive support and encouragement that I have received along the way. This is a topic that brings together a range of individuals and groups who are enthusiastic about the value of the insights that this history brings.

I am very grateful for the support of successive bailiffs of Jersey and especially to Sir Philip Bailhache. I am also grateful for the support of the law officers and their team in the Civil Division of the Law Officers' Department (especially Matt Berry), who have been advocates both for this project and the imperative to understand the charters in their modern context. The support and proactive engagement of the Jersey Legal Information Board has been vital to the work; their programme director, Marcus Ferbrache, has been particularly generous with his advice and insight.

My work has been made more straightforward by librarians and archivists, including those at the Jersey Archive, St Helier; Lord Coutanche Library, Société Jersiaise, St Helier; Jersey Public Library; Island Archive Service, St Peter Port, Guernsey (especially Dr Darryl Ogier); Brotherton Library, University of Leeds; my own colleagues in the University Library in Huddersfield; and HM Greffier in Guernsey, Jon Torode, and his predecessor Ken Tough, and their staff, especially Keith Robilliard and Steven Payne.

The staff of The National Archives of the United Kingdom at Kew have been consistently helpful, notably Dr Sean Cunningham, Head of Medieval Records, and Paul Johnson, Image Library Manager. I am grateful for the permission of The National Archives to use the images of the royal charters that appear here.

I have also been generously assisted by members of the legal profession in Jersey and in Guernsey, in particular Dr John Kelleher of Carey Olsen and Gordon Dawes of Mourant Ozannes.

I have been consistently fortunate in the support of colleagues at the University of Huddersfield, especially the Vice-Chancellor Professor Bob Cryan, and also my fellow historians and others in the School of Arts and Humanities.

The most important acknowledgements, however, are the most personal: the love and support of my wife Sue Johns, and our children Carys and Gwyn, have been a constant factor in whatever I have done.

Errors and omissions remain my own responsibility.

ABBREVIATIONS

ABSJ	*Annual Bulletin of the Société Jersiaise / Bulletin Annuel de la Société Jersiaise*
BL	London, British Library
CCR	*Calendar of the Close Rolls Preserved in the Public Record Office* (London, 1892–)
CFR	*Calendar of the Fine Rolls Preserved in the Public Record Office* (London, 1911–)
CPR	*Calendar of the Patent Rolls Preserved in the Public Record Office* (London, 1891–)
CSPD	*Calendar of State Papers, Domestic Series*, ed. Mary Anne Everett Green [et al.] (London, 1856–).
JA	St Helier, Jersey, Jersey Archive
ODNB	H. C. G. Matthew and Brian Harrison (eds), *Oxford Dictionary of National Biography* (61 vols, Oxford, 2004)
Prison Board	Papers Connected with the Privy Council's Consideration of the Jersey Prison Board Case (3 vols, printed but not published; [London], 1891–94)
TNA	Kew, The National Archives of the United Kingdom

TIMELINE

Normans
William I	1066–87
William II	1087–1100
Henry I	1100–35
Stephen	1135–54
Empress Matilda	1141

Plantagenets
Henry II	1154–89	
Richard I	1189–99	
John	1199–1216	
Henry III	1216–72	
Edward I	1272–1307	
Edward II	1307–27	
Edward III	1327–77	Charter 1341
Richard II	1377–99	Charters 1378; 1394

House of Lancaster
Henry IV	1399–1413	Charter 1400
Henry V	1413–22	Charter 1414
Henry VI	1422–61	Charter 1442

House of York
Edward IV	1461–83	Charter 1469
Edward V	1483	
Richard III	1483–85	Charter 1484

Tudors

Henry VII	1485–1509	Charter 1486
Henry VIII	1509–47	Charter 1510
Edward VI	1547–53	Charter 1549
Jane Grey	1553	
Mary I	1553–58	
Elizabeth I	1558–1603	Charter 1562

Stuarts

| James I | 1603–25 | Charter 1604 |
| Charles I | 1625–49 | Charter 1628 |

Commonwealth

| Oliver Cromwell | 1649–58 |
| Richard Cromwell | 1658–59 |

Stuarts (restored)

| Charles II | 1660–85 | Charter 1662 |
| James II | 1685–88 | Charter 1687 |

GLOSSARY

assizes sittings of justices, setting up courts and summoning juries
bailli the king's administrative representative during the ancien régime in northern France
bailiff senior justice in Jersey and Guernsey, after the cessation of visits of justices in eyre; with the jurats constituted the Royal Court
extente assessment on land
eyre a circuit travelled by an itinerant justice (a justice in eyre), or the circuit court over which they presided
fossage service of maintaining ditches of castle or town, or payment in lieu
hanaper the office of the clerk in the English king's Chancery responsible for the fees paid for the issue of documents under the Great Seal
jurat after the cessation of visits of justices in eyre, a lay juror / justice; all judgements were rendered and all fines assessed by them, and, with the bailiff, the jurats constituted the Royal Court
livres/sols/deniers in the monetary system of the Channel Islands in the middle ages, the livre tournois was worth 20 sols, and each sol was worth 12 deniers; these were often abbreviated as l/s/d
murage toll or tax levied for the erection, maintenance, or repair of town walls
panage fee for pasturage (as a translation of pan(n)agium; an alternative reading of this might be 'pauagium', a tax for paving roads)
Patent Rolls English royal administrative record of the grants made by the monarch in the form of an open letter
pontage bridge-toll or tax for bridge repairs
quo warranto a prerogative writ requiring the person to whom it is directed to show by what authority they exercise some right, power, or franchise
seigneur lord, especially in a feudal context
staple (especially the Calais staple) market, or market town, especially with official royal sanction; the Calais wool staple was the staple through which all English wool exports had to be directed from the mid-fourteenth century
tallage tax levied on feudal dependents by their superiors
warden official entrusted with the government of the Channel Islands, often as a subordinate to a Lord of the Isles

FOREWORD

It gives me great pleasure to write the foreword to this book and to introduce the author.

I am confident that this book will be of interest to many people in the Island who wish to better understand the development not only of our unique legal system, but also of Jersey's autonomy and system of Government. As the contents reflect, Jersey's autonomy, and the rights and privileges that it was built on through the developments in the Charters, were not simply gifts from the Crown. As exemplified in the Charter of Charles II, the rights and privileges contained in the Charters were earned, considering '*how courageously and loyally the said islanders and inhabitants have behaved themselves in our own and in our progenitors' service, and considering what great detriments, losses and dangers they have sustained.*' The story of the Charters is then the story of the challenges that were overcome, and sacrifices that were made, to forge Jersey's independent identity.

I hope that it will become a text which is regularly referenced by scholars, lawyers, judges and anyone with an interest in, not only the historical relationship between the Crown and Jersey, but also its evolution and the relevance of the Royal Charters today.

As some readers of this book will be aware, Jersey has had the benefit of greater access to the Charter documents in recent years. The Royal Charters were granted by sixteen English (and subsequently British) Sovereigns from Edward III in 1341 to James II in 1687. In view of the importance of the Charters to Jersey's constitutional position, the Law Officers commissioned the preparation of authoritative translations of all the Royal Charters, which were prepared by the author of this book. To commemorate the 250th Anniversary of the Code of 1771 and to make accessible this important source of Jersey's ancient constitutional rights, these translations have in recent years been published on the Jersey Legal Information Board's website. The Charters are presented there in a tabular form, with the original Latin or Anglo-Norman French text in a left-hand column and a translation into English in the right-hand column for ease of reference.

This book includes a photo of each of the manuscripts, the originals of which are kept at the National Archives at Kew, and which are produced by their kind permission. There is a translation of each of the Charters along with a timeline for the monarchs and a glossary of terms.

The Charters granted various rights to islanders, including the right for the people of Jersey to be governed by their own laws and adjudicated on by their own courts. They also exempted islanders from all forms of tributes or taxation and import duties on exports of Jersey goods to England (and latterly Great Britain) except in extreme circumstances, such as the Monarch personally being taken prisoner. The confirmation of these rights is foundational to the economic and legal independence that Jersey has now enjoyed for many centuries. This book provides the historical context for each of the Charters and vital insights into the purpose behind the confirmation of rights. These matters remain of importance to all Islanders since the Charters have continuing legal force.

The legal force of the Charters derives in part from the incorporation of the rights conferred into other constitutional documents or enactments in the intervening period. For example, the Code of Laws of 1771 – which is an Order in Council and central feature of Jersey's constitution – states expressly that Orders, Warrants and Letters of any nature shall not be executed in Jersey if they are presented to the Royal Court for registration as part of Jersey law, but are found contrary to the Charters. Another example is the Charter of Elizabeth I of 27 June 1562, which confirms privileges with respect to the status of warrants or orders in English proceedings and is referenced in the preamble to the Judgments (Reciprocal Enforcement) (Jersey) Law 1960, which makes further statutory provision for such matters.

Statutory entrenchment of Charter rights is not limited to Jersey. Following a dispute over the extent of the Charter right to export goods to England, legislation was put in place during the reign of George I in 1717 to safeguard the right for the Channel Islands to export to England, free from duty, *any goods which are the produce or growth of any of the Channel Islands or which have been manufactured in any of those islands*. As referenced later in this book, through a long series of successive statutes that right remains a feature of UK law to this day.

Courts in Jersey and in England have also referred to Royal Charter rights as a source of law. In Jersey this point was illustrated in the recent decision of the Royal Court in the case of Want v Minister for Infrastructure [2024] JRC083. In that case, the Court considered the Charters of Elizabeth I and James II and concluded that the Appellant's rights under those charters had not been infringed.

In concluding this foreword, I would like to acknowledge the contributions of both the Attorney General and lawyers within the Law Officers' Department who have contributed to this work, and the Jersey Legal Information Board, without whose support it would not have been possible for this book to be published.

Sir Timothy Le Cocq KC, Bailiff of Jersey
June 2024

Introduction

The distinctive position of Jersey and the other Channel Islands, culturally, socially, economically, politically and constitutionally, has deep roots. Historically part of the duchy of Normandy since the capture of the Cotentin in the early days under the Viking dynasty founded by Rollo as count of Rouen at the start of the tenth century, the duchy was divided by the seizure of its continental elements by Philip Augustus, king of France from 1180 to 1223. This separation in 1204 was not seen as final at the time, by any of the parties involved.[1] There were successful French invasions of the islands in 1204 and again in 1216, and English kings continued to aspire to restore their control over the duchy as a whole, an aspiration that came close to achievement at several times in the Hundred Years War, either specifically as the duchy or as part of a wider claim to the throne of France. There was therefore a creative tension between the reality of separation and aspirations for reunification that ran across a society that remained Norman in its language and customs, and with significant interchange socially, economically and ecclesiastically, given the continued authority of the bishop of Coutances over the islands, as part of the province of Rouen. This meant that Jersey and its neighbours retained much of their Norman character while beginning to develop distinctive legal and administrative and political relationships.[2]

The law of Normandy continued to be the law of the islands, with additional elements that seem to have begun with additions from King John himself in the immediate aftermath of the events of 1204. This was expressed in the 'Constitutions of King John', which survive from a document written in the

---

[1] For general accounts of this period from 1204 to the late thirteenth century, see J. A. Everard and J. C. Holt, *Jersey 1204: The Forging of an Island Community* (London, 2004); John Le Patourel, *The Medieval Administration of the Channel Islands, 1199–1399* (London, 1937), pp. 36–45.

[2] Le Patourel, *Medieval Administration of the Channel Islands*, pp. 32–5; Everard and Holt, *Jersey 1204*, pp. 140–9; Trevor Williams, 'The Importance of the Channel Islands in British Relation [sic] with the Continent during the Thirteenth and Fourteenth Centuries: A Study in Historical Geography', *ABSJ*, 11 (1928–31), [xxxix–xl], 1–89, esp. pp. 1–55.

late thirteenth or fourteenth century, but which are evidenced closer to the time of their probable grant in the response to a writ of September 1248.[3]

Authority over the islands, stated as custody or wardenship, was granted to a succession of figures with wider interests across the Angevin territories of the king of England, men referred to by a range of titles depending on the aspect of authority invoked. This might be warden, or bailiff. During the thirteenth century, this authority began to segment into a separate role for a leading local man as bailiff with responsibility for justice under the laws applying in the island. The system of jurors to advise on the specific local custom applicable in the island, which reflected the growing importance of such a system in continental Normandy under the control of the parlement of Paris perhaps linked with the role of leading local landholders holding direct from the crown as suitors of the court, and leading men called as jurors at an inquest, increasingly took formal shape as a group of 12 jurats.[4]

Many of these developments contrasted with the experience of English communities in England. There, for example, the influence of local custom, while not obliterated, was being reduced in the face of the common application of the law of England. In the last quarter of the thirteenth century and the first four decades of the fourteenth century English courts and other institutions were at their most assertive of wide-ranging geographical authority, the role of the core English royal kin-group and associated court circle was most expansive, the English parliament aspired to make practical interventions in a range of non-English territories, and Anglo-centric networks of crown servants and of noble families encompassing communications and service spanned across the king's dominions.[5]

The challenge for the leading islanders, especially those who held land directly from the king, and who had gained most from the developments of the decades after 1204, was to secure these local arrangements. Increasingly the question was asked, by what right did the island's community possess this body of custom and its operation and oversight in local hands. The resolution of that question soon gained a simple answer, in the grant of a charter of liberties by the English crown. That grant and its successors, which consolidated and expanded on it, rapidly gained a currency in the minds of islanders, and islanders beyond those who most immediately exercised power under it. For rich and poor, for those owning extensive lands or none, for men or

---

[3] Le Patourel, *Medieval Administration of the Channel Islands*, pp. 105–10; Everard and Holt, *Jersey 1204*, pp. 156–65.

[4] Le Patourel, *Medieval Administration of the Channel Islands*, pp. 88–93; Everard and Holt, *Jersey 1204*, pp. 150–5, 166–70.

[5] R. R. Davies, *The First English Empire: Power and Identities in the British Isles 1093–1343* (Oxford, 2000); Robin Frame, *The Political Development of the British Isles, 1100–1400*, new edn (Oxford, 1995).

women, old and young, the charters of liberties took on a talismanic significance. They cited them, as Helier de la Roque did early in Henry VIII's reign, at points of stress in their personal and communal lives. De la Roque argued that substance of his dispute 'is clerely determynable within the kynges Ile of Jarsey in the said bill named after the Course and ordre of the lawes and Customes there vsed *whiche the kynges highnes vndre his grete seall of Englond hath confermed* and ought nott to be determyned in this honorable Court [of Chancery] ne in noo place els owt of thesame'.[6] The charters created a tradition that, even when they ceased to be renewed and developed after 1688, formed a central part of local legal, social and political dialogue, and in debate with the crown and its representatives. Jersey's charters, presented fully for the first time here in the original and in translation, with commentaries, are some of the most important documents in the island's past and present.

Note on editorial method

The texts presented here are taken from the enrolments of the charters held at the National Archives of the United Kingdom at Kew, with additional material from surviving copies of the charters held in Jersey and Guernsey.

Abbreviations have been silently expanded. In translation, personal and place names are modernised. While the original texts are presented in one continuous sequence of clauses, for ease of interpretation and use both the editions and translations have been structured around numbered sections. Names are given as in the original texts, although in the translations most placenames have been modernised. Dates are presented in the editions and translations as in the original texts, and in some cases this means they appear 'old style', with the year taken as beginning not on 1 January but on 25 March ('Lady Day', the feast of the Annunciation).

---

[6] TNA, C 1/491/15–16 (my emphasis). A similar formula citing that the laws of Guernsey had been 'by his highnesse vnder his great seale ratyfyed allowed and approvyd' appears in C 1/771/44 (1533–38).

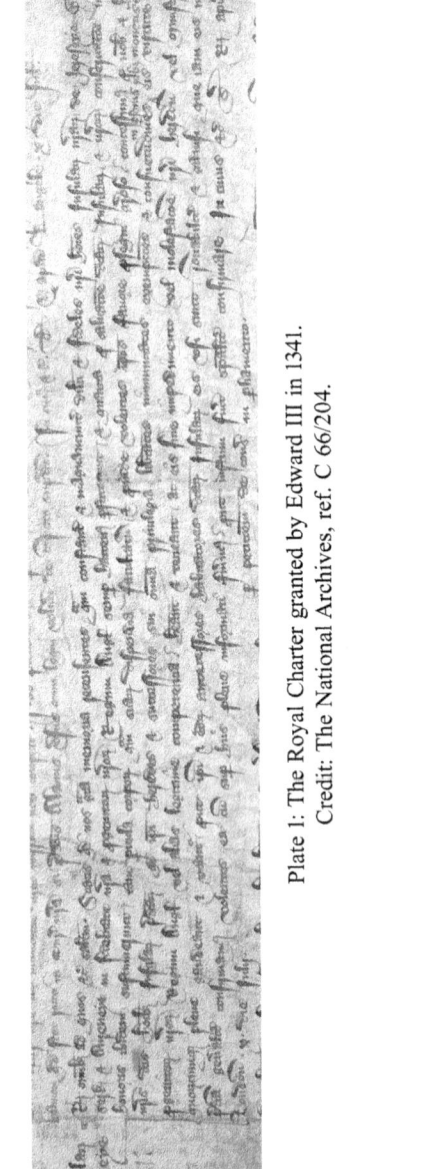

Plate 1: The Royal Charter granted by Edward III in 1341.
Credit: The National Archives, ref. C 66/204.

Edward III: 1341

Commentary

Jersey's original royal charter of liberties was shaped in the depths of crisis as the island and its neighbours bore the brunt of the first campaigns of the Hundred Years War.

The island's traditional form of government and its relationship with the crown had developed slowly in the years after 1204 and the disruption of its previous ties to continental Normandy. For several decades, peace returned to the relationships between England and France and to the Channel Islands' environments in the Bay of Saint-Malo and the western approaches to the English Channel. The islanders grew more confident in a view that they were governed neither by the laws of England nor those of Normandy without qualification. But the peaceful context began to break down seriously for the first time in several generations when, in the 1290s, Edward I of England and Philip IV of France fought a war over the English possessions in south-west France, in Edward's duchy of Aquitaine.[1] Some of the earliest exchanges in the conflict had arisen from clashes between Norman shipping and forces from Aquitaine, and the Channel Islands' key role as a safe harbour on the long sea voyage between England and Aquitaine meant they were strategically important in this wider conflict and suffered heavily in French raids.

The warden of the islands, Otto de Grandison, a figure of European importance and a close ally of Edward I, made increasingly ruthless attempts to extract the maximum possible return from them. This was most dramatically seen in a series of judicial eyres starting in 1299, when a commission combined what had previously usually been separate commissions to take the assizes and all other pleas on the one hand, and of inquiry on the other. By

---

[1] For the context of development in the century since the loss by the English king of continental Normandy in 1204, see John Le Patourel, *The Medieval Administration of the Channel Islands, 1199–1399* (London, 1937), pp. 36–45; J. A. Everard and J. C. Holt, *Jersey 1204: The Forging of an Island Community* (London, 2004), esp. pp. 150–76.

1323 and 1331, these took the form of the exceptionally powerful and intrusive general eyre.[2]

Even without Otto's interest, it is likely that Jersey's rights would have been under threat. Across the territories ultimately controlled by the English crown, the reigns of Edward I and his son Edward II represent a highpoint in a tendency to extend the control of English institutions and courts, and to see the English parliament and politics more generally becoming more extensive in their aspirations and impact. Any individual or community that seemed to hinder the exercise of royal power was challenged. For example, these were years often typified by legal proceedings driven by a writ of *quo warranto*, essentially asking by what warrant privileges were exercised.[3] Otto de Grandison died at an advanced age in 1328, but he had been granted the islands for five years after his death for the payment of his debts, and challenges to island privileges continued.

The island communities petitioned repeatedly in defence of their privileges and customs during this period. The most important instance of this occurred in 1333, requesting that the judgments of most recent eyre (in 1331) should be suspended and reviewed, and that the islands' privileges and customs be confirmed. The petitioners provided a clear and precise statement of the islands' laws and how they differed from those of Normandy. Although Edward III did suspend the judgments of the eyre, he did not at that stage confirm the islands' privileges and customs.[4]

From the accession of Edward III, English interest in France grew. Edward inherited from his father a claim to many lands in France; but he had also acquired from his mother Queen Isabella a claim to the French throne itself. That claim to the throne became immediately relevant when in February 1328 Isabella's last surviving brother Charles IV of France died without a son, and the crown was taken by his cousin, Philip of Valois. Although Edward did not strongly press his claim initially, he was finally prompted to do so when

---

[2] Le Patourel, *Medieval Administration of the Channel Islands*, pp. 45–61; L. James Marr, *A History of the Bailiwick of Guernsey: The Islanders' Story* (Chichester, 1982), pp. 76–7.

[3] Donald W. Sutherland, *Quo Warranto Proceedings in the Reign of Edward I, 1278–1294* (Oxford, 1963).

[4] Alexander Kelleher, 'Petitions from the Channel Islands in the Thirteenth and Fourteenth Centuries', *Jersey and Guernsey Law Review* (2021), pp. 31–61, at pp. 56–7; Julien Havet, *Les cours royales des îles Normandes*, (Paris, 1878), pp. 228–33. There is a copy of these articles, with some variation, in [G. F. B. de Gruchy, R. R. Marett, and E. T. Nicolle (eds)], *Cartulaire des îles Normandes: recueil de documents concernant l'histoire de ces îles, conservés aux archives du département de la Manche et du Calvados, de la Bibliothèque nationale, du Bureau des rôles, du château de Warwick, etc*, ([St Helier] Jersey, 1924 [i.e. 1918–24]), item no. 2, pp. 2–5.

in May 1337 the French attempted to seize one of those territories inherited from his father, in Gascony.[5] In this capacity, he began a war that had an immediate impact on Jersey.

Deteriorating Anglo-French relations in the 1330s were compounded by Edward's renewal of English attacks on Scottish independence. Hundreds of miles to the north though this might have been, Jersey was among the first to feel its effects on the relationship between England and France. Forces associated with the exiled claimant to the Scottish throne, David Bruce (in France since Edward's victory at Halidon Hill in 1333), had already raided the islands in 1336, and attacked Sark in 1337. In the spring of 1338, a French naval force under Nicolas Béhuchet attacked Jersey, causing widespread damage, and besieged Mont Orgueil Castle. September 1338 saw a force of galleys under Robert Bertrand, marshal of France and seigneur of Briquebec, attack Guernsey; Castle Cornet surrendered on 8 September, and Alderney and Sark were also taken.[6] The French king gave the islands to his son Jean, who had been created duke of Normandy in 1332 at the age of 13. Jean in turn gave the islands to Bertrand. With Guernsey already in French hands, in March 1339 Bertrand invaded Jersey.[7] The promise was made by the French attackers that

---

[5] Jonathan Sumption, *The Hundred Years War* (5 vols, London: 1990–2023), vol. 1, pp. 69–184.

[6] G. R. Balleine, *History of Jersey*, rev. Marguerite Syvret and Joan Stevens (Chichester, 1981), pp. 40–1; Marr, *History of the Bailiwick of Guernsey*, pp. 77–8, 136–7; Sumption, *Hundred Years War*, vol. 1, pp. 156–61, 226, 247. For the context for the raid of 1336 in Franco-Scottish relations and their interactions with England, see Michael A. Penman, 'The Kingship of David II, 1329–71' (Unpublished Ph.D. thesis, University of St Andrews, 1999), pp. 90–2 (though Penman does not mention the islands); *CPR 1334–38*, pp. 337, 413 show a ship being sent to reinforce the islands in November 1336, and measures to fortify castles in April 1337; for the attack on Sark by Scots in May 1337, see Thomas Rymer and Robert Sanderson (eds), *Foedera, conventiones, litterae, et cujuscunque generis acta publica*, rev. John Caley and Frederick Holbrooke (4 vols in 7; London, 1816–69), ii. 969 (*CPR 1334–38*, p. 451).

[7] Sumption, *Hundred Years War*, vol. 1, p. 260; Anne Merlin-Chazelas (ed.), *Documents relatifs au clos des galées de Rouen et aux armées de mer du Roi de France de 1293 a 1418* (2 vols, Paris, 1978), vol. 1, nos 227–8; Paul Bertrand de La Grassière, *Le Chevalier au Vert Lion: le maréchal de France Robert Bertrand, sire de Bricquebec (1273–1348) et l'intégration de la Normandie au royaume de France* (Paris, 1969), pp. 74–6, 160–2. For attacks on the islands and their desperate state, see on Bertrand's attack TNA, SC 8/118/5880 (*'Ancient Petitions of the Chancery and the Exchequer': ayant trait aux îles de la Manche, conservées au 'Public Record Office' à Londres*, Société Jersiaise, publication spéciale (St Helier: Labey et Blampied, 1902), pp. 67–9; also in M. H. Marret-Godfray, 'Documents relatifs aux attaques sur les îles de la Manche, 1338–1345', *ABSJ*, 93 (1891–96), 11–53, esp. pp. 14–16; and in similar terms from the period TNA, SC 8/157/7814 [c. 1340] (*'Ancient Petitions'*, pp. 69–70); TNA, SC 8/118/5884 (*'Ancient Petitions'*, p. 61; complaint of poor islanders, having

if Mont Orgueil was surrendered, the island community would be given its lands and liberties, and the French king would confirm whatever franchises they desired.[8] Although on this occasion Bertrand's threats and blandishments were ignored by the castle's defenders, some islanders were attracted by this offer, amid ongoing raiding that saw areas of Jersey destroyed and burnt three times in the year. Jurat William Payn, who had helped the invaders and fled to Normandy, and Guillaume de St Hilaire, seigneur of Samarès and vicomte of the island, who was also found to be disloyal,[9] both had their property seized in 1340: de St Hilaire was compensated by the French with lands in the Cotentin that belonged to Renaud de Carteret.[10] In this period from 1339 into 1340, Edward III's active interest in the fate of Jersey is evident from the activity of Thomas le Cerf, a king's clerk who originated from Jersey and who was sent on missions to the island and elsewhere.[11] In 1340, however, English control of the Channel was reinforced thanks to a naval victory at Sluys on 24 June. The following month Thomas de Ferrers was sent to Guernsey and, in the autumn of that year, the island, though not Castle Cornet, was recaptured.[12]

---

their customs removed during time of peace and being attacked during time of war, and have been harshly ruled by previous guardians; could be from *c.* 1297 or *c.* 1340).

[8] TNA, SC 8/118/5880, referring to the attack of 12 March 1339, printed in Marret-Godfray, 'Documents relatifs aux attaques sur les îles de la manche', pp. 14–16, translated in *'Ancient Petitions'*, pp. 67–9.

[9] *CPR 1317–21*, p. 590 (25 May 1321 inspeximus & confirmation of letters patent of Otto de Grandison, dated 22 March 1317, granting Guillot de Sancto Hillario the viscounty of Jersey for life at the request of Mary, queen of France). Guillaume held the manor of Samarès by homage at the Extente of 1331: *Extente de l'Ile de Jersey* (St Helier, 1876), p. 40, fragments p. 6. When Guillaume switched his allegiance to the king of France the manor was confiscated by Edward III; but in 1340 the bailli of the Cotentin assigned Guillaume 78 livres 10 sols 2 deniers of rente on the lands of Renaud de Carteret in recognition of the loss of his lands in Jersey. Peter Bisson, 'The Fief and Seigneurs of Samarès in the Middle Ages', *ABSJ*, 24 (1985–88), 339–53, at p. 347; C. Langton, 'The Seigneurs of Samarès', *ABSJ*, 11 (1928–31), 376–427, at pp. 380–1. For the Payn jurats of this period, see J. A. Messervy, 'Liste de jurés-justiciers de la cour royale de Jersey', *ABSJ*, 4 (1897–1901), 213–36, at p. 214.

[10] Balleine, *History*, rev. Syvret and Stevens, p. 41; *CCR 1339–41*, p. 359; G. R. Balleine, *A Biographical Dictionary of Jersey* (London, 1948), pp. 187–91 (Reginald de Carteret, d. 1349). For the investigation into the Payn inheritance in 1341–42, see TNA, SC 8/210/10479 (the resulting report is SC 8/210/10476 (*'Ancient Petitions'*, pp. 70–3)) and Peter Bisson, 'Philippe de Barentin and the Payns of Samarès', *ABSJ*, 26 (1993–96), 537–52.

[11] Mary Lyon (ed.), *The Wardrobe Book of William de Norwell, 12 July 1338 to 26 May 1340* (Bruxelles, 1983), pp. 293, 299, 430; see also ibid., pp. 233, 303, 352, 392; *CPR 1338–40*, pp. 533–4; *CPR 1340–43*, pp. 238, 240; *CCR 1339–41*, pp. 161, 292.

[12] *CPR 1334–38*, p. 451; *CPR 1338–40*, p. 530; *CPR 1340–43*, p. 20; *Documents relatifs au clos des galées de Rouen*, ii. nos 589, 596, 603; Marr, *History of the*

These traumatic years brought home to Edward the importance of Jersey and Guernsey and the loyalty (or not) of their people. In 1341, with Castle Cornet still in the hands of the French, Edward faced one of his greatest crises. Whatever the recent progress his troops had won in the islands, he had spent many months, and large sums of money, in the Low Countries, trying in vain to assemble an alliance to take on the French king.[13] In parliament in 1340, Edward had been subject to severe criticism. Returning to England at the end of the year, Edward dramatically attempted to make scapegoats of some of his ministers, but the result was further confrontation in parliament in the spring of 1341.[14] On top of this, David Bruce returned to Scotland from his French exile, and hostilities on the northern frontier resumed.[15]

The pressures on the communities of the islands were very severe in these years, and it soon became evident that the English government was willing to make concessions to support them and maintain their loyalty. For example, in April 1337 the king granted the islanders exemption from the toll of 3*d.* in the pound on merchandise brought into and taken out of England, and this was extended for two years in July 1340.[16]

When the Truce of Esplechin was agreed by the English and French regimes on 25 September 1340, it bought some respite for those involved in the fighting. There was a nine-month pause in hostilities, to 24 June 1341. This meant humiliation for Edward, however, and it was during the period of the truce, as Edward desperately attempted to recover his position, that Jersey received its confirmation of customs.[17]

The grant made on 10 July 1341 was short but sweeping and transformative in its effects.[18] The king simply gave the islanders the right to be governed

---

Bailiwick of Guernsey, p. 137; Sumption, *Hundred Years War*, vol. 1, pp. 346, 363.

[13] W. M. Ormrod, *The Reign of Edward III: Crown and Political Society in England, 1327–1377* (New Haven CT, 1990), p. 13; W. Mark Ormrod, *Edward III* (New Haven CT, 2012), pp. 192–211.

[14] Michael Prestwich, *The Three Edwards: War and State in England, 1272–1377* (London, 1980), pp. 217–23. Ormrod, *Edward III*, pp. 214–41 (January 1340 no tax; March more generous through compromise; July cautious in spite of Sluys; purge begins 1 December; April 1341 confrontation in parliament, but concessions and credit rebuilt and new taxes offered).

[15] Michael A. Penman, *David II, 1329–71* (East Linton, 2004), pp. 76–84; Sumption, *Hundred Years War*, vol. 1, p. 363.

[16] *CPR 1334–38*, p. 416; *CPR 1340–43*, p. 18.

[17] Sumption, *Hundred Years War*, vol. 1, pp. 358–63, emphasises the dire situation of Edward at this point – the effects of the truce include the abandonment of the siege of Castle Cornet and an acceptance at least temporarily of French control there.

[18] TNA, C 66/204, m. 38; *CPR 1341–43*, p. 237; Tim Thornton, *The Charters of Guernsey* (Bognor Regis, 2004), pp. 1–4. The grant is noted as being by petition of the Commons in Parliament: C. Given-Wilson *et al.* (eds), *The Parliament Rolls of*

by their own law and customs, and not to be subject to courts outside the island. When in 1342 war flared again Edward was able to attempt to redress his losses in the islands, and he was apparently able to do that with renewed local support. Thomas of Hampton, who had bought the wardenship of the isles, attempted to recapture Castle Cornet. The siege lasted for three years, and Jerseymen were involved in the campaign.[19] A new focus on the islands' liberties was evident: when Henry de la More, Hampton's lieutenant, caused resentment, Edward responded.[20] This continued to reinforce local loyalties and security into the next decade.

It was more than a decade later that Anglo-French hostilities again affected Jersey and its neighbours. In the 1350s, the ambiguous role of Jean II's brother-in-law, Charles of Navarre, and his interests in Normandy, and especially in the Cotentin, saw, for example, Charles offer to meet the English commander Henry, duke of Lancaster in the islands in person in 1355, when he held out the possibility that his army might combine with Lancaster's in the Cotentin and then campaign in Normandy.[21] Then, as Jean II made a pre-emptive but rash strike against Charles in 1356, seizing some of his major centres in Normandy, the French and their allies seized Castle Cornet. A Jersey force raised under Sir Renaud de Carteret, Bailiff Raoul Lemprière, and Richard de St Martin, seigneur of Trinity, having captured the invading captain, released him in exchange for the surrender to them of Castle Cornet, when they could have personally taken 80,000 moutons d'or for his ransom. The potential for conflicted loyalties reared its head when, in the course of the struggle, a Guernseyman was slain as a traitor, and the Guernsey court ordered the arrest of those Jerseymen who were responsible. The warden got the trial transferred to the Privy Council. The Guernseyman's widow went to London and advocated for him, and the Guernsey jurats threatened to resign if justice, as they saw it, was not done. All this led to the alleged perpetrators of the murder spending two years in a Guernsey dungeon, until they were released

---

Medieval England, 1275–1504 (16 vols, Woodbridge and London, 2005), vol. 4, pp. 301–24, at p. 324 (noting petition not extant). The parliament had been in session from 23 April to 28 May 1341.

[19] *CPR 1340–43*, pp. 159 (appointment to survey castles, fortlets and estates of islands, 25 March 1341), 467 (18 May 1342 activity) 484 (13 July 1342, indicating his background, as clerk, of co Warwick).

[20] '*Ancient Petitions*', pp. 74, 75 (complaints against Hampton, TNA SC 8/245/12212 (early 1343); SC 8/158/7856 (1342)); Balleine, *Biographical Dictionary of Jersey*, pp. 137, 187. Complaints continued through the 1340s, expressed in petitions: in January 1345 when the king was crossing to France, Jerseymen intercepted him in the golfe du Morbihan and presented a petition regarding de la More. TNA, SC 8/245/12212 ('*Ancient Petitions*', pp. 74–5).

[21] Sumption, *Hundred Years War*, vol. 2, p. 141.

in 1359 in recognition of the islanders' contribution to the recovery of island and castle.[22]

This resumption of conflict therefore highlighted again the costs of loyalty, the threat of treason to the English crown, and the opportunity to promote the islands' liberties. In 1357 the island communities successfully sought confirmation of their freedom from a custom of 3*d.* in the pound on their goods and merchandise brought to and from the king's realm, and there was a confirmation of Guernsey liberties in the face of the recent disruption to the continuity of authority in the island.[23] As Edward III entered his final years on the throne, the conflicts he had helped unleash had rebalanced power in the islands in favour of their communities, and the charters were the clearest expression of that shift.

Text

Edward III granted the people of the Islands confirmation of their privileges, liberties, immunities, exemptions, and customs. Common to Guernsey, Sark and Alderney; text [A] expanded from [B] enrolment in The National Archives, C 66/204, m. 38, with reference to the edition presented in Prison Board.

[[A]Edwardus Dei Gracia Rex Anglie et Francie et Dominus Hibernie Omnibus ad quos presentes litere pervenerint Salutem:] [[B]Rex omnibus ad quos etc. salutem.] Sciatis quod nos grata memoria recensentes quam constanter et magnanimiter dilecti et fideles nostri homines Insularum nostrarum de Jereseye Gernereye Serk et Aureneye in fidelitate nostra et progenitorum nostrorum Regum Anglie semper hactenus perstiterunt et quanta pro saluacione dictarum Insularum et nostrorum conseruacione iurium et honoris ibidem sustinuerunt tam pericula corporum quam suarum dispendia facultatum et proinde volentes ipsos fauore prosequi gracioso concessimus pro nobis et heredibus nostris dictis

---

[22] Balleine, *History*, rev. Syvret and Stevens, p. 45; Sumption, *Hundred Years War*, vol. 2, pp. 198–226; T. M. W. de Guérin, 'An Account of the Families of de St Martin and de la Court (Seigneurs of Trinity)', *ABSJ*, 9 (1919–22), 54–95, at pp. 60–2; *CPR 1354–58*, pp. 515, 562, 590; *CCR 1354–60*, pp. 372–3, 374, 384 (15 August 1357 order to stay process, and also order to release; 12 November 1357 Wm le Febvre's wife Nicholaa get order for trial if he was true liegeman); Balleine, *Biographical Dictionary of Jersey*, pp. 191–4. The mouton was about 40 grains weight and worth 5 *s.* – so the claim was they had foregone no less than £20,000.

[23] *CPR 1354–58*, pp. 510, 562, 590; Trevor Williams, 'The Importance of the Channel Islands in British Relation [sic] with the Continent during the Thirteenth and Fourteenth Centuries: A Study in Historical Geography', *ABSJ*, 11 (1928–31), [xxxix–xl], 1–89, at pp. 82–3. The grant of 1357 was a precedent for the similar grant of 1370 regarding tolls, for which see below pp. 16.

hominibus Insularum predictarum quod ipsi heredes et successors sui omnia priuilegia libertates immunitates exempciones et consuetundines in personis rebus monetis et aliis eis virtute concessionum progenitorum nostrorum Regum Anglie vel alias legitime competencia habeant et teneant ac eis sine impedimento vel molestacione nostri heredum vel ministrorum quorumcumque plene gaudeant et vtantur prout ipsi et eorum antecessores habitatores dictarum Insularum eis vsi sunt racionabiliter et gauisi que iam eis in forma predicta generaliter confirmamus volentes ea cum super hiis plene informati fuerimus prout iustum fuerit specialiter confirmare. In cuius [rei testimonium has literas nostras fieri fecims Patentes.] [etc.] [ATESTE ME ipse apud Turrim Londonii decimo die Julii anno Regni nostri Anglie quinto decimo Regni vero nostri Francie secundo.] [BTeste Rege apud Turrim Londonii. x die Julii.]

Per peticionem de concilio in parliament.

Translation

AEdward, by the grace of God king of England and France and lord of Ireland, to all to whom these present letters shall come, greeting. [BThe King to all to whom, etc., greeting.] Know ye, that we recalling with grateful memory with what constancy and high spirit our beloved and faithful men of our islands of Guernsey, Jersey, Sark and Alderney have always hitherto continued in their faithfulness to us and our progenitors kings of England; and how great dangers to their bodies, as well as costs to their property they have borne for the safety of the said islands, and conservation of our laws and honour therein, and in like manner desiring to follow after them with our gracious favour, we have granted for ourselves and our heirs to the said men of the aforesaid islands, that they themselves, their heirs and successors, may have and hold all privileges, liberties, immunities, exemptions, and customs, in respect of their persons, goods, moneys, and other matters, by virtue of the grant of our progenitors kings of England, or otherwise lawfully by agreement, and, without impediment or molestation from us, our heirs, or our officers whomsoever, may fully enjoy and use them, according as they themselves and their predecessors, the inhabitants of the said islands, have reasonably enjoyed and used them. Which things we do now confirm to them generally in the aforesaid form, being willing after we have enquired into them to confirm them as may be just. AIn testimony whereof we have had these letters made patent, myself as witness at the Tower of London the tenth day of July, in the year of our reign in England the fifteenth, but of our reign in France the second. [BIn relation, etc.; the King as witness at the Tower of London the tenth day of July]

By petition of the Council in Parliament.

Richard II: 1378 and 1394

Commentary

Edward III reigned for another 36 years after the grant of his charter to the bailiwicks. In that time, the English struggle against the French, which had provided the conditions for the original grant, went from one of desperation, through the heights of success in the battles of Crécy and Poitiers and the

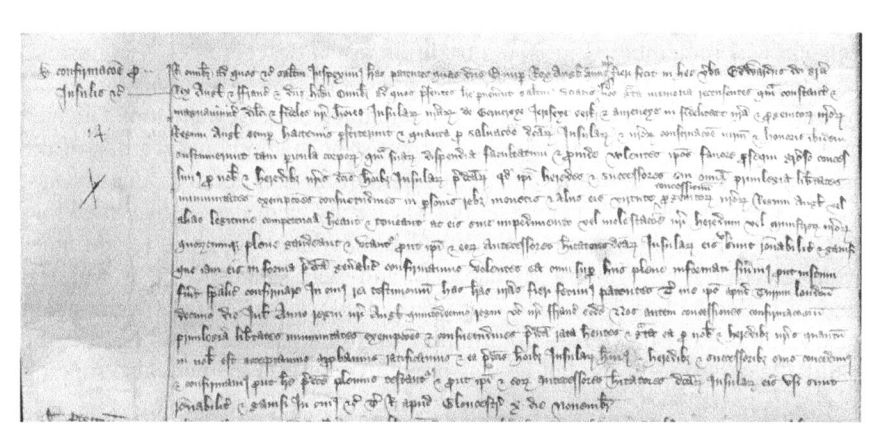

Plate 2: The Royal Charter granted by Richard II in 1378.
Credit: The National Archives, ref. C 76/63.

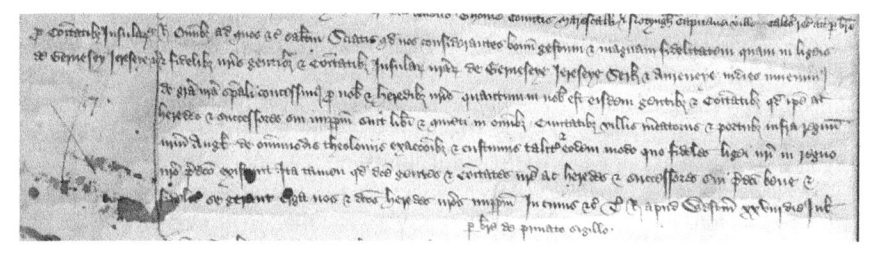

Plate 3: The Royal Charter granted by Richard II in 1394.
Credit: The National Archives, ref. C 76/79.

treaty of Brétigny, to, once again, desperation. Edward's grandson, Richard II, inherited a situation in which the English were struggling to maintain their position in south-western France and in which their alliances in the north-west, especially in Brittany, on which the position of the islands so closely depended, were in tatters.

Under Richard's grandfather, peace had followed the treaty of Brétigny, concluded on 8 May 1360, for nine years. It eventually broke down thanks to a challenge to the English position in Aquitaine and, in the early 1370s, the French were increasingly successful.[1] Very quickly, the decline in English fortunes started to have an effect on the islands. In 1372, Guernsey was attacked by a force led by the Welsh princely claimant in exile in France, Owain ap Thomas ap Rhodri (known as Owen of Wales); Jerseymen petitioned desperately to the crown for protection, and the sheriffs of Southampton and Portsmouth were ordered to hold ships in readiness. In Guernsey, it was the newly arrived captain of Mont Orgueil, Sir Edmund Rose, who moved to rally the defence, but his force, including many local people, was defeated, and they were driven back into Castle Cornet, where they held out long enough for the invaders to be summoned away, towards the French south-west. The episode was remembered in island tradition as 'la descente des Aragousais', commemorated in a ballad.[2]

In 1373 Bertrand du Guesclin led a further attack on Jersey and took Grosnez castle. Sir William Asthorp, who had only just been appointed warden of the isles in succession to Walter Huwet (although he had acted as deputy first in 1367), led the island's response, but his forces were driven back to Mont Orgueil. Their position was so difficult that they had to commit to surrender if they were not relieved by Michaelmas, and were saved by the arrival of a fleet on 2 September. The successive years of attacks raised the spectre again of treason among the Jersey community, and charges were laid against the bailiff, Jean de St Martin, but he was not convicted.[3] They were also sapping

---

[1] Jonathan Sumption, *The Hundred Years War* (5 vols, London, 1990–2023), vol. 2, pp. 455–585; vol. 3, pp. 18–211.

[2] G. R. Balleine, *History of Jersey*, rev. Marguerite Syvret and Joan Stevens (Chichester, 1981), p. 46; Edmund Toulmin Nicolle, *Mont Orgueil Castle: Its History and Description* (Jersey, 1921), pp. 19–22, 167–70; Jean Froissart, *Oeuvres: Chroniques*, ed. baron Kervyn de Lettenhove (25 vols in 26, Brussels, 1867–77), vol. 8, pp. 140–3; Siméon Luce (ed.), *Chronique des quatre premiers Valois (1327–1393)* (Paris, 1862), pp. 230–2; Sumption, *Hundred Years War*, vol. 3, p. 136; A. D. Carr, *Owen of Wales: The End of the House of Gwynedd* (Cardiff, 1991), pp. 29–30.

[3] Thomas Rymer, *Fœdera, conventiones, litteræ, et cujuscunque generis acta publica* (London, 1816–69), vol. 3, part 2, p. 997; Nicolle, *Mont Orgueil Castle*, pp. 20–2, 168–71; Sumption, *Hundred Years War*, vol. 3, pp. 184–5; Richard Vernier, *The Flower of Chivalry: Bertrand Du Guesclin and the Hundred Years War* (Woodbridge, 2003), p. 173; Georges Minois, *Du Guesclin* (Paris, 1993), pp. 412–13; Jean d'Orronville

of the islands' resources, as in April 1374 du Guesclin agreed a ransom with Jersey and, for two years, payments were regularly made to him.[4]

The Anglo-French treaty of Bruges of July 1375 brought a year's peace, extended in March 1376 through to June 1377.[5] The French were nonetheless still extracting ransom from Jersey, and they were soon preparing further attacks on Jersey and the other islands. The French agreed with their Castilian allies in February 1378 on an assault that would utterly destroy the islands: 'ils fassent leur loyal pouvoir de destruire les Isles de Huic, Iarsi, & Garnizi, & mettre tout en feu, tailler les arbres, & faire la plus grande destruction que faire se pourra bonnement'.[6]

One indication of the heightening tensions of these years was the appointment of Sir Hugh de Calveley as warden of the isles in 1376. This vastly experienced military commander rearrested Bailiff Jean de St Martin for treason, and he was held in prison for four years.[7]

Even the involvement of such an outstanding campaigner as Calveley could not address the imminence of the threat faced by the English and their allies. By the end of June 1377, days after the truce had expired, French and Castilian troops landed on the English coast at Winchelsea. Towns including Hastings and Lewes were destroyed before the invaders pulled back.[8] The English recognised that French control of the Channel and of its key ports represented a threat to the whole of the south of England, and adopted a policy of defence via what was referred to as the establishment of 'barbicans', strategic

---

dit Cabaret, *La chronique du bon duc Loys de Bourbon*, ed. A.-M. Chazaud (Paris, 1876), pp. 45–6 (1429; translated in 'How the Duke of Bourbon, the Constable and the Marshal took the Islands of Jersey and Guernsey which face Brittany', *ABSJ*, 16 (1953–56), 281–3); *The Guernsey and Jersey Magazine*, 2 (1836), 169; Jean Lemoine, 'du Guesclin à Jersey (1373–1376)', *Revue Historique*, 61 (1896), 45–61.

[4] Lemoine, 'du Guesclin à Jersey', pp. 52, 59–60; Nicolle, *Mont Orgueil Castle*, pp. 171–2; Minois, *Du Guesclin*, p. 421; Thomas Rymer and Robert Sanderson (eds), *Foedera, conventiones, litterae, et cujuscunque generis acta publica*, rev. John Caley and Frederick Holbrooke (4 vols in 7, London, 1816–69), vol. 3ii, p. 1068.

[5] Sumption, *Hundred Years War*, vol. 3, pp. 212–80.

[6] Lemoine, 'du Guesclin à Jersey', pp. 59–60; Gustave Dupont, *Histoire du Cotentin et de ses îles* (4 vols, Caen, 1870–85), vol. 2, p. 451; Paul Hay, sieur du Chastelet, junior, *Histoire de Bertrand Du Guesclin, connétable de France et des royaumes de Léon, de Castille* (Paris, 1666), pp. 403–5, at p. 404 which has date in text of 4 February 1378; Dupont indicates it must be pre-hostilities, and chroniclers say hostilities commenced on the death of Edward III.

[7] *CPR 1374–77*, p. 394; *CCR 1374–77*, p. 392. In January 1387 Jean de St Martin's case was reinvestigated and he was found innocent, but he was not restored to the bailiffship. Balleine, *Biographical Dictionary of Jersey*, p. 223; Nicolle, *Mont Orgueil Castle*, p. 24.

[8] Sumption, *Hundred Years War*, vol. 3, pp. 281–3, 286–8.

locations that stood for England in rather the same way as outer defences and powerful gateways did for castles and towns. Both Jersey and Guernsey were provided with sizeable garrisons.[9] Brest was reinforced and, although an attempt to take Saint-Malo was unsuccessful, Cherbourg was occupied under a deal with the weakened Charles of Navarre, who had lost almost all of his duchy of Normandy.[10]

This effort to bolster the 'barbicans' of English defence along the French coastline unsurprisingly included the islands. As part of this effort, the rights and privileges of the islanders accepted by Edward III were confirmed by Richard in November 1378 when the new king was at Gloucester.

English weakness had already encouraged the island communities to press for confirmation and extension of their privileges. In about 1370, in the last years of the reign of Richard's grandfather, a petition had been submitted to the king and council on behalf of the community of Guernsey requesting a charter of the franchises of the island, confirming freedom from customs and other charges. This seems to relate to a grant of freedom from tolls for Jersey, Guernsey, Alderney and Sark for 20 years on 7 May 1370, recorded on the Patent Rolls.[11] In practice this was not the first attempt of this type – probably some time in the second quarter of the century a petition in the names of the communities of both Guernsey and Jersey requested a charter making them free from all charges and quayage that they were forced to pay when trading in England. The islanders asserted that their islands were part of the king's ancient heritage and therefore they should not be forced to make such payments as aliens.[12]

After further months of reverses in England's conflict with France, a failed alliance with Brittany in 1380 was the precursor to a period in which the momentum of conflict slowed. In England, there was dissatisfaction at the cost of the conflict. Richard's preference for peace with France became apparent, provoking a violent response from some of his noble opponents, the Appellants. But when Richard skilfully re-established his personal control from the spring of 1389, he was able to resume peace negotiations in earnest. The result was the truce of Leulinghem of August 1389.[13] In the parliament of November 1390, a petition in the names of Guernsey, Jersey, Sark and Alderney

---

[9] Sumption, *Hundred Years War*, vol. 3, pp. 304–5.

[10] Sumption, *Hundred Years War*, vol. 3, pp. 304–16.

[11] TNA, SC 8/113/5611 (*'Ancient petitions of the Chancery and the Exchequer': ayant trait aux îles de la Manche, conservées au 'Public Record Office' à Londres*, Société Jersiaise, publication spéciale (St Helier, 1902), pp. 85–6); *CPR 1367–70*, p. 401. See the precedent set in the 1350s, above pp. 11.

[12] TNA, SC 8/114/5676 (*'Ancient Petitions'*, p. 86).

[13] L. James Marr, *A History of the Bailiwick of Guernsey: The Islanders' Story* (Chichester, 1982), pp. 141–3; Sumption, *Hundred Years War*, vol. 3, pp. 351–623.

recognised that the king had granted them to be quit of tolls etc., by letters patent, for 12 years. The island communities requested further letters patent, to last as long as they remained lieges to the king and his kingdom; and they asked that it be borne in mind that they were ransomed and had paid annually to the admiral of France more than 6,000 francs, both in time of truce and of war. In response the king granted the privilege, but for eight years, not 12.[14]

The three-year truce of 1389 was followed by negotiations in search of a final peace. Major obstacles to this were the French insistence on the surrender or dismantling of Calais, which was unacceptable to the English, and their assertion of ultimate French sovereignty over all lands retained by the English, with implications for the islands. Eventually, a truce was agreed in 1396, for the long term of 28 years, and Richard married the French princess Isabella.[15]

Much had therefore changed since 1378 when Richard II again came to act on the rights of the islanders. On 28 July 1394, Richard granted a considerable increase to the privileges of the communities of Jersey and Guernsey. In a brief charter issued from Westminster, he conceded to them the right to exemption from tolls, duties and customs in England, as if they were English. In conjunction with the grant of Edward III, earlier confirmed by Richard, this effectively gave Guernsey and Jersey the financial privileges of being English while at the same time allowing the islands their own customs and exemption from English laws.[16]

The context of this charter is to be found more broadly in the way Richard attempted to reformulate English royal authority in what turned out to be the last five years of his reign.

Later in 1394 Richard was to embark on an expedition to Ireland, which was to prove a success. On his return to England he began a period of assertion of royal rights, which some have seen as a tyranny. One key element of that assertion was the role of the non-English territories over which Richard

---

[14] C. Given-Wilson et al. (eds), *The Parliament Rolls of Medieval England, 1275–1504* (16 vols, Woodbridge and London, 2005), vol. 7, p. 184.

[15] Marr, *History of the Bailiwick of Guernsey*, p. 79; J. J. N. Palmer, 'The Anglo-French Peace Negotiations, 1390–6', *Transactions of the Royal Historical Society*, 5th ser., 16 (1966), 81–94, esp. p. 93 (local objections, not English intransigence, as the obstacle to settlement); idem, 'The Background to Richard II's Marriage to Isabel of France (1396)', *Bulletin of the Institute of Historical Research*, 44 (1971), 1–17; Sumption, *Hundred Years War*, vol. 3, pp. 788–93, 806–14, 826–7.

[16] TNA, C 76/79 (Chancery: Treaty Rolls, 18 Richard II), m. 10, printed in *Prison Board*, pp. 158–9; Tim Thornton, *The Charters of Guernsey* (Bognor Regis, 2004), pp. 5–9 (calendared in Thomas Carte, *Catalogue des rolles gascons, normans et françois conservés dans les archives de la Tour de Londres: et contenant le précis & le sommaire de tous les titres qui s'y trouvent concernant la Guienne, la Normandie & les autres provinces de la France sujettes autrefois aux rois d'Angleterre* (2 vols, Paris, 1743), vol. 2, p. 170).

ruled. Whether through systematic policy, or through their own reassertion of their rights and influence, Richard became particularly associated with Cheshire, Ireland, and others, including Jersey.[17] While noting that there were limits to the generosity of the regime, as when in July 1394 Robert Markele, king's serjeant at arms, and Henry Ryther (the lieutenant governor) were commissioned to act against merchants importing material into Guernsey that should have passed through the Calais staple, Richard's policy meant a greater prominence for Jersey and Guernsey and their enhanced privileges.[18]

One sign of this is the eminence of the men chosen as warden or governor of Jersey. Sir Hugh de Calverley, who had been warden/governor until 1393, was succeeded by Sir John de Golafre of Langley until 1396, and then by Edward, earl of Rutland. Golafre, a chamber knight, was very close to the king, who had him buried at Westminster immediately beside his own tomb.[19] Rutland was also very close to Richard. Soon to be promoted to the duchy of Aumale, he was the son and heir of the duke of York, a younger brother of Richard's father, Edward the Black Prince; one well-informed observer noted that there was no-one 'whom Richard loved better' and Richard may have seen him as his own heir.[20]

Richard's reign had already by 1394 seen exceptional internal political division. Given their close association with Richard's key supporters, their strengthened privileges and their existing status, it is not surprising that the islands were to serve as a place of exile and imprisonment for one of Richard's bitterest enemies. From the time when he had replaced Sir Simon de Burley as Richard's tutor or personal guardian, through his prominent membership of the commissions and councils that had attempted to restrain the king in 1385–86, John, Lord Cobham had become ever more clearly a man hated by Richard.[21] When the time came for Richard to assert his personal control,

---

[17] Michael J. Bennett, 'Richard II and the Wider Realm', in Anthony Goodman and James L. Gillespie (eds), *Richard II: The Art of Kingship* (Oxford, 1999), pp. 187–204 (although he mentions none of the Channel Islands in this connection).

[18] *CFR, 1391–99*, p. 88; for Ryther, see TNA, SC 8/218/10854.

[19] N. E. Saul, 'The Fragments of the Golafre Brass in Westminster Abbey', *Transactions of the Monumental Brass Society*, 15/i (1992), 19–32.

[20] J. T. Webb (ed.), 'Translation of a French Metrical History of the Deposition of Richard II', *Archaeologia*, 20 (1824), 1–423, at p. 309; Saul, *Richard II*, p. 345.

[21] J. S. Roskell, *The Impeachment of Michael de la Pole Earl of Suffolk in 1386 in the Context of the Reign of Richard II* (Manchester, 1984), pp. 24, 61, 74; T. F. Tout, *Chapters in the Administrative History of Medieval England: The Wardrobe, the Chamber and the Small Seals* (6 vols, Manchester, 1920–33), vol. 3, p. 349; Anthony Tuck, *Richard II and the English Nobility* (London, 1973), pp. 43–4, 76, 100, 106–7; Chris Given-Wilson, 'Richard II and the Higher Nobility', in Anthony Goodman and James L. Gillespie (eds), *Richard II: The Art of Kingship* (Oxford, 1999), pp. 107–28, at pp. 112–14; Christopher Fletcher, *Richard II: Manhood, Youth, and Politics, 1377–1399*

Cobham was clearly a marked man. On the same day in September 1397 when another of Richard's bêtes noires, Richard Fitzalan, earl of Arundel, was arrested and executed, Cobham's trial was ordered, and he was convicted during the second, Shrewsbury, session of the parliament then sitting – and sent into exile in Jersey.[22]

It is therefore unsurprising that when in 1399 Richard was deposed, and his supporters were being challenged in their turn, Cobham was active and Aumale his target. When on Friday 17 October the question was put whether Richard's supporters, the three dukes of Surrey, Exeter and Aumale, should be arrested, Cobham was the first to reply, emphasising 'the evils of recent years'.[23] Those attitudes were to have an impact on the islands in the new reign.

Text (1378)

Richard confirms the charter of his grandfather and immediate predecessor as king, Edward III. Common to Guernsey, Sark and Alderney; text taken from ^A charter in Jersey archive, D/AP/Z/1 – some damage towards end – and ^B enrolment in The National Archives, C 76/63, m. 11, as presented in Prison Board.

[1] [^ARichardus Dei Gratia Rex Anglie et ffrancie et Dominus Hibernie Omnibus ad quos presentes litere pervenerint salutem.] [^BRex omnibus ad quos etc. salutem.] Inspeximus literas patentes quas dominus Edwardus nuper Rex Anglie auus noster fieri fecit in hec verba.

[2] Edwardus dei gratia Rex Anglie et ffrancie et dominus Hibernie Omnibus ad quos presentes litere peruenerint salutem. Sciatis quod nos grata memoria recensentes quam constanter et magnanimiter dilecti et fideles nostri homines Insularum nostrarum de Gernereye Jereseye Serk et Aureneye in fidelitate nostra et progenitorum nostrorum Regum Anglie semper hactenus perstiterunt et quanta pro saluacione dictarum Insularum et nostrorum conseruacione iurium et honoris ibidem sustinuerunt tam pericula corporum quam suarum dispendia

---

(Oxford, 2008), pp. 81, 141–2, 154, 178; Nigel Saul, *Richard II* (New Haven CT, 1997), pp. 28, 163–4, 196, 381; idem, *Death, Art, and Memory in Medieval England: The Cobham Family and their Monuments 1300–1500* (Oxford, 2001), pp. 21–5.

[22] George B. Stow, Jr (ed.), *Historia vitae et regni Ricardi Secundi* ([Philadelphia PA], 1977), p. 144; Chris Given-Wilson (ed.), *Chronicles of the Revolution, 1397–1400: The Reign of Richard II* (Manchester, 1993), pp. 60, 126, 174.

[23] 'Annales Ricardi Secundi et Henrici Quarti Regis Angliae', in *Chronica Monasterii S. Albani: Johannis de Trokelowe, et Henrici de Blaneforde ... Chronica et Annales*, ed. H. T. Riley, Rolls Ser., 28(3) (London, 1866), pp. 153–420, at pp. 306–7; Given-Wilson (ed.), *Chronicles of the Revolution*, pp. 204–5.

facultatum et proinde volentes ipsos fauore prosequi gracioso concessimus pro nobis et heredibus nostris dictis hominibus Insularum predictarum quod ipsi heredes et successores sui omnia priuilegia libertates immunitates exempciones consuetudines in personis rebus monetis et aliis eis virtute concessionum progenitorum nostrorum Regum Anglie vel alias legitime competencia habeant et teneant ac eis sine impedimento vel molestacione nostri heredum vel Minstrorum quorumcumque plene gaudeant et vtantur prout ipsi et antecessores habitatores dictarum Insularum eis vsi sunt rationabiliter et gauisi que iam illis in forma predicta generaliter confirmamus Volentes ea cum super hiis plene informati fuerimus prout iustum fuerit specialiter confirmare. In cuius rei testimonium has literas nostras fieri fecimus patentes. Teste me ipso apud Turrim Londonii decimo die Julii Anno regni nostri Anglie quintodecimo regni vero nostri ffrancie secundo.

[3] Nos autem concessiones confirmacionem priuilegia libertates immunitates exempciones et consuetudines predicta rata habentes et grata ea pro nobis et heredibus nostris quantum in nobis est acceptamus approbamus ratificamus et ea predictis hominibus Insularum habemus heredibus et successoribus suis concedimus et confirmamus prout litere predicte plenius testantur et prout ipsi et eorum antecessores habitatores dictarum Insularum eis vsi sunt rationabiliter et gauisi [^A In cuius rei testimonium has literas nostras fieri fecimus patentes. Teste me ipso apud Gloucestriam decimo die Nouembris anno Regni nostri secundo.] [^B In cuius etc. Teste Regis apud Gloucestriam x die Nouembris.] [^A Middelton]

Translation (1378)

[1] [^A Richard by the grace of God king of England and France and lord of Ireland to all those to whom these present letters shall come, greeting [^B The King to all those to whom, etc., greeting] We have inspected the Letters Patent which the Lord Edward lately king of England our grandfather caused to be made in these words.

[2] Edward by the grace of God king of England and France and lord of Ireland, to all to whom these present letters shall come, greeting. Know ye, that we recalling with grateful memory with what constancy and high spirit our beloved and faithful men of our islands of Guernsey, Jersey, Sark and Alderney have always hitherto continued in their faithfulness to us and our progenitors kings of England; and how great dangers to their bodies, as well as costs to their property they have borne for the safety of the said islands, and conservation of our laws and honour therein, and in like manner desiring to follow after them with our gracious favour, we have granted for ourselves and our heirs to the said men of the aforesaid islands, that they themselves, their

heirs and successors, may have and hold all privileges, liberties, immunities, exemptions, and customs, in respect of their persons, goods, moneys, and other matters, by virtue of the grant of our progenitors kings of England, or otherwise lawfully by agreement, and, without impediment or molestation from us, our heirs, or our officers whomsoever, may fully enjoy and use them, according as they themselves and their predecessors, the inhabitants of the said islands, have reasonably enjoyed and used them. Which things we do now confirm to them generally in the aforesaid form, being willing after we have enquired into them to confirm them as may be just. In testimony whereof we have had these letters made patent, myself as witness at the Tower of London the tenth day of July, in the year of our reign in England the fifteenth, but of our reign in France the second.

[3] We, moreover, holding the concessions, confirmations, privileges, liberties, immunities, and customs to be reasonable and seasonable, accept, approve, and ratify them for us and our heirs, as far as in us lies, and concede and confirm them to the aforesaid men of the islands in the same manner to their heirs and successors as the aforesaid Letters more fully testify and as they and their predecessors inhabitants of the said Islands have reasonably used and enjoyed them. [A]In witness whereof we have had these our Letters made Patent. Myself as witness at Gloucester the tenth day of November in the second year of our reign. [[B]In relation to which, etc. The King as witness at Gloucester the tenth day of November]

[A]Middelton

Text (1394)

Richard II grants freedom from tolls, duties and customs in his kingdom. Common to Guernsey, Sark and Alderney; text taken from [A] charter in Guernsey Greffe and [B] enrolment in The National Archives, C 76/79, m. 10, as presented in Prison Board.

[[A]Richardus dei gracia Rex Anglie et ffrancie et Dominus Hibernie Omnibus ad quos presentes litere peruenerint Salutem:] [[B]Rex omnibus ad quos etc. salutem.] Sciatis quod nos considerantes bonum gestum et magnam fidelitatem quam in ligeis et fidelibus nostris gentibus et Communitatibus Insularum nostrarum de Gerneseye Jereseye Serk et Aureneye indies inuenimus de gratia nostra speciali concessimus pro nobis et heredibus nostris quantum in nobis est eisdem gentibus et Communitatibus quod ipse ac heredes et successores sui imperpetuum sint liberi et quieti in omnibus Ciuitatibus villis mercatoriis et portubus infra regnum nostrum Anglie de omnimodis theoloniis exaccionibus et custumis taliter et eodem modo quo fideles ligei nostri in regno nostro predicto existunt. Ita tamen quod dicte gentes et Communitates nostre ac heredes et successores sui predicti bene et fideliter se gerant erga nos et dictos heredes nostros imperpetuum. [^AIn cuius rei testimonium has literas nostras fieri fecimus patentes. Teste me ipso apud Westmonasterium vicesimo octauo Julii anno regni nostri decimo octauo.

Hertilpole

[^BIn cuius etc. Teste Regis apud Westmonasterium xxviii die Julii.]

Per breve de priuato sigillo.

Translation (1394)

[^ARichard, by the grace of God king of England and France and lord of Ireland, to all to whom these present letters may come, greeting [^BThe King to all to whom, etc., greeting]: Know ye that we in consideration of the good behaviour and the great loyalty which we have ever found in our liege and faithful peoples and communities of our islands of Guernsey, Jersey, Sark and Alderney, have of our special grace granted for ourselves and our heirs, as far as in us lies, to the said peoples and communities, that they, their heirs and successors shall for ever be free and quit from all tolls, duties, and customs of whatsoever kind in all our cities, market towns, and ports within our kingdom of England, in the same manner as our faithful liege people in our aforesaid kingdom are. Provided always, however, that our said peoples and communities, their heirs and successors aforesaid shall well and faithfully conduct themselves towards us and our heirs aforesaid for ever. [^AIn witness whereof we have caused these our Letters to be made patent. Witness myself at Westminster this twenty-eighth day of July in the eighteenth year of our reign.

Hertilpole

[^BIn relation to which, etc. Witness the King at Westminster the twenty-eighth day of July.]

By warrant of the Privy Seal.

Henry IV: 1400

Commentary

Henry IV's reign was dominated by the circumstance of his accession. Richard II's second expedition to Ireland in the summer of 1399 meant that most of his strongest supporters were with him and out of England at the point that Henry, then as duke of Lancaster, returned from exile, initially claiming only his inheritance, from which he had been disinherited by Richard after his father John of Gaunt's death. Henry soon moved to claim the throne and, after returning to Wales with only a few followers, Richard resigned the

Plate 4: The Royal Charter granted by Henry IV in 1400.
Credit: The National Archives, ref. C 76/84.

throne in September. Henry was crowned in Westminster Abbey in October 1399; Richard was apparently murdered in the February of the following year when it became apparent that he would be the focus of rebellion against the new regime.

The insecurity inherent in such a controversial accession influenced Henry's policy from the start. Henry was thrown almost immediately into a war against the Scots, as well as facing rebellion at home. He was in many people's eyes a usurper and, although an account of the voluntary vacation of the throne by Richard was vigorously and effectively promoted, there remained a challenge for his regime to establish its legitimacy.

One of the pressures on the new king was the potential for conflict with the French and their allies. Not long after Henry's accession the French confirmed the truce with England that had been instigated by Richard II, although they avoided acknowledging Henry as king for several years.[1] Relations with the French soon deteriorated, however; when Henry made his eldest son duke of Aquitaine, the French king Charles VI responded by making his son duke of Guyenne. And although the French regime was hampered by financial problems and political division, and therefore keen to maintain the principle of the truce, it was willing to use third parties and privateers to attack and discomfort the English. In particular, the Bretons were regarded as allies of Charles VI and not his subjects, thereby allowing them to escalate conflict with the English, even to the point of attacks on each other's territory, without this implying an outright breach of the truce. And so the early years of the new reign saw raiding along the Channel coast of England and affecting the islands.[2]

This threat interacted with the potential for rebellion and treason among those whom Henry IV hoped to enlist in his support. Very quickly, the rebellion of the three earls of Huntingdon, Kent and Salisbury in January 1400 shook the new regime with its demonstration that many who had apparently switched their allegiance from Richard to the new king could not be relied upon. The warden of the islands, from 1396, was Edward, earl of Rutland, son of Edmund of Langley, duke of York and therefore grandson of Edward III. He navigated Richard's fall and, unlike other close royal kin, was not implicated in the conspiracy of January 1400. Although on 23 January John Sperston was sent

---

[1] Christopher Philpotts, 'The Fate of the Truce of Paris, 1396–1415', *Journal of Medieval History*, 24 (1998), 61–80, at pp. 68–70; J. L. Kirby, *Henry IV of England* (London, 1970), p. 161; Jonathan Sumption, *The Hundred Years War* (5 vols, London, 1990–2023), vol. 4, pp. 45–52; Chris Given-Wilson, *Henry IV* (New Haven CT, 2016), pp. 165–6, 171–3.

[2] Philpotts, 'Fate of the Truce of Paris', pp. 70–1; C. J. Ford, 'Piracy or Policy: The Crisis in the Channel 1400–03', *Transactions of the Royal Historical Society*, 5th ser., 29 (1979), 63–77; Sumption, *Hundred Years War*, vol. 4, pp. 89–129; Given-Wilson, *Henry IV*, pp. 202–3.

urgently to Guernsey and Jersey, only a month later armour was sent to the islands in Rutland's own name.[3] Jersey was not immune from the pressure caused by ongoing plotting against the crown. From 1400, the coalition of the Percies in the north of England, Owain Glyndŵr in Wales and the representatives of the Mortimers, whose young heir Edmund, fifth earl of March, inherited a strong claim to the English throne through Philippa, daughter of King Edward III's son Lionel of Antwerp, who married Edmund Mortimer, third earl of March, started to make itself felt. By 1403 Glyndŵr's forces were fighting widely across Wales; in July, the Percies challenged the king. From March 1403 there were signs of a concern in Westminster as to developments in the islands and, on 6 June 1403, the king ordered his warden (Aumale/Rutland, who had now succeeded his father as duke of York) to repress rebellion there.[4]

In the islands this uncertainty, in the threat of revolt or betrayal, combining with increasing offensive action against the islands, made the challenges of Henry IV's reign particularly acute.[5] In this situation, Henry needed the support of Jersey, along with Guernsey, and it appeared straightforward in May 1400 to confirm the privileges that had been granted by Edward III in 1341 and earlier confirmed by Richard in 1378 soon after the start of his reign.[6]

The wisdom of this approach became apparent as the level of hostilities in the western channel and approaches escalated. The small-scale raiding of 1402 moved in 1403 to larger-scale operations. The severity of the crisis is indicated by the fate of ecclesiastical property belonging to mainland French institutions on the islands, taken into the king's hands for the duration of the war.[7] In 1403, a raid led by Jean de Penhoët, admiral of Brittany, hit Jersey.[8]

---

[3] *CCR 1399–1402*, pp. 40, 49. Sperston was from Bristol: *CCR 1399–1402*, pp. 207, 516; *CCR 1405–09*, p. 80.

[4] *CCR 1402–05*, pp. 53, 59, 70; Thomas Rymer and Robert Sanderson (eds), *Foedera, conventiones, litterae, et cujuscunque generis acta publica*, rev. John Caley and Frederick Holbrooke (4 vols in 7, London, 1816–69), vol. 4i, p. 45.

[5] Paul Strohm, *England's Empty Throne: Usurpation and the Language of Legitimation, 1399–1422* (New Haven CT, 1998); Ian Mortimer, *The Fears of Henry IV: The Life of England's Self-Made King* (London, 2007).

[6] TNA, C 76/84, m. 7; Tim Thornton, *The Charters of Guernsey* (Bognor Regis, 2004), pp. 11–14.

[7] On 28 March 1403 Robert Thresk, clerk, and Roger Lughtburgh were given the keeping of Vale priory, for the duration of the war with France: *CFR, 1399–1405*, p. 205. On 24 May 1403, Nicholas Burton, king's clerk, was given the chapel of St Mary de la Marreys: *CPR 1401–05*, p. 228. In January 1405, Peter Julian, parson of St Clement, Jersey, ensured he had a ratification of his estate entered on the English patent rolls: *CPR 1405–08*, p. 92; he did this again in July 1413, following the accession of Henry V: *CPR 1413–16*, p. 4.

[8] Michel Pintoin, *Chronique du religieux de Saint-Denys: contenant le règne de Charles VI, de 1380 à 1422*, ed. L. Bellaguet and Prosper Brugière baron de Barante

And in 1406 there was extensive destruction as a result of another raid, this time inspired by a desire to limit the raiding by Jerseymen in the roads of Saint-Malo and to release the more than 30 prisoners they were holding. The price Jersey paid for removing the raiders was 10,000 golden crowns.[9]

Richard's grant of custody of the islands to Aumale was not challenged by Henry on his accession.[10] But the critics of the Ricardian regime, including one with particular understanding of Jersey, soon made themselves felt. As we have seen, very early in the new reign, those who had suffered most were prominent in demanding change, and John, Lord Cobham took the opportunity to raise 'the evils of recent years', which for him had meant an uncomfortable exile in Jersey.[11] As elsewhere in his dominions, the accession of Henry IV did not fundamentally undermine the consolidation of local liberties. But the 1394 charter granted by Richard was not confirmed. And so the islanders lost, for the moment, their right to be treated as Englishmen in terms of customs and other tolls.

(6 vols, Paris, 1839–52), vol. 3, p. 113; Given-Wilson, *Henry IV*, p. 237; Colin Platt, *A Concise History of Jersey: A New Perspective* (St Helier, 2009), p. 33; G. R. Balleine, *History of Jersey*, rev. Marguerite Syvret and Joan Stevens (Chichester, 1981), p. 49; Gustave Dupont, *Histoire du Cotentin et de ses îles* (4 vols, Caen, 1870–85), vol. 2, p. 497; *Le Cotton manuscrit Galba B.I.*, transcribed Edward Scott, ed. M. L. Gilliodts-Van Severen (Bruxelles, 1896), pp. 77–8; Edmund Toulmin Nicolle, *Mont Orgueil Castle: Its History and Description* (Jersey, 1921), pp. 25–8.

[9] Juan de Mata Carriazo (ed.), *El Victorial: crónica de Don Pero Niño, Conde de Buelna* (Madrid, 1940); Paul de Gibon, *Un archipel Normand: les îles Chausey et leur histoire*, 2nd edn (Évreux, 1935), pp. 80–1; A. C. Saunders, *Jersey in the 15th and 16th Centuries* (Jersey, 1933), pp. 13–14; F. Joüon des Longrais, 'La lutte sur mer au xive siècle et la prise de Jersey en 1406 par Hector de Pontbriand', *Bulletin Archéologique de l'Association Bretonne*, 3rd ser., 10 (1891), 145–205. E. T. Nicolle, '"Le Victorial" and the Attack on Jersey in 1406', *ABSJ*, 10 (1923–27), 32–46, gives material from parlement of Paris 9 March 1407 (showing decision to act against 'pirates' – Pierre de Pontbriand assembled ships inc. 3 galleys under Niño; Jerseymen gave up their French prisoners and paid 8,000 livres, part cash and part under surety of hostages) and 11 April 1409.

[10] *CPR 1399–1401*, p. 106 (23 November 1399).

[11] H. T. Riley (ed.), 'Annales Ricardi Secundi et Henrici Quarti Regis Angliae', in *Chronica Monasterii S. Albani: Johannis de Trokelowe, et Henrici de Blaneforde ... Chronica et Annales*, Rolls Ser., 28(3) (London, 1866), pp. 153–420, at pp. 306–07; Chris Given-Wilson (ed.), *Chronicles of the Revolution, 1397–1400: The Reign of Richard II* (Manchester, 1993), pp. 204–5.

Text

Henry IV confirmed the charter of his predecessor, Richard II, granted in 1378, and hence Richard's confirmation of the charter of his grandfather, Edward III. Common to Guernsey, Sark and Alderney; text taken from enrolment in The National Archives, C 76/84, m. 7, with reference to the edition presented in Prison Board.

[1] Rex Omnibus ad quos &c. salutem. Inspeximus literas patentes domini Ricardi nuper Regis Anglie secundi post conquestum de confirmacione factas in hec verba.

[2] Ricardus Dei gratia Rex Anglie et ffrancie et Dominus Hibernie Omnibus ad quos presentes litere peruenerint salutem. Inspeximus literas patentes quas dominus Edwardus nuper Rex Anglie auus noster fieri fecit in hec verba

[3] Edwardus Dei gratia Rex Anglie et ffrancie et Dominus Hibernie Omnibus ad quos presentes litere peruenerint salutem. Sciatis quod nos grata memoria recensentes quam constanter et magnanimiter dilecti et fideles nostri homines Insularum nostrarum de Jereseye Gernereye Serk et Aureneye in fidelitate nostra et progenitorum nostrorum Regum Anglie semper hactenus perstiterunt et quanta pro saluacione dictarum Insularum et nostrorum conseruacione iurium et honoris ibidem sustinuerunt tam pericula corporum quam suarum dispendia facultatum et proinde volentes ipsos fauore prosequi gracioso concesssimus pro nobis et heredibus nostris dictis hominibus Insularum predictarum quod ipsi heredes et successores sui omnia priuilegia libertates immunitates exempciones consuetudines in personis rebus monetis et aliis eis virtute concessionum progenitorum nostrorum Regum Anglie vel alias legitime competencia habeant et teneant ac eis sine impedimento vel molestacione nostri heredum vel Ministrorum nostrorum quorumcumque plene gaudeant et vtantur prout ipsi et eorum antecessores habitatores dictarum Insularum eis vsi sunt rationabiliter et gauisi que iam eis in forma predicta generaliter confirmamus Volentes ea cum super hiis plene informati fuerimus prout iustum fuerit confirmare. In cuius rei testimonium has literas nostras fieri fecimus patentes Teste me ipso apud Turrim Londonii decimo die Julii anno regni nostri Anglie quintodecimo regni vero nostri ffrancie secundo.

[4] Nos autem concessiones confirmacionem priuilegia libertates immunitates et consuetudines predicta rata habentes et grata ea pro nobis et heredibus nostris quantum in nobis est acceptamus approbamus ratificamus et ea prædictis hominibus Insularum huiusmodi heredibus et successoribus suis concedimus et confirmamus prout litere predicte plenius testantur et prout ipsi et eorum antecessores habitatores dictarum Insularum eis vsi sunt rationabiliter et gauisi.

In cuius rei testimonium has literas nostras fieri fecimus patentes. Teste me ipso apud Gloucestriam decimo die Nouembris anno regni nostri secundo.

[5] Nos autem concessiones confirmacionem priuilegia libertates immunitates et consuetudines predicta rata habentes et grata ea pro nobis et heredibus nostris quantum in nobis est acceptamus approbamus ratificamus et ea dilectis nobis nunc hominibus Insularum predictarum heredibus et successoribus suis de gratia nostra speciali concedimus et confirmamus prout litere predicte rationabiliter testantur et prout ipsi et eorum antecessores habitatores dictarum Insularum eis vsi sunt rationabiliter et gauisi. In cuius &c Teste Regis apud Westmonasterium viii die Maii.
Per breve de privato sigillo et pro sex marcis solutis in Hanaperio.

Translation

[1] The King to all to whom, etc., greeting [Henry by the grace of God king of England and France and lord of Ireland to all to whom these present letters may come, greeting]: We have inspected the Letters Patent of the Lord Richard lately king of England the second after the conquest in confirmation made in these words.

[2] Richard by the grace of God king of England and France and lord of Ireland to all to whom these present letters may come, greeting. We have inspected the Letters Patent which the Lord Edward lately king of England our grandfather caused to be made in these words.

[3] Know ye, that we recalling with grateful memory with what constancy and high spirit our beloved and faithful men of our islands of Guernsey, Jersey, Sark and Alderney have always hitherto continued in their faithfulness to us and our progenitors kings of England; and how great dangers to their bodies, as well as costs to their property they have borne for the safety of the said islands, and conservation of our laws and honour therein, and in like manner desiring to follow after them with our gracious favour, we have granted for ourselves and our heirs to the said men of the aforesaid islands, that they themselves, their heirs and successors, may have and hold all privileges, liberties, immunities, exemptions, and customs, in respect of their persons, goods, moneys, and other matters, by virtue of the grant of our progenitors kings of England, or otherwise lawfully by agreement, and, without impediment or molestation from us, our heirs, or our officers whomsoever, may fully enjoy and use them, according as they themselves and their predecessors, the inhabitants of the said islands, have reasonably enjoyed and used them. Which things we do now confirm to them generally in the aforesaid form, being willing after we have enquired into them to confirm them as may be just. In testimony whereof we

have had these letters made patent, myself as witness at the Tower of London the tenth day of July, in the year of our reign in England the fifteenth, but of our reign in France the second.

[4] We, moreover, holding the concessions, confirmations, privileges, liberties, immunities, and customs to be reasonable and seasonable, accept, approve, and ratify them for us and our heirs, as far as in us lies, and concede and confirm them to the aforesaid men of the islands in the same manner to their heirs and successors as the aforesaid Letters more fully testify and as they and their predecessors inhabitants of the said Islands have reasonably used and enjoyed them. In witness whereof we have had these our Letters made Patent. Myself as witness at Gloucester the tenth day of November in the second year of our reign.

[5] We, moreover, holding the concessions, confirmations, privileges, liberties, immunities, and customs to be reasonable and seasonable, accept, approve, and ratify them for us and our heirs, as far as in us lies, and concede and confirm them to the aforesaid men of the islands in the same manner to their heirs and successors as the aforesaid Letters more fully testify and as they and their predecessors inhabitants of the said Islands have reasonably used and enjoyed them. In witness whereof, &c.. Witness the King at Westminster the eighth day of May [In witness whereof we have caused these our letters to be made patent. Witness myself at Westminster the eighth day of May in the first year of our reign.]

By writ of Privy Seal and for six marks paid into the Hanaper.

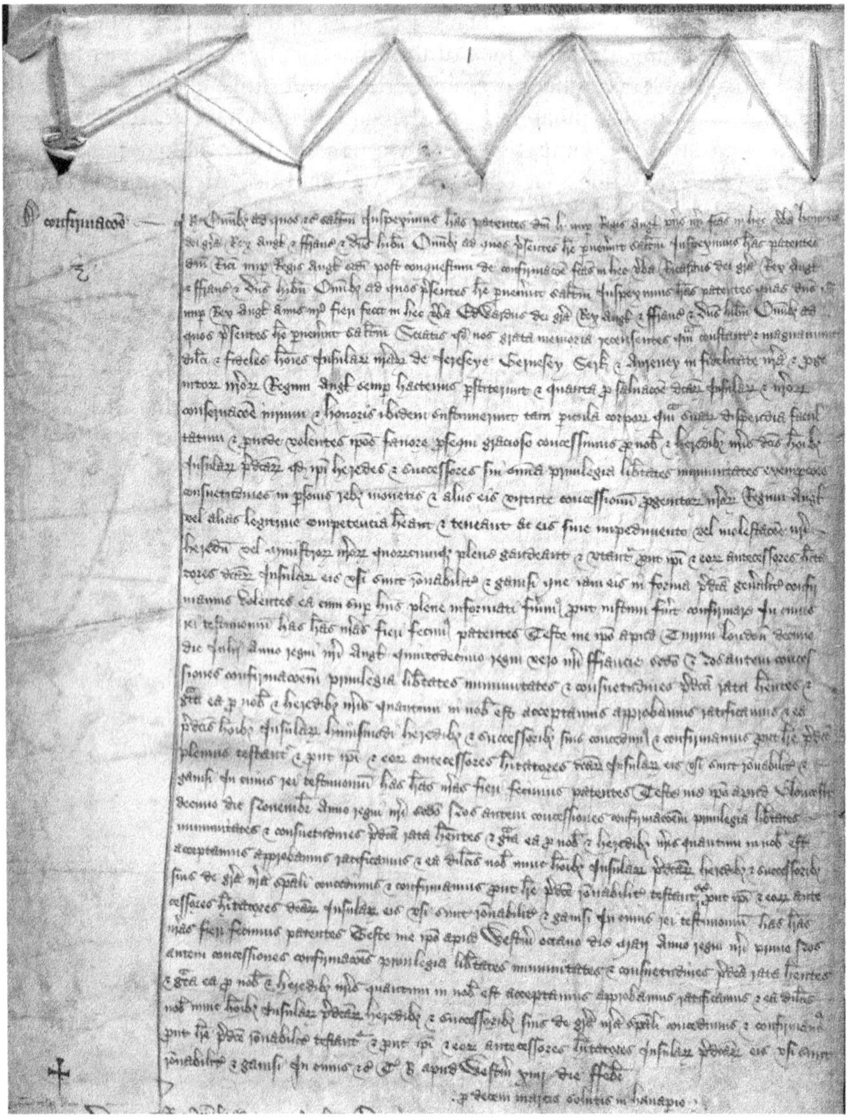

Plate 5: The Royal Charter granted by Henry V in 1414.
Credit: The National Archives, ref. C 76/96.

Henry V: 1414

Commentary

Even if Henry V's policy after his accession in 1413 seemed to represent a shifting pattern of attempts to extend alliances and truces, the new king rapidly transformed England's relationship with France, and with Normandy in particular. The last years of his father's reign had seen Henry IV continue his pursuit of security for English interests in the south-west of France on terms similar to those established in the treaty of Brétigny. Henry V's focus was the recovery of the old Norman-Angevin empire, including feudal superiority over Brittany. While in January 1414 Henry's representatives were seeking for him a marriage with the French princess Catherine, and they agreed a truce of a year, this was allied with demands for a dowry of one million crowns and the reassertion of their territorial ambitions.[1] The confirmation of the islands' rights came in February of 1414.[2] May 1414 saw the final meeting, in Guernsey, between English and Breton commissioners charged with making arrangements for the renewal of the truce between the king and the duke.[3] By the summer of that year, Henry was in complex negotiation with both of the rival French parties, the Burgundians and the Armagnacs, skilfully seeking to play them off for the best advantage. Jersey and the other islands were much more likely to take an important part in the new king's campaigns, given the role that Normandy played within them. A specific aspiration to reclaim the

---

[1] Jonathan Sumption, *The Hundred Years War* (5 vols, London, 1990–2023), vol. 4, pp. 366–400; Christopher Allmand, *Henry V*, new edn (New Haven CT, 1997), pp. 67–71.

[2] TNA, C 76/96 (Chancery: Treaty Rolls, 1 Henry V), m. 1, no. 3, printed in *Prison Board*, pp. 160–1 (Thomas Carte, *Catalogue des Rolles gascons, normans et françois conservés dans les archives de la Tour de Londres : et contenant le précis & le sommaire de tous les titres qui s'y trouvent concernant la Guienne, la Normandie & les autres provinces de la France sujettes autrefois aux rois d'Angleterre* (2 vols, Paris, 1743), vol. 2, p. 212); Tim Thornton, *The Charters of Guernsey* (Bognor Regis, 2004), pp. 15–19.

[3] J. H. Wylie and W. T. Waugh, *The Reign of Henry V* (3 vols, Cambridge, 1914–29), vol. 1, p. 102.

duchy of Normandy more or less independently of the French crown does not seem to have been evident in the early years of the reign, although it became more apparent at times, especially from 1417.[4] Still, even if Henry's opening military move, against Harfleur in the summer of 1415, was largely dictated by the pragmatic recognition of that port's prominent and disruptive role over the previous decade and a half, Normandy was to be the focus of his campaigning for some time. Yet although this meant that, in a relatively short time, the islands would once again neighbour a Norman coast that acknowledged an English duke, Henry V confirmed their privileges as his father had done, without the extension of rights they had briefly acquired under Richard II.

Text

Henry V confirmed the charter of his father, Henry IV, and hence his confirmation of that of his predecessor, Richard II, in 1378, and in turn Richard's confirmation there of the charter of his grandfather, Edward III. Common to Guernsey, Sark and Alderney; text taken from enrolmentA in The National Archives, C 76/96, m. 1, with reference to the edition presented in Prison Board.

[1] [Henricus dei gracia Rex Anglie & ffrancie & Dominus Hibernie Omnibus ad quos presentes litere peruenerint Salutem.] [ARex Omnibus ad quos &c., salutem.] Inspeximus literas patentes domini Henrici nuper Regis Anglie patris nostri factas in hec verba.

[2] Henricus dei gratia Rex Anglie et ffrancie et Dominus Hibernie Omnibus ad quos presentes litere peruerint salutem. Inspeximus literas patentes domini Ricardi nuper Regis Anglie secundi post conquestum de confirmacione factas in hec verba.

[3] Ricardus dei gratia Rex Angelie et ffrancie et Dominus Hibernie Omnibus ad quos presentes litere pervenerint salutem. Inspeximus literas patentes quas dominus Edwardus nuper Rex Anglie auus noster fieri fecit in hec verba.

[4] Edwardus Dei gratia Rex Anglie et ffrancie et Dominus Hibernie Omnibus ad quos presentes litere pervenerint salutem Sciatis quod nos grata memoria recensentes quam constanter et magnanimiter dilecti et fideles nostri homines Insularum nostrarum de Jeresey Gernesey Serk et Aureney in fidelitate nostra et progenitorum nostrorum Regum Anglie semper hactenus perstiterunt et

---

[4] Anne Curry, 'Lancastrian Normandy: The Jewel in the Crown?', in David Bates and Anne Curry (eds), *England and Normandy in the Middle Ages* (London and Rio Grande, 1994), pp. 235–52; Allmand, *Henry V*, pp. xii–xiii.

quanta pro salvacione dictarum Insularum et nostrorum conservacione jurium et honoris ibidem sustinuerunt tam pericula corporum quam suarum dispendia facultatum et proinde volentes ipsos fauore prosequi gracioso concessimus pro nobis et heredibus nostris dictis hominibus Insularum predictarum quod ipsi heredes et successores sui omnia priuilegia libertates immunitates exempciones consuetudines in personis rebus monetis et aliis eis virtute concessionum progenitorum nostrorum Regum Anglie vel alias ligitime competencia habeant et teneant ac eis sine impedimento vel molestacione nostri heredum aut Ministrorum nostrorum quorumcumque plene gaudeant et utantur prout ipsi et eorum antecessores habitatores dictarum Insularum eis vsi sunt rationabiliter et gauisi que iam eis in forma predicta generaliter confirmamus Volentes ea cum super hiis plene informati fuerimus prout justum fuerit confimare. In cuius rei testimonium has literas nostras fieri fecimus patentes. Teste me ipso apud Turrim Londonii decimo die Julii anno regni nostri Anglie quintodecimo regni vero nostri ffrancie secundo.

[5] Nos autem concessiones confirmacionem priuilegia libertates immunitates et consuetudines predicta rata habentes et grata ea pro nobis et heredibus nostris quantum in nobis est acceptamus approbamus ratificamus et ea predictis hominibus Insularum hujusmodi heredibus et successoribus suis concedimus et confirmamus prout litere predicte plenius testantur et prout ipsi et eorum antecessores habitatores dictarum Insularum eis vsi sunt rationabiliter et gauisi. In cuius rei testimonium has literas nostras fieri fecimus patentes. Teste me ipso apud Gloucestriam decimo die Novembris anno regni nostri secundo.

[6] Nos autem concessiones confirmacionem privilegia libertates immunitates et consuetudines predicta rata habentes et grata ea pro nobis et heredibus nostris quantum in nobis est acceptamus approbamus ratificamus et ea dilectis nobis nunc hominibus Insularum predictarum heredibus et successoribus suis de gratia nostra speciali concedimus et confirmamus prout litere predicte rationabiliter testantur et prout ipsi et eorum antecessores habitatores dictarum Insularum eis vsi sunt rationabiliter et gauisi. In cujus rei testimonium has literas nostras fieri fecimus patentes. Teste me ipso apud Westmonasterium octauo die Maii anno regni nostri primo.

[7] Nos autem concessiones confirmaciones privilegia libertates immunitates et consuetudines predicta rata habentes et grata ea pro nobis et heredibus nostris quantum in nobis est acceptamus approbamus ratificamus et ea dilectis nobis nunc hominibus Insularum predictarum heredibus et successoribus suis de gratia nostra speciali concedimus et confirmamus prout litere predicte rationabiliter testantur et prout ipsi et eorum antecessores habitatores Insularum predictarum eis vsi sunt rationabiliter et gauisi. [In cuius rei testimonium has literas nostras fieri fecimus patentes. Teste me ipso apud Westmonasterium

quartodecimo die ffebruarii Anno regni nostri primo] [^In cuius &c. Teste Regis apud Westmonasterium xiiij die ffebruarii.]

pro decem marcis solutis in Hanaperio.

Clerck

[Ex p Ricu Gabriell Johem Clerk clericos.]

Translation

[1] Henry, by the grace of God king of England and France and lord of Ireland, to all to whom these present letters may come, greeting [^The King to all to whom etc., greeting.] We have inspected the Letters Patent of the Lord Henry lately king of England, our father, made in these words.

[2] Henry by the grace of God king of England and France and lord of Ireland, to all to whom these present letters may come, greeting. We have inspected the Letters Patent of the Lord Richard lately king of England the second after the conquest in confirmation made in these words.

[3] Richard by the grace of God king of England and France and lord of Ireland to all to whom these present letters may come, greeting. We have inspected the Letters Patent which the Lord Edward lately king of England our grandfather, caused to be made in these words.

[4] Edward by the grace of God king of England and France and lord of Ireland to all to whom these present letters may come, greeting. Know ye, that we recalling with grateful memory with what constancy and high spirit our beloved and faithful men of our islands of Guernsey, Jersey, Sark and Alderney have always hitherto continued in their faithfulness to us and our progenitors kings of England; and how great dangers to their bodies, as well as costs to their property they have borne for the safety of the said islands, and conservation of our laws and honour therein, and in like manner desiring to follow after them with our gracious favour, we have granted for ourselves and our heirs to the said men of the aforesaid islands, that they themselves, their heirs and successors, may have and hold all privileges, liberties, immunities, exemptions, and customs, in respect of their persons, goods, moneys, and other matters, by virtue of the grant of our progenitors kings of England, or otherwise lawfully by agreement, and, without impediment or molestation from us, our heirs, or our officers whomsoever, may fully enjoy and use them, according as they themselves and their predecessors, the inhabitants of the said islands, have reasonably enjoyed and used them. Which things we do now confirm to them generally in the aforesaid form, being willing after we have

enquired into them to confirm them as may be just. In testimony whereof we have had these letters made patent, myself as witness at the Tower of London the tenth day of July, in the year of our reign in England the fifteenth, but of our reign in France the second.

[5] We, moreover, holding the concessions, confirmations, privileges, liberties, immunities, and customs to be reasonable and seasonable, accept, approve, and ratify them for us and our heirs, as far as in us lies, and concede and confirm them to the aforesaid men of the islands in the same manner to their heirs and successors as the aforesaid Letters more fully testify and as they and their predecessors inhabitants of the said Islands have reasonably used and enjoyed them. In witness whereof we have had these our Letters made Patent. Myself as witness at Gloucester the tenth day of November in the second year of our reign.

[6] We, moreover, holding the concessions, confirmations, privileges, liberties, immunities, and customs to be reasonable and seasonable, accept, approve, and ratify them for us and our heirs, as far as in us lies, and concede and confirm them to the aforesaid men of the islands in the same manner to their heirs and successors as the aforesaid Letters more fully testify and as they and their predecessors inhabitants of the said Islands have reasonably used and enjoyed them. In witness whereof we have caused these our letters to be made patent. Witness myself at Westminster the eighth day of May in the first year of our reign.

[7] We, moreover, holding the concessions, confirmations, privileges, liberties, immunities, and customs to be reasonable and seasonable, accept, approve, and ratify them for us and our heirs, as far as in us lies, and concede and confirm them to the aforesaid men of the islands in the same manner to their heirs and successors as the aforesaid Letters more fully testify and as they and their predecessors inhabitants of the said Islands have reasonably used and enjoyed them. In witness whereof we have caused these our letters to be made Patent. Witness myself at Westminster the fourteenth day of February in the first year of our Reign. [^AIn witness whereof, etc. Witness the King at Westminster the fourteenth day of February.]

For ten marks paid into the Hanaper.

Clerck

[On behalf of Richard Gabriel and John Clark clerks.]

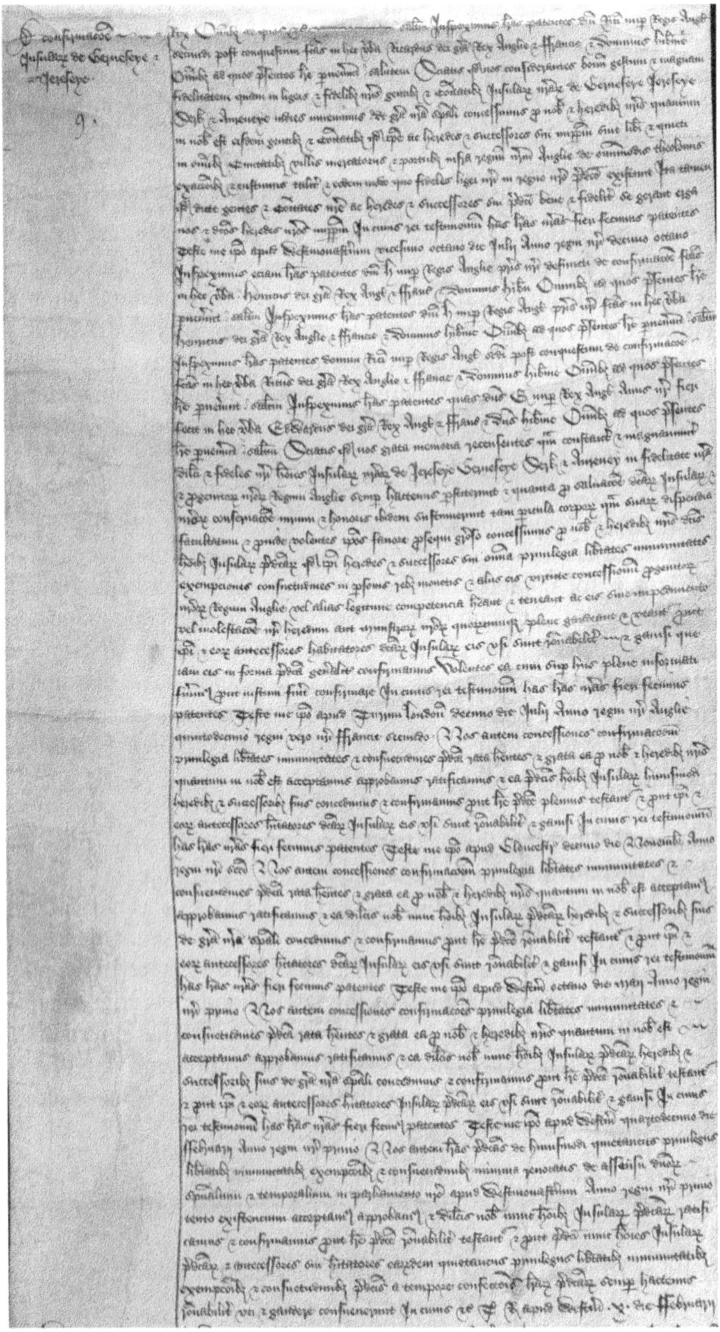

Plate 6: The Royal Charter granted by Henry VI in 1442.
Credit: The National Archives, ref. C 76/124.

Henry VI: 1442

Commentary

When Henry V died at Vincennes, on 31 August 1422, he left an heir who was only eight months old. Henry VI's infancy dictated a period of regency council, led, in England, by his uncle Humphrey, duke of Gloucester.[1] English practice relating to the end of royal minorities was never fixed and, after a period of attempted compromises, by early 1441 conciliar rule had been effectively abandoned.[2] A few months later, on 10 February 1442, Henry confirmed the privileges of the communities of the bailiwicks of Jersey and Guernsey.

The grant to Jersey and Guernsey was more generous than those made in 1400 and 1414 because, as well as reciting Henry V's confirmation of the sequence of charters beginning in 1341, Henry VI's charter confirmed the grant by Richard II in 1394 of exemption from English tolls, duties and customs. This generosity was perhaps characteristic of Henry's approach to government, but other factors played a role in the decision.

One was the gradual rehabilitation of Richard II in the reigns of Henry V and VI. After his death in custody, Richard's body had been buried at King's Langley, but in 1413 he was re-interred in the tomb Richard himself had always intended, in Westminster Abbey. As well as a still urgent need to prove that Richard was truly dead, the move sprang from a desire to atone for Henry IV's actions and to claim, on Henry V's part, to be in some sense Richard's heir. The rehabilitation continued through Henry V's reign and into Henry VI's.[3]

Next, we must consider the ongoing importance of the islands' strategic position. Early in Henry V's campaigns to conquer Normandy, that position

---

[1] Ralph A. Griffiths, *The Reign of Henry VI: The Exercise of Royal Authority, 1422–1461* (London, 1981), pp. 189–94; B. P. Wolffe, *Henry VI* (London, 1981), pp. 54–62.

[2] J. L. Watts, 'When did Henry VI's Minority End?' in Dorothy J. Clayton, Richard G. Davies, and Peter McNiven (eds), *Trade, Devotion and Governance: Papers in Later Medieval History* (Stroud, 1994), pp. 116–39, esp. p. 129.

[3] Nigel Saul, *Richard II* (New Haven CT, 1997), p. 428; Paul Strohm, *England's Empty Throne: Usurpation and the Language of Legitimation, 1399–1422* (New Haven CT and London, 1998), pp. 115–25.

had been evident, for example, when naval support was required for the siege of Cherbourg.[4] By 1442, the military situation had deteriorated, and defence and support for the remaining English positions in Normandy was more of a question.[5]

Another was the fact that Jersey and Guernsey were no longer in the king's hands. First his eldest surviving uncle, John, duke of Bedford had become lord of the isles, and then, following Bedford's death in 1435, the islands were granted (in 1437) to the surviving uncle, Humphrey, duke of Gloucester.[6] Further, the years before 1442 had tested the position and liberties of the islanders. In 1440, the English government had levied a tax on aliens in England, including Irishmen and Channel Islanders. There was considerable opposition to this move and, for islanders, exemption was quickly secured before the end of the year on 22 November 1440. So in 1442, when a further alien subsidy was granted, islanders were recognised as the king's subjects and henceforth exempt.[7] Parliament sat from 25 January to 27 March 1442, so the grant of privileges to Jersey and Guernsey occurred as it was in session, and probably as the alien taxation was being discussed. A confirmation and re-extension of liberties, to include exemption from tolls, duties and customs, was clearly aligned with the decisions of parliament.

The alien subsidy legislation also demonstrated not English and parliamentary control over the islands (since it was islanders in England who were targeted) but an instinctive English assumption that even the king's subjects might be treated as 'other' if they did not live in England and adopt English

---

[4] Titus Livius, *Vita Henrici Quinti* (Oxford, 1716), p. 52; Kenneth Hotham Vickers, *Humphrey, Duke of Gloucester: A Biography* (London, 1907), p. 62.

[5] Griffiths, *Reign of Henry VI*, pp. 443–66, 470–3; Jonathan Sumption, *The Hundred Years War* (5 vols, London, 1990–2023), vol. 5, pp. 1–596, esp. 530–96.

[6] *Proceedings and Ordinances of the Privy Council of England*, ed. Harris Nicolas (7 vols, London, 1834–37), vol. 5, p. 5; *48th Report of the Deputy Keeper of the Public Records* (London, 1887), appendix, p. 317; Vickers, *Humphrey, Duke of Gloucester*, p. 248.

[7] C. Given-Wilson et al. (eds), *The Parliament Rolls of Medieval England, 1275–1504* (16 vols, Woodbridge and London, 2005), vol. 11, pp. 253–4, 330–1; TNA, E 159/217, Brevia directa baronibus, Michaelmas, r. 61d; W. Mark Ormrod, Bart Lambert, and Jonathan Mackman, *Immigrant England, 1300–1550* (Manchester, 2018), pp. 83–4; W. Mark Ormrod and Jonathan Mackman, 'Resident Aliens in Later Medieval England: Sources, Contexts, and Debates', in Mark Ormrod, Nicola McDonald, and Craig Taylor (eds), *Resident Aliens in Later Medieval England* (Turnhout, 2017), pp. 3–32; R. A. Griffiths, 'The English Realm and Dominions and the King's Subjects in the Later Middle Ages', in J. G. Rowe (ed.), *Aspects of Late Medieval Government and Society: Essays Presented to J. R. Lander* (Toronto (Ont), 1986), pp. 83–105, reprinted in R. A. Griffiths, *King and Country: England and Wales in the Fifteenth Century* (London, 1991), pp. 33–54, at pp. 44–5.

manners and customs. The legislation and the charter are therefore consistent with another important development of the decade, the grant on 24 November 1445 of the reversion of the lordship of the islands to Henry Beauchamp, earl of Warwick, who was one of the king's closest friends.[8] The grant was part of an effort to give Warwick near-royal status, which included (according to the family chronicle compiled at Tewkesbury) the earl's crowning as king of the Isle of Wight.[9]

From islanders' perspectives, this meant that privileges sat in a wider context too, not simply in relation to the English parliament, courts, taxation and customs officials. This perspective is clear from the contemporary statement made in the Guernsey *précepte d'assize*. Dated 30 September 1441, the *précepte* stated the rights of the islanders as they were then understood, in relation to the determination of *extente* of 1331. The circumstances of 1441/42 helped shape this claim, for example, protecting the islanders from being forced to go out of the islands on an appeal or otherwise to the Exchequer at Rouen as part of the duchy of Normandy.[10]

Henry Beauchamp was not to live to enjoy the islands' lordship. He died in June 1446, and so when Gloucester followed him to the grave in suspicious circumstances in February 1447, it was Anne, Warwick's daughter and heir, who benefited from the reversion[11] and, with her death in June 1449, the islands' lordship passed to her aunt, Henry Beauchamp's full sister Anne.[12] Anne's marriage to Richard Neville, heir of Richard, earl of Salisbury, brought him Jersey and Guernsey as part of the complex provisions for the division of

---

[8] *CPR 1441–46*, p. 400.

[9] Tim Thornton, 'Lordship and Sovereignty in the Territories of the English Crown: Sub-kingship and Its Implications, 1300–1600', *Journal of British Studies*, 60 (2021), 848–66, at p. 854.

[10] Havilland de Sausmarez (ed.), *The Extentes of Guernsey 1248 and 1331, and other Documents Relating to the Ancient Usages and Customs in that Island* (St Peter Port, Guernsey, 1934), pp. 130–50, esp. p. 135, re-edited by D. M. Ogier as 'Guernsey's *précepte d'assize* of 1441: Translation and Notes', *Jersey and Guernsey Law Review*, 12 (2008), 207–19. The notarial element is dated 11 September 1482, and collation 25 September 1489 (pp. 138–9).

[11] G. E. C[ockayne], *The Complete Peerage of England, Scotland, Ireland, Great Britain and the United Kingdom, Extant, Extinct and Dormant*, rev. Vicary Gibbs, ed. H. A. Doubleday, D. Warrand, and Lord Howard de Walden (new edn, 13 vols in 14, London, 1910–59), vol. 12/ii, pp. 383–4; *CPR 1446–52*, p. 42; James Gairdner (ed.), *The Paston Letters*, reprinted (6 vols in 1, Gloucester, 1983, from the Library Edition of 1904), vol. 2, pp. 78–9.

[12] Richard Beauchamp had had three daughters by his wife Elizabeth (Berkeley): Margaret, Eleanor and Elizabeth; by his other wife, Isabel, Baroness Burghersh, as well as his son Henry, he had had another daughter, the Anne in question here: C[ockayne], *Complete Peerage*, vol. 12/ii, pp. 381–2; Griffiths, *Reign of Henry VI*, pp. 572–4.

the Warwick inheritance.[13] And so Richard, earl of Warwick was soon acting as lord of the isles, in right of his wife.[14] The privileges of the islands might therefore be strengthened not just in the hands of members of the royal family, but in those of the king's closest friend, and even those of a nobleman without obvious direct ties to the crown.

Text

Henry VI confirmed the charter of his father, Henry V, and hence his confirmation of that of Henry IV; through that, he confirmed the charter of his predecessor, Richard II, in 1378, and in turn Richard's confirmation there of the charter of his grandfather, Edward III. Common to Guernsey, Sark and Alderney; text taken from [A] charter in Guernsey Greffe and [B] enrolment in The National Archives, C 76/124, m. 14, with reference to the edition presented in Prison Board.

[1] [[A]Henricus dei gracia Rex Anglie & ffrancie & Dominus Hibernie Omnibus ad quos presentes litere peruenerint salutem.] [[B]Rex omnibus ad quos &c. salute.] Inspeximus literas patentes domini Ricardi nuper Regis Anglie secundi post conquestum factas in hec verba.

[2] Ricardus dei gracia Rex Anglie et ffrancie et Dominus Hibernie Omnibus ad quos presentes litere peruenerint salutem. Sciatis quod nos considerantes bonum gestum et magnam fidelitatem quam in ligeis et fidelibus nostris gentibus et communitatibus Insularum nostrarum de Gerneseye Jereseye Serk et Aureneye indies inuenimus de gratia nostra speciali concessimus pro nobis et heredibus nostris quantum in nobis est eisdem gentibus et communitatibus quod ipse [sic] ac heredes et successores sui imperpetuum sint liberi et quieti in omnibus Ciuitatibus villis mercatoriis et portubus infra regnum nostrum Anglie de omnimodis theoloniis exaccionibus et custumis taliter et eodem modo quo fideles ligei nostri in regno nostro predicto existunt. Ita tamen quod dicte gentes et Communitates nostre ac heredes et successores sui predicti bene et fideliter se gerant erga nos et dictos heredes nostros imperpetuum. In cuius rei testimonium has literas nostras fieri fecimus patentes. Teste me ipso apud Westmonasterium vicesimo octauo die Julii anno regni nostri decimo octauo.
[3] Inspeximus eciam literas patentes domini Henrici nuper Regis Anglie patris nostri defuncti de confirmacione factas in hec verba.

[4] Henricus Dei gratia Rex Anglie et ffrancie et Dominus Hibernie Omnibus ad quos presentes litere peruenerint salutem. Inspeximus literas patentes

---

[13] *CPR 1446–52*, p. 262.
[14] E.g. in letters patent issued on 18 January 1452: *CPR 1452–61*, pp. 571–2.

domini Henrici nuper Regis Anglie patris nostri defuncti de confirmacione factas in hec verba.

[5] Henricus Dei gratia Rex Anglie et ffrancie et Dominus Hibernie Omnibus ad quos presentes litere peruenerint salutem. Inspeximus literas patentes domini Ricardi nuper Regis Anglie secundi post conquestum de confirmacione factas in hec verba.

[6] Ricardus Dei gratia Rex Anglie et ffrancie et Dominus Hibernie. Omnibus ad quos presentes litere peruenerint salutem. Inspeximus literas patentes quas Dominus Edwardus nuper Rex Anglie auus noster fieri fecit in hec verba.

[7] Edwardus Dei gratia Rex Anglie et ffrancie et Dominus Hibernie Omnibus ad quos presentes litere peruenerint salutem Sciatis quod nos grata memoria recensentes quam constanter et magnanimiter dilecti et fideles nostri Homines Insularum nostrarum de Jereseye Gerneseye Serk et Aureney in fidelitate nostra et progenitorum nostrorum Regum Anglie semper hactenus perstiterunt et quanta pro saluacione dictarum Insularum et nostrorum conseruacione iurium et honoris ibidem sustinuerunt tam pericula corporum quam suarum dispendia facultatum et proinde volentes ipsos fauore prosequi gracioso concessimus pro nobis et heredibus nostris dictis hominibus Insularum predictarum quod ipsi heredes et successores sui omnia priuilegia libertates immunitates exempciones consuetudines in personis rebus monetis et aliis eis virtute concessionum progenitorum nostrorum Regum Anglie vel alias legitime competencia habeant et teneant ac eis sine impedimento vel molestacione nostri heredum aut ministrorum nostrorum quorumcumque plene gaudeant et vtantur prout ipsi et eorum antecessores habitatores dictarum Insularum eis vsi sunt rationabiliter et gauisi que iam eis in forma predicta generaliter confirmamus volentes ea cum super hiis plene informati fuerimus prout justum fuerit confirmare In cuius rei testimonium has literas nostras fieri fecimus patentes. Teste me ipso apud Turrim Londonii decimo die Julii anno regni nostri Anglie quinto decimo regni vero nostri ffrancie secundo.

[8] Nos autem concessiones confirmacionem priuilegia libertates immunitates et consuetudines predicta rata habentes et grata ea pro nobis et heredibus nostris quantum in nobis est acceptamus approbamus ratificamus et ea predictis hominibus Insularum huiusmodi heredibus et successoribus suis concedimus et confirmamus prout litere predicte plenius testantur et prout ipsi et eorum antecessores habitatores dictarum Insularum eis vsi sunt rationabiliter et gauisi. In cuius rei testimonium has literas nostras fieri fecimus patentes Teste me ipso apud Gloucestriam decimo die Nouembris Anno regni nostri secundo.

[9] Nos autem concessiones confirmacionem priuilegia libertates immunitates et consuetudines predicta rata habentes et grata ea pro nobis et heredibus nostris quantum in nobis est acceptamus approbamus ratificamus et ea dilectis nobis nunc hominibus Insularum predictarum heredibus et successoribus suis de gratia nostra speciali concedimus et confirmamus prout litere predicte rationabiliter testantur et prout ipsi et eorum antecessores habitatores dictarum Insularum eis vsi sunt rationabiliter et gauisi. In cuius rei testimonium has literas nostras fieri fecimus patentes. Teste me ipso apud Westmonasterium octauo die Maii anno regni nostri primo.

[10] Nos autem concessiones confirmaciones priuilegia libertates immunitates et consuetudines predicta rata habentes et grata ea pro nobis et heredibus nostris quantum in nobis est acceptamus approbamus ratificamus et ea dilectis nobis nunc hominibus Insularum predictarum heredibus et successoribus suis de gratia nostra speciali concedimus et confirmamus prout litere predicte rationabiliter testantur et prout ipsi et eorum antecessores habitatores Insularum predictarum eis vsi sunt rationabiliter et gauisi. In cuius rei testimonium has literas nostras fieri fecimus patentes Teste me ipso apud Westmonasterium quartodecimo die ffebruarii anno regni nostri primo.

[11] Nos autem literas predictas de huiusmodi quietanciis priuilegiis libertatibus immunitatibus exempcionibus et consuetudinibus minime reuocatis de assensu dominorum spiritualium et temporalium in Parliamento nostro apud Westmonasterium Anno regni nostri primo tento existencium acceptamus approbamus & dilectis nobis nunc hominibus Insularum predictarum ratificamus et confirmamus prout litere predicte rationabiliter testantur et prout predicti nunc homines Insularum predictarum et antecessores sui habitatores earundem quietanciis priuilegiis libertatibus immunitatibus exempcionibus et consuetudinibus predictis a tempore confeccionis literarum predictarum semper hactenus rationabiliter vti et gaudere consueuerunt. [AIn cuius rei testimonium has literas nostras fieri fecimus patentes. Teste me ipso apud Westmonasterium decimo die ffebruarii Anno regni nostri vicesimo.] [BIn cuius &c. Teste Regis apud Westmonasterium x die ffebruarii.]

[AEx p Johem Bate Thomas Shipton clericos]

Translation

[1] AHenry by the grace of God, king of England and France and lord of Ireland. To all those to whom these present letters shall come, greeting. [BThe King to all to whom etc., greeting]
We have seen the Letters Patent of the Lord Richard late king of England the second after the Conquest made in these words.

[2] Richard, by the grace of God king of England and France and lord of Ireland, to all to whom these present letters may come, greeting. Know ye that we in consideration of the good behaviour and the great loyalty which we have ever found in our liege and faithful peoples and communities of our islands of Guernsey, Jersey, Sark and Alderney, have of our special grace granted for ourselves and our heirs, as far as in us lies, to the said peoples and communities, that they, their heirs and successors shall for ever be free and quit from all tolls, duties, and customs of whatsoever kind in all our cities, market towns, and ports within our kingdom of England, in the same manner as our faithful liege people in our aforesaid kingdom are. Provided always, however, that our said peoples and communities, their heirs and successors aforesaid shall well and faithfully conduct themselves towards us and our heirs aforesaid for ever. In witness whereof we have caused these our Letters to be made patent. Witness myself at Westminster this twenty-eighth day of July in the eighteenth year of our reign.

[3] We have seen also the Letters Patent of Confirmation of the Lord Henry late king of England our deceased father, made in these words.

[4] Henry, by the grace of God king of England and France and lord of Ireland, to all to whom these present letters may come, greeting. We have inspected the Letters Patent of the Lord Henry lately king of England, our father, made in these words.

[5] Henry by the grace of God king of England and France and lord of Ireland, to all to whom these present letters may come, greeting. We have inspected the Letters Patent of the Lord Richard lately king of England the second after the conquest in confirmation made in these words.

[6] Richard by the grace of God king of England and France and lord of Ireland to all to whom these present letters may come, greeting. We have inspected the Letters Patent which the Lord Edward lately king of England our grandfather, caused to be made in these words.

[7] Edward by the grace of God king of England and France and lord of Ireland to all to whom these present letters may come, greeting. Know ye, that we recalling with grateful memory with what constancy and high spirit our beloved and faithful men of our islands of Guernsey, Jersey, Sark and Alderney have always hitherto continued in their faithfulness to us and our progenitors kings of England; and how great dangers to their bodies, as well as costs to their property they have borne for the safety of the said islands, and conservation of our laws and honour therein, and in like manner desiring to follow after them with our gracious favour, we have granted for ourselves and

our heirs to the said men of the aforesaid islands, that they themselves, their heirs and successors, may have and hold all privileges, liberties, immunities, exemptions, and customs, in respect of their persons, goods, moneys, and other matters, by virtue of the grant of our progenitors kings of England, or otherwise lawfully by agreement, and, without impediment or molestation from us, our heirs, or our officers whomsoever, may fully enjoy and use them, according as they themselves and their predecessors, the inhabitants of the said islands, have reasonably enjoyed and used them. Which things we do now confirm to them generally in the aforesaid form, being willing after we have enquired into them to confirm them as may be just. In testimony whereof we have had these letters made patent, myself as witness at the Tower of London the tenth day of July, in the year of our reign in England the fifteenth, but of our reign in France the second.

[8] We, moreover, holding the concessions, confirmations, privileges, liberties, immunities, and customs to be reasonable and seasonable, accept, approve, and ratify them for us and our heirs, as far as in us lies, and concede and confirm them to the aforesaid men of the islands in the same manner to their heirs and successors as the aforesaid Letters more fully testify and as they and their predecessors inhabitants of the said Islands have reasonably used and enjoyed them. In witness whereof we have had these our Letters made Patent. Myself as witness at Gloucester the tenth day of November in the second year of our reign.

[9] We, moreover, holding the concessions, confirmations, privileges, liberties, immunities, and customs to be reasonable and seasonable, accept, approve, and ratify them for us and our heirs, as far as in us lies, and concede and confirm them to the aforesaid men of the islands in the same manner to their heirs and successors as the aforesaid Letters more fully testify and as they and their predecessors inhabitants of the said Islands have reasonably used and enjoyed them. In witness whereof we have caused these our letters to be made patent. Witness myself at Westminster the eighth day of May in the first year of our reign.

[10] We, moreover, holding the concessions, confirmations, privileges, liberties, immunities, and customs to be reasonable and seasonable, accept, approve, and ratify them for us and our heirs, as far as in us lies, and concede and confirm them to the aforesaid men of the islands in the same manner to their heirs and successors as the aforesaid Letters more fully testify and as they and their predecessors inhabitants of the said Islands have reasonably used and enjoyed them. In witness whereof we have caused these our letters to be made Patent. Witness myself at Westminster the fourteenth day of February in the first year of our Reign.

[11] We, moreover, accept and approve the aforesaid letters, concerning acquittances, privileges, liberties, immunities, exemptions, and customs (in no ways revoked), with the assent of the lords spiritual and temporal assembled in our parliament held at Westminster in the first year of our reign, and ratify and confirm the same now to our aforesaid beloved men of the said islands, as the aforesaid letter rationally testify, and as the inhabitants of the aforesaid islands and their ancestors, inhabitants of the same, have possessed and enjoyed, those acquittances, privileges, liberties, immunities, exemptions, and customs from the time that the aforesaid Letters Patent were granted them. [A]In witness whereof we have caused these our letters to be made patent. Witness myself at Westminster the tenth day of February the twentieth year of our reign. [[B]In witness whereof, etc. Witness the King at Westminster the tenth day of February.]

[[A]Examined by John Bate and Thomas Shipton clerks]

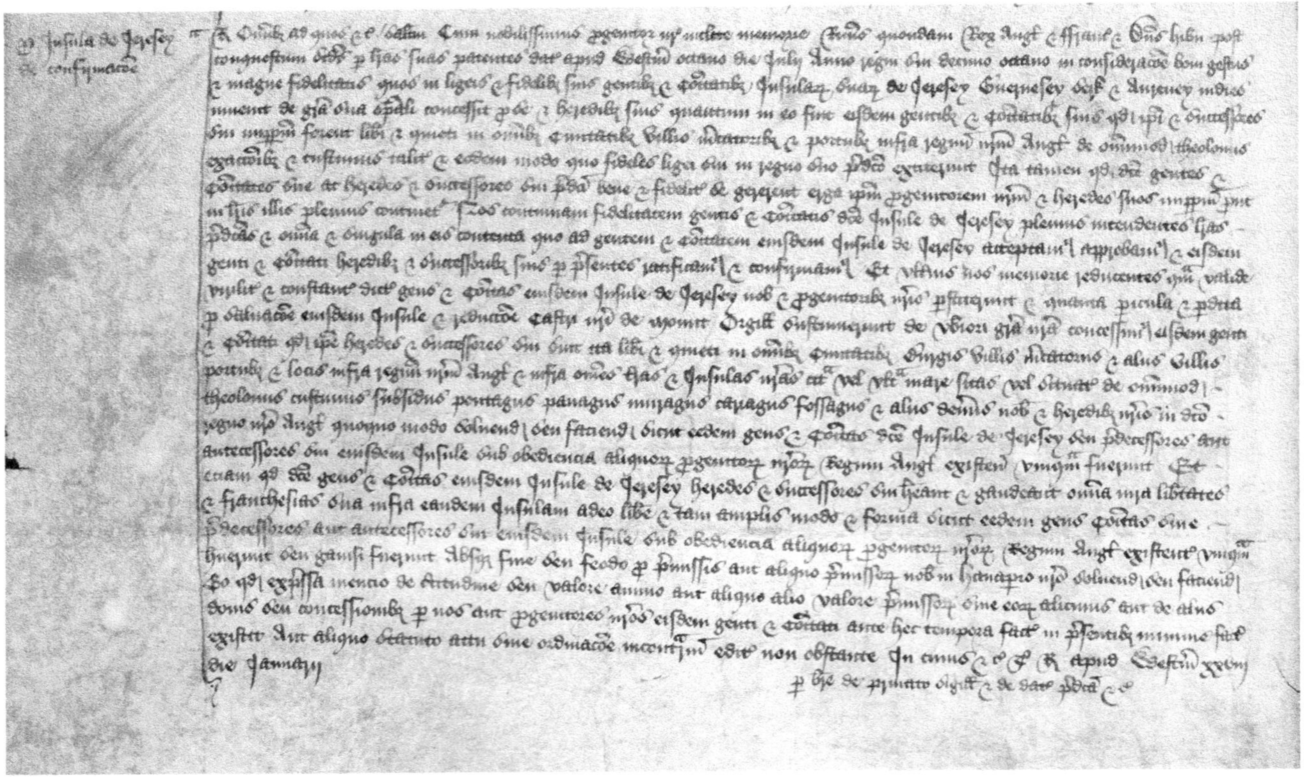

Plate 7: The Royal Charter granted by Edward IV in 1469.
Credit: The National Archives, ref. C 66/522.

Edward IV: 1469

Commentary

The reign of Edward IV represents very clearly some of the most important factors shaping the evolution of Jersey's royal charters of liberties. Edward had seized the English throne in 1461, and to many he was no more than a usurper. The threat and reality of internal opposition to his claims remained real through all of his first reign to 1470, and for much of his second reign after his return from exile in 1471. These conflicts, which we call the Wars of the Roses, also had an international dimension. Henry VI's queen, Margaret of Anjou, represented this very clearly, given her close connections in her native France; and that international challenge grew in complexity because of the often-fraught internal politics of France in the 1460s and 1470s. The international military threat to the islands therefore grew and coalesced with the domestic strife that was increasingly taking hold in the English king's dominions. In this situation, internal strife and the eagerness (or perhaps urgent need) of all parties to respond to the French threat interacted with the potential for liberties to be renegotiated. As might be expected, the loyalty of the islands in these circumstances was valuable, and it was bargained for chiefly in the context of requests for the charter of liberties.

Edward inherited a high degree of confusion and conflict in the islands. It appears that in the early 1450s this reached a high-point with the French raiding the islands to take hostages and apparently extorting considerable sums from the islanders.[1] The 1450s also saw the lord of the islands, Richard Neville (from 1449 earl of Warwick), moving from a position of loyal support for the court to one of opposition, sparked by dislike of the influence of Queen Margaret and others around King Henry. In 1460, after the battle of Blore Heath and after the triumph of the court party pushed Warwick into exile,

---

[1] TNA, SC 8/118/5892 (printed in *'Ancient Petitions of the Chancery and the Exchequer': ayant trait aux îles de la Manche, conservées au 'Public Record Office' à Londres*, Société Jersiaise, publication spéciale (St Helier, 1902), pp. 89–90). For the progress of the conflict more generally, see Jonathan Sumption, *The Hundred Years War* (5 vols, London, 1990–2023), vol. 5, pp. 656–762.

Warwick's position in the islands was challenged by appointments to office made by the king under the influence of the court.[2]

When Edward IV was victorious in 1461 and took the throne, Jersey came under further threat. Richard, earl of Warwick played a central role in the new regime, but as lord of the islands he quickly lost the opportunity to recover practical control there. Jersey was seized by Jean Carbonnel, cousin and standard-bearer of Pierre de Brézé, comte de Maulevrier, who had been the dominant figure in the regime of the French king, Charles VII, until 1450, after which he focused his activity in Normandy. De Brézé's initiative was possibly agreed with the governor, John Nanfan, given the willingness of Henry VI's exiled queen, Margaret of Anjou, to make concessions in return for French support against the new king. There were certainly accusations at the time that Guillaume de St Martin had helped betray the island.[3] While suggestions that the occupation of the island was limited in geographic extent are later inventions to protect the reputation of the de Carteret family,[4] the new regime was far from uncomplicated. A few months after the island fell, Louis XI wrote a sequence of letters on 3–5 December 1461 to the baillis of the Cotentin and of the isle of Jersey (or to the governor and jurats of Jersey) concerning the problems being experienced by French monasteries in asserting their rights in Jersey. The seizure of the island by de Brézé did not mean its straightforward absorption by a centralised French regime.[5] The

---

[2] Tim Thornton, 'The English King's French Islands: Jersey and Guernsey in English Politics and Administration, 1485–1642', in George W. Bernard and Steven J. Gunn (eds.), *Authority and Consent in Tudor England: Essays Presented to C. S. L. Davies* (Aldershot, 2002), pp. 197–217, at pp. 198–201.

[3] Thornton, 'English King's French Islands', pp. 201–2; G. R. Balleine, *History of Jersey*, rev. Marguerite Syvret and Joan Stevens (Chichester, 1981), p. 57; Ed. Toulmin Nicolle, 'L'occupation de Jersey par les comtes de Maulevrier de 1461 à1468', *ABSJ*, 9 (1919–22), 168–88, at pp. 169–72; R. R. Lemprière, 'L'occupation de Jersey par le comte de Maulevrier', *ABSJ*, 10 (1923–27), 102–55, esp. pp. 150–1 (Musée Condé, Chantilly, MS 1340); N. V. L. Rybot, *Gorey Castle (Le Château Mont Orgueil): Official Guide Book* ([St Helier?], 1933), p. 65; 'Documents Concerning the Proceedings of the Royal Commissioners of 1531', *ABSJ*, 6 (1906–09), 87–110, at p. 108; G. R. Balleine, *A Biographical Dictionary of Jersey* (London, 1948), p. 218.

[4] Balleine, *History of Jersey*, rev. Syvret and Stevens, pp. 57–8; *Les Chroniques de Jersey*, ed. Bronwyn Matthews (St Helier, 2017), pp. 30–3; A. J. Eagleston, 'The Chroniques de Jersey in the Light of Contemporary Documents', *ABSJ*, 13 (1936–39), 37–62, at pp. 38–40; 'Contrat de 1513', *ABSJ*, 6 (1906–09), 210–11; C.-P. Le Cornu, 'Le chateau de Grosnez, *ABSJ*, 4 (1897–1901), 14–48, at pp. 26–7; Lemprière, 'L'occupation de Jersey par le comte de Maulevrier', p. 104.

[5] [G. F. B. de Gruchy, R. R. Marett, and E. T. Nicolle (eds)], *Cartulaire des îles Normandes: recueil de documents concernant l'histoire de ces îles, conservés aux archives du département de la Manche et du Calvados, de la Bibliothèque nationale,*

negotiations between de Brézé and Margaret of Anjou implied that he would receive the islands in his own right, free from the sovereignty of the king of England.[6] There is no explicit mention of his intended relationship with the French crown. This may reflect the sensitivity of the negotiations and hence a French desire to deny complicity. What was probably more significant was the continuing tradition of Norman autonomy. De Brézé's identification with this cause had been strengthened in preceding years, as grand seneschal of the duchy; even stronger was the commitment of his agents in Jersey, such as Jean de Carbonnel, seigneur of Sourdeval. The treason of which the de St Martin family and other islanders were accused, for plotting to support de Brézé, or simply accepting his regime, may have been because they saw it as representing a secure expression of their Norman identity, not subjection to the French monarchy.

That complexity grew almost immediately, because de Brézé fell from favour on the death of Charles VII in July 1461, as the dauphin Louis XI – his enemy of some years' standing – acceded to the throne. De Brézé was, however, given the opportunity to support Margaret of Anjou's expedition to the north of England in 1462 and he sailed for Northumberland on 9 October. In the meantime, his officers on the island issued two important documents in his name, the ordinances of 3 October and orders dated 22 October for the defence of Mont Orgueil.[7] The ordinances represent a further example of the successful assertion of the island community's determination to be governed by the custom of Normandy as understood in Jersey: de Brézé's

---

du Bureau des rôles, du château de Warwick, etc ([St Helier], 1924 [i.e. 1918–24]), pp. 272–7, items 192–3, and pp. 326–9, item 244 (Louis XI to baillis of Cotentin and Jersey re St Pierre priory detained by Pierre de Brézé from abbey of St Sauveur le Vicomte, 3 December 1461; same to bailli of Cotentin, governor and jurats of Jersey re rights of St Sauveur 5 December 1461; Louis XI to baillis of Cotentin and Jersey, and vicomte of Valognes re priory of l'islet, and restoring Cherbourg's interest there 4 December 1461).

[6] Thomas Basin, *Histoire des règnes de Charles VII et de Louis XI*, ed. J. Quicherat (4 vols, Paris, 1855–59), vol. 4, p. 358, pièce VIII.

[7] Balleine, *History of Jersey*, rev. Syvret and Stevens, p. 58; 'Ordonnance de 1462 pour la garde du château de Montorgueil et la police de l'île de Jersey', *ABSJ*, 7 (1910–14), 187–92 (from 'Mémoires de Pierre Mangon, Vicomte de Valognes' [d. 1705], Grenoble, Bibliothèque Municipale, MS 1392, tome III, ff. 387ff); Edmund Toulmin Nicolle, *Mont Orgueil Castle: Its History and Description* (Jersey, 1921), p. 32; John Patriarche Ahier, *Tableaux historiques de la civilization à Jersey* (Jersey, 1852), pp. 247–51; *Prison Board*, pp. 163–71. Jehan de Waurin, *Recueil des Croniques et anchiennes istories de la Grant Bretaigne, a present nomme Engleterre*, ed. William Hardy & Edward L. C. P. Hardy, Rolls Ser., 39 (5 vols, London, 1864–91), vol. 5, p. 431, makes the motivation for Brézé's involvement no more than the jealousy of Louis XI towards him.

commission of six representatives held an assize, and the island clergy and notables present were successful in their request to be governed 'as of old by the custom of Normandy with certain exceptions which were granted some time ago in writing'. And the ordinances were issued in de Brézé's name alone: the sovereignty of Louis or the kingdom of France was not acknowledged.[8]

The issue of sovereignty in Jersey was thrown into even sharper relief by the outbreak in 1465 of the War of the Public Weal in France, pitting Louis again many leading noblemen. Among them was his brother Charles, duc de Berry, who was granted the duchy of Normandy as part of the peace of Conflans in October 1465. In rebellion again soon afterwards, Charles proved unable to maintain control of mainland Normandy. In this conflict de Brézé and his son supported Louis XI.[9] In Jersey, however, Jean de Carbonnel would not. Weak though the hold of Charles, duke of Normandy might have been, he did attempt to revictual the island in October 1468.[10] By that stage, however, English interest in the island was reasserting itself.

Some islanders did not accept the de Brézé regime, and there was plotting aimed at seizing Mont Orgueil involving Renaud Lemprière, seigneur of Rozel and others. This was detected and foiled, leading to a court case that sheds detailed light on conditions in the island, but during the turbulent years of Norman rebellion contacts were made with English agents.[11] In the spring of 1468, Richard Harliston, a vice admiral, visited St Ouen secretly and agreed to invade, and the English resupplied his forces during a 19-week siege of Mont Orgueil.[12]

As so often in Jersey, this intervention was as much associated with English ambitions in France as with English politics alone. By the early months of 1468, Edward IV had achieved almost complete control over the territories ruled by his predecessor, Henry VI; for example, the long siege of Harlech in

---

[8] Nicolle, 'L'occupation de Jersey par les Comtes de Maulévrier', pp. 179–80 – a *vidimus* of Maulévrier's letters patent, 21 August 1462, ordering the holding of assizes in Jersey; *Prison Board*, pp. 163–71; *Chroniques*, ed. Matthews, pp. 32–41. Nicolle, *Mont Orgueil Castle*, pp. 32–3 makes the point about the 'intentionally vague' position regarding ultimate sovereignty.

[9] The agreement is printed in Nicolle, 'L'occupation de Jersey par le Comte de Maulévrier', pp. 181–3 (January 1466).

[10] Nicolle, 'L'occupation de Jersey par les Comtes de Maulévrier', pp. 184–8 (from Paris, Bibliothèque Nationale, MS 26,092, no. 764; 29 October 1468); Nicolle, *Mont Orgueil Castle*, pp. 34–5.

[11] Balleine, *History of Jersey*, rev. Syvret and Stevens, pp. 59–60 refers to new material identified since 1924 and transcribed by Dr Doug J. Shone in the Société Jersiaise Library, but in practice this is a transcript of the material edited and published in 1924.

[12] Balleine, *History of Jersey*, rev. Syvret and Stevens, pp. 60–1; *Chroniques*, ed. Matthews, pp. 42–51; Nicolle, *Mont Orgueil Castle*, pp. 35–6.

north Wales was approaching its final days with the castle's fall in August. In parliament in May 1468 Edward declared his intention to defeat Louis, whom he described as the usurping king of France and, more specifically, to recover his duchy of Normandy.[13] The intervention in Jersey in the spring of 1468 was led by Edmund Weston and Richard Harliston, who pursued the siege of Mont Orgueil alongside local forces. The king seems to have followed events closely.

Meanwhile the king's plans for war against France were taking shape and rivalry was developing for control of Mont Orgueil and Jersey if and when they were recaptured. English forces under the command of Anthony Woodville, Lord Scales, the brother of Edward's queen, Elizabeth, and Walter Blount, Lord Mountjoy were about to set sail in support of Breton resistance to the French (forestalled by a Franco-Breton truce) when, on 23 September, Scales received a grant of Jersey. The English regained control of the island and of Mont Orgueil before November was out.[14] In the face of Warwick's claims to the lordship of both Jersey and Guernsey, the grant of the recaptured Jersey to Scales spoke volumes.[15] Richard Harliston, who led the English contribution to the recovery of Jersey, was a long-standing Yorkist servant, whose father John had been receiver of the key York honour of Clare as early as 1447/48: in the words of the Chroniques de Jersey, 'nourri le temps de sa jeunesse en la maison du Duc d'York'. He was not an adherent of Warwick and was

---

[13] C. Given-Wilson *et al.* (eds), *The Parliament Rolls of Medieval England, 1275–1504* (16 vols, Woodbridge and London, 2005), vol. 13, pp. 253, 362–4; *Letters and Papers Illustrative of the Wars of the English in France during the Reign of Henry the Sixth, King of England*, ed. Joseph Stevenson, Rolls Ser., 22 (2 vols in 3, London, 1861–64), vol. 2, p. 789; Balleine, *Biographical Dictionary*, pp. 159–60; Charles Ross, *Edward IV*, new edn (New Haven CT, 1997), pp. 110–12.

[14] *Chroniques*, ed. Matthews, pp. 130–1, only in a later part of the narrative refers back to Weston's involvement with Harliston. But see TNA, E 404/74/2/35 (5 July 1469) indicating Thomas Dobney was sent to the island with letters to Harliston and Weston three times. Two Fowey ships served 20 or 22 weeks there, along with one ship of Southampton: Issue roll, Easter 8 Ed. IV 13 July; TNA, E 404/74/1/138, /141 (9 and 14 December 1468). *CCR, 1468–76*, nos 210, 214 (rewards for local people in relation to the retaking of Jersey – to John Peryn and others of Guernsey, and Peter Leserkees and others of Jersey itself – of right to take goods custom free to the islands up to £140 yearly, 10 March 1469). Grant: TNA, C 81/821, no. 2555; there was no enrolment on the Patent or French Rolls. Cora L. Scofield, *The Life and Reign of Edward the Fourth. King of England and France and Lord of Ireland* (2 vols, London, 1923), vol. 1, p. 479 (suggests the grant may have been made contingent on the taking of Mont Orgueil, as the king's writ was not delivered to the chancellor until 25 November, by which time castle had probably fallen and Scales returned to England); Ross, *Edward IV*, pp. 112–13.

[15] Michael Hicks, *Warwick the Kingmaker* (Oxford, 1998), p. 264, thinks the grant to Scales tactless and hints at possible resumption of the isles.

therefore a clear break with Warwick's previous regime in the islands.[16] After the recovery of Jersey and Mont Orgueil, it was Harliston who was appointed as captain there.[17] Warwick's activity as lord of the isles had nonetheless continued through the 1460s, and he issued letters patent as lord throughout the period of Jersey's occupation. The tradition of autonomy represented by the lordship of the isles under English allegiance remained strong.[18] In the spring following the recapture of Mont Orgueil, supporters of the Nevilles in Yorkshire were fomenting trouble that would eventually lead to the flight of Edward and the re-adeption of Henry VI in October 1470.[19]

It is also clear that the French did not accept the English capture of Jersey in 1468. The opportunity presented by the break between the earl of Warwick and Edward IV allowed for further negotiation with the new alliance connecting the Nevilles, the exiled Lancastrians around Margaret of Anjou, and Edward IV's own brother George, duke of Clarence. In the treaties of 16 February 1471, the French negotiators did not initially include Jersey, Guernsey or Alderney in the territories listed as possessions of Henry VI. While England, Ireland, and the town and march of Calais, Guisnes and Hammes, were all specified, along with

---

[16] P. A. Johnson, *Duke Richard of York 1411–1460*, corrected paperback reprint (Oxford, 1991), p. 233: receiver in 1447/48 and 1450/51; *Chroniques*, ed. Matthews, pp. 48–9. Edmund Weston was the son of Peter Weston, of Boston (Lincolnshire), so the association with Harliston (from Humberstone in the same county) was probably at least in part a geographical one: S. T. Bindoff (ed.), *The House of Commons, 1509–1558* (3 vols, London, 1982), vol. 3, pp. 590–2; Balleine, *Biographical Dictionary*, pp. 612–14.

[17] The grant to Harliston on 13 January 1477 was probably a renewal of an earlier one, as the *Chroniques*, ed. Matthews, pp. 54–5, say he was captain for 16 years: Scofield, *Edward the Fourth*, vol. 1, p. 479; TNA, C 76/160, m. 3 (Thomas Carte, *Catalogue des Rolles gascons, normans et françois conservés dans les archives de la Tour de Londres : et contenant le précis & le sommaire de tous les titres qui s'y trouvent concernant la Guienne, la Normandie & les autres provinces de la France sujettes autrefois aux rois d'Angleterre* (2 vols, Paris, 1743), vol. 2, p. 368); it was superseded on 3 June 1477 by a joint grant, with William Hareby 'his brother': *CPR 1476–85*, p. 40.

[18] T. W. M. de Guérin, 'An Account of the Families of de St Martin and de la Court (Seigneurs of Trinity)', *ABSJ*, 9 (1919–22), 54–95, at pp. 69, 83–4 (Thomas de la Court is granted the possessions of the de St Martin family in Jersey, 21 March 1463). Warwick also acted in this capacity in Guernsey, with more effect: *ibid.*, pp. 69–70 (letters patent 1 April 1465); J. H. Lenfestey (ed.), *List of Records in the Greffe, Guernsey*, vol. 2, *Documents under Bailiwick Seal*, List and Index Society, special ser., 11 (1978), p. 19 (no. 53, 30 September 1466).

[19] Ross, *Edward IV*, pp. 125–30.

'autres plus ysles terres et seigneuries', Jersey, Guernsey and Alderney were only added by name later, as an interlineation, probably at English insistence.[20]

The predecessor of Edward IV's charter to Jersey was his grant to the bailiff, jurats and people of Guernsey and its bailiwick of 1465. It may be that the occupation of Jersey and questions about the loyalty of the remaining islands helped delay that grant for several years into his reign. The confirmation was issued, on 29 March 1465, at the time of the rebellion against Louis XI, known as the League of the Public Weal: it was on 4 March that Louis' brother, the duc de Berry, had left his company under the pretence of going hunting, and the following fortnight saw the rapid transformation of France into a political system again at war with itself.[21] This rebellion was to emphasise the split between Jersey and the French crown, and ultimately its identification once again with the duke of Normandy. The beneficiaries of the charter were the bailiff and jurats of Guernsey, and the communities of their bailiwick. Jersey was not mentioned in the confirmation clauses, but it is likely to be significant that Edward IV's regime signalled its support for island privileges when the connections between Jersey's regime and the French government were fractured, and opportunities to cultivate a pro-English party in the island grew. The Guernsey charter of 1465 confirmed the privilege originally granted by Edward III in 1341 on laws and customs, and notably added confirmation of the grant of 1394, which provided for freedom from English tolls, duties and customs, as Henry VI had done in 1442, but which Henry's father and grandfather had omitted to do.[22]

Once Jersey had been recovered by the English crown, a further confirmation of charters was issued on 28 January 1469. This was authorised by a privy seal writ of 11 December 1468 and explicitly recognised contributions to the recovery of Mont Orgueil.[23] It took the form of a reassertion, specifically for Jersey, of the previous grant of Richard II to the communities of both bailiwicks regarding tolls, duties and customs. There were dynastic reasons for this: Edward was ignoring the charters of Henry IV, V and VI, and confirmed directly the charters of 1378 and 1394 issued by Richard II. Edward's regime viewed the Lancastrian monarchs as illegitimate – the consequence of the interruption to legitimate succession resulting from the usurpation of

---

[20] TNA, E 30/540; J. Calmette and G. Périnelle, *Louis XI et l'Angleterre, 1461–1483* (Paris, 1930), p. 132, n. 2.

[21] Paul Murray Kendall, *Louis XI: The Universal Spider*, paperback edn (London, 2001), pp. 139–54.

[22] Tim Thornton, *The Charters of Guernsey* (Bognor Regis, 2004), pp. 28–35. The grant is also related to concerns about non-observance of safe conducts for island shipping in Devon and Cornwall, which resulted in royal action on 15 April 1464: TNA, C 81/797/1379.

[23] TNA, C 81/823/2692; C 66/522, m. 3.

1399. The king and his father, Richard, duke of York, were presented as the true heirs of Richard II. At the start of Edward's reign parliament recorded Edward's claim to that inheritance and denounced the tyranny of the three Lancastrian kings.[24] The charters to the islands represent the same message: in 1465 and 1469 Edward returned to the charters of Richard II, omitting the previous 70 years of history. But there were also pragmatic reasons for this approach, recognising the contribution of the local communities to the English king's recovery of the island. The terms of the grant not only confirmed the substance of Richard's charter but extended it, using forms of words that were much more complex and inclusive, covering 'all tolls, customs, subsidies, pontages, pannages, murages, tallages, fossages and other dues'. This echoed the grants of the period to favoured corporations and other local communities, recognised as 'ancient demesne' of the crown.[25] An Angevin creation aimed at enhancing revenue, ancient demesne became an opportunity for communities to assert extensive freedom from customs and dues.[26] It may not have been an entirely appropriate parallel to draw for those seeking and granting liberties in the islands in the late 1460s, but that it was used emphasises the extensive and generous intent to the 1469 charter.

---

[24] Paul Strohm, *England's Empty Throne: Usurpation and the Language of Legitimation, 1399–1422* (New Haven CT, 1998), pp. 126–7; *Parliament Rolls of Medieval England*, vol. 13, pp. 13–21, at pp. 15–17; Edward's use of Ricardian symbolism: J. L. Laynesmith, *Cecily, Duchess of York* (London, 2017), pp. 120–1.

[25] E.g. *CPR 1467–77*, pp. 61, 600; *CPR 1476–85*, pp. 190, 358, 484, 500. Even more precisely comparable is the generous grant to the burgesses and inhabitants of Bewdley (now Worcestershire), 30 October 1472: *CPR 1467–77*, pp. 361–2 (printed in John Richard Burton, *A History of Bewdley; with Concise Accounts of Some Neighbouring Parishes* (London, 1883), p. xlii). Bewdley was growing in status as a town outside wider local government control and with an important sanctuary: Shannon McSheffrey, *Seeking Sanctuary: Crime, Mercy, and Politics in English Courts, 1400–1550* (Oxford, 2017), pp. 17, 109–10, 182.

[26] Robert S. Hoyt, 'The Nature and Origins of the Ancient Demesne', *English Historical Review*, 65 (1950), 145–74; Marjorie Keniston McIntosh, 'The Privileged Villeins of the English Ancient Demesne', *Viator*, 7 (1976), 295–328; R. J. Faith, 'The "Great Rumour" of 1377 and Peasant Ideology', in R. H. Hilton and T. H. Aston (eds), *The English Rising of 1381* (Cambridge, 1984), pp. 43–73; Miriam Müller, 'The Aims and Organisation of a Peasant Revolt in Early Fourteenth-century Wiltshire', *Rural History*, 14 (2003), 1–20.

Text

Edward IV recognised the contribution of the Jersey community to the recovery of his control of the island. His charter confirmed the privileges granted by Richard II in respect of the islanders' freedom from tolls, duties and customs, added a wider exemption from subsidies and other dues such as pontages, and finally, in unspecific terms, confirmed all earlier (unspecified) grants of rights, liberties and franchises. Specific to Jersey; text taken from enrolment in The National Archives, C 66/522, m. 3, with reference to the edition presented in Prison Board.

[1] Rex Omnibus ad quos etc salutem. Cum nobilissimus progenitor noster inclite memorie Ricardus quondam Rex Anglie et ffrancie et Dominus Hibernie post conquestum secundus per literas suas patentes datas apud Westmonasterium octauo die Julii anno regni sui decimo octauo in consideratione boni gestus et magne fidelitatis quos in ligeis et fidelibus suis gentibus et communitatibus Insularum suarum de Jeresey Guernesey Serk et Aureney indies inuenit de gratia sua speciali concessit pro se et heredibus suis quantum in eo fuit eisdem gentibus et communitatibus suis quod ipsi et successores sui imperpetuum forent liberi et quieti in omnibus Ciuitatibus villis mercatoribus et portubus infra regnum nostrum Anglie de omnimodis theoloniis exaccionibus et custumis taliter et eodem modo quo fideles ligei sui in regno suo predicto extiterunt Ita tamen quod dictæ gentes et Communitates sue ac heredes et successores sui predicti bene et fideliter se gererent erga ipsum progenitorem nostrum et heredes suos imperpetuum prout in literis illis plenius continetur. Nos continuam fidelitatem gentis et communitatis dicte Insule de Jeresey plenius intendentes literas predictas et omnia et singula in eis contenta quo ad gentem et communitatem eiusdem Insule de Jeresey acceptamus approbamus et eisdem genti et Communitati heredibus et successoribus suis per presentes ratificamus et confirmamus.

[2] Et vlterius nos memorie reducentes quam valide viriliter et constanter dicte gens et Communitas eiusdem Insule de Jeresey nobis et progenitoribus nobis perstiterunt et quanta pericula et perdita pro saluacione eiusdem Insule et reductione Castri nostri de Mount Orgill sustinuerunt de vberiori gratia nostra concessimus eisdem genti et Communitati quod ipse heredes et successores sui sint ita liberi et quieti in omnibus Ciuitatibus Burgis villis mercatoriis et aliis villis portubus et locis infra regnum nostrum Anglie et infra omnes terras et Insulas nostras citra vel vltra mare sitas vel situatas de omnimodis theoloniis custumis subsidiis pontagiis pauagiis muragiis cariagiis fossagiis et aliis denariis nobis et heredibus nostris in dicto regno nostro Anglie quoquo modo soluendis seu faciendis sicut eedem gens et Communitas dicte Insule de

Jeresey seu predecessores aut antecessores sui eiusdem Insule sub obediencia aliquorum progenitorum nostrorum Regum Angliæ existentes vmquam fuerunt.

[3] Et eciam quod dicte gens et Communitas eiusdem Insule de Jeresey heredes et successores sui habeant et gaudeant omnia iura libertates et franchesias sua infra eandem Insulam adeo libere et tam amplis modo et forma sicut eedem gens et Communitas sive predecessores aut antecessores sui eiusdem Insule sub obediencia aliquorum progenitorum nostrorum Regum Anglie existentes vmquam habuerunt seu gauisi fuerunt absque fine seu feodo pro premissis aut aliquo premissorum nobis in hanaperio soluendis seu faciendis Eo quod expressa mencio de certitudine seu valore annuo aut aliquo alio valore premissorum sive eorum alicuius aut de aliis donis seu concessionibus per nos aut progenitores nostros eisdem genti et communitati ante hec tempora factis in presentibus minime facta existit aut aliquo Statuto actu siue ordinacione in contrarium edito non obstante. In cuius &c. Teste Regis apud Westmonasterium xxviii die Januarii

Per breve de privato sigillo et de data predicta &c.

Translation

[1] Edward by the grace of God king of England and France and lord of Ireland: to all to whom these presents may come, greeting. Whereas our most noble progenitor of glorious memory Richard the Second after the Conquest, lately king of England and France and lord of Ireland, by his Letters Patent given at Westminster on the eighth day of July in the eighteenth year of his reign in consideration of the good behaviour and great loyalty which he always found among his liege and faithful peoples and communities of the islands of Jersey, Guernsey, Sark and Alderney, of his special grace granted on behalf of himself and his heirs, as far as in him lay, to these his same peoples and communities that they themselves and their successors should be for ever in all cities, market towns, and ports within the kingdom of England free and quit of all tolls, duties and customs of whatsoever kind in such wise and in such manner as his own faithful lieges have continued in his own aforesaid kingdom. Provided always that they his said people and communities, their heirs and successors aforesaid should conduct themselves well and faithfully towards himself and his heirs for ever as is more fully contained in those Letters. We considering more fully the continuous loyalty of the said island of Jersey, the aforesaid Letters and all and singular contained therein as regards the people and community of the same island of Jersey, do accept approve and by these presents to these same people and community their heirs and successors, do ratify and confirm them.

[2] And, further, calling to mind how valiantly, manfully and steadfastly the said people and community of the said island of Jersey have stood out for us and our progenitors and what great dangers and losses they have sustained for the safety of the said island and for the recapture of our castle of Mont Orgueil, of our more abundant grace have granted to the same people and community that they, their heirs and successors shall likewise be free and quit in all cities, boroughs, market towns and other towns, ports and places within our kingdom of England and within all our lands and islands lying or situated on this side or beyond the sea from all tolls, customs, subsidies, pontages, pavages, murages, tallages, fossages, and other dues in whatever way to be discharged or made to us and our heirs in our said kingdom of England just as the same people and community of the said island of Jersey or their predecessors, or ancestors of the same island living under the obedience of any of our progenitors the kings of England, have ever been.

[3] And further that the said people and community of the same island of Jersey, their heirs and successors, should enjoy all the rights, liberties and franchises as freely and fully as their predecessors and ancestors living under the obedience of any of our progenitors the kings of England have ever had or enjoyed them, without fine or fee in the premises or any of the premises to be paid or made to us in the Hanaper so far as express mention exists of the surety or annual value or any other value in the matter of the premises or of any of them or of other gifts or concessions by us or our progenitors to the same people and community, whether such mention has been made before these times or is expressly set forth in these present letters, or any statute, act or ordinance published to the contrary notwithstanding. In witness whereof we have caused these out Letters to be made Patent. Witness the king at Westminster the twenty-eighth day of January [in the eighth year of our reign].

By writ of privy seal and of the date aforesaid, etc.

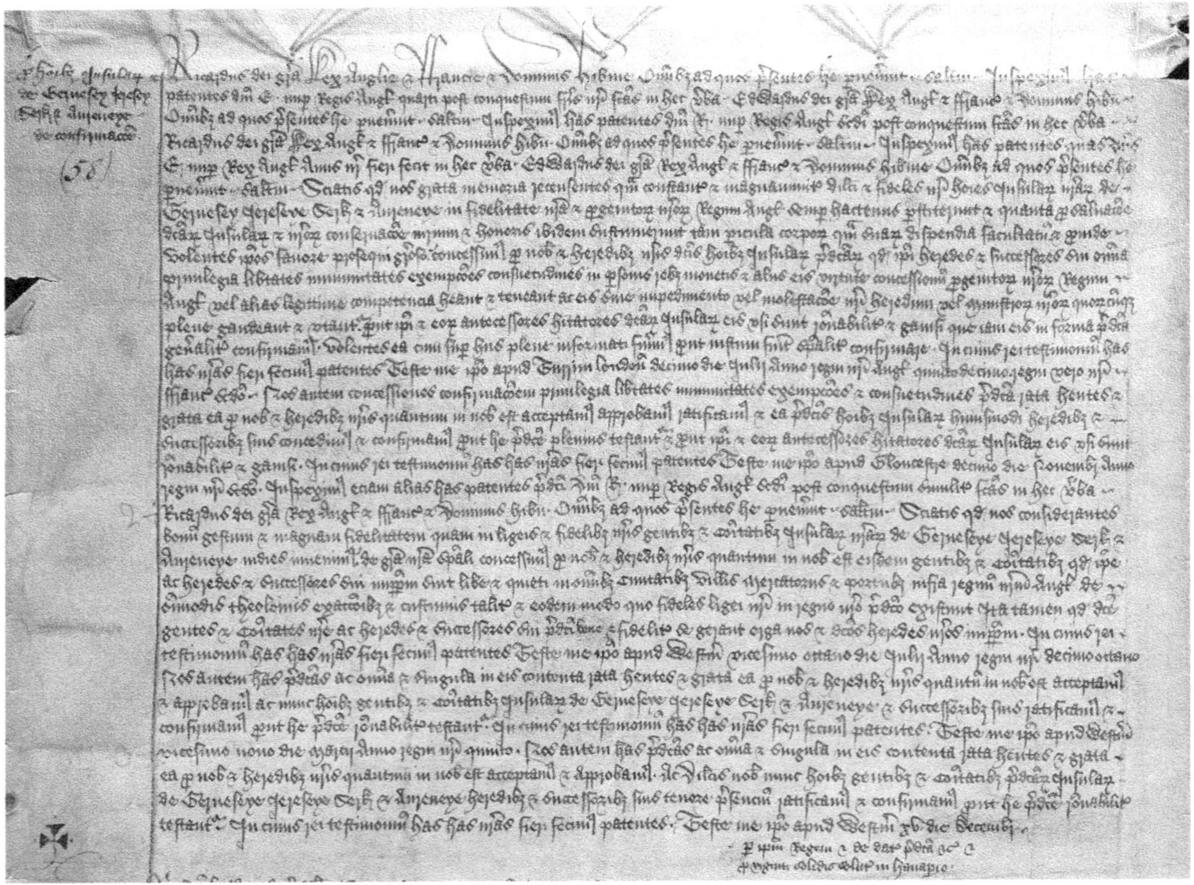

Plate 8: The Royal Charter granted by Richard III in 1483.
Credit: The National Archives, ref. C 66/554.

Richard III: 1483

Commentary

After nearly a century of internal strife and a sequence of contested successions, the seizure of the English throne by Richard, duke of Gloucester added further instability. The events of April–June 1483 surrounding Richard's coup had very direct relevance to the situation and privileges of Jersey and its neighbours, and the repercussions lasted through his reign and beyond. Political strife in England and destabilised relationships with Brittany and France heightened the focus on Jersey's loyalty and privileges.

The English Channel and Brittany were immediately an issue for Richard. Richard's capture of the throne displaced the party grouped round Edward IV's widow, Elizabeth Woodville. Before Richard's coup became apparent, Elizabeth's brother, Sir Edward Woodville, was sent to sea in the Channel with a fleet, and he managed to avoid capture as Richard took control of English ports. The governor of Guernsey, Edward Brampton, was one of those commissioned to arrest Edward.[1] But the attempt failed and Edward Woodville found refuge in Brittany. There, Duke François II was already the protector of Henry Tudor. Having become king on 26 June and been crowned on 6 July, Richard almost immediately, on 13 July 1483, sent Thomas Hutton, one of his clerks, to Brittany to negotiate on issues of piracy, Edward Woodville's position, and almost certainly Tudor exiles there.[2]

---

[1] Cecil Roth, 'Perkin Warbeck and his Jewish Master', *Transactions of the Jewish Historical Society of England*, 9 (1918–20), 143–62; Christopher Wilkins, *The Last Knight Errant: Edward Woodville and the Age of Chivalry* (London, 2009); Rosemary Horrox, *Richard III: A Study in Service*, corrected paperback edn (Cambridge, 1991), pp. 102–3; C. S. L. Davies, 'Richard III, Henry VII and the Island of Jersey', *The Ricardian*, 9 (1991–93), 334–42, at p. 335; Michael Hicks, *Richard III: The Self-Made King* (New Haven CT, 2019), pp. 238, 253.

[2] Thomas Rymer (ed.), *Foedera, conventiones, litterae, et cujuscunque generis acta publica*, rev. George Holmes, 3rd edn (10 vols, The Hague, 1739–45), vol. 5/iii, p. 134; James Gairdner (ed.), *Letters and Papers Illustrative of the Reigns of Richard III and Henry VII*, Rolls Ser., 24 (2 vols, London, 1861–63), vol. 1, pp. 22–3; Wilkins, *Last Knight Errant*; Ralph A. Griffiths and Roger S. Thomas, *The Making of the Tudor Dynasty*, paperback edn (Stroud, 1993), p. 86; S. B. Chrimes, *Henry VII*, corrected

Hutton's mission was not successful, and the consequence was François II's support for Henry Tudor's attempt to capitalise on the rebellion of Richard's erstwhile ally, the duke of Buckingham, in the autumn of 1483. Tudor launched his ill-fated bid to join Buckingham's rebellion from Paimpol, close to the islands; he may even have passed through Jersey on his return from England in November 1483.[3]

Edward Woodville's role was also significant of another aspect of the complex international relationships surrounding the islands. In the last days of Edward IV's reign, Woodville had been charged with assembling a 2,000-strong force to attack France.[4] Since the treaty of Picquigny of 1475, a seven-year truce had been in force between England and France, generously facilitated with French gold for Edward IV and leading members of his regime. Richard, as duke of Gloucester, had objected to the arrangement. And now the treaty of Arras of December 1482 between France and Burgundy had ended that peace.[5] In what were to be the closing days of Edward's reign, relationships with the French deteriorated and, once on the throne, Richard was even more determined on a reversal of policy and a more aggressive posture towards Louis XI's regime.[6]

It was in this period that Richard's confirmation of the islands' privileges occurred, on 15 December 1483. During the last weeks of 1483, Richard was reacting to the aftermath of Breton assistance for Henry Tudor. The islands were strategically crucial in English attempts to influence Brittany and retrieve Tudor. They acted as a forward listening post, a potential base from which to launch a kidnap. There was a significant coincidence between the capture by the French of dispatches from Richard Harliston in Jersey, in late August 1484, and the departure of Tudor for France in October.[7] Richard

---

paperback edn (London, 1977), p. 19; C. S. L. Davies, 'Richard III, Brittany and Henry Tudor', *Nottingham Mediaeval Studies*, 37 (1993), 110–26; Davies, 'Richard III, Henry VII and the Island of Jersey', p. 335; Anne F. Sutton, 'England and Brittany 1482–86: Politics, Trade and War', *Nottingham Medieval Studies*, 62 (2018), 137–82.

[3] Griffiths and Thomas, *Making of the Tudor Dynasty*, pp. 102–3; Chrimes, *Henry VII*, pp. 26–7; Horrox, *Richard III*, pp. 255–6; Davies, 'Richard III, Henry VII and the Island of Jersey', p. 335; I. Arthurson and N. Kingwell, 'The Proclamation of Henry Tudor as King of England, 3 November 1483', *BIHR*, 63 (1990), 100–6.

[4] Horrox, *Richard III*, p. 91; Wilkins, *The Last Knight Errant*; Hicks, *Richard III: The Self-Made King*, p. 238. Immediately after Edward's death, Woodville was commanded to take ships to attack French pirates in the Channel.

[5] Philippe de Commynes, *Memoirs: The Reign of Louis XI, 1461–83*, trans. Michael Jones (Harmondsworth, 1972), pp. 258–9; Hicks, *Richard III: The Self-Made King*, p. 238; Charles Ross, *Edward IV*, new edn (New Haven CT, 1997), p. 292.

[6] Charles Ross, *Richard III*, new edn (New Haven CT, 1999), pp. 192, 194–5.

[7] Davies, 'Richard III, Henry VII and the Island of Jersey', p. 335. It may also be that Margaret Beaufort was the route for a leak of the regime's intentions to her son.

was working successfully to turn the previously hostile Breton regime in his favour, supporting Pierre Landais, treasurer of Brittany, as his instrument in reversing Breton policy in 1484. This campaign saw an increasing frequency of visits to the islands by leading figures from among Richard's supporters, including James Nesfield in December 1484, Thomas Maunsell in March 1485 and, most notably, Thomas Hutton in May 1485, the latter ostensibly to consider the papal bull protecting the islands from piracy but more likely with a view to Breton and French politics as they related to Tudor.[8] Hutton had been Richard's agent in Brittany at the very start of his reign and had recently been one of the group that had negotiated an alliance with the duke, and his presence in the islands in the spring of 1485 highlights the connections between them and the king's policy towards the duchy.

The charter that Richard confirmed was that granted by his brother to Guernsey in 1465, however, and not that of 1469 to Jersey – the 1465 charter being more traditional and a direct reassertion of the original grants of Richard II, without the more specific and extensive wording, and without the fulsome praises for the islanders' assistance in the recovery of Mont Orgueil. It was also, it should be noted, the charter that had been granted to the islands when his father-in-law, Richard Neville, had been undisputed lord, and not that which had been granted in connection with the recapture of Jersey and its grant to Anthony Woodville, an opponent whom Richard had in 1483 recently executed in the most controversial of circumstances.

Text

Richard III confirmed Edward IV's 1465 charter of liberties granted to Guernsey, Sark and Alderney alone, and which confirmed both the 1378 charter of Richard II and hence that of Edward III, and the 1394 charter, which granted exemptions for tolls, duties and customs. Common to Guernsey, Sark and Alderney; text as enrolled in The National Archives, C 66/554, m. 21, with variations from a charter in the Guernsey Greffe.

[1] Ricardus dei gracia Rex Anglie et ffrancie et Dominus Hibernie omnibus ad quos presentes litere peruenerint Salutem. Inspeximus literas patentes Domini

---

Griffiths and Thomas, *Making of the Tudor Dynasty*, pp. 110–12; Chrimes, *Henry VII*, pp. 28–9; Ross, *Richard III*, pp. 196–200; Davies, 'Richard III, Brittany and Henry Tudor'.

[8] Rosemary Horrox and P. W. Hammond (eds), *British Library Harleian Manuscript 433* (4 vols, Upminster and Gloucester, 1979–83), vol. 2, p. 178; Rymer (ed.), *Foedera* (1739–45), vol. 5iii, p. 164; Griffiths and Thomas, *Making of the Tudor Dynasty*, p. 86; Chrimes, *Henry VII*, p. 19; Davies, 'Richard III, Brittany and Henry Tudor', pp. 110–26.

Edwardi nuper Regis Anglie quarti post conquestum fratris nostri defuncti de confirmacione factas in hec verba. Edwardus Dei gratia Rex Anglie et ffrancie et Dominus Hibernie Omnibus ad quos presentes Litere peruenerint Salutem. Inspeximus literas patentes domini Ricardi nuper Regis Angliae Secundi post conquestum factas in hec verba.

[2] Ricardus dei gratia Rex Anglie et ffrancie et Dominus Hibernie Omnibus ad quos presentes litere peruenerint salutem. Inspeximus literas patentes quas Dominus Edwardus nuper Rex Anglie Auus noster fieri fecit in hec verba.

[3] Edwardus dei gratia Rex Anglie et ffrancie et Dominus Hibernie Omnibus ad quos presentes litere peruenerint salute. Sciatis quod nos grata memoria recensentes quam constanter et magnanimiter dilecti et fideles nostri homines Insularum nostrarum de Gernesey Jereseye Serk et Aureneye in fidelitate nostra et progenitorum nostrorum Regum Anglie semper hactenus perstiterunt et quanta pro saluacione dictarum Insularum et nostrorum conseruacione iurium et honoris ibidem sustinuerunt tam pericula corporum quam suarum dispendia facultatum et proinde volentes ipsos fauore prosequi gracioso concessimus pro nobis et heredibus nostris dictis hominibus Insularum predictarum quod ipsi heredes et successores sui omnia priuilegia libertates immunitates exempciones consuetudines in personis rebus monetis et aliis eis virtute concessionum Progenitorum nostrorum Regum Anglie vel alias legitime competencia habeant et teneant ac eis sine impedimento vel molestacione nostri heredum vel Ministrorum nostrorum quorumcumque plene gaudeant et vtantur prout ipsi et eorum antecessores habitatores dictarum Insularum eis vsi sunt racionabiliter et gauisi que iam eis in forma predicta generaliter confirmamus Volentes ea cum super hiis plene informati fuerimus prout iustum fuerit confirmare. In cuius rei testimonium has literas nostras fieri fecimus patentes Teste me ipso apud Turrim Londonii decimo die Julii anno regni nostri Anglie quintodecimo regni vero nostri ffrancie secundo.

[4] Nos autem concessiones confirmacionem priuilegia libertates immunitates exempciones et consuetudines predicta rata habentes et grata ea pro nobis et heredibus nostris quantum in nobis est acceptamus approbamus ratificamus et ea predictis hominibus Insularum huiusmodi heredibus et successoribus suis concedimus et confirmamus prout litere predicte plenius testantur et prout ipsi et eorum antecessores habitatores dictarum Insularum eis vsi sunt racionabiliter et gauisi. In cuius rei testimonium has literas nostras fieri fecimus patentes Teste me ipso apud Gloucestre decimo die Novembris Anno regni nostri secundo.

[5] Inspeximus eciam alias literas patentes predicti domini Ricardi nuper Regis Anglie secundi post conquestum similiter factas in hec verba. Ricardus

dei gracia Rex Anglie et ffrancie et Dominus Hibernie Omnibus ad quos presentes litere peruenerint salutem. Sciatis quod nos considerantes bonum gestum et magnam fidelitatem quam in ligeis et fidelibus nostris gentibus et communitatibus Insularum nostrarum de Gerneseye Jerseye Serk et Aureneye indies inuenimus de gratia nostra speciali concessimus pro nobis et heredibus nostris quantum in nobis est eisdem gentibus et Communitatibus quod ipse ac heredes et successores sui imperpetuum sint liberi et quieti in omnibus Ciuitatibus Villis mercatoriis et portubus infra regnum nostrum Anglie de omnimodis theoloniis exaccionibus et custumis taliter et eodem modo quo fideles ligei nostri in regno nostro predicto existunt. Ita tamen quod dicte gentes et Communitates nostre ac heredes et successores sui predicti bene et fideliter se gerant erga nos et dictos heredes nostros imperpetuum. In cuius rei testimonium has literas nostras fieri fecimus patentes Teste me ipso apud Westmonasterium vicesimo octauo die Julii anno regni nostri decimo octauo.

[6] Nos autem literas predictas ac omnia et singula in eis contenta rata habentes et grata ea pro nobis et heredibus nostris quantum in nobis est acceptamus et approbamus ac nunc hominibus Gentibus et Communitatibus Insularum de Gernesey Jereseye Serk et Aureneye et successoribus suis ratificamus et confirmamus prout litere predicte rationabiliter testantur. In cuius rei testimonium has literas nostras fieri fecimus patentes. Teste me ipso Rege apud Westmonasterium vicesimo nono die Marcii anno regni nostri quinto.

[7] Nos autem literas predictas ac omnia et singula in eis contenta rata habentes et grata ea pro nobis et heredibus nostris quantum in nobis est acceptamus et approbamus ac nunc hominibus Gentibus et Communitatibus Insularum de Gerneseye Jereseye Serk et Aureneye et successoribus suis ratificamus et confirmamus prout litere predicte rationabiliter testantur. In cuius rei testimonium has literas nostras fieri fecimus patentes. Teste me ipso apud Westmonasterium xv die Decembris [Anno regni nostri primo].

[ELIOT]

Per ipsum Regem et de data predicta etc. [auctoritate Parliamenti] et pro viginti solidis solutis in hanaperio.

[Examinata per Willielmum Morland Willielmum Kelet Clericos]

[Ex p Johem Bate Thomas Shipton clericos]

Translation

[1] Richard by the grace of God, king of England and France and lord of Ireland to all those to whom these present letters come, greeting. We have inspected the letters patent of our Lord Edward lately king of England our

brother made in these words: Edward by the grace of God, king of England and France and lord of Ireland to all those to whom these present letters come, greeting. We have inspected the letters patent of Lord Richard late king of England, the second after the Conquest, made in these words.

[2] Richard by the grace of God king of England and France and lord of Ireland to all those to whom these present letters shall come, greeting. We have inspected the Letters Patent which the Lord Edward lately king of England, our ancestor, caused to be made in these words.

[3] Edward, by the Grace of God King of England and France and Lord of Ireland. To all to whom these present letters shall come, greeting. Know ye, that we recalling with grateful memory with what constancy and high spirit our beloved and faithful men of our islands of Guernsey, Jersey, Sark and Alderney have always hitherto continued in their faithfulness to us and our progenitors kings of England; and how great dangers to their bodies, as well as costs to their property they have borne for the safety of the said islands, and conservation of our laws and honour therein, and in like manner desiring to follow after them with our gracious favour, we have granted for ourselves and our heirs to the said men of the aforesaid islands, that they themselves, their heirs and successors, may have and hold all privileges, liberties, immunities, exemptions, and customs, in respect of their persons, goods, moneys, and other matters, by virtue of the grant of our progenitors kings of England, or otherwise lawfully by agreement, and, without impediment or molestation from us, our heirs, or our officers whomsoever, may fully enjoy and use them, according as they themselves and their predecessors, the inhabitants of the said islands, have reasonably enjoyed and used them. Which things we do now confirm to them generally in the aforesaid form, being willing after we have enquired into them to confirm them as may be just. In testimony whereof we have had these letters made patent, myself as witness at the Tower of London the tenth day of July, in the year of our reign in England the fifteenth, but of our reign in France the second.

[4] We, moreover, holding the concessions, confirmations, privileges, liberties, immunities, and customs to be reasonable and seasonable, accept, approve, and ratify them for us and our heirs, as far as in us lies, and concede and confirm them to the aforesaid men of the islands in the same manner to their heirs and successors in the same manner as the aforesaid letter more fully testify and as they and their predecessors inhabitants of the said islands have reasonably used and enjoyed them. In witness whereof we have had these our letters made patent. Myself as witness at Gloucester the tenth day of November in the second year of our reign.

[5] We have also inspected other letters patent of our aforesaid Lord Richard formerly king of England, the second after the Conquest, similarly made in these words. Richard, by the grace of God king of England and France and lord of Ireland, to all to whom these present letters may come, greeting. Know ye that we in consideration of the good behaviour and the great loyalty which we have ever found in our liege and faithful peoples and communities of our islands of Guernsey, Jersey, Sark and Alderney, have of our special grace granted for ourselves and our heirs, as far as in us lies, to the said peoples and communities, that they, their heirs and successors shall for ever be free and quit from tolls, duties and customs of whatsoever kind in all our cities, market towns, and ports within our kingdom of England, in the same manner as our faithful liege people in our aforesaid kingdom are. Provided always, however, that our said peoples and communities, their heirs and successors aforesaid shall well and faithfully conduct themselves towards us and our heirs aforesaid for ever. In witness whereof, we have caused these our letters to be made patent. Witness myself at Westminster this twenty-eighth day of July in the eighteenth year of our reign.

[6] We, moreover, holding the aforesaid letters, and all and singular contained therein, to be reasonable and seasonable, accept and approve them same for us and our heirs, as far as in us lies, and now ratify and confirm them to the men, peoples and communities of the islands of Guernsey, Jersey, Sark and Alderney, and to the successors as the aforesaid letters more fully testify. In witness whereof we have caused these our letters to be made patent. Witness myself at Westminster the twenty-ninth day of March in the fifth year of our reign.

[7] We, moreover, holding the aforesaid letters, and all and singular contained therein, to be reasonable and seasonable, accept and approve them same for us and our heirs, as far as in us lies, and now ratify and confirm them to the men, peoples and communities of the islands of Guernsey, Jersey, Sark and Alderney, and to the successors as the aforesaid letters more fully testify. In witness whereof we have caused these our letters to be made patent. Witness myself at Westminster the fifteenth day of December in the first year of our reign.

ELIOT

By the king himself and according to the aforesaid authority of Parliament and for forty shillings paid into the hanaper.

Examined by William Morland William Kelet clerks

[Examined by John Bate and Thomas Shipton clerks]

Plate 9: The Royal Charter granted by Henry VII in 1486.
Credit: The National Archives, ref. C 56/8.

Henry VII: 1486

Commentary

Given the circumstances of Henry VII's accession, it is no surprise that the instabilities and insecurities that so often characterised the position of Jersey and its neighbours were very evident again. Henry seized the throne in battle, in the context of civil war, and he did so from an exile in France and before that in Brittany, which emphasised the tensions between the powers surrounding the Bay of Saint-Malo and the western Channel approaches. At the same time, the context for Henry's victory placed a spotlight on their inherent interconnectedness and the importance of the islands.

Henry's exile in Brittany had begun in 1471, as a desperate young fugitive from the disastrous collapse of the regime of the restored Henry VI. There were times, especially in the first half dozen years of this exile, when his freedom of movement and association were severely curtailed but, after a narrow escape from an attempt by English agents to take him on board ship in Saint-Malo in 1476, he was more generously supported at the Breton court. Richard III's reign saw renewed and vigorous efforts to take him back to England, but the negotiations with Pierre Landais, duke Francis's treasurer, were leaked to Henry, and he escaped over the border into France in the autumn of 1484. It was from the mouth of the Seine that Henry launched his invasion at the start of August 1485, which was to end in victory at Bosworth Field.

These years left a significant imprint on Henry in ways that mattered for Jersey and the other islands. Henry understandably placed great reliance on the men and women who had shared his exile, and he was comfortable with those whose Norman-French speech was familiar to him after his long sojourn in Brittany and France. The circle of Henry's heir, Prince Arthur, was particularly influenced by the king's associates from the Channel Islands. The prince's premier usher was Thomas de St Martin; Edouard de Carteret was among the prince's gentlemen carvers.[1] The dean of Arthur's chapel was the Jerseyman

---

[1] St Martin: William Campbell (ed.), *Materials for a History of the Reign of Henry VII. from Original Documents preserved in the Public Record Office*, Rolls Ser., 60 (2 vols, London, 1873–75), vol. 2, pp. 45 (already a gentleman usher of the chamber in 1486), 80, 141. See also the lasting impact on Henry's religious outlook and practice:

Jean Neele, who had been educated in Paris before becoming treasurer to William Waynflete, bishop of Winchester.[2] This interest in the islands, and Jersey in particular, had very personal roots too, for he may have passed through the Channel Islands in 1471, as he fled into exile,[3] and when, late in 1483, Henry made an abortive attempt to land in the south-west of England, it seems very probable that he did so as he sailed back towards Brittany. There is a good chance that, as storms blew him back across the Channel, he first found refuge in Jersey. Henry's apparent knowledge of and trust in Edmund Weston, Thomas de St Martin and Clement le Hardy, appointed bailiff of Jersey not long after Bosworth, is suggestive of the personal connections that might have been made during a visit to the island.[4] A later grant of office in Guernsey recalled St Martin and Weston's service to Henry at great personal cost, perhaps during that episode,[5] and a later tradition tells of Clement le Hardy assisting Henry during his return from England in November 1483. Clement le Hardy was certainly later one of the closest associates of Matthew Baker, captain of Jersey from 1488 and one of the men closest to Henry during his exile: when Henry escaped from Brittany into France in the autumn of 1484 he was disguised as Baker's servant.[6]

The context for events in 1485–86 was therefore informed by Henry's time in Brittany and France, but it was also a time of continuing civil conflict in England and the other territories of the English crown. There was continuing resistance in some parts of the north of England, and in April 1486 Henry heard of a planned rebellion by Humphrey Stafford in Worcestershire. Some of the participants in this rising believed that the earl of Warwick, son of Edward IV

Virginia K. Henderson, 'Rethinking Henry VII: The Man and his Piety in the Context of the Observant Franciscans', in Douglas Biggs, Sharon D. Michalove, and Compton Reeves (eds), *Reputation and Representation in Fifteenth-Century Europe* (Leiden, 2004), pp. 317–47, esp. pp. 320–5, 340.

[2] Neele died in March 1498. A. B. Emden, *A Biographical Register of the University of Oxford to 1540* (3 vols, Oxford, 1957–59), pp. 1340–41; G. R. Balleine, *A Biographical Dictionary of Jersey* (London, 1948), pp. 512–13; J. de la Croix, *Jersey: ses antiquités, ses institutions, son histoire* (3 vols, Jersey, 1859–61), vol. 3, pp. 174–5.

[3] Ralph A. Griffiths and Roger S. Thomas, *The Making of the Tudor Dynasty*, rev. edn (Stroud, 2005), p. 77; S. B. Chrimes, *Henry VII*, new edn (New Haven CT, 1999), p. 17.

[4] Balleine, *Biographical Dictionary of Jersey*, pp. 398–401; G. R. Balleine, *History of Jersey*, rev. Marguerite Syvret and Joan Stevens (Chichester, 1981), p. 63.

[5] *Materials for a History of the Reign of Henry VII.*, vol. 1, p. 186 (28 November 1485).

[6] *Materials for a History of the Reign of Henry VII.*, vol. 2, pp. 338–9; Denys Hay, *Polydore Vergil* (Oxford, 1952), p. 198; C. S. L. Davies, 'Richard III, Henry VII and the Island of Jersey', *The Ricardian*, 9 (1991–4), 334–42, at pp. 338, 340 (n. 8); cf. p. 337 on de St Martin.

and Richard III's brother George, duke of Clarence, had been released from imprisonment and had travelled from Guernsey into England.[7] And, most importantly for the context of the royal charter grant of 1486, Henry also encountered serious opposition in Jersey. Richard Harliston, who had been captain of Jersey probably since he led its recapture in 1469 and combined this captaincy with that of Guernsey since 1473, was initially confirmed by Henry in his role. But before long he rebelled, apparently looking for support to Margaret of Burgundy, sister of the Yorkist kings Edward IV and Richard III. On 6 September 1485 Henry sent Edmund Weston and Thomas de St Martin to Guernsey in haste; in November they were made joint governors, with reference to their exceptional service.[8] The siege of Mont Orgueil must have begun before 28 February 1486, when Mathew Baker and David Philips were jointly made governors of Jersey and Mont Orgueil.[9] Mont Orgueil apparently held out for six months. Eventually it fell,[10] however, and in the wake of this fall the relationship of the islands to each other was further changed.

Henry VII confirmed Jersey's charters in February 1486. The new king's choice of which charters to confirm is very significant. Like Edward IV and Richard III, Henry made a point about his relationship with his predecessors

---

[7] *CPR 1485–94*, pp. 119, 132–4; Paul L. Hughes and James F. Larkin (eds), *Tudor Royal Proclamations* (3 vols, New Haven CT, 1964–69), vol. 1, no. 8; *CPR 1485–94*, pp. 119, 133–4; Michael Bennett, *The Battle of Bosworth* (Gloucester, 1985), pp. 111–12; Anthony Goodman, *The Wars of the Roses: Military Activity and English Society, 1452–97* (London, 1981), pp. 97–101; C. H. Williams, 'The Rebellion of Humphrey Stafford in 1486', *English Historical Review*, 43 (1928), 181–9, esp. p. 183.

[8] *Materials for a History of the Reign of Henry VII.*, vol. 1, pp. 186, 316. Weston was appointed alone less than six months later: *ibid.*, pp. 372–3 (8 March 1486).

[9] *Materials for a History of the Reign of Henry VII.*, vol. 1, p. 320; *CPR 1485–94*, p. 80; warrant for Baker's guns: M. Oppenheim (ed.), *Naval Accounts and Inventories of the Reign of Henry VII, 1485–8 and 1495–7*, Navy Records Society, 8 (1896), p. 77 (25 February 1486).

[10] Davies, 'Richard III, Henry VII and the Island of Jersey', pp. 336–7; Charles le Quesne, *A Constitutional History of Jersey* (London, 1856), pp. 562–3; Balleine, *History of Jersey*, rev. Syvret and Stevens, pp. 63–5; *Biographical Dictionary of Jersey*, p. 614; Edmund Toulmin Nicolle, *Mont Orgueil Castle: Its History and Description* (Jersey, 1921), p. 38. Harliston's pardon covers offences to 4 September 1486 (*Materials for a History of the Reign of Henry VII.*, vol. 2, p. 30; *CPR 1485–94*, pp. 139, 141). Cecil Roth, 'Perkin Warbeck and his Jewish Master', *Transactions of the Jewish Historical Society of England*, 9 (1918–20), 143–62, esp. pp. 155–6 (was Sir Edward Brampton, captain of Guernsey 1482–84, the connection between Harliston and Margaret of Burgundy?). Bronwyn Matthews (ed.), *Les Chroniques de Jersey* (St Helier, 2017), pp. 52–5, thanks to the connection between Harliston and the de Carterets, who married his heiress, makes an attempt to justify the latter's departure from the island for Burgundy.

when he confirmed the charters. It was Edward IV's charters that were confirmed, ignoring Richard III's – and, as a consequence, also omitting the Lancastrian kings. Henry was Edward IV's successor far more than he was a Lancastrian revivalist in this respect as in others. And by confirming the 1469 charter of Edward IV rather than that of 1465, he ensured that the incipient separation of the bailiwicks was confirmed and reinforced. In 1469, thanks to the recent occupation of Jersey and the divisions Edward IV's regime, the two bailiwicks for the first time received separate charters of privileges. Since 1478, the islands had had different captains, although Richard Harliston retained the overall title of captain in chief. Now, with Harliston's fall, Henry allowed the position of the islands' separation to continue in the form of separate charters of confirmation, as also through different captains.

In February 1486, when the charters were sealed, Mont Orgueil was almost certainly still in the hands of Harliston and Henry's opponents. While this makes the celebration of the islanders' recovery of the castle in Edward's charter appear a touch ironic, there was a powerful message too about the significance of Jersey and its community's loyalty for the new regime. That sensitivity to Jersey's position may also have led to a conscious decision to separate the approach to each bailiwick. The previous few years had demonstrated to Henry the Channel Islands' importance. And, since a key diplomatic challenge of the first years of Henry's reign remained focused on the fate of Brittany and resistance to its absorption by France, careful management of relationships with the island communities continued.[11]

Text

Henry VII confirmed the privileges originally granted in 1341 by Edward III and the further rights in respect of tolls, duties and customs granted by Richard II, as confirmed and extended in Edward IV's charter of 1465. The grant of 1465 was to Guernsey, Sark and Alderney, and in 1486 it was confirmed specifically for those islands and their communities – and therefore not for Jersey. As a result, it was necessary to provide a further confirmation, this time of the 1394 privileges, specifically to Jersey, Guernsey, Sark and Alderney, to which was appended an indication of a grant of the earlier privileges of 1341 to the island communities now including Jersey, in the form already confirmed more narrowly, mutatis mutandis. Taken from the enrolment in The National Archives, C 56/8, m. 12; it should be noted that the version in Prison Board is heavy abbreviated.

---

[11] John M. Currin, 'Henry VII and the Treaty of Redon (1489): Plantagenet Ambitions and Early Tudor Foreign Policy', *History*, 81 (1996), 343–58.

[1] [Henricus dei gratia Rex Anglie et Francie et Dominus Hibernie] Rex Omnibus ad quos etc [presentes litere peruenerint] Salutem. Inspeximus literas patentes domini Edwardi nuper Regis Anglie quarti factas in hec verba: Edwardus Dei gratia Rex Anglie et ffrancie et Dominus Hibernie Omnibus ad quos presentes litere peruenerint Salutem].

[2] Cum nobilissimus progenitor noster inclite memorie Ricardus quondam Rex Anglie et ffrancie et Dominus Hibernie post conquestum secundus per literas suas patentes datas apud Westmonasterium octauo die Julii Anno regni sui decimo octauo in consideracione boni gestus et magne fidelitatis quos in ligeis et fidelibus suis gentibus et Communitatibus Insularum suarum de Jeresey Guernesey Serk et Aureney indies inuenit de gracia sua speciali concessit pro se et heredibus suis quantum in eo fuit eisdem gentibus et Communitatibus suis quod ipsi et successores sui imperpetuum forent liberi et quieti in omnibus Ciuitatibus villis mercatoriis et portubus infra Regnum Anglie de omnimodo Theoloniis exaccionibus et Custumis taliter et eodem modo quo fideles ligei sui in Regno suo predicto extiterunt. Ita tamen quod dicte gentes et Communitates sue ac heredes et successores sui predicti bene et fideliter se gererent erga ipsum progenitorem nostrum et heredes suos imperpetuum prout in literis illis plenius continetur. Nos continuam fidelitatem gencium et communitatum dicte Insularum de Guernesey Serk et Aureney plenius intendentes literas predictas de omnia et singula in eis contenta quoad gentes et Communitates earundem Insularum de Guernesey Serk et Aureney acceptamus approbamus et eisdem gentibus et comunitatibus heredibus et successoribus suis per presentes ratificamus et confirmamus.

[3] Et vlterius nos memorie Reducentes quam valide viriliter et constanter dicte Gentes et Communitates earundem Insularum de Guernesey Serk et Aureney nobis et progenitoribus nostris perstiterunt et quanta pericula et perdita pro saluacion earundem Insularum et reductione Castri nostri de Mount Orgill sustinuerunt de vberiori gracia nostra concessimus eisdem gentibus et Communitatibus quod ipse heredes et successores sui sint liberi et quieti in omnibus Ciuitatibus Burgis Villis Mercatoriis et aliis Villis portubus et locis infra regnum nostrum Anglie et infra omnes terras et insulas nostras citra vel vltra mare sint vel situatum de omnibus Theoloniis Custumis subsidiis pontagiis pauagiis muragiis cariagiis fossagiis et aliis deneris nobis et heredibus nostris in dicto regno nostro Anglie quoquomodo soluendo seu faciendo sicut eedem gentes et Communitates dictarum Insularum de Guernesey Serk et Aureney seu predecessores aut antecessores sui earundem Insularum sub obediencia aliquorum progenitorum nostrorum Regum Anglie existentum vmquam fuerunt.

[4] Et eciam quod dicte gentes et Communitates earundem Insularum de Guernesey Serk et Aureney heredes et successores sui habeant et gaudeant omnia iura libertates et franchesias sua infra easdem Insulas adeo libere et tam amplis modo et forma sicut eedem gentes et communitates siue predecessores aut antecessores sui earundem Insularum sub obediencia aliquorum progenitorum nostrorum Regum Anglie existentum vnquam habuerunt seu gauisi fuerunt absque fine seu feodo per premissis aut aliquo premissorum nobis in Hanaperio nostro soluendo seu faciendo. Eo quod expressa mencio de certitudine seu valore annuo aut aliquo alio valore premissorum siue eorum alicuius aut de aliquis donis seu concessionibus per nos aut progenitores nostros eisdem gentibus et Communitatibus ante hec tempora facta in presentibus minime facta existit. Aut aliquo statuto actu siue ordinacione incontrarium editum non obstante. In cuius rei testimonium has literas nostras fieri fecimus patentes. Teste me ipso apud Westmonasterium vicesimo octauo die Januarii anno regni nostri octauo.

[5] Nos autem literas predictas ac omnia et singula in eisdem contenta rata habentes et grata ea pro nobis et heredibus nostris quantum in nobis est acceptamus approbamus et prefatis gentibus et Communitatibus Insularum de Guernesey Serk et Aureney predictarum heredibus et successoribus suis tenore presencium ratificamus concedimus et confirmamus prout litere predicte in se racionabiliter testantur In cuius etc [rei testimonium has literas nostras fieri fecimus patentes]. Teste Regis [me ipso] apud Westmonasterium x die ffebruarii [anno regni nostri primo].

Per ipsum Regem et de data predicta etc.

et pro quadraginta solidis solutis in hanaperio

[6] Rex omnibus ad quos &c. salute. Cum nobilissimus progenitor noster inclite memorie Ricardus quondam Rex Anglie et ffrancie et Dominus Hibernie post conquestum secundus per literas suas patentes datas apud Westmonasterium octauo die Julii Anno regni sui decimo octauo in consideracione boni gestus et magne fidelitatis quos in ligeis et fidelibus suis gentibus et Communitatibus Insularum suarum de Jeresey Guernesey Serk et Aureney indies inuenit de gracia sua speciali concessit pro se et heredibus suis quantum in eo fuit eisdem Gentibus et Communitatibus suis quod ipsi et successores sui imperpetuum forent liberi et quieti in omnibus Ciuitatibus villis mercatoriis et portubus infra Regnum Anglie de omnimodo Theoloniis exaccionibus et Custumis taliter et eodem modo quo fideles ligei sui in Regno suo predicto extiterunt. Ita tamen quod dicte gentes et Communitates sue ac heredes et successores sui predicti bene et fideliter se gererent erga ipsum progenitorem nostrum et heredes suos imperpetuum prout in literis illis plenius continetur. Nos continuam fidelitatem gentis et communitatis dicte Insule de Jeresey plenius intendentes literas

predictas de omnia et singula in eis contenta quoad gentem et Communitatem dicte Insule de Jeresey acceptamus approbamus et eisdem genti et comunitati heredibus et successoribus suis per presentes ratificamus et confirmamus. Et vlterius etc. vt supra mutantis mutandis. In cuius etc. Teste vt supra.

Per ipsum Regem et de data predicta etc.

et pro quadraginta solidis solutis in hanaperio

Translation

[1] Henry by the grace of God king of England and France and lord of Ireland, to all to whom these present letters may come, greeting. We have inspected the Letters Patent of the Lord Edward the Fourth, lately king of England, made in these words: Edward by the grace of God king of England and France and lord of Ireland to all to whom these present letters may come, greeting.

[2] Whereas our most noble progenitor of glorious memory Richard the Second after the Conquest, lately king of England and France and lord of Ireland, by his Letters Patent given at Westminster on the eighth day of July in the eighteenth year of his reign in consideration of the good behaviour and great loyalty which he always found in his liege and faithful peoples and communities of the islands of Jersey, Guernsey, Sark, and Alderney, of his special grace granted for himself and his heirs, as far as in him lay, to these his same peoples and communities that they themselves and their successors should be for ever in all cities, market towns, and ports within the kingdom of England free and quit of all tolls, duties, and customs of whatsoever kind in such wise and in such manner as his own faithful lieges have continued in his own aforesaid kingdom. Provided always that they his said peoples and communities, their heirs and successors aforesaid should conduct themselves well and faithfully towards himself and his heirs for ever as is more fully contained in those Letters. We considering more fully the continuous loyalty of the said islands of Guernsey, Sark and Alderney, the aforesaid Letters and all and singular contained therein as regards the peoples and communities of the same islands of Guernsey, Sark and Alderney, do accept, approve, and by these presents to these same peoples and communities, their heirs and successors do ratify and confirm them.

[3] And, further, calling to mind how valiantly, manfully, and steadfastly the said peoples and communities of the said islands of Guernsey, Sark, and Alderney have stood out for us and our progenitors and what great dangers and losses they have sustained for the safety of the said island and for the recapture of our castle of Mont Orgueil, of our more abundant grace we have granted to the same peoples and communities that they, their heirs and

successors shall likewise be free and quit in all cities, boroughs, market towns, and other towns, ports, and places within our kingdom of England and within all our lands and islands lying or situated on this side or beyond the sea from all tolls, customs, subsidies, pontages, pavages, murages, tallages, fossages, and other dues in whatever way to be discharged or made to us and our heirs in our said kingdom of England just as the same peoples and communities of the said islands of Guernsey, Sark, and Alderney or their predecessors, or ancestors of the same islands, living under the obedience of any of our progenitors the kings of England, have ever been.

[4] And further that the said peoples and communities of the same islands of Guernsey, Sark, and Alderney, their heirs and successors, should enjoy all the rights, liberties and franchises as freely and fully as their predecessors and ancestors living under the obedience of any of our progenitors the kings of England have ever had or enjoyed them, without fine or fee in the premises or any of the premises to be paid or made to us in the Hanaper so far as express mention exists of the surety or annual value or any other value in the matter of the premises or of any of them or of other gifts or concessions by us or our progenitors to the same peoples and communities, whether such mention has been made before these times or is expressly set forth in these present letters, or any statute, act or ordinance published to the contrary notwithstanding. In witness whereof we have caused these out Letters to be made Patent. Witness myself at Westminster this twenty-eighth day of January in the eighth year of our reign.

[5] We, moreover, finding the aforesaid letters and all and singular therein contained to be reasonable and seasonable, accept and approve them for us and our heirs, as far as in us lies, and now ratify and confirm them to the aforesaid peoples and communities of the islands of Guernsey, Sark, and Alderney aforesaid, and to their heirs and successors, in the tenor of the present letters, as the aforesaid letters reasonably testify. In witness whereof we have caused these our letters to be made patent. Witness myself at Westminster the tenth day of February [in the first year of our reign].

By the king himself and of the aforesaid date, etc.

And for forty shillings paid in the Hanaper

[6] The King to all to whom etc., greeting. Whereas our most noble progenitor of glorious memory, Richard the Second after the Conquest, lately king of England and France and Lord of Ireland, by his Letters Patent given at Westminster on eighth day of July in the eighteenth year of his reign in consideration of the good behaviour and great loyalty which we have ever found in his liege and faithful peoples and communities of our islands of

Jersey, Guernsey, Sark and Alderney, of his special grace granted for himself and his heirs, as far as in him lay, to these his same peoples and communities, that they themselves and their successors should be for ever in all the cities, market towns, and ports within our kingdom of England free and quit from all tolls, duties, and customs of whatsoever kind, in the such wise and in such manner as his own faithful lieges have continued in his own aforesaid kingdom. Provided always, however, that his said peoples and communities, their heirs and successors aforesaid should conduct themselves well and faithfully towards us and our heirs and successors aforesaid for ever as is more fully contained in those letters. We more fully understanding the continuous loyalty of the people and community of the aforesaid island of Jersey by these present letters accept and approve the aforesaid letters in all and singular contained in them in relation to the people and community of the aforesaid island of Jersey, and ratify and confirm to the same people and community and their successors by these present letters. And further, etc. as above, with details changed as necessary.

In relation to which, etc. Witness as above.

By the king himself and of the aforesaid date, etc.

And for forty shillings paid in the Hanaper

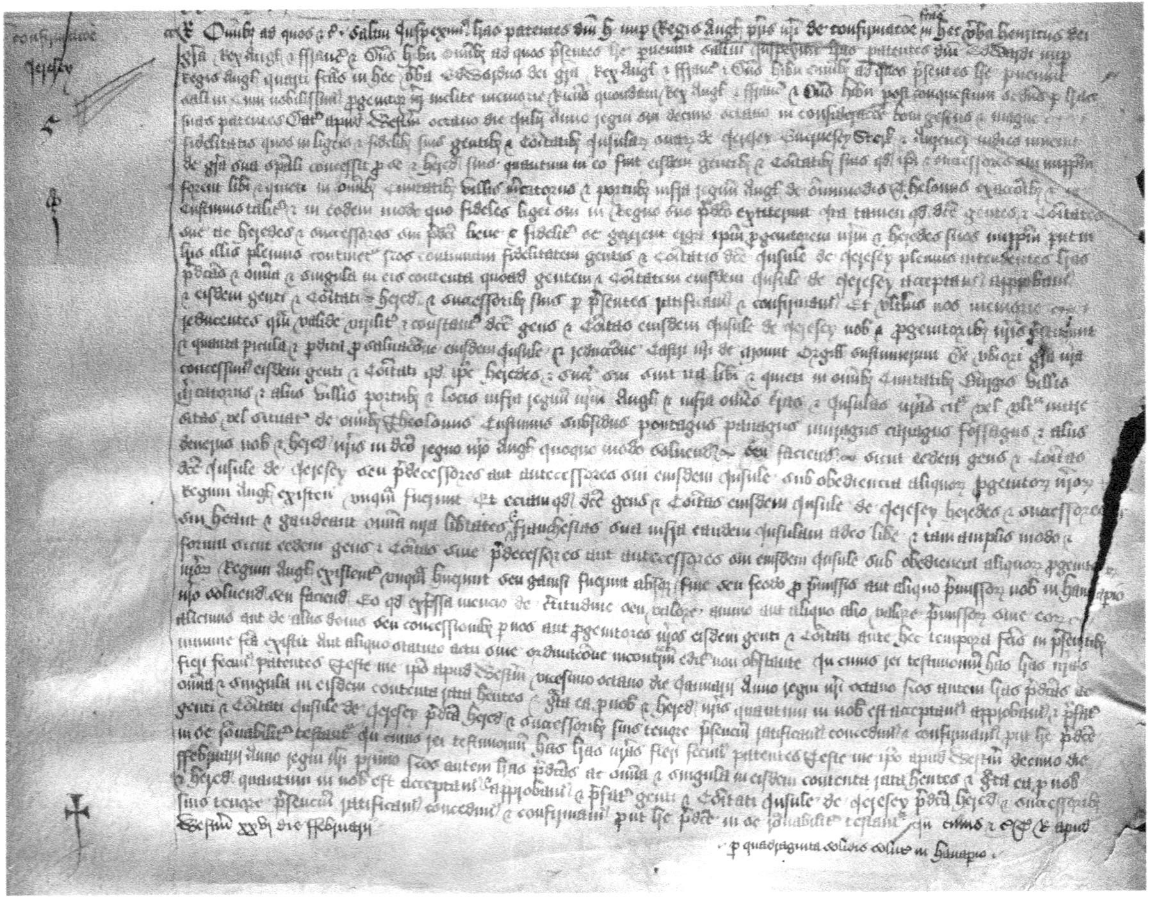

Plate 10: The Royal Charter granted by Henry VIII in 1510.
Credit: The National Archives, ref. C 56/25.

Henry VIII: 1510

Commentary

Henry VIII confirmed the Jersey charter of his father soon after his accession. The last years of Henry VII's reign had in many ways been difficult ones, as some of the more suspicious and acquisitive elements of the king's character came to the fore. They were difficult in Jersey too and, although Henry VIII came to the throne in relatively uncomplicated circumstances and allowed for continuity in the local regime in the island, the new king's ambitions in France and the underlying instability in the rule of governor Sir Hugh Vaughan meant Jersey's distinctive position retained its importance.

Henry VII was fortunate that he survived long enough to have a near-adult heir in spite of the loss of his eldest son Arthur in 1502. Speculation about the succession, including in strategically important centres such as Calais, was not unknown, and the days immediately following Henry's death were tense ones.[1] But once he was proclaimed, even at the age of only 17, Henry was able to establish himself successfully on the throne.

There was also continuity in the growing authority of some of the most prominent families in Jersey. Edmund Weston had first come to Jersey in 1468 and served there until he died in 1505. Edmund was the son of Peter Weston, of Boston (Lincolnshire), so the association with Richard Harliston, with whom he had arrived in 1468, who was from Humberstone in the same county, was at least in part a geographical one. If anything, Edmund Weston was better connected than Harliston, because his brother John was a hospitaller who rose to become prior of the Order of St John in England from 1476 to 1489. Edmund had established himself in Jersey, marrying Catherine, widow of Renaud Lemprière. Within a few months of Henry VII's accession, Edmund, first jointly, and then very swiftly alone, was appointed governor of Guernsey and appeared as an esquire for the body.[2] Edmund and Catherine's eldest

---

[1] S. J. Gunn, 'The Accession of Henry VIII', *Historical Research*, 64 (1991), 278–88.

[2] C. S. L. Davies, 'Richard III, Henry VII and the Island of Jersey', *The Ricardian*, 9 (1991–93), 334–42; William Campbell (ed.), *Materials for a History of the Reign of Henry VII.*, Rolls Ser., 60 (2 vols, London, 1873–77), vol. 1, pp. 186 (28 November 1485; with Thomas de St Martin), 372–3 (8 March 1486).

son, Richard, was born at Rozel (Jersey) in 1469. Richard's success was made through Henry VII's favour for his followers from the Channel Islands, some of whom, as has been explained, may have provided valued service even before Bosworth. Richard made his first appearance at court probably in the early months of 1499 and by 1501 he was winning at chess and the dice against the king. He seems to have been initially a groom of the king's chamber, although also closely associated with the service of the queen, Elizabeth of York, for whom he bought 'certain harnesses of gyrdelles ... beyond the see'. About this time, he married one of the queen's gentlewomen, Anne, daughter of Oliver Sandys of Shere (Surrey). Richard Weston demonstrated that the fate of others from Guernsey and Jersey, many of whom lost position with the death of Prince Arthur, was not inevitable. Before Henry VIII's coronation Richard had already succeeded his father as governor of Guernsey. His eminence in the king's service is demonstrated by the offices he held – including lieutenant of the forest and castle of Windsor (1508), and knight of the body (1518).[3]

A peaceful succession to the English throne and a reduction in the risk of civil strife in England and its associated territories did not, of course, reduce the threat of war between England and France. Given Henry VIII's determination to make war on France, the islands would remain strategically important. Henry initially confirmed the French peace, in place since 1502, inherited from his father. But in 1511, Henry's forces intervened alongside Ferdinand of Aragon against his Moorish enemies and with the troops of Margaret of Savoy, governor of the Netherlands, against the duke of Guelders. Success in the latter campaign at least encouraged Henry's ambitions.[4] In 1512 the English fleet operated with some impunity in the Channel and in raiding in Brittany, before in 1513 Guyon le Roy, seigneur du Chillou, was given

[3] TNA, E 101/414/16, ff. 62r, 64v, 73r; E 101/415/3, ff. 30r, 62r, 83r; Nicholas Harris Nicolas (ed.), *Wardrobe Accounts of Edward the Fourth: With a Memoir of Elizabeth of York* (London, 1830), p. 84; J. S Brewer, J. Gairdner and R. H. Brodie (eds), *Letters and Papers, Foreign and Domestic, of the Reign of Henry VIII* (21 vols in 37, London, 1864–1932), vol. 1, no. 54(71), p. 438 (2 m. 25); Stanford Lehmberg, 'Weston, Sir Richard (*c.* 1465–1541), Courtier', *ODNB*, vol. 58, pp. 295–6; S. T. Bindoff (ed.), *The House of Commons, 1509–1558* (3 vols, London, 1982), vol. 2, pp. 590–2 (NB the latter two authorities put Richard's birth at *c.* 1465, probably based on Frederic Harrison, *Annals of an Old Manor-House: Sutton Place, Guildford* (London, 1899), p. 36); G. R. Balleine, *A Biographical Dictionary of Jersey* (London, 1948), pp. 612–14; S. J. Gunn, *Henry VII's New Men and the Making of Tudor England* (Oxford, 2016), pp. 195, 221, 319; Joan Kirby (ed.), *The Plumpton Letters and Papers*, Camden Soc., 5th ser., 8 (1996), p. 170.

[4] C. G. Cruickshank, *Army Royal: Henry VIII's Invasion of France, 1513* (Oxford, 1969), pp. 1–5; J. J. Scarisbrick, *Henry VIII* (London, 1968), pp. 27–8; R. B. Wernham, *Before the Armada: The Growth of English Foreign Policy 1485–1588* (London, 1966), pp. 81–3.

command by Louis XII and a new sense of urgency was apparent on the French side.[5] An early sign of the impact of the war with France was an increased interest in the garrison of Guernsey, seen in Thomas Wolsey's order, issued in February 1513, to pay wages for 40 soldiers for three months.[6] There were significant attempts to moderate this impact, for example in the safe conduct for the inhabitants of Guernsey granted on 27 March of that year by Guyon le Roy as lieutenant general of the French fleets in Normandy and Brittany.[7] A little later, on 20 April, Louis, lord of Granville granted Guillaume Fabien, 'natif du païx et duché de Normandie', curé of Alderney, on his own behalf and that of the island's other inhabitants, freedom to travel to Normandy until 1 January next; he noted that in times past during time of war the inhabitants had been 'en bonne paix'.

Further, the success of the Weston family was achieved in the context of an increasingly problematic regime in Jersey as a result of the abuses of the governor, Hugh Vaughan, from 1502.[8] Against the background of the increasing tension and move to war between England and France, the situation within Jersey deteriorated.[9] Bailiff Thomas Lemprière went to England in 1513 to complain against Vaughan.[10] His action is reflective of a greater openness on the part of the English court of Chancery to Channel Islands cases. Vaughan in 1513 allied himself with the de Carterets of St Ouen – Richard and Jean were in his service, and Vaughan offered Helier the bailiffship. In a letter of 30 April 1513, Vaughan emphasised the daily threat from the French when reporting his grant of the bailiffship to Helier de Carteret, who carried a gift of Norman

[5] Alfred Spont (ed.), *Letters and Papers relating to the War with France, 1512–1513*, Publications of the Navy Records Society, 10 (London, 1897), pp. xv–xxxi; Neil Murphy, 'Henry VIII's First Invasion of France: The Gascon Expedition of 1512', *English Historical Review*, 130 (2015), 25–56.

[6] BL, Stowe MS 146, ff. 39, 108 (*Letters and Papers*, vol. 1, nos 1605–06). Kenneth James Barton, 'Excavations at the Vale Castle, Guernsey, C. I.', *Report and Transactions of La Société Guernesiaise*, 21 (1981–85), 485–538, suggests that the enclosure there is fifteenth- and early sixteenth-century in date, and may arise because of the situation in 1512, or in the subsequent two decades.

[7] *Letters and Papers*, vol. 1, no. 1742.

[8] Balleine, *History of Jersey*, rev. Syvret and Stevens, p. 67; A. J. Eagleston, 'The Chroniques de Jersey in the Light of Contemporary Documents', *ABSJ*, 13 (1936–39), 37–62, at pp. 44–55, 61–2; *Chroniques*, ed. Matthews, pp. 92–3.

[9] Cf. Colin Platt, *A Concise History of Jersey: A New Perspective* (St Helier, 2009), p. 39, for an alternative emphasis on the situation of Jersey in these years as relatively peaceful, which therefore fails to provide the necessary context for the drawn-out contest between Vaughan and de Carteret.

[10] *Chroniques*, ed. Matthews, pp. 90–129, provides an extended account of this struggle.

cloth for sheets for Thomas Wolsey's servants, seeking royal confirmation.[11] In May 1514, the deposition of Lemprière and his replacement by de Carteret was confirmed by the king.[12] This seems to have met with passive resistance in the island, for in August and September 1514 Lemprière was still acting as bailiff.[13] A 1515 commission, made up of two English lawyers, George Treheyron and Reginald Meynours, found mainly against Lemprière.[14] Vaughan's triumph seemed complete, but it was overturned when a dispute over Trinity Manor led to a complete reversal in allegiances in the island.

Henry VIII's confirmation of the charter of his father, granted in February 1510 when his reign was still in its first year, was therefore in many ways more straightforward than those of the previous half century and more. Yet his ambitions in France, and the underlying fragility of the regime in Jersey itself, made the continuation of the island's privileges just as important as those granted by its predecessors.

Text

Henry VIII confirmed the charter of his father, Henry VII, and thereby the privileges granted by Edward IV in 1465. This grant by Edward included and extended those rights granted by Richard II in 1394 relating to tolls, duties and customs. Henry VIII confirmed all these rights and liberties specifically for Jersey. The Jersey charter is taken from the enrolled version TNA, C 56/25, m. 14A; it was issued slightly earlier than the equivalent Guernsey charter. The latter, which survives in the Greffe in St Peter Port in a more extensive form, provides fuller readingsB, amended as relevant for the Jersey context.

[1] BHenricus dei gratia Rex Anglie et ffrancie et Dominus hibernie Omnibus ad quos presentes litere pervenerint Salutem [ARex omnibus ad quos etc salutem.] Inspeximus literas patentes domini Henrici nuper Regis Anglie [Apatris nostri de confirmacione; Bseptimi] factas in hec verba: Henricus dei gratia Rex Anglie et ffrancie et Dominus hibernie Omnibus ad quos presentes litere peruenerint Salutem. Inspeximus literas patentes domini Edwardi nuper Regis Anglie quarti factas in hec verba: Edwardus Dei gratia Rex Anglie et ffrancie et Dominus hibernie Omnibus ad quos presentes litere peruenerint Salutem.

---

[11] *Letters and Papers*, vol. 1, no. 1829.
[12] *Letters and Papers*, vol. 1, no. 2964(30) from TNA, C 76/196 (French Roll, 6 Henry VIII, p. 2), m. 4.
[13] St Helier, Société Jersiaise, Lord Coutanche Library, de St Martin Contrat, unnumbered: 12 Aug. 1514; Lord Coutanche Library, 'I 1500 to 1560 Soc. Jers.': 16 September 1514.
[14] *Letters and Papers*, vol. 2, no. 854.

[2] Cum nobilissimus progenitor noster inclite memorie Ricardus quondam Rex Anglie et ffrancie et Dominus hibernie post conquestum secundus per literas suas patentes datas apud Westmonasterium octavo die Julii Anno regni sui decimo octavo in consideracione boni gestus et magne fidelitatis quos in ligeis et fidelibus suis gentibus et Communitatibus Insularum suarum de [^AJeresey] Guernesey Serk [^ASterk – sic] et Aureney indies inuenit de gracia sua speciali concessit pro se et heredibus suis quantum in eo fuit eisdem gentibus et Communitatibus suis quod ipsi et successores sui imperpetuum forent liberi et quieti in omnibus Ciuitatibus villis mercatoriis et portubus infra Regnum Anglie de omnimodo Theoloniis exaccionibus et Custumis taliter et eodem modo quo fideles ligei sui in Regno suo predicto extiterunt. Ita tamen quod dicte gentes et Communitates sue ac heredes et successores sui predicti bene et fideliter se gererent erga ipsum progenitorem nostrum et heredes suos imperpetuum prout in literis illis plenius continetur. Nos continuam fidelitatem gentis et Communitatis dicte Insule de Jeresey plenius intendentes literas predictas de omnia et singula in eis contenta quoad gentem et Communitatem eiusdem Insule de Jeresey acceptamus approbamus et eisdem gentibus et Comunitatibus heredibus et successoribus suis per presentes ratificamus et confirmamus.

[3] Et vlterius nos memorie Reducentes quam valide viriliter et constanter dicte gens et Communitas eiusdem Insule de Jersey et progenitoribus nostris perstiterunt et quanta pericula et perdita pro saluacione eiusdem Insule et reduccione Castri nostri de Mount Orgill sustinuerunt de vberiori gracia nostra concessimus eisdem genti et Communitati quod ipse heredes et successores sui sint liberi et quieti in omnibus Ciuitatibus Burgis Villis Mercatoriis et aliis Villis portubus et locis infra regnum nostrum Anglie et infra omnes terras et insulas nostras citra vel ultra mare sint vel situatum de omnibus Theoloniis Custumis subsidiis pontagiis pauagiis muragiis cariagiis fossagiis et aliis deneris nobis et heredibus nostris in dicto regno nostro Anglie quoquomodo soluendo seu faciendo sicut eedem gens et Communitas dicte Insule de Jeresey seu predecessores aut antecessores sui eiusdem Insule sub obediencia aliquorum progenitorum nostrorum Regum Anglie existentum vmquam fuerunt.

[4] Et eciam quod dicte gens et Communitas eiusdem Insule de Jeresey heredes et successores sui habeant et gaudeant omnia jura libertates et franchesias sua infra eandem Insulam adeo libere et tam amplis modo et forma sicut eedem gens et communitas sive predecessores aut antecessores sui eiusdem Insule sub obediencia aliquorum progenitorum nostrorum Regum Anglie existentum vnquam habuerunt seu gauisi fuerunt absque fine seu feodo per premissis aut aliquo premissorum nobis in Hanaperio nostro solvendo seu faciendo. Eo quod expressa mencio de certitudine seu valore annuo aut aliquo alio valore premissorum sive eorum alicuius aut de aliquis donis seu concessionibus per

nos aut progenitores nostros eisdem genti et Communitati ante hec tempora facta in presentibus minime facta existit. Aut aliquo statuto actu sive ordinacione incontrarium editum non obstante. In cuius rei testimonium has literas nostras fieri fecimus patentes. Teste me ipso apud Westmonasterium vicesimo octavo die Januarii anno regni nostri octavo.

[5] Nos autem literas predictas ac omnia et singula in eisdem contenta rata habentes et grata ea pro nobis et heredibus nostris quantum in nobis est acceptamus approbamus et prefati genti et Communitati Insule de Jeresey predicta heredibus et successoribus suis tenore presencium ratificamus concedimus et confirmamus prout litere predicte in se racionabiliter testantur In cuius rei testimonium has literas nostras fieri fecimus patentes. Teste me ipso apud Westmonasterium decimo die ffebruarii anno regni nostri primo.

[6] Nos autem literas predictas ac omnia et singula in eisdem contenta rata habentes et grata ea pro nobis et heredibus nostris quantum in nobis est acceptamus approbamus et prefati genti et Communitati Insule de Jeresey predicta heredibus et successoribus suis tenore presencium ratificamus concedimus et confirmamus prout litere predicte in se racionabiliter testantur [BIn cujus rei testimonium has literas nostras fieri fecimus patentes.] [AIn cujus etc..] [BTeste me ipso apud Westmonasterium quinto die Martii anno regni nostri primo.] [ATeste Rege apud Westmonasterium xxvj die ffebruarii.]

[HANNYNGTON

Per ipsum Regem et de data predicta auctoritate parliamenti et pro quadraginta solidis solutes in Hanaperio.]

[pro quadraginta solidis solutes in Hanaperio.]

Ex. per William Morland Francis Skipton clericos

Translation

[1] BHenry by the grace of God king of England and France and lord of Ireland: to all to whom these presents may come, greeting [AThe King to all to whom etc., greeting]. We have inspected the Letters Patent [Aof confirmation] of the Lord Henry [Bthe Seventh], lately king of England [A, our father,] made in these words: Henry by the grace of God king of England and France and lord of Ireland, to all to whom these presents may come, greeting. We have inspected the Letters Patent of the Lord Edward the Fourth, lately king of England, made in these words: Edward by the grace of God king of England and France and lord of Ireland, to all to whom these presents may come, greeting.

[2] Whereas our most noble progenitor of glorious memory Richard the Second after the Conquest, lately king of England and France and lord of Ireland, by his Letters Patent given at Westminster on the eighth day of July in the eighteenth year of his reign in consideration of the good behaviour and great loyalty which he always found among his liege and faithful peoples and communities of the island of Jersey, Guernsey, Sark, and Alderney, of his special grace granted for himself and his heirs, as far as in him lay, to these his same peoples and communities that they themselves and their successors should be for ever in all cities, market towns, and ports within the kingdom of England free and quit of all tolls, duties, and customs of whatsoever kind in such wise and in such manner as his own faithful lieges have continued in his own aforesaid kingdom. Provided always that they his said peoples and communities, their heirs and successors aforesaid should conduct themselves well and faithfully towards himself and his heirs for ever as is more fully contained in those Letters. We considering more fully the continuous loyalty of the said island of Jersey, the aforesaid Letters and all and singular contained therein as regards the people and community of the same island of Jersey, do accept, approve, and by these presents to these same people and community their heirs and successors, do ratify and confirm them.

[3] And, further, we calling to mind how valiantly, manfully, and steadfastly the said people and community of the said island of Jersey have stood out for us and our progenitors and what great dangers and losses they have sustained for the safety of the said island and for the recapture of our castle of Mont Orgueil, of our more abundant grace have granted to the same people and community that they, their heirs and successors shall likewise be free and quit in all cities, boroughs, market towns, and other towns, ports, and places within our kingdom of England and within all our lands and islands lying or situated on this side or beyond the sea from all theolonies, customs, subsidies, pontages, pavages, murages, tallages, fossages, and other dues in whatever way to be discharged or made to us and our heirs in our said kingdom of England just as the same people and community of the said island of Jersey or their predecessors or ancestors of the same islands, living under the obedience of any of our progenitors the kings of England have ever been.

[4] And further that the said people and community of the same island of Jersey, their heirs and successors, should enjoy all their rights, liberties and franchises as freely and fully as their predecessors and ancestors living under the obedience of any of our progenitors the kings of England have ever had or enjoyed them, without fine or fee in the premises or any of the premises to be paid or made to us in the Hanaper so far as express mention exists of the surety or annual value or any other value in the matter of the premises or of any of them or of other gifts or concessions by us or our progenitors

to the same people and community, whether such mention has been made before these times or is expressly set forth in these present letters, or any statute, act or ordinance published to the contrary notwithstanding. In witness whereof we have caused these out Letters to be made Patent. Witness myself at Westminster this twenty-eighth day of January in the eighth year of our reign.

[5] We, moreover, holding the aforesaid letters, and all and singular contained therein, to be reasonable and seasonable, accept and approve them for us and our heirs, as far as in us lies, and now ratify and confirm them to the aforesaid people and community of the island of Jersey aforesaid, and to their heirs and successors, in the tenor of the present letters, as the aforesaid letters reasonably testify. In witness whereof we have caused these our letters to be made patent. Witness myself at Westminster the tenth day of February in the first year of our reign.

[6] We, moreover, finding the aforesaid letters and all and singular contained therein, to be reasonable and seasonable, accept and approve them for us and our heirs, as far as in us lies, and now ratify, grant, and confirm them to our aforesaid people and community of the island of Jersey aforesaid, and to their heirs and successors, in the tenor of the present letters, as the aforesaid letters reasonably testify. [BIn witness whereof we have caused these out letters to be made patent.] [AIn witness whereof, etc..] [BWitness myself at Westminster this fifth day of March in the first year of our reign.] [AWitness the King at Westminster this twenty-sixth day of February.]

[HANNYNGTON

By the king himself, and the aforesaid authority of parliament and forty shillings paid into the Hanaper.]

[For forty shillings paid into the Hanaper.]

Examined by William Morland and Francis Skipton clerks

Edward VI: 1548

Commentary

Edward VI's charter to Jersey and Guernsey for the first time provides specific evidence of the process of negotiation that lay behind the grant of these documents. It continued the islands' earlier charter privileges, but it also added further elements, highlighting the way in which negotiation and its context, including the development of the regime in England and its relationships with France and other powers, impacted on the new form of the islands' charter.

Edward VI made his grant confirming the islands' privileges on 6 March 1548. This was a period of rapid change in the policy of the English government, both in its relationships with its neighbours and in religion. Edward's charter confirmed Henry VIII's, which in turn confirmed his father's confirmation of the Edward IV charter of 1469, confirming and developing the grants of Richard II. It did so, unlike these predecessors, for both Jersey and Guernsey together – the charters confirmed are those for Jersey specifically, but Edward's charter summarised and confirmed for both bailiwicks. This reintegration, which, with the exception of Richard III's charter, returns to the pattern that had not been seen for a century since the grant of Henry VI, probably occurred through the influence of Edward Seymour, duke of Somerset, the king's uncle and protector of the realm. The charter specifically refers to its having been granted 'on the advice and with the agreement of our dearest uncle Edward, duke of Somerset, governor of our person and Protector of our realms, lordships, and subjects'. Seymour had a long-standing and genuine interest in the islands dating back over ten years, from the time he had bought the governorship of Jersey in 1536, meaning that, for the first time since the fall of Richard Harliston in the 1480s, one individual had a dominant interest in all the islands. That interest was expressed in a variety of sometimes innovative ways; for example in 1541–42 in the invitation issued to the island communities to send representatives to the English parliament in an attempt to redress then current issues with the export of goods from England.[1]

---

[1] TNA, C 66/814, m. 7; Tim Thornton, *The Charters of Guernsey* (Bognor Regis, 2004), pp. 57–67; *Letters and Papers, Foreign and Domestic, of the Reign of Henry VIII, 1509–47*, ed. J. S. Brewer, J. Gairdner and R. H. Brodie (London, 1862–1910);

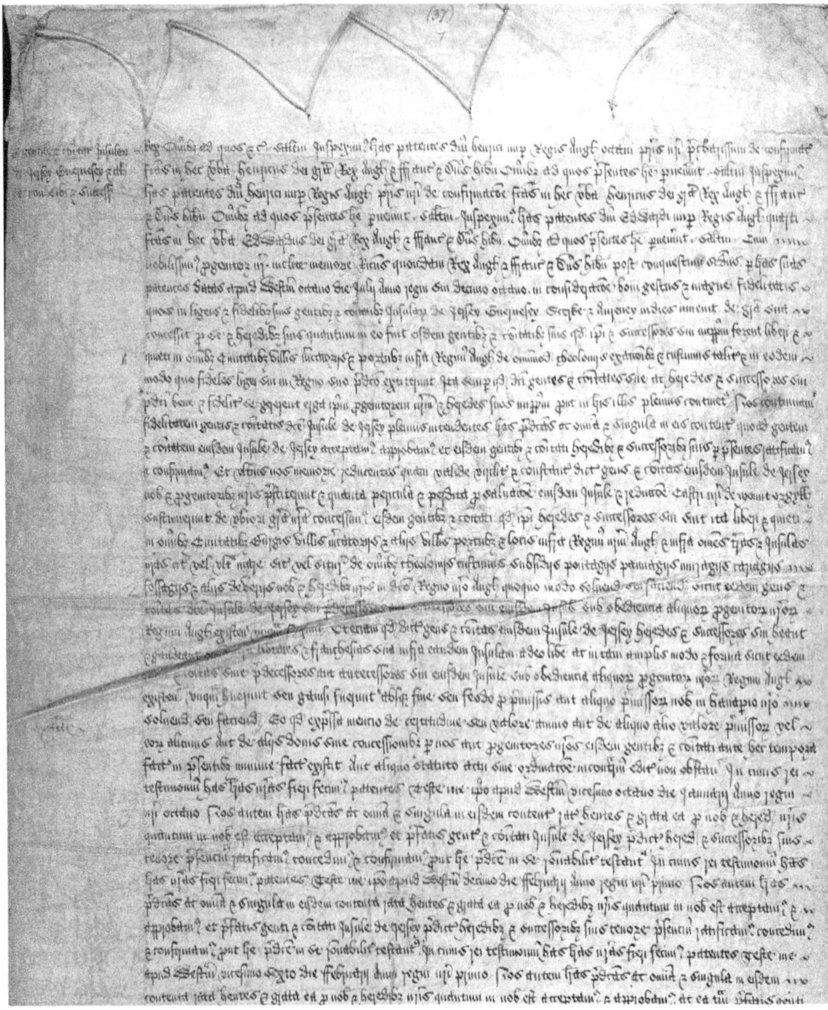

Plate 11 (i): The Royal Charter granted by Edward VI in 1548.
Credit: The National Archives, ref. C 66/814.

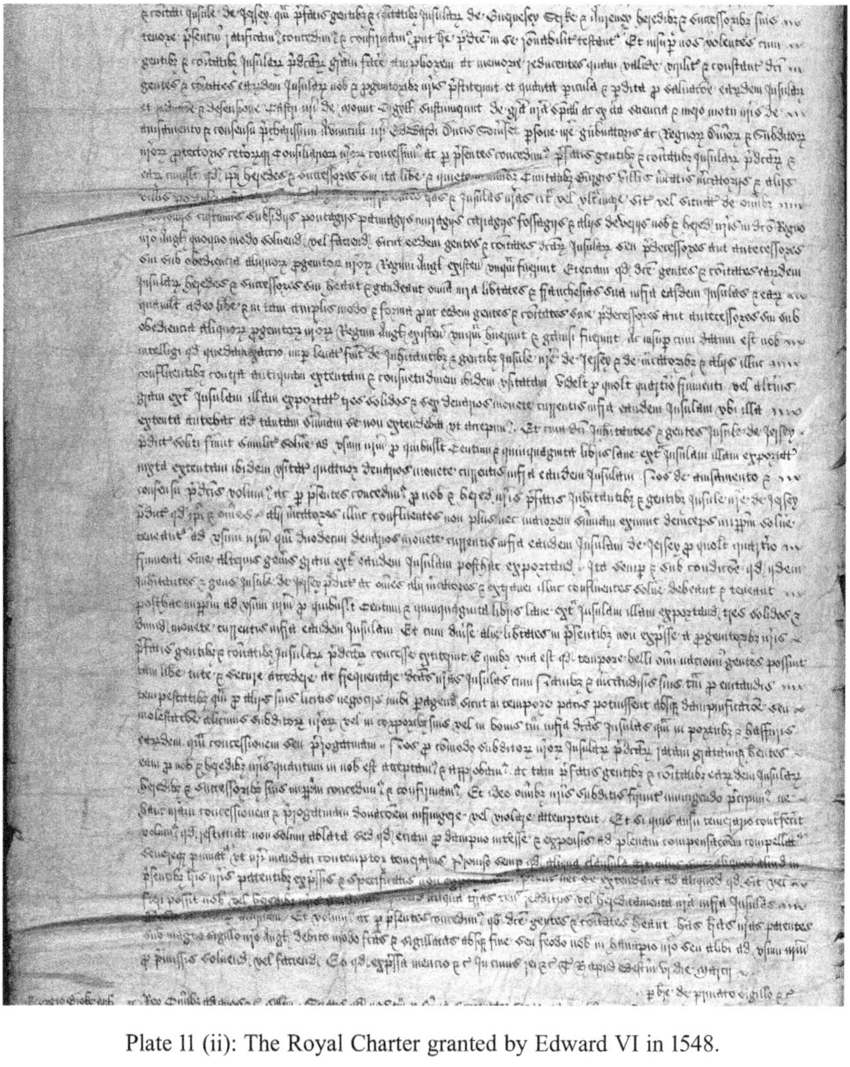

Plate 11 (ii): The Royal Charter granted by Edward VI in 1548.

Edward's confirmation in the charter of the privileges granted by his father, his grandfather, and his great-grandfather (ultimately confirming the grants of Edward III and Richard II) recalled the bravery of the island communities in the recapture of Mont Orgueil, apparently in reference to the much earlier events of Edward IV's reign. The charter indicated that this was on the advice of Edward Seymour, the king's uncle and protector, a man with a record of interest in the islands since 1536.[2] There was then a confirmation of all the liberties and franchises that any of the island communities had before enjoyed. Edward VI's charter then further dealt with customs charged on the merchants of Jersey for exports. In each case, the charter moderated recent demands, which in the first instance were described as 'against the ancient extent and custom used there'. This custom was being imposed on each quarter of grain at the rate of 3*s.* 6*d.*, in the islands' currency. The charter indicated that the rate would now be held at 1 *s.* only. In addition, a custom on wool, which had traditionally been levied at 4*d.* per 150 pounds of wool and evidently had been raised significantly, was to be levied at no more than 3*s.* 6*d.*

The latter measures provide a powerful clue as to the origins of the charter. An undated petition of the inhabitants of the islands to Somerset ends with a call for the ending or mitigation of the custom on wheat exports, and the charter evidently responds directly. This was not a straightforward transaction, however; although this request was granted, there were others in the petition that were not accepted, relating to royal lands, to partible inheritance, to repair of ports, for the captain, bailiff, dean and others to decide petty causes, and for writs and commissions from Chancery.[3]

The petition also refers to free access and trade for all merchants coming to the islands, even in time of war. In response, Edward VI's charter confirmed the neutrality of the islands in any conflict, along with the right of the island communities to continue trading with all parties, whether they were friends or enemies of the king of England. The origin of this privilege was a papal

---

Addenda, I (London, 1929–32), vol. 9, nos 202(22), 385(16); vol. 10, no. 226(12); vol. 11, no. 202(12); Bronwyn Matthews (ed.), *Les Chroniques de Jersey* (St Helier, 2017), pp. 134–51. Parliament: *Actes des Etats de l'Ile de Jersey 1524–1596*, 12e publication de la Société Jersiaise (St Helier, 1897), pp. 9–10; A. J. Eagleston, *The Channel Islands under Tudor Government, 1485–1642: A Study in Administrative History* (Cambridge, 1949), p. 34; A. D. K. Hawkyard, 'The Enfranchisement of Constituencies, 1504–1558', *Parliamentary History*, 10 (1991), 1–26, at p. 21; C. S. L. Davies, 'Tournai M.P.s at Westminster?' *Parliamentary History*, 20 (2001), 233–5; Tim Thornton, *The Channel Islands, 1370–1640: Between England and Normandy* (Woodbridge, 2012), pp. 72–3.

[2] *Letters and Papers, Foreign and Domestic, of the Reign of Henry VIII*, vol. 9, nos 202(22), 385(16); Eagleston, *Channel Islands under Tudor Government*, p. 34.

[3] Royal Commission on Historical Manuscripts, *Calendar of the Manuscripts of the Most Honourable the Marquess of Salisbury* (24 vols, London, 1883–1976), vol. 13, p. 31.

monition of February 1481, which was directed against piracy and had come to be interpreted as placing the islands in a form of neutral status.[4] The break with Rome had made a papal foundation for this privilege unacceptable, however effective it had been initially in regulating the behaviour of competing powers. Henry VIII had dealt piecemeal with many of the consequences of his ending of the pope's authority and, when the people of Jersey petitioned in July 1543 with the support of Edward Seymour for confirmation of their privileges under the bull of Sixtus IV, they expressed a lack of confidence in the papal authority but did not reframe their request.[5] Edward's regime, however, adamant in its rejection of any papal pretensions, chose to restate the privilege, but without reference to any part of the papal contribution to its development and rather associating it with grants of his predecessors as kings of England: 'in time of war people of all nations have been able to visit and frequent our said islands with their ships and merchandise, both to escape storms and to conduct their other their lawful business there, as freely, safely, and securely as they have been able to in time of peace'.

The insistence on a continued form of the neutrality of previous decades had a particular relevance early in 1548. These were challenging months for English diplomacy and especially for her intervention in Scotland. From the beginning of Edward's reign, Protector Somerset had led England into a vigorous attempt to conquer and garrison Scotland. He had built his reputation in the preceding years substantially in leading attacks on Scotland. That intervention in 1547 had always carried the danger of bringing France into the conflict to support its traditional Scottish ally. In the early days of 1548, in Scotland the queen mother, Mary of Lorraine, was seeking French support, and negotiations began for a match between the infant Mary, queen of Scots

---

[4] J. A. Twemlow (ed.), *Calendar of Entries in the Papal Registers Relating to Great Britain and Ireland: Papal Letters*, vol. 13, *1471–84* (2 vols, London, 1955), vol. 1, p. 258 (monition of 27 February 1480/81); B.-A. Pocquet du Haut-Jussé, *François II, Duc de Bretagne, et l'Angleterre (1458–1488)* (Paris, 1929), p. 323. D. M. Ogier, *Reformation and Society in Guernsey* (Woodbridge, 1996), pp. 37–8, points out the error in attributing the bull to 1483 (as in J. C. Appleby, 'Neutrality, Trade and Privateering, 1500–1689', in A. G. Jamieson (ed.), *A People of the Sea: The Maritime History of the Channel Islands* (London, 1986), pp. 59–64; Raoul Lemprière, *History of the Channel Islands* (London, 1974), pp. 39–40 (says reissued as Bull on 1 March 1483); G. R. Balleine, *History of Jersey*, rev. Marguerite Syvret and Joan Stevens (Chichester, 1981), pp. 64–5; Eagleston, *Channel Islands under Tudor Government*, pp. 43–9). On this (and the problematic reference to papal action in 1483 made in Henry VIII's confirmation), see also Bernard Jacqueline, 'Sixte IV et la piraterie dans les Iles Anglo-Normandes (1480)', *Revue du département de la Manche*, 20 (1978), 197–202.

[5] *Letters and Papers, Foreign and Domestic, of the Reign of Henry VIII*, vol. 18/i, no. 915.

and the dauphin François.[6] The English possessions on the French mainland at Calais and Boulogne were soon experiencing heightened security concerns.[7] Although war between France and England was in the end not declared until August 1549, the prompts to French aggression found in the Somerset regime's difficulties in Scotland and eventually in rebellion at home were obvious.[8] The consequent threat to the islands was evidently appreciated by the regime early in 1548, for the Privy Council warranted the delivery of ordinance to Helier de Carteret for the defence of Jersey in the February of that year.[9] Anxiety in the islands about their safety was fully justified by the fact that, when war came, it affected the islands even before any official declaration. On 21 July 1549, the day after the French king Henri II had assured the English ambassador of his love for England, there was an attack on Sark (leading to a nine-year occupation), followed on 31 July by an attack on Guernsey. This was repulsed and so the French troops headed for Bouley Bay, where they landed until they were defeated by a local force.[10]

Edward's charter, granted tin March 1548, therefore helped to consolidate the English position in the islands at a time of substantial weakness at home and of serious threat from France. The charter's silence on the papal origins of neutrality hints at another driver of change and instability in Jersey and in England: radical Protestantism. Under Henry VIII there were few signs of early progress for Protestant ideas and, if anything, the implementation of religious policies at the command of the English king showed even less sign of success than was achieved in Guernsey. While the early administrative stages of the reformation were implemented in Guernsey, with the commissioners compiling the relevant sections of the *Valor Ecclesiasticus* (albeit without listing many of the religious foundations in the bailiwick),

---

[6] W. K. Jordan, *Edward VI – The Young King: The Protectorship of the Duke of Somerset* (London, 1968), pp. 270–80; Michael L. Bush, *The Government Policy of Protector Somerset* (London, 1975), pp. 25–7.

[7] Jordan, *Edward VI – The Young King*, pp. 280–2; David Grummitt, *The Calais Garrison: War and Military Service, 1436–1558* (Woodbridge, 2008), p. 18.

[8] Bush, *Government Policy of Protector Somerset*, pp. 87, 94.

[9] John Roche Dasent (ed.), *Acts of the Privy Council of England*, new ser., vol. 2, *1547–1550* (London, 1890), p. 171. Appleby, 'Neutrality, Trade and Privateering', pp. 65–7.

[10] Balleine, *History of Jersey*, rev. Syvret and Stevens, p. 76; E. Toulmin Nicolle, 'The Capture of Sark by the French in 1549 and its Re-capture in 1553 by a Flemish Corsair', *ABSJ*, 10 (1923–27), 157–73; Matthews (ed.), *Chroniques*, pp. 142–7; W. K. Jordan (ed.), *The Chronicle and Political Papers of King Edward VI* (London, 1966), p. 13; Wm. Laird Clowes, *The Royal Navy: A History, from the Earliest Times to the Present* (7 vols, London, 1897–1903), vol. 1, p. 469; N. A. M. Rodger, *The Safeguard of the Sea: A Naval History of Britain, 660–1649* (London, 1997), p. 478.

no record of their action in Jersey, if any, survives.[11] Still, it seems the rapid progress of Protestantism in Lower Normandy in the 1540s was reflected in Jersey, given the close connections between the communities there. Those connections were relied on by many who had to flee Normandy in 1547 and 1549, due to the restrictions attempted against Protestants in edicts in those years.[12] Otherwise it is hard to explain the success of measures to advance Protestantism in Jersey early in Edward's reign. In 1548, Jersey's rectors were required to bring their books and rent rolls to the castle, but there is no similar evidence for Guernsey. And the sale of religious property, often to provide for investment in defence, quickened in 1548–49.[13] Also in Jersey in 1548, the Royal Court made a payment to two reformed ministers to preach the gospel.[14] And the interruption to the St Saviour parish register, starting in 1548 and running through to 1554, demonstrates the reality of 'le tumulte' that affected the parish, including the deposition of the traditionalist incumbent and the transformation of local religious life.[15]

Edward VI's reign was a time of extensive disruption, when the islands were threatened by French intervention and by religious change and conflict. Edward's charter demonstrates the ability of the charter tradition to respond flexibly to new concerns while at the same time carrying established privileges forward into a new world of reformation.

---

[11] Ogier, *Reformation*, pp. 42–3; J. Hunter and J. Caley (ed.), *Valor Ecclesiasticus* (6 vols, London, 1810–34), vol. 2, p. 27 (NB the process for Guernsey, subscribed by the lieutenant and bailiff, was very different from that for the rest of the diocese, which involved bishop and commissioners (*ibid.*, vol. 2, p. 1)).

[12] David Nicholls, 'Social Change and Early Protestantism in France: Normandy, 1520–62', *European Studies Review*, 10 (1980), 279–308; Fernand de Schickler, *Les églises du refuge en Angleterre* (3 vols, Paris, 1892), vol. 2, pp. 365–6.

[13] JA, D/Y/F1/2 (J. A. Messervy, 'Extraits des anciens roles de la cour royale', *ABSJ*, 4 (1897–1901), 294–314, at p. 297); Balleine, *History*, rev. Syvret and Stevens, pp. 74–5; S. W. Bisson (ed.), *The Jersey Chantry Certificate of 1550* (St Helier, 1975), pp. 7–10; Matthews (ed.), *Chroniques*, pp. 152–5, used by Eagleston, *Channel Islands under Tudor Government*, p. 36.

[14] Helen Mary Elizabeth Evans, 'The Religious History of Jersey, 1558–1640' (Unpublished Ph.D. thesis, University of Cambridge, 1991), pp. 23–4; Matthews (ed.), *Chroniques*, pp. 154–5; G. R. Balleine, *A Biographical Dictionary of Jersey* (London and New York, 1948), pp. 146–7. Fernand de Schickler notes significant immigration in 1547, 1549, and 1551, due to the proscriptive edicts of those years: *Les églises du refuge en Angleterre*, vol. 2, pp. 365–6: this does not seem to be taken into account by Evans (p. 49 sees mention in a note).

[15] JA, G/C/09/A1/1; Evans, 'Religious History of Jersey', pp. 23–4.

Text

Edward VI confirmed the royal charter of his father, Henry VIII, thereby confirming its predecessors from the reigns of Henry VII, Edward IV and Richard II. Edward's charter further addressed customs on the export of grain and wool, and the rights of people of all nations to visit the islands in time of war. Common to Guernsey, Sark and Alderney; text taken from enrolment in The National Archives, C 66/818, m. 7, with reference to the edition presented in Prison Board.

[1] Rex Omnibus ad quos &c. Salutem Inspeximus literas patentes domini Henrici nuper Regis Anglie octaui patris nostri precharissimi de confirmacione factas in hec verba.

[2] Henricus Dei gracia Rex Anglie et ffrancie et Dominus Hibernie Omnibus ad quos presentes Iitere peruenerint salutem. Inspeximus Iiteras patentes domini Henrici nuper Regis Anglie patris nostri de confirmacione factas in hec verba.

[3] Henricus Dei gracia Rex Anglie et ffrancie et Dominus Hibernie Omnibus ad quos presentes Iitere peruenerint salutem. Inspeximus Iiteras patentes domini Edwardi nuper Regis Anglie quarti factas in hec verba.

[4] Edwardus Dei gracia Rex Anglie et ffrancie et Dominus Hibernie Omnibus ad quos presentes Iitere peruenerint salutem Cum nobilissimus progenitor noster inclite memorie Ricardus quondam Rex Anglie et ffrancie et Dominus Hibernie post conquestum secundus per Iiteras suas patentes datas apud Westmonasterium octauo die Julii anno regni sui decimo octauo in consideracione boni gestus et magne fidelitatis quos in ligeis et fidelibus suis gentibus et communitatibus Insularum de Jersey Guernesey Scerke et Aureney indies inuenit de gracia sua concessit pro se et heredibus suis quantum in eo fuit eisdem gentibus et communitatibus suis quod ipsi successores sui imperpetuum forent liberi et quieti in omnibus Ciuitatibus villis mercatoriis et portubus infra Regnum Anglie de omnimodis theoloniis exaccionibus et custumis taliter et in eodem modo quo fideles ligei sui in Regno suo predicto extiterunt Ita semper quod dicti gentes et communitates sue ac heredes et successores sui predicti bene et fideliter se gererent erga ipsum progenitorem nostrum et heredes suos imperpetuum prout in Iiteris illis plenius continetur Nos continuam fidelitatem gentis et communitatis dicte Insule de Jersey plenius intendentes Iiteras predictas ac omnia et singula in eis contenta quoad gentem et communitatem ejusdem Insule de Jersey acceptamus approbamus et eisdem gentibus et communitati heredibus et successoribus suis per presentes ratificamus et confirmamus.

[5] Et ulterius nos memorie reducentes quam valide viriliter et constanter dicta gens et communitas ejusdem Insule de Jersey nobis et progenitoribus nostris perstiterunt et quanta pericula et perdita pro saluacione eiusdem Insule et reduccione Castri nostri de Mount Orgyll sustinuerunt de uberiori gracia nostra concessimus eisdem gentibus et communitati quod ipsi heredes et successores sui sint ita liberi et quieti in omnibus Ciuitatibus Burgis villis mercatoriis et aliis villis portubus et locis infra Regnum nostrum Anglie et infra omnes terras et Insulas nostras citra vel ultra mare sitas vel situatas de omnibus theoloniis custumis subsidiis pontagiis pannagiis muragiis cariagiis fossagiis et aliis deveriis nobis et heredibus nostris in dicto Regno nostro Anglie quoquo modo soluendis seu faciendis sicut eedem gens et communitas dicte Insule de Jersey seu predecessores aut antecessores sui eiusdem Insule sub obediencia aliquorum progenitorum nostrorum Regum Anglie existentes vnquam fuerunt.

[6] Et eciam quod dicta gens et communitas ejusdem Insule de Jersey heredes et successores sui habeant et gaudeant omnia jura libertates et franchesias sua infra eandem Insulam adeo libere ac in tam amplis modo et forma sicut eedem gens et communitas sive predecessores aut antecessores sui ejusdem Insule sub obediencia aliquorum progenitorum nostrorum Regum Anglie existentium vnquam habuerunt seu gauisi fuerunt absque fine seu feodo pro premissis aut aliquo premissorum nobis in hanaperio nostro solvendo seu faciendo Eo quod expressa mencio de certitudine seu valore annuo aut de aliquo alio valore premissorum vel eorum alicuius Aut de aliis donis sive concessionibus pro nos aut progenitores nostros eisdem gentibus et comunitati ante hec tempora factis in presentibus minime factis existit aut aliquo statuto actu sive ordinacione in contrarium edita non obstantibus. In cuius rei testimonium has literas nostras fieri fecimus patentes. Teste me ipso apud Westmonasterium vicesimo octauo die Januarii Anno regni nostri octavo.

[7] Nos autem literas predictas ac omnia et singula in eisdem contenta rata habentes et grata ea pro nobis et heredibus nostris quantum in nobis est acceptamus et approbamus et prefatis gentibus et communitati Insule de Jersey predicte heredibus et successoribus suis tenore presencium ratificamus concedimus et confirmamus prout litere predicte in se racionabiliter testantur. In cuius rei testimonium has literas nostras fieri fecimus patentes. Teste me ipso apud Westmonasterium decimo die ffebruarij Anno regni nostri primo.

[8] Nos autem literas predictas ac omnia et singula in eisdem contenta rata habentes et grata ea pro nobis et heredibus nostris quantum in nobis est acceptamus et approbamus et prefatis gentibus et communitati Insule de Jersey predicte heredibus et successoribus suis tenore presencium ratificamus concedimus et confirmamus prout litere predicte in se racionabiliter testantur.

In cuius rei testimonium has literas nostras fieri fecimus patentes. Teste me apud Westmonasterium vicesimo sexto die ffebruarii Anno regni nostri primo.

[9] Nos autem literas predictas ac omnia et singula in eisdem contenta rata habentes et grata ea pro nobis et heredibus nostris quantum in nobis est acceptamus et approbamus ac ea tam prefatis gentibus et communitati Insule de Jersey quam prefatis gentibus et communitatibus Insularum de Guernesey Serke et Aureney heredibus et successoribus suis tenore presencium ratificamus concedimus et confirmamus prout litere predicte in se racionabiliter testantur.

[10] Et insuper nos volentes cum gentibus et communitatibus Insularum graciam facere ampliorem ac memorie reducentes quam valide viriliter et constanter dicti gentes et communitates earundem Insularum nobis et progenitoribus nostris perstiterunt et quanta pericula et perdita pro saluacione earundem Insularum et reduccione et defensione Castri nostri de Mount Orgyll sustinuerunt de gracia nostra speciali ac ex certa sciencia et mero motu nostris de avisamento et consensu precharissimi Avunculi nostri Edwardi Ducis Somerset persone nostre gubernatoris ac Regnorum Dominiorum et Subditorum nostrorum protectoris ceterorumque Consiliariorum nostrorum concessimus ac per presentes concedimus prefatis gentibus et communitatibus Insularum predictarum et earum cuiuslibet quod ipsi heredes et successores sui ita libere et quiete in omnibus Ciuitatibus Burgis villis mercetis mercatoriis et aliis villis portubus infra Regnum nostrum Anglie ac infra omnes terras et Insulas nostras citra vel vltra mare sitas vel situatas de omnibus theoloniis custumis subsidiis pontagiis pannagiis muragiis cariagiis fossagiis et aliis deueriis nobis et heredibus nostris in dicto Regno nostro Anglie quoquo modo soluendis vel faciendis sicut eedem gentes et communitates dictarum Insularum seu predecessores aut antecessores sui sub obediencia aliquorum progenitorum nostrorum Regum Anglie existentium vnqam fuerunt.

[11] Et eciam quod dicte gentes et communitates earundem Insularum heredes et successores sui habeant et gaudeant omnia iura libertates et franchesias sua infra easdem Insulas et earum quamlibet adeo libere et in tam amplis modo et forma prout eedem gentes et communitates sive predecessores aut antecessores sui sub obediencia aliquorum progenitorem nostrorum Regum Anglie existentem unquam habuerunt et gauisi fuerunt.

[12] Ac insuper cum datum est nobis intelligi quod quedam exaccio nuper leuato fuerit de inhabitantibus et gentibus Insule nostre de Jersey et de mercatoribus et aliis illuc confluentibus contra antiquam extentam et consuetudinem ibidem vsitatam videlicet per quolibet quarterio frumenti vel alterius grani extra Insulam illam exportato tres solidos et sex denarios monete currentis infra

eandem Insulam ubi illa extenta antehac ad tantam summam se non extendebat ut accepimus Et cum dicti Inhabitantes et gentes Insule de Jersey predicte soliti fuerint similiter soluere ad vsum nostrum per quibuslibet Centum et quinquaginta libris lane extra Insulam illam exportatis juxta extentam ibidem vsitatam quatuor denarios monete currentis infra eandem Insulam Nos de auisamento et consensu predicto volumus ac per presentes concedimus pro nobis et heredibus nostris prefatis Inhabitantibus et gentibus Insule nostre de Jersey predicte quod ipsi et omnes alii mercatores illuc confluentes non plus nec majorem summam exnunc deinceps imperpetuum solvere teneantur ad vsum nostrum quam duodecim denarios monete currentis infra eandem Insulam de Jersey per quolibet quarterio frumenti siue alterius generis grani extra eandem Insulam posthac exportando Ita semper et sub condicione quod iidem Inhabitantes et gens Insule de Jersey predictas ac omnes alii mercatores et extranei illuc confluentes soluere debeant et teneant posthac imperpetuum ad vsum nostrum per quibus libet Centum et quinquaginta libris lane extra Insulam illam exportandis tres solidos et dimidium monete currentis infra eandem Insulam.

[13] Et cum diuerse alie libertates in presentibus non expresse a progenitoribus nostris prefatis gentibus et communitatibus Insularum predictarum concesse extiterint e quibus una est quod tempore belli omnium nacionum gentes possint tam libere tute et secure accedere ac frequentare dictas nostras Insulas cum Navibus et mercandisis suis tam pro evitandis tempestatibus quam pro aliis suis licitis negociis inibi peragendis sicut in tempore pacis potuissent absque dampnificacione seu molestacione alicuius subditorum nostrorum vel in corporibus suis vel in bonis tam infra dictas Insulas quam in portubus et haffuris earundem quam concessionem seu prerogativam Nos pro commodo subditorum nostrorum Insularum predictaram ratam gratamque habentes eam pro nobis et heredibus nostris quantum in nobis est acceptamus et approbamus ac tam prefatis gentibus et communitatibus earundem Insularum heredibus et successoribus suis imperpetuum concedimus et confirmamus.

[14] Et ideo omnibus nostris subditis firmiter iniungendo precipimus ne hanc nostram concessionem et prerogativam donacionem infringere vel violare attemptent Et si quis ausu temerario contrafecerit volumus quod restituat non solum ablata sed quod eciam pro dampno interesse et expensis ad plenam compensacionem compellatur severeque puniatur ut nostri mandati contemptor temerarius.

[15] Proviso semper quod aliqua clausula articulus sive aliquod aliud in presentibus literis nostris patentibus expressis et specificatis non exponantur interpretentur nec se extendant ad aliquod quod sit vel fieri possit nobis vel heredibus

nostris preiudiciale quoad aliqua terras tenementa redditus vel hereditamenta nostra infra Insulas predictas sive earum aliquam.

[16] Et volumus ac per presentes concedimus quod dicte gentes et communitates habeant has Iiteras nostras patentes sub magno sigillo nostro Anglie debito modo factas et sigillatas absque fine seu feodo nobis in hanaperio nostro seu alibi ad usum nostrum per premissis solvendis vel faciendis Eo quod expressa mencio etc In cujus etc Teste Regis apud Westmonsterium vj die Marcij.

Per breve de privato sigillo &c.

Translation

[1] The king, to all to whom these present letters come, greeting. We have inspected the Letters Patent of the Lord Henry the Eighth, lately king of England, our most dearly beloved father, made in these words.

[2] Henry by the grace of God king of England and France and lord of Ireland, to all those to whom these present letters may come, greeting. We have inspected the Letters Patent of the Lord Henry the Seventh, our father, lately king of England, made in these words.

[3] Henry by the grace of God king of England and France and lord of Ireland, to all those to whom these present letters may come, greeting. We have inspected the Letters Patent of the Lord Edward the Fourth, lately king of England, made in these words.

[4] Edward by the grace of God king of England and France and lord of Ireland to all to whom these present letters may come, greeting. Whereas our most noble progenitor of glorious memory Richard the Second after the Conquest, lately king of England and France and lord of Ireland, by his Letters Patent given at Westminster on the eighth day of July in the eighteenth year of his reign in consideration of the good behaviour and great loyalty which he always found in his liege and faithful peoples and communities of the islands of Jersey, Guernsey, Sark and Alderney, of his special grace granted for himself and his heirs, as far as in him lay, to these his same peoples and communities that they themselves and their successors should be for ever in all cities, market towns, and ports within the kingdom of England free and quit of all tolls, duties, and customs of whatsoever kind in such wise and in such manner as his own faithful lieges have continued in his own aforesaid kingdom. Provided always that they his said people and communities, their heirs and successors aforesaid should conduct themselves well and faithfully towards himself and his heirs for ever as is more fully contained in those

Letters. We considering more fully the continuous loyalty of the said island of Jersey, the aforesaid Letters and all and singular contained therein as regards the people and community of the same island of Jersey, do accept, approve, and by these presents to these same people and community, their heirs and successors, do ratify and confirm them.

[5] And, further, calling to mind how valiantly, manfully and steadfastly the said people and community of the said island of Jersey have stood out for us and our progenitors and what great dangers and losses they have sustained for the safety of the said islands and for the recapture of our castle of Mont Orgueil, of our more abundant favour we have granted to the same people and community that they, their heirs and successors shall likewise be free and quit in all cities, boroughs, market towns, and other towns, ports, and places within our kingdom of England and within all our lands and islands lying or situated on this side or beyond the sea from all tolls, customs, subsidies, pontages, panages, murages, tallages, fossages, and other dues in whatever way to be discharged or made to us and our heirs in our said kingdom of England just as the same people and community of the said island of Jersey, or their predecessors or ancestors of the same island, living under the obedience of any of our progenitors the kings of England, have ever been.

[6] And further that the said people and community, their heirs and successors, should have and enjoy all their rights, liberties, and franchises within the same island as freely and in as full a manner and form as the same people and community, or their predecessors and ancestors in the same island living under the obedience of any of our progenitors the kings of England have ever had or enjoyed them, without fine or fee in the premises or any of the premises to be paid or made to us in the hanaper; so far as express mention exists of the surety or annual value or any other value in the matter of the premises, or of any of them, or of other gifts or concessions by us or our progenitors to the same people and community, whether such mention has been made before these times or is expressly set forth in these present letters, or any statute, act or ordinance published to the contrary, notwithstanding. In witness whereof we have caused these out Letters to be made Patent. Myself as witness at Westminster this twenty eighth day of January in the eighth year of our reign.

[7] We, moreover, holding the aforesaid letters, and all and singular contained therein, to be reasonable and seasonable, accept and approve them for us and our heirs, as far as in us lies, and now ratify and confirm them to the aforesaid people and community of the island of Jersey, and to their heirs and successors, in the tenor of the present letters, as the aforesaid letters reasonably testify. In witness whereof we have caused these our letters to be made patent. Witness myself at Westminster this tenth day of February in the first year of our reign.

[8] We, moreover, holding the aforesaid letters, and all and singular contained therein, to be reasonable and seasonable, accept and approve them for us and our heirs, as far as in us lies, and now ratify, grant and confirm them to the aforesaid people and community of the island of Jersey, and to their heirs and successors, in the tenor of the present letters, as the aforesaid letters reasonably testify. In witness whereof we have caused these our letters to be made patent. Witness myself at Westminster this twenty-sixth day of February in the first year of our reign.

[9] We, moreover, holding the aforesaid letters, and all and singular contained therein, to be reasonable and seasonable, accept and approve them for us and our heirs, as far as in us lies, and ratify, grant and confirm them both to the aforesaid people and community of the island of Jersey and to the aforesaid peoples and communities of the islands of Guernsey, Sark, and Alderney, and to their heirs and successors, in the tenor of the present letters, as the aforesaid letters in themselves reasonably testify.

[10] And above this, we wishing to show the peoples and communities of the islands our fuller favour, and calling to mind how valiantly, manfully and steadfastly the said peoples and communities of the same islands have stood out for us and our progenitors and what great dangers and losses they have sustained for the salvation of the same islands and the reduction and defence of our castle of Mont Orgueil, of our special grace, certain knowledge, and mere motion, on the advice and with the agreement of our dearest uncle Edward, duke of Somerset, governor of our person and Protector of our realms, lordships, and subjects, and of our other councillors we have granted and by these present letters we grant to the foresaid peoples and communities of the aforesaid islands, and to each of them, that they themselves, their heirs and successors, be as free and quit, in all the cities, boroughs, fairs, mart-towns, and other towns and ports sited and situate within our kingdom of England and within all our lands and islands on this side of or beyond the sea, from all tolls, customs, subsidies, pontage, panage, murage, fossage, and all other duties to us and our heirs in our said kingdom of England, howsoever to be paid or made, as the same peoples and communities of the said islands or their predecessors or ancestors living under the obedience of any of our predecessors the kings of England ever were.

[11] And, furthermore, that the said peoples and communities of the said islands, their heirs and successors, should have and enjoy all their rights, liberties, and franchises within the same islands and any of them as freely and in as full a manner and form as the same peoples and communities or their predecessors and ancestors living under the obedience of any of our progenitors kings of England ever had and enjoyed them.

[12] And, above this, since it is given to us to understand that a certain exaction has recently been levied of the inhabitants and peoples of our island of Jersey and of merchants and others gathering there, against the ancient extent and custom used there, viz. for each quarter of wheat or other grain exported out of that island three shillings and six pence of money current in the same island, where that extent previously did not extend to such a great sum, as we understand; and since the said inhabitants and peoples of the aforesaid island of Jersey have been accustomed similarly to pay to our use for each 150 pounds of wool exported out of that island, according to the extent used in that place, four pence of money current within the same island; we, by the advice and consent aforesaid will, and by the present letters grant, for us and our heirs, to the aforesaid inhabitants and peoples of our aforesaid island of Jersey that they themselves and all other merchants gathering there should not be held to pay more nor greater sum from now henceforth for ever to our use than twelve pence of money current within the same island of Jersey for each quarter of wheat or of other type of grain henceforth to be exported out of the same island. Thus always and on condition that the same inhabitants and people of the island of Jersey aforesaid and all other merchants and outsiders gathering there ought and hold to pay henceforth for ever to our use for each 150 pounds of wool exported out of the same island three and a half shillings of money current within the same island.

[13] And since various other liberties not expressed in the present letters exist, conceded by our progenitors to the aforesaid peoples and communities of the aforesaid island, of which one is that in time of war people of all nations have been able to visit and frequent our said islands with their ships and merchandise, both to escape storms and to conduct their other their lawful business there, as freely, safely, and securely as they have been able to in time of peace, without condemnation or interference from any of our subjects either in their bodies or in their goods, both within the said islands and in the ports and harbours of the same; finding this concession or prerogative reasonable and acceptable, for the benefit of our subjects of the aforesaid islands, we accept and approve, for us and our heirs, as far as in us lies, and we concede and confirm it both to the aforesaid peoples and communities of the same islands, and to their heirs and successors for ever.

[14] And therefore firmly enjoining all our subjects we order that they should not attempt to infringe or violate this our concession and prerogative grant; and if anyone, in their rashness and daring, should contravene it, we wish that he should not only restore that taken away but that he should be compelled to give full compensation for the costs, interest, and damages, and be severely punished for his audacious contempt of our order.

[15] Provided always that any clause, article or anything other expressed and specified in our present letters patent should not be set forth, interpreted or extend itself to anything which should or could be prejudicial to us or our heirs in relation to any our lands, tenements, rents or inheritances within the foresaid islands or of any of them.

[16] And we wish and by these present [letters] we grant that the same peoples and communities should have these our letters patent under our great seal of England in due manner made and sealed, without fine or fee paid or made to us in our hanaper or elsewhere to our use by the premises. So that express mention, &c. In testimony whereof, &c. Witness the king at Westminster, 6 March.

Elizabeth I: 1562

Commentary

The critical conjunction of French threat, internal division, uncertainty in English policy and leadership, and religious turmoil, which had shaped the grant of a charter to Jersey under Edward VI, was evident again at the start of Elizabeth I's reign. Although the charter that was eventually granted in 1562 was very similar to the one obtained by Guernsey in 1560, the precise circumstances differed.

The early 1560s were years of dramatic change in the islands and further afield. The reign opened in the aftermath of the loss of Calais to the French, and with English military efforts in difficulty. Reports from Jersey highlight the uncertainty of these months. In April 1559 a report from the island indicated that a French threat was imminent, and that there had been suspicious conversations between Jerseymen and their French contacts. Such reports took a more specific form in December 1559, indicating that there was treasonous correspondence involving Peter de Rocquier of Jersey.[1] Close to Jersey, however, in Lower Normandy Protestantism was making rapid progress.[2] This stimulated the radical Protestants around Elizabeth to plan for intervention, resulting, in the year after the grant of Jersey's charter, in the Newhaven expedition of 1563, in which Ambrose Dudley, earl of Warwick, brother of Elizabeth's favourite Robert Dudley, earl of Leicester, as captain general and governor was commissioned to rally the queen's subjects in the duchy of Normandy, and to take and hold Le Havre ('Newhaven'), in part to provide a port through which to supply Protestants in the duchy.[3]

---

[1] TNA, SP 1/59/1, fol. 80 (*CSPD 1601–03, Addenda, 1547–65*, pp. 490–1, 494). Peter's correspondent, described as the 'seigneur de Glatigni' (Glatigny, south of Portbail on the west coast of the Cotentin), was probably Martin du Bellay, seigneur de Langey and de Glatigny, Prince d'Yvetot, although he died in March 1559.

[2] D. Nicholls, 'Social Change and Early Protestantism in France: Normandy, 1520–62', *European Studies Review*, 10 (1980), 279–308.

[3] *CPR 1560–63*, pp. 252–3; Wallace T. MacCaffrey, 'The Newhaven Expedition, 1562–1563', *Historical Journal*, 40 (1997), 1–21.

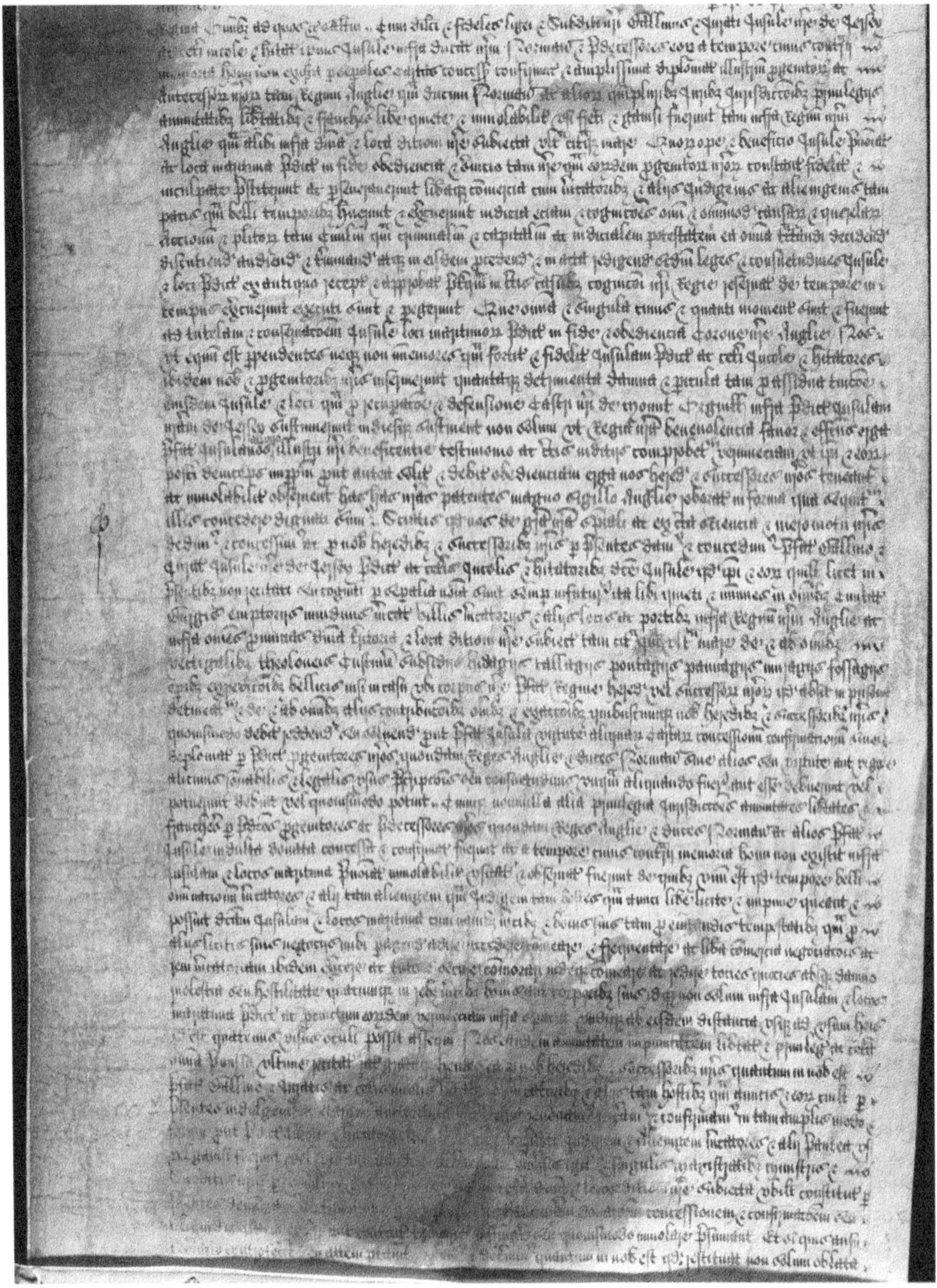

Plate 12 (i): The Royal Charter granted by Elizabeth I in 1562.
Credit: The National Archives, ref. C 66/978.

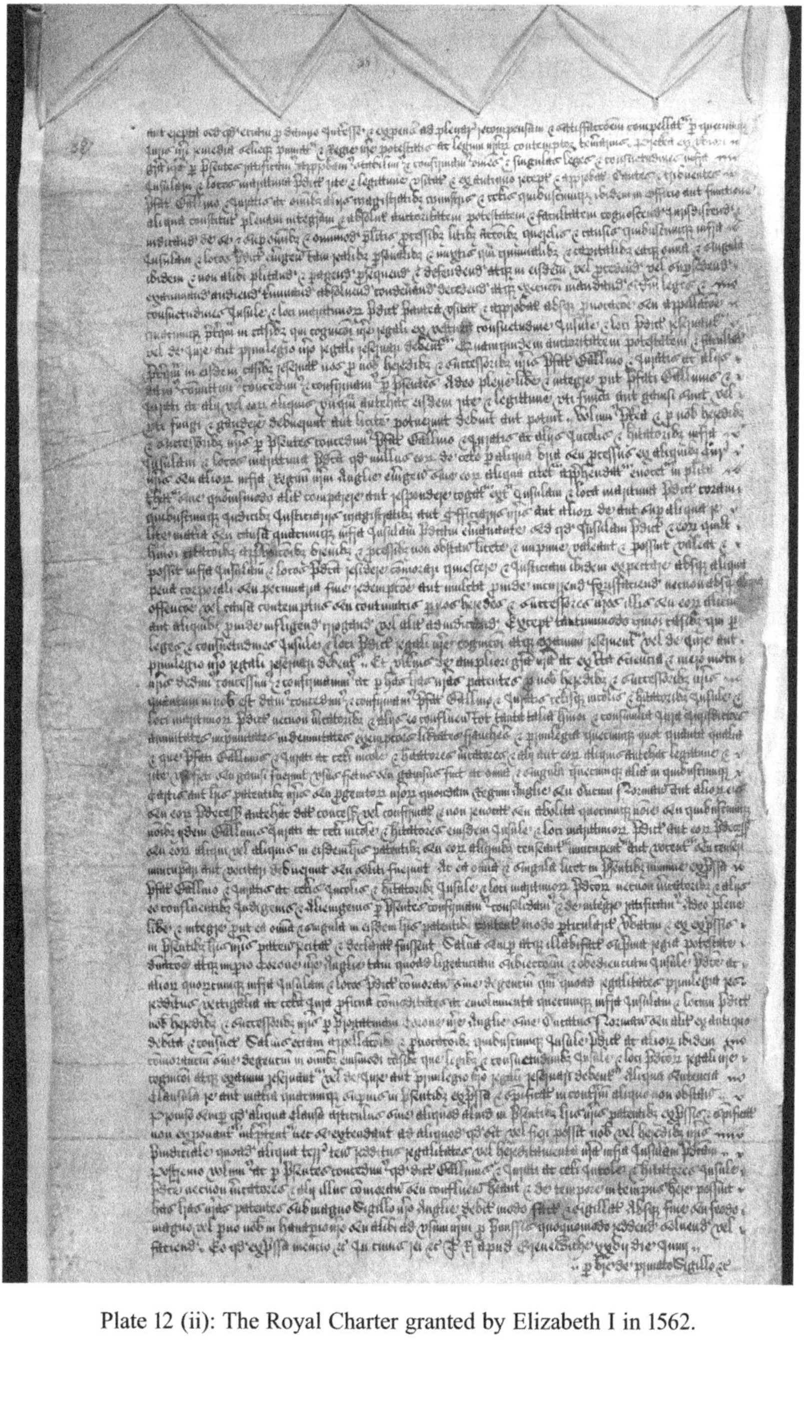

Plate 12 (ii): The Royal Charter granted by Elizabeth I in 1562.

This action to support Protestants in Normandy and the references to the duchy in the islands' charters demonstrates a renewed interest in Normandy among some in England in the early 1560s. The Dudley connection seems to have maintained and even increased this interest in subsequent years. As Edward Coke was to write a few decades later, the islands were the surviving elements, and therefore proof, of the queen's ownership of Normandy.[4]

Guernsey had seen a very high-profile confrontation between Catholicism and reform under Mary. But by 1562 this was slowly being resolved in favour of the party of reform, and a reform strongly under Genevan influence and more radical than anything Elizabeth would permit in England.[5] This change was made possible by the recent experience of the distinctively violent and assertive regime in Guernsey under Mary, of which there was no equivalent in Jersey. The echoes of the horrific burning of Catherine Cauches for heresy under Mary were soon reverberating in England, and a small but increasingly powerful party of reform, including some who had been in exile, like Guillaume de Beauvoir, in Geneva, were working to overthrow the Marian establishment. There was growing awareness in England of the degree to which Guernsey's Royal Court had not co-operated with earlier demands for the dissolution of religious foundations in the island, and this, along with the associated question of who continued to hold influence in Guernsey, needed to be addressed. Commissions were therefore appointed, starting in January 1561, although the first to make a real impact in the island was that of 25 May 1563.[6]

The inhabitants of Jersey sought additions to their rights early in Elizabeth's reign. On 6 December 1559, they were granted the right to import, duty free, 100 tuns of beer and other commodities for the defence of the island. A very similar grant had been made to Guernsey on 13 October 1559, and a further comparator was explicitly recognised in the charter, in the form of a grant to Berwick-upon-Tweed.[7] Further, in July 1559, Guernsey had received a straightforward confirmation of the charter granted them by Mary. Then, less than eight months later in March 1560, Guernsey was granted a charter stating the bailiwick's liberties in a very different form: the islands' laws and customs were confirmed, as was freedom from English customs and duties; then, neutrality and freedom of trade in times of war was reaffirmed. The charter added, for the first time, clear confirmations of the jurisdiction of bailiff, jurats and other officers, and the right to justice exclusively in

---

[4] Edward Coke, *The Fourth Part of the Institutes of the Laws of England: Concerning the Jurisdiction of Courts* (London, 1648), pp. 286–7.

[5] D. M. Ogier, *Reformation and Society in Guernsey* (Woodbridge, 1996), pp. 59–62.

[6] Ogier, *Reformation and Society*, pp. 64–7.

[7] *CPR 1558–60*, pp. 45, 247.

Guernsey, free from the threat of summons to appear before any court in England. This was the most extensive reformulation of the island's privileges to occur in the sixteenth century. It was a clear and conscious break from the past, especially the past of Mary's reign, and most obviously the failure to continue the Marian charter's reliance for freedom of movement to and from the islands in time of war and associated 'neutrality' on the papal action of 1481.[8] This charter was in some ways the manifesto of a party that was yet to achieve complete control in Guernsey. It was not until nearly six years later that the costs of obtaining the charter were eventually met, when on 8 May 1566 the Royal Court agreed a tax of £60, partly accounted for by these charges.[9] This was possible following the revolution in the membership of Guernsey's Royal Court represented by the dismissal of seven jurats in 1565, and their replacement in such a way as to create a Protestant majority there.[10]

The eventual progress of reformation in Guernsey was possible in large part due to the earlier success of the reformist regime in Jersey, and notably to the influence of the captain of Jersey Sir Hugh Paulet.[11] In Jersey the group of jurats acting in the last years of Edward VI's reign appears to have almost unanimously demonstrated Protestant sympathies and, while this might not have found local expression during the reign of Mary, many leading men and women chose to travel to Saint-Lô and elsewhere in Normandy to partake in Protestant services.[12] There may be a suggestion of the progress achieved by the reforming group in 1562 in the grant of the charter of June that year to Jersey, which followed closely the example set by the 1560 Guernsey charter.[13]

---

[8] *CPR 1558–60*, p. 337; Tim Thornton, *The Charters of Guernsey* (Bognor Regis, 2004), pp. 74–94.

[9] John Le Patourel, D. H. Gifford and R. H. Videlo (eds), *List of Records in the Greffe, Guernsey*, vol. 1, *Jugements, Ordonnances et Ordres de Conseil*, List and Index Society, special ser., 2 (London, 1969), p. 248; Ogier, *Reformation and Society*, pp. 72–3.

[10] A. J. Eagleston, 'The Dismissal of the Seven Jurats in 1565', *Report and Transactions of La Société Guernesiaise*, 12 (1933–36), 508–16; Ogier, *Reformation and Society*, pp. 70–1.

[11] For Paulet's contribution in Jersey, see Bronwyn Matthews (ed.), *Les Chroniques de Jersey* (St Helier, 2017), pp. 152–5; and on his family's background in Somerset, Simon Edwardes John Lambe, 'The Paulet Family and the Gentry of Early Tudor Somerset, 1485–1547' (Unpublished Ph.D. thesis, University of Surrey, 2014).

[12] Matthews (ed.), *Chroniques*, pp. 158–9. A reference early in 1559 to a gathering of 5,000 people in the court of a gentleman's house to hear the gospel preached almost certainly refers to Caen and its hinterland, rather than to Jersey, but indicates the opportunity to join this larger expression of reformed religion (TNA, SP 15/9/1, fol. 51 (*CSPD, 1601–03, Addenda 1547–65*, pp. 490–1)).

[13] TNA, C 66/978 (Patent Roll, 4 Elizabeth I), part 3, mm. 37–8 (*CPR 1560–63*, p. 270), printed in *Prison Board*, pp. 216–20.

The situation in Jersey becomes much clearer in the later months of 1562, considering St Helier at least. The arrival from Anjou of a Protestant minister, Guillaume Morise, seigneur de la Ripaudière, allowed for the formation of a clearly reformed congregation that had strong political support. As early as February 1563, the royal court prosecuted a man for describing Morise as a 'meschant', arguing that his doctrine was 'meschant', and suggesting that all those who went to his sermons, including the bailiff himself, were 'meschantz'.[14] The situation in St Helier was sufficiently established by 12 May 1563 for a meeting to take place between Morise, lieutenant-governor Amyas Paulet (Sir Hugh's son) and bailiff Hostes Nicolle, with jurats, deacons and elders, and Guernsey representatives minister Nicolas Bonhomme, elder Guillaume de Beauvoir, deacon Nicholas Martin and Thomas le Marchant, at which they promised mutual aid.[15]

Jersey's charter of 1562 also picked up a theme that had appeared in the Guernsey 1560 charter of liberties: the assertion of Queen Elizabeth's right to the duchy of Normandy, not simply historically but indicating the islands were still in the 1560s 'within our duchy of Normandy'. On this theme, the 1562 charter included among Elizabeth's predecessors not just kings of England but also dukes of Normandy. Notably, however, where the 1560 charter in Guernsey refers to its being granted by authority granted by parliament (perhaps reflecting some of the inherent gendered weakness of a female monarch), that for Jersey in 1562 did not do so.

Text

Elizabeth I confirmed the grants of her predecessors in this charter and specified more precisely the island's rights and privileges with regard to tolls, subsidies and other payments, its law and customs, freedom of trade, and its exemption from legal processes originating in English courts and others elsewhere. As enrolled in The National Archives, C 66/978, m. 37. I have respected the edition and translation as provided in the Jersey and Guernsey

---

[14] JA, D/Y/F1/6 (J. A. Messervy, 'Listes des recteurs de l'Ile de Jersey: recteurs de Saint-Hélier', *ABSJ*, 7 (1910–14), 75–98, at p. 85); Helen Mary Elizabeth Evans, 'The Religious History of Jersey, 1558–1640' (Unpublished Ph.D. thesis, University of Cambridge, 1991), pp. 48–9; Fernand de Schickler, *Les églises du refuge en Angleterre* (3 vols, Paris, 1892), vol. 2, p. 372 (burning Catholic texts, 26 May). Matthews (ed.), *Chroniques*, pp. 204–7, recognises the importance of these events, but places them 'Viron l'an 1563'.

[15] Matthews (ed.), *Chroniques*, ed., pp. 204–11; Northamptonshire Record Office, Finch Hatton 312, p. 306. Evans, 'Religious History', pp. 45–8, makes the meeting of May 1563 'the inauguration of the *église dressée* in Saint Helier', although the latter source allows for the existence of deacons and elders in advance of the meeting.

Law Review in 2016 *(the translation being from c. 1960, and with notes by Sir Philip Bailhache), with limited exceptions – most importantly amending the translation of* civitas *from state to city, otherwise e.g. adding a little punctuation and some missing articulation.*

Pro Balliuo et Juratis Insule de Jersey

Regina Omnibus ad quos &c. salutem

[1] Cum dilecti et fideles ligei et Subditi nostri Balliuus et Jurati Insule nostre de Jersey ac ceteri incole et habitatores ipsius Insule infra Ducatum nostrum Normannie et predecessores eorum a tempore cuius contrarii memoria hominum non existit per separales Cartas concessiones confirmaciones et amplissima diplomata illustrium progenitorum ac antecessorum nostrorum tam Regum Anglie quam Ducum Normannie ac aliorum quam pluribus Juribus Jurisdiccionibus Priuilegiis annuitatibus libertatibus et franchesiis libere quiete et inuiolabiliter vsi freti et gauisi fuerunt tam infra Regnum nostrum Anglie quam alibi infra dominia et loca ditioni nostre subiecta vltra citraque mare Quorum opere et beneficio Insule prenominate ac loca maritima predicta in fide obediencia et seruicio tam nostre quam eorundem progenitorum nostrorum constanter fideliter et inculpate prestiterunt ac perseuerauerunt liberaque commercia cum mercatoribus et aliis indigenis ac alienigenis tam pacis quam belli temporibus habuerunt et exercuerunt iudicia eciam et cogniciones omnium et omnimodorum causarum et querelarum accionum et placitorum tam Ciuilium quam criminalium et capitalium ac iudicialem potestatem ea omnia tractandi decidendi discutiendi audendi et terminandi atque in eisdem procedendi et in acta redigendi secundum leges et consuetudines Insule et loci predictorum ex antiquo receptas et approbatas preterquam in certis casubus cognicioni nostri [sic] regie reseruatis de tempore in tempus exercuerunt executi sunt et peregerunt.

[2] Que omnia et singula cuius et quanti momenti sunt et fuerunt ad tutelam et conseruacionem Insule [et] loci maritimorum predictorum in fide et obediencia Corone nostre Anglie Nos vt equum est perpendentes neque non immemores quam fortiter et fideliter Insulani predicti ac ceteri incole et habitatores ibidem nobis et progenitoribus nostris inseruierunt quantaque detrimenta damna et pericula tam pro assidua tuicione eiusdem Insule et loci quam pro recuperacione et defensione Castri nostri de Mount Orguill' infra predictam Insulam nostram de Jersey sustinuerunt indiesque sustinent non solum vt regia nostra beneuolencia fauor et effectus erga prefatos Insulanos aliquo illustri nostri beneficientie testimonio ac certis inditiis comprobetur verum eciam vt ipsi et eorum posteri deinceps imperpetuum prout antea solitam et debitam obediendenciam erga nos heredes et successores nostros teneant ac inuiolabiliter

obseruent has literas nostras patentes magno sigillo Anglie roboratas in forma qua sequitur illis concedere dignati sumus.

[3] Sciatis quod nos de gratia nostra speciali ac ex certa sciencia et mero motu nostris dedimus et concessimus ac pro nobis heredibus et successoribus nostris per presentes damus et concedimus prefatis Balliuo et Juratis Insule nostre de Jersey predicte ac ceteris Incolis et Habitatoribus dicte Insule quod ipsi et eorum quilibet licet in presentibus non recitati seu cogniti per seperalia nomina sunt semper in futuro ita liberi quieti et immunes in omnibus Ciuitatibus Burgis emptoriis nundinis mercatis villis mercatoriis et aliis locis ac portibus infra Regnum nostrum Anglie ac infra omnes prouincias dominia territoria et loca ditioni nostre subiecta tam citra quam vltra mare de et ab omnibus vectigalibus theoloneis custumis subsidiis hidagiis tallagiis pontagiis pannagiis muragiis fossagiis operibus expedicionibus bellicis nisi in casu vbi corpus nostre prefate Regine heredum vel successorum nostrorum quod absit in prisona detineatur et de et ab omnibus aliis contribucionibus oneribus et exccionibus quibuscumque nobis heredibus et successoribus nostris quouismodo debitis reddendis seu soluendis prout prefata Insula virtute aliquarum Cartarum concessionum confirmacionum siue deplomatum per predictos progenitores nostros quondam Reges Anglie et Duces Normannie siue alios seu virtute aut vigore alicuius rationabilis et legalis vsus prescripcionis seu consuetudinis vnquam aliquando fuerunt aut esse debuerunt vel potuerunt debuit vel quouismodo potuit.

[4] Cumque nonnula alia Priuilegia Jurisdicciones annuitates libertates et franchesie per predictos progenitores ac predecessores nostros quondam Reges Anglie et Duces Normannie ac alios prefate Insule indulta donata concessa et confirmata fuerunt ac a tempore cuius contrarii memoria hominum non existit infra Insulam et locos maritima prenominata inuiolabiliter vsitata et obseruata fuerunt de quibus vnum est quod tempore belli omnium nacionum mercatores et alii tam alienigeni quam Indigeni tam hostes quam amici libere licite et impune queant et possint dictam Insulam et locos maritima cum nauibus mercibus et bonis suis tam pro euitandis tempestatibus quam pro aliis licitis suis negociis inibi peragendis adire accedere commeare et frequentare ac libera commerica negociacionis ac rem mercatoriam ibidem exercere ac tuto et secure commorari indeque commeare ac redire tocies quocies absque damno molestia seu hostilitate quacumque in rebus mercibus bonis aut corporibus suis idque non solum infra Insulam et locos marittima predicta ac procinctum eorundem verum eciam infra spacia vndique ab eisdem distancia vsque ad vsum hominis id est quatenus visus oculi possit assequi Nos eandem annuitatem impunitatem libertates et priuilegia ac cetera omnia premissa vltime recitata rata grataque habentes ea pro nobis heredibus et successoribus nostris quantum in nobis est prefatis Balliuo et Juratis ac ceteris incolis habitatoribus mercatoribus et aliis tam hostibus quam amicis et eorum cuilibet per presentes

indulgemus ac elargimur auctoritate nostra regia renouamus reiteramus et confirmamus in tam amplis modo et forma prout predicti incole et habitatores Insule predicte ac predicti indigeni et alienigeni mercatores et alii preantea vsi vel gauisi fuerunt vel vti aut gaudere debuerunt vniuersis igitur et singulis Magistratibus Ministris et Subditis nostris per vniuersum Regnum nostrum Anglie ac cetera dominia et locos ditioni nostre subiecta vbilibet constitutis per presentes denunciamus ac firmiter iniungendo precipimus ne hanc nostram donacionem concessionem et confirmacionem seu aliquid in eisdem expressum aut contentum temerarie infringere seu quouismodo inuiolare presumant. Et si quis ausu temerario controfecerit seu attemptauerit volumus et decernimus quantum in nobis est quod restituat non solum oblata aut erepta sed quod eciam pro damno interesse et expensas ad plenariam recompensam et satisfaccionem compellatur per quecumque iuris nostri remedia seuereque puniatur et regie nostre potestatis ac legum nostrarum contemptor temerarius.

[5] Preterea ex vberiori gratia nostra per presentes ratificamu approbamus stabilimus et confirmamus omnes et singulas leges et consuetudines infra Insulam et locos marittima predicta rite et legittime vsitatas et ex antiquo receptas et approbatas Dantes et tribuentes prefatis Balliuo et iuratis ac omnibus aliis Magistratibus Ministris et ceteris quibuscumque ibidem in officio aut functione aliqua constitutis plenam integram et absolutam auctoritatem potestatem et facultatem cognoscendi iurisdiscendi et iudicandi de se et super omnibus et omnimodis placitis processibus litibus accionibus querelis et causis quibuscumque infra Insulam et locos predictos emergentibus tam realibus personalibus et mixtis quam criminalibus et capitalibus eaque omnia et singula ibidem et non alibi placitandi et peregendi prosequendi et defendendi atque in eisdem vel procedendi vel supersedendi examinandi audiendi terminandi absoluendi condenandi decidendi atque execucioni mandandi secundum leges et consuetutines Insule et loci marittimorum predictorum preantea vsitatas et approbatas absque prouocacione seu appellacione quacumque preterquam in casibus qui cognicioni nostre regali ex vetusta consuetudine Insule et loci predictorum reseruantur vel de iure aut priuilegio nostro regali reseruari debentur. Quam quidem auctoritatem potestatem et facultatem (preterquam in eisdem casibus reseruatas) nos pro nobis heredibus et successoribus nostris prefatis Balliuo et Juratis ac aliis damus committimus concedimus et confirmamus per presentes adeo plene libere et integre prout prefati Balliuus et Jurati ac alii vel eorum aliquis vnquam antehac eisdem rite et legittime vti functi aut gauisi sunt velu ti fungi et gaudere debuerunt aut licite potuerunt debuit aut potuit.

[6] Volumus preterea et pro nobis heredibus et successoribus nostris per presentes concedimus prefatis Balliuo et Juratis ac aliis incolis et habitatoribus infra Insulam et locos marittima predicta quod nullus eorum de cetero

per aliqua breuia sen processus ex aliquibus Curiis nostris seu aliorum infra Regnum nostrum Anglie emergencia siue eorum aliqua citetur apprehendatur euocetur in placita trahatur siue quouismodo aliter comparere aut respondere cogatur extra Insulam et loca maritima predicta coram quibuscumque Judicibus Justiciariis Magistratibus aut Officiariis nostris aut aliorum de aut super aliqua relite materia seu causa quacumque infra Insulam predictam emanante sed quod Insulam predictam et eorum quilibet huiusmodi citacionibus apprehencionibus breuibus et processibus non obstantibus licete et impune valeant et possint valeat et possit infra Insulam et locos predicta residere commorari quiescere et Justiciam ibidem expectare absque aliqua pena corporali seu pecuniaria fine redempcione aut mulcta proinde incurrenda forisfacienda necnon absque aliqua offencione vel causa contemptus seu contumacis per nos heredes et successores nostros illis seu eorum alicui aut aliquibus proinde infligenda irroganda vel aliter adiudicanda. Exceptis tantummodo huiusmodi casibus qui per leges et consuetudines Insule et loci predictorum regali nostre cognicioni atque examini reseruentur vel de iure aut priuilegio nostro regali reseruari debentur.

[7] Et vlterius de ampliori gratia nostra ac ex certa sciencia et mero motu nostris dedimus concessimus et confirmauimus ac per has literas nostras patentes pro nobis heredibus et successoribus nostris quantum in nobis est damus concedimus et confirmamus prefatis Balliuo et Juratis ceterisque incolis et habitatoribus Insule et loci maritimorum predictorum necnon mercatoribus et aliis eo confluentibus tot tanta talia huiusmodi et consimilia Jura Jurisdicciones annuitates impunitates indemnitates exempciones libertates franchesias et priuilegia quecumque quot quanta qualia et que prefati Balliuus et Jurati ac ceteri incole et habitatores mercatores et alii aut eorum aliquis antehac legittime et rite vsi freti seu gauisi fuerunt vsus fretus seu gauisus fuit ac omnia et singula quecumque alia in quibuscumque Cartis aut literis patentibus nostris seu progenitorum nostrorum quondam Regum Anglie seu Ducum Normannie aut aliorum eis seu eorum predecessoribus antehac data concessa vel confirmata et non reuocata seu abolita quocumque nomine seu quibuscumque nominibus iidem Balliuus Jurati ac ceteri incole et habitatores eiusdem Insule et loci marittimorum predictorum aut eorum predecessores seu eorum aliqui vel aliquis in eisdem literis patentibus seu eorum aliquibus censeantur nuncupentur aut vocentur seu censeri nuncupari aut vocitari debuerunt seu soliti fuerunt ac ea omnia et singula licet in presentibus minime expressa prefatis Balliuo et Juratis ac ceteris incolis et habitatoribus Insule et loci marittimorum predictorum necnon mercatoribus et aliis eo confluentibus Indigenis et Alienigenis per presentes confirmamus consolidamus et de integre ratificamus adeo plene libere et integre prout ea omnia et singula in eisdem literis patentibus contenta modo particulariter verbatim et ex expressis in presentibus literis nostris patentibus recitatata et declarata fuissent.

[8] Salua semper atque illabifacta suprema regia potestate dominacione atque imperio Corone nostre Anglie tam quoad ligeanciam subieccionem et obedienciam Insule predicte ac aliorum quorumcumque infra Insulam et locos predictos commorancium siue degencium quam quoad regalitates priuilegia res redditus vectigalia ac cetera Jura proficua commoditates ac emolumenta quecumque infra Insulam et locum predictos nobis heredibus et successoribus nostris per prerogatiuam Corone nostre Anglie siue Ducatus Normannie seu aliter ex antiquo debita et consueta Saluis eciam appellacionibus et prouocacionibus quibuscumque Insule predicte ac aliorum ibidem commorancium siue degencium in omnibus eiusmodi casibus que legibus et consuetudinibus Insule et loci predictorum regali nostre cognicioni atque examini reseruantur vel de iure aut priuilegio nostro regali reseruari debentur aliqua sentencia clausula re aut materia quacumque superius in presentibus expressa et specificata in rontrarium aliquo non obstante Prouiso semper quod Aliqua clausa articulus siue aliquod aliud in presentibus literis nostris patentibus expressis et specificatis non exponantur interpretentur nec se extendant ad aliquod quod sit vel fieri possit nobis vel heredibus nostris preiudiciale quoad aliqua terras tenementa redditus regalitates vel hereditamenta nostra infra Insulam predictam.

[9] Postremo volumus ac per presentes concedimus quod dicti Balliuus et Jurati ac ceteri incole et habitatores Insule predicte necnon mercatores et alii illuc commorantes seu confluentes habeant et de tempore in tempus habere possint has literas nostras patentes sub magno Sigillo nostro Anglie debito modo factas et sigillatas absque fine seu feodo magno vel paruo nobis in Hanaperio nostro seu alibi ad vsum nostrum pro premissis quoquomodo reddendis soluendis vel faciendis.

[10] Eo quod expressa mencio etc. In cuius rei etc. Teste Regine apud Grenewiche xxvii die Iunii.

per breue de priuato Sigillo.

Translation

For the Bailiff and Jurats of the Island of Jersey

The Queen to all to whom these Presents shall come, greeting

[1] Whereas our beloved and faithful lieges and subjects the Bailiff and Jurats of our Island of Jersey and other inhabitants of and dwellers in that Island within our duchy of Normandy and their predecessors have from time immemorial by special charters, grants, confirmations, and most ample writs of our illustrious progenitors and predecessors as well kings of England as dukes of Normandy and others used, enjoyed and been in possession of very

many rights, jurisdictions, privileges, immunities, liberties, and franchises freely, quietly, and without molestation as well within our realm of England as elsewhere within the dominions and places subject to our government beyond and on this side of the sea, by the help and benefit of which the before mentioned Island and maritime places before named have steadfastly, faithfully, and unblameably continued and persevered in their allegiance, obedience, and service as well to us as to those same ancestors of ours and have enjoyed and gone on in their free trade with merchants and others, natives and foreigners, as well in times of peace as of war, and have moreover exercised and executed and carried through judgment and cognisance of all and every sort of causes, complaints, actions, and pleas, as well civil as criminal and capital and have received the judicial power of taking into consideration, deciding, discussing, hearing, and determining all those things and of proceeding in the same and keeping records of their proceedings according to the laws and customs of the Island and before mentioned places accepted and approved of old except in certain cases from time to time reserved to our royal cognisance.

[2] And we as is just considering of how great advantage and moment all and singular the premises are and have been for the safety and preservation of the Island and maritime places before mentioned in their fidelity and obedience to our crown of England and being not unmindful how bravely and faithfully the aforesaid Islanders and other inhabitants and dwellers in the same place have been devoted to us and our ancestors and how great losses damages and dangers they have sustained and do still sustain as well for the constant defence of the same Island and places as for the recovery and defence of our castle of Mont Orgueil within our aforesaid Island of Jersey. So that not only our royal benevolence, favour, and affection toward the aforesaid Islanders may be shown by some remarkable testimony and evident proof of our beneficence but also that they and their posterity may hereafter for ever as formerly retain and inviolably observe their wonted and due obedience to us our heirs and our successors, we have thought fit to grant to them these our letters patent confirmed under the Great Seal of England in the following form.

[3] Know ye that we of our special grace and certain knowledge and mere motion have given and granted and by these presents we give and grant for us our heirs and successors to the said Bailiff and Jurats of our aforesaid Island of Jersey and the other natives and inhabitants of the said Island that they and any one of them although not mentioned in these presents or specified by their separate names be ever in future as free quit and exempt in all cities, boroughs, markets, trading towns, fairs, mart-towns, and other places and ports within our kingdom of England and within all provinces, dominions, territories, and places subject to our rule as well on this side of as beyond the sea, of and from all tributes, tolls, customs, subsidies, hidage, taylage,

pontage, panage, murage, fossage, works and warlike expeditions, except in case our aforesaid royal person or that of our heirs or successors should be detained in prison, which God forbid, and of and from all other contributions burdens and exactions whatsoever, actually due or which are to be paid or given to us our heirs and successors in any manner, as the before mentioned Islanders by virtue of any charters, grants, confirmations, and princely writs of our said progenitors formerly kings of England and dukes of Normandy or others or by virtue or force of any reasonable and legal usage prescription or custom have ever been or ought to be or could be or any of them ought to be or in any way could be.

[4] And whereas some other privileges, jurisdictions, immunities, liberties, and franchises were conferred upon given, granted, and confirmed to the aforesaid Island by our before mentioned progenitors and predecessors formerly kings of England and dukes of Normandy and others and have from time immemorial been inviolably used and observed within the Island and maritime places before mentioned, one of which is that in time of war the merchants and others of all nations as well foreigners as natives, as well enemies as friends, could and might freely lawfully and without fear of punishment resort to, come to, visit, and frequent the said Island and maritime places with their ships, merchandises, and goods as well to avoid storms as to carry on their other lawful business there, and there to exercise a free commerce, trade and traffic and safely and quietly to remain there and thence to depart and there to return as often as they think fit without any harm molestation or hurt whatsoever to their wares, goods, or persons and that not only within the Island and maritime places aforesaid and the precincts of the same but also farther on all sides at such space and distance from them as the sight of man goes to, that is as far as the sight of the eye can reach. We holding the same immunity, impunity, liberties, and privileges and all other the premises last mentioned as fixed and acceptable do by these presents grant and bestow the same for us our heirs and successors as much as in us lies unto the said Bailiff and Jurats and other natives, inhabitants, merchants, and others as well enemies as friends and to each one of them and by our royal authority do renew reiterate and confirm the same in as ample a manner and form as the said natives and inhabitants of the said Island and the said natives and foreigners merchants and others have in time passed used or enjoyed or ought to have used or enjoyed the same. Therefore by these presents we order and strictly enjoin all and singular our magistrates, officers, and subjects throughout our whole realm of England and other dominions and places subject to our rule wheresoever constituted that they do not presume rashly to infringe or in any way to violate this our grant, concession, and confirmation or anything therein expressed or contained, and if anyone should rashly dare do anything to the contrary or attempt to do we will and decree as much as in our power lies that he restore not only

the things he has taken and seized but also that he be compelled by every remedy of our law to make full restitution and satisfaction for the loss interest and expense and that he be severely punished as a rash despiser of our royal authority and of our laws.

[5] Further of our further grace by these presents we ratify approve establish and confirm all and singular the laws and customs duly and lawfully used in the Island and maritime places before mentioned and received and approved of old giving and granting to our aforesaid Bailiff and Jurats and all other magistrates officers of justice and any other persons appointed there in any office or duty full absolute and complete authority power and faculty to have the cognisance, jurisdiction, and judgment concerning and touching all and all sorts of pleas, processes, lawsuits, actions, disputes, and causes of any kind whatsoever arising in the Island and before mentioned places as well real, personal, and mixed as criminal and capital and there and not elsewhere to plead, proceed with, prosecute and defend all these things and every one of them and in the same matters either to proceed or supersede, to examine, hear, end, acquit, condemn, decide, and put their sentences in execution according to the laws and customs of the Island and before mentioned maritime places heretofore used and approved without any challenge or appeal whatsoever except in cases which according to the ancient custom of the Island and before mentioned places are reserved to our royal cognisance or which by our right or royal privilege ought to be reserved, which authority power and faculty except in those cases reserved we for ourselves our heirs and successors give entrust grant and confirm by these presents to our said Bailiff and Jurats and others as fully freely and completely as the said Bailiff and Jurats and others or any of them have ever up to the present rightly and lawfully used practised or enjoyed the same or ought or could legitimately have used performed or enjoyed the same or any one of them ought or could.

[6] Moreover we desire and for us our heirs and successors by these presents we grant to the aforesaid Bailiff and Jurats and others, natives and inhabitants within the Island and other maritime places before mentioned, that none of them for the future should be cited, apprehended or drawn into a lawsuit by any writs or process issued from any of our courts or other courts within our kingdom of England or any of them or in any other way be compelled to appear or reply without the Island and maritime places aforesaid before any judges, courts, magistrates, or officers of justice of ours or of others concerning or touching any thing, suit, matter, or cause whatsoever arising within the aforesaid Island but that the said Islanders and any one of them notwithstanding citations, apprehensions, writs, and processes of the kind mentioned may and might lawfully and with impunity in the Island and aforesaid places reside remain be at rest and there await justice without any corporal punishment or

pecuniary fine, ransom, or loss on that account to be incurred or suffered and without any offence or cause of contempt or contumacy as far as concerns our heirs and successors on them or on any one or more of them on that account to be inflicted imposed or otherwise adjudged. Except only such cases as by the laws and customs of the Island and aforesaid places may be reserved to our royal cognisance and examination or by our royal right or privilege ought to be reserved.

[7] And moreover of our fuller grace and certain knowledge and mere motion we have given granted and confirmed and by these our letters patent for ourselves our heirs and successors as much as in us lies we give grant and confirm to the said Bailiff and Jurats and the other natives of and dwellers in the Island and maritime places before mentioned as also to merchants and others resorting thither such great similar or like rights, jurisdictions, immunities, impunities, indemnities, exemptions, liberties, franchises, and privileges whatsoever as the said Bailiff and Jurats and other natives and inhabitants merchants and others or any one of them have heretofore legally and rightfully used practised and enjoyed or any one of them has used practised or enjoyed and all and every other thing that has been given granted and confirmed heretofore to them or their predecessors in whatever charters or letters patent of ours or of our progenitors formerly kings of England or dukes of Normandy or others and not revoked or abolished by whatsoever name or names the said Bailiff, Jurats and other natives and inhabitants of the said Island and maritime places aforesaid or their predecessors or some or any of them may be described, called, or named or ought to be described, called, or named or have been wont to be in the said letters patent or any of them and all and singular which things although not expressly mentioned we do by these presents confirm, consolidate, and ratify anew to the said Bailiff and Jurats and other residents and inhabitants of the said Island and before mentioned maritime places as well as to merchants as others natives and foreigners coming together there as fully freely and entirely as if all and singular the things contained in those letters patent were just now particularly expressly and clearly recited and declared in our present letters patent.

[8] Saving always entire and unimpaired the supreme royal power dominion and empire of our crown of England as much as to what may concern the allegiance and obedience of the aforesaid Island and of others whoever they may be sojourning or living in the Island and above named places as to what may concern the regalities, privileges, interests, revenues, tributes, and other rights, profits, commodities, and emoluments whatever in the Island and said places anciently due and accustomed to be paid to us our heirs and successors by the prerogative of our crown of England or dukedom of Normandy or otherwise; saving also every possible right of appeal of the said Island and

of others dwelling or being there in all kinds of cases which by the laws and customs of the Island and aforesaid places are reserved to our royal cognisance and examination or ought by law or our royal prerogative to be reserved; notwithstanding any sentence, clause, thing, or matter whatever expressed above in these presents and set out to the contrary. Provided always that no clause article or any other thing expressed and set out in these our present letters patent should be explained or understood or should enlarge themselves in some way which might be or might possibly become prejudicial to us or our heirs as regards any tenements, lands, revenues, regalities, or inheritances of ours within the aforesaid Island.

[9] Lastly our pleasure is and by these presents we grant that the said Bailiff and Jurats and others, natives and inhabitants of the aforesaid Island, as well merchants as others dwelling or coming together there, should have and from time to time should be able to have these our letters patent made and sealed under our great seal of England in the required manner without yielding, paying, or rendering any fine or fee whether great or small to us in our Hanaper or elsewhere to our use for the same.

[10] And that although express mention [Editor's note, in the *JGLR* edition: The translator has completed the text that did not appear in the version printed in the *Prison Board* case] of the fine annual value or of the certainty of the premises or of any of them or of the other gifts or grants before this time made by us or by some of our progenitors or predecessors to the aforesaid Bailiff and Jurats and other natives and inhabitants of the said Island or to any of them do not appear clearly in these presents or notwithstanding any statute, act, ordinance, proviso, edict, or restriction to the contrary thereof up to the present had, made, decreed, ordained, or provided or any other thing, cause, or matter whatsoever in any way notwithstanding.

In witness whereof We have caused these our Letters to be made patent

At Greenwich the twenty-seventh day of June [in the fourth year of our reign].

By writ of Privy Seal.

James I: 1604

Commentary

James I succeeded Elizabeth on 24 March 1603. His journey from Scotland took several weeks, and he arrived in London on 7 May. James' charter for Jersey followed on 7 April 1604. In it, he confirmed the contents of the island's charter of 1562, without mentioning specifically Elizabeth's grant, but in almost precisely similar wording. The only additions were a strengthened proviso protecting the crown's rights, and a clause rehearsed the fixing of customs for wool and grain, in practice another restatement of earlier concessions. This early grant of a charter in that form reflected some of the insecurities and instabilities arising from the accession of a Scottish king to the English throne, and therefore to rule over the islands. The grant also reflected the more dynamic religious, political and economic environment in Jersey, compared to Guernsey and other neighbouring islands.

When a little later James issued his first confirmation of liberties to Guernsey (on 18 December 1604), he similarly confirmed the effect of Elizabeth's charter, in the case of Guernsey that being the grant of 1560. More than a year later, in June 1605, in a further charter, James confirmed Guernsey's rights with regard to law and customs in similar terms, before going on to recognise a number of specific rights in several more clauses, across a range of topics. First, his charter granted what was in practice a long-standing concession, providing Nicholas Baudouin, rector of St Peter Port, and his successors, with 60 quarters of wheat per annum in perpetuity from the crown's possessions in the parish of St Saviour.[1] Control over the Petit Coutume, granted to the Royal Court of Guernsey in 1563, was confirmed as supporting the construction of a new harbour.[2] Finally, the charter gave Guernsey's bailiff and jurats, or

---

[1] Tim Thornton, *The Charters of Guernsey* (Bognor Regis, 2004), pp. 95–115; D. M. Ogier, *Reformation and Society in Guernsey* (Woodbridge, 1996), p. 73.

[2] Ogier, *Reformation and Society*, p. 65; J. H. Lenfestey (ed.), *List of Records in the Greffe, Guernsey*, vol. 2, *Documents under Bailiwick Seal*, List and Index Society, special ser., 11 (London, 1978), p. 65, no. 447; Havilland de Sausmarez (ed.), *The Extentes of Guernsey 1248 and 1331: And Other Documents Relating to Ancient Usages and Customs in that Island* (Guernsey, 1934), p. 70.

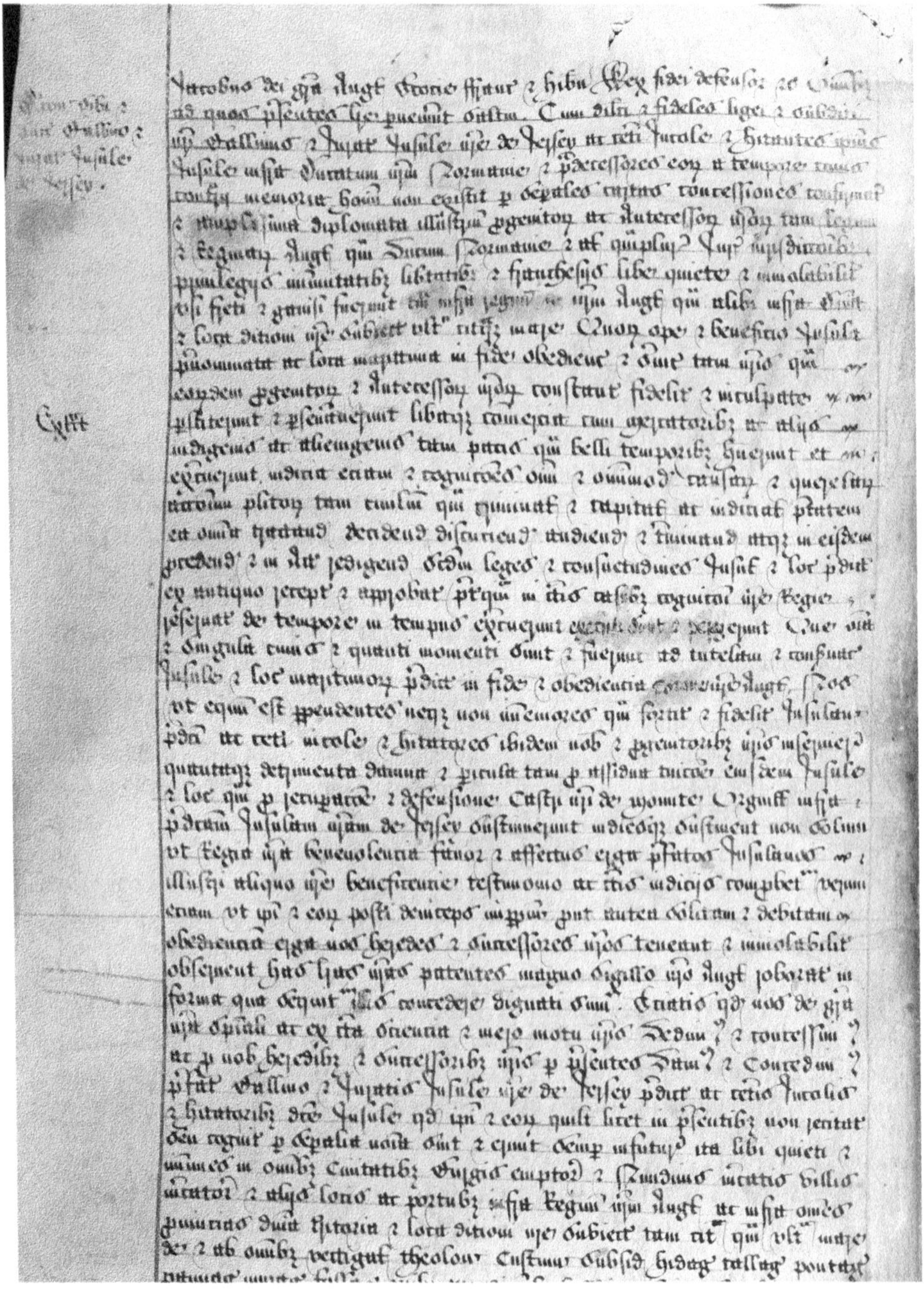

Plate 13 (i): The Royal Charter granted by James I in 1604.
Credit: The National Archives, ref. C 66/1654.

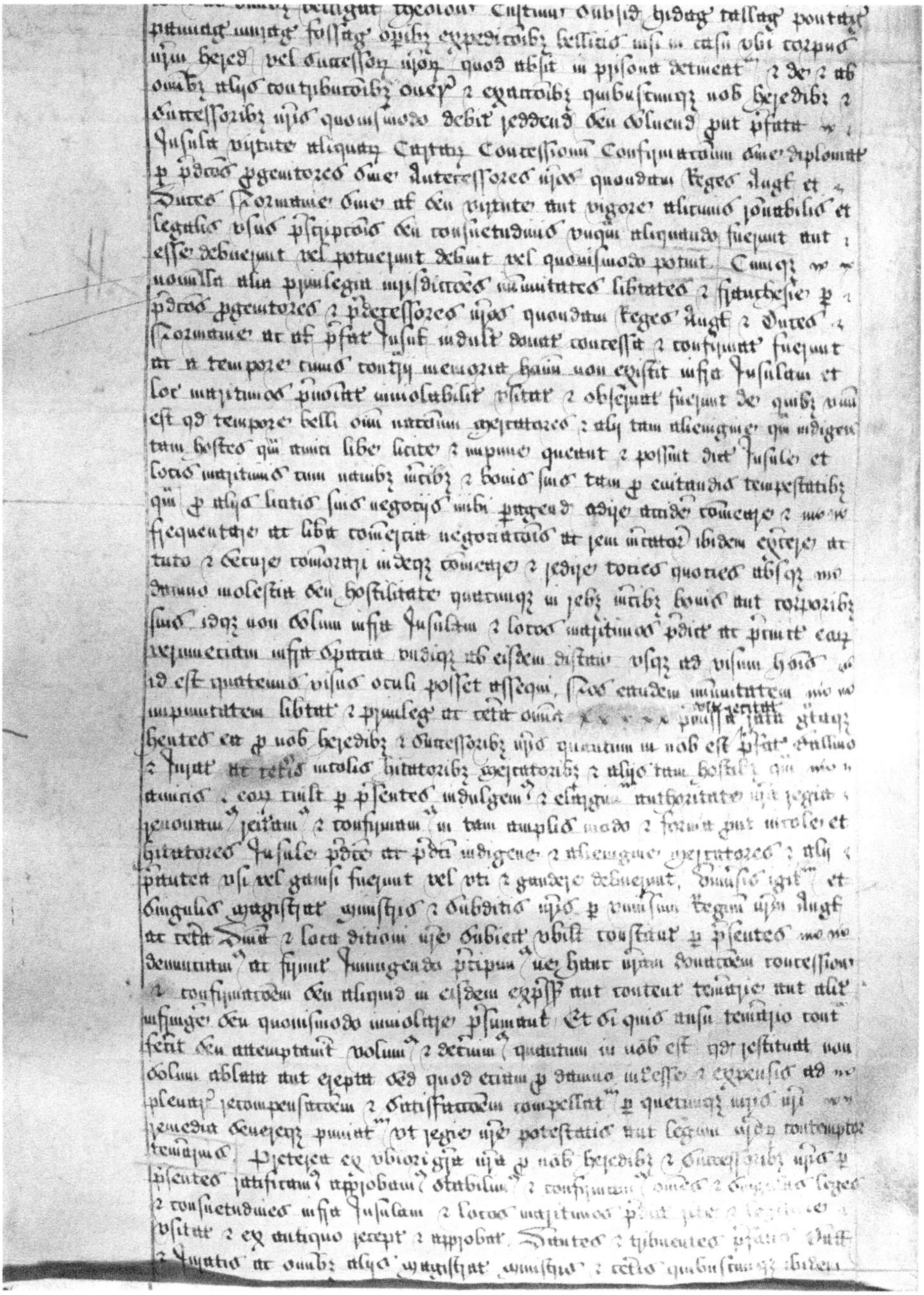

Plate 13 (ii): The Royal Charter granted by James I in 1604.

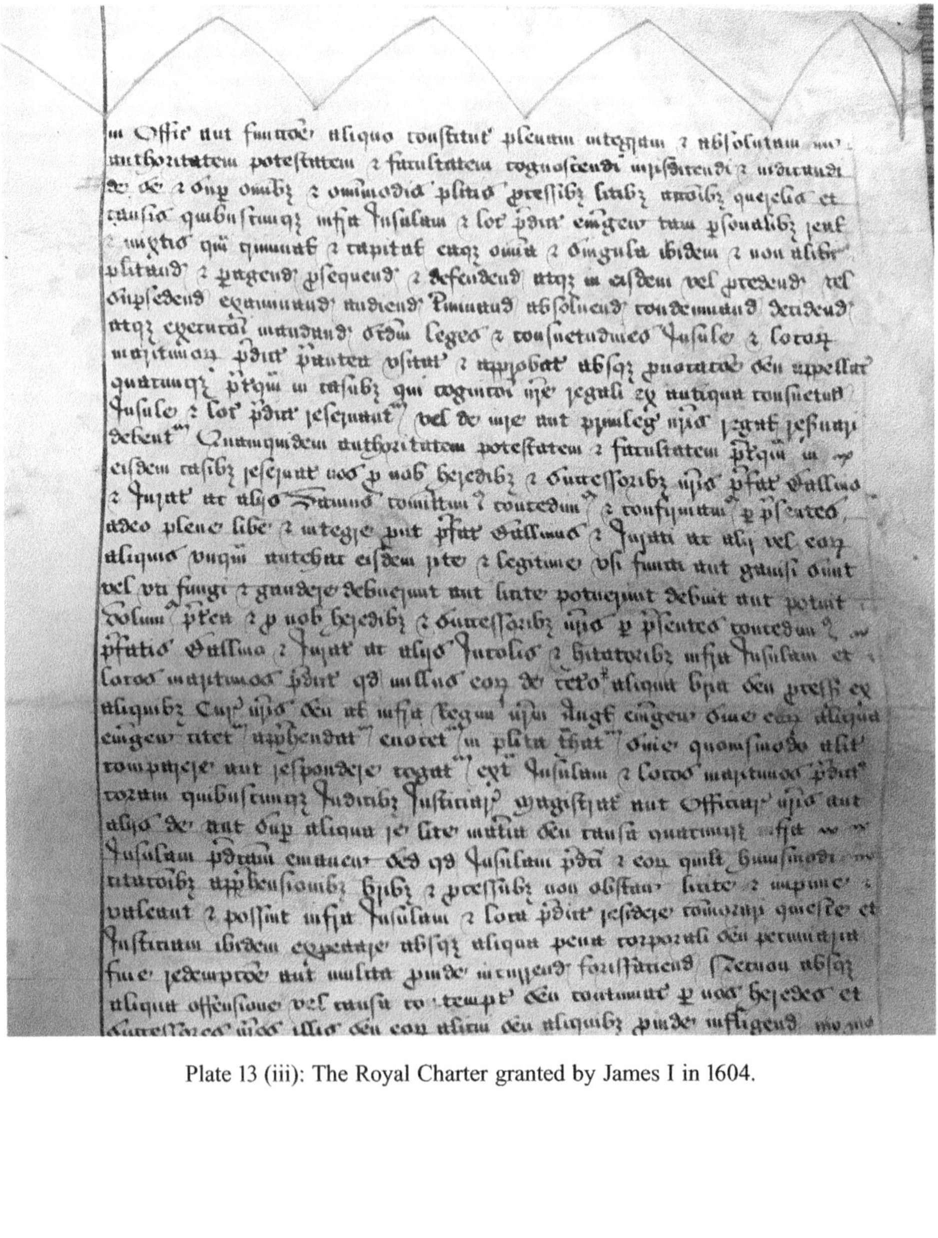

Plate 13 (iii): The Royal Charter granted by James I in 1604.

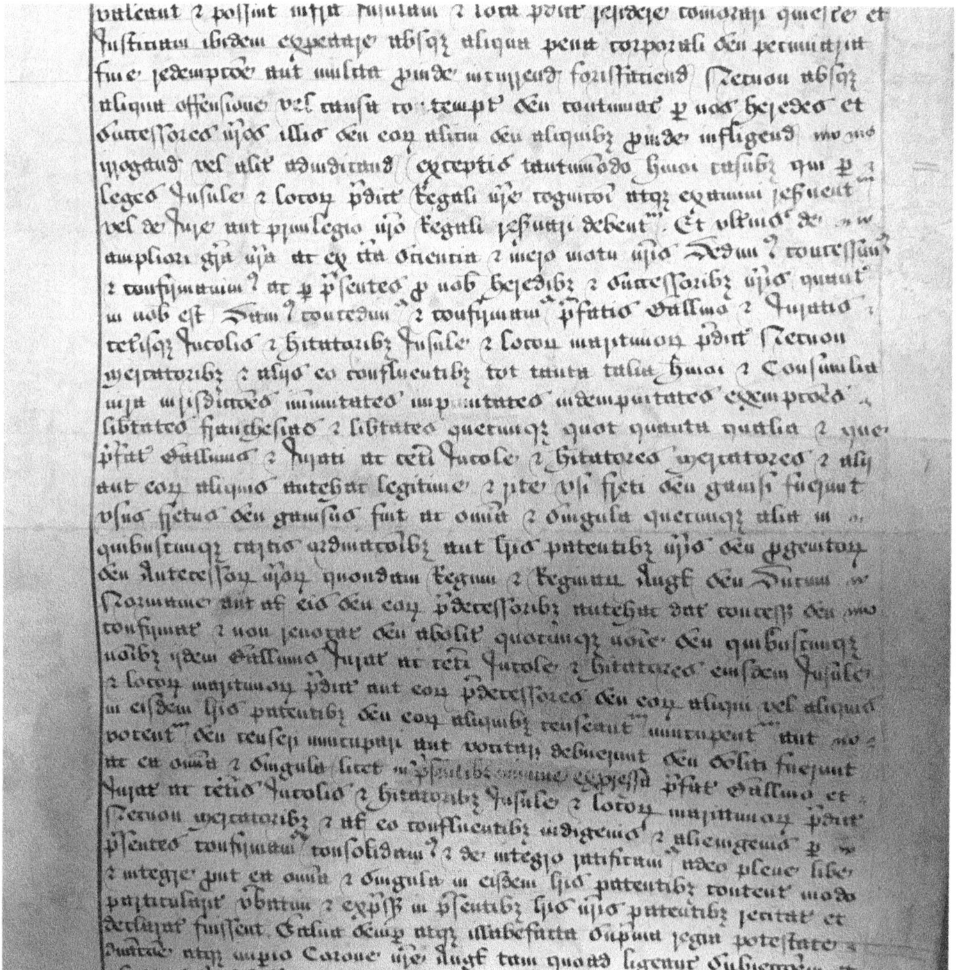

Plate 13 (iv): The Royal Charter granted by James I in 1604.

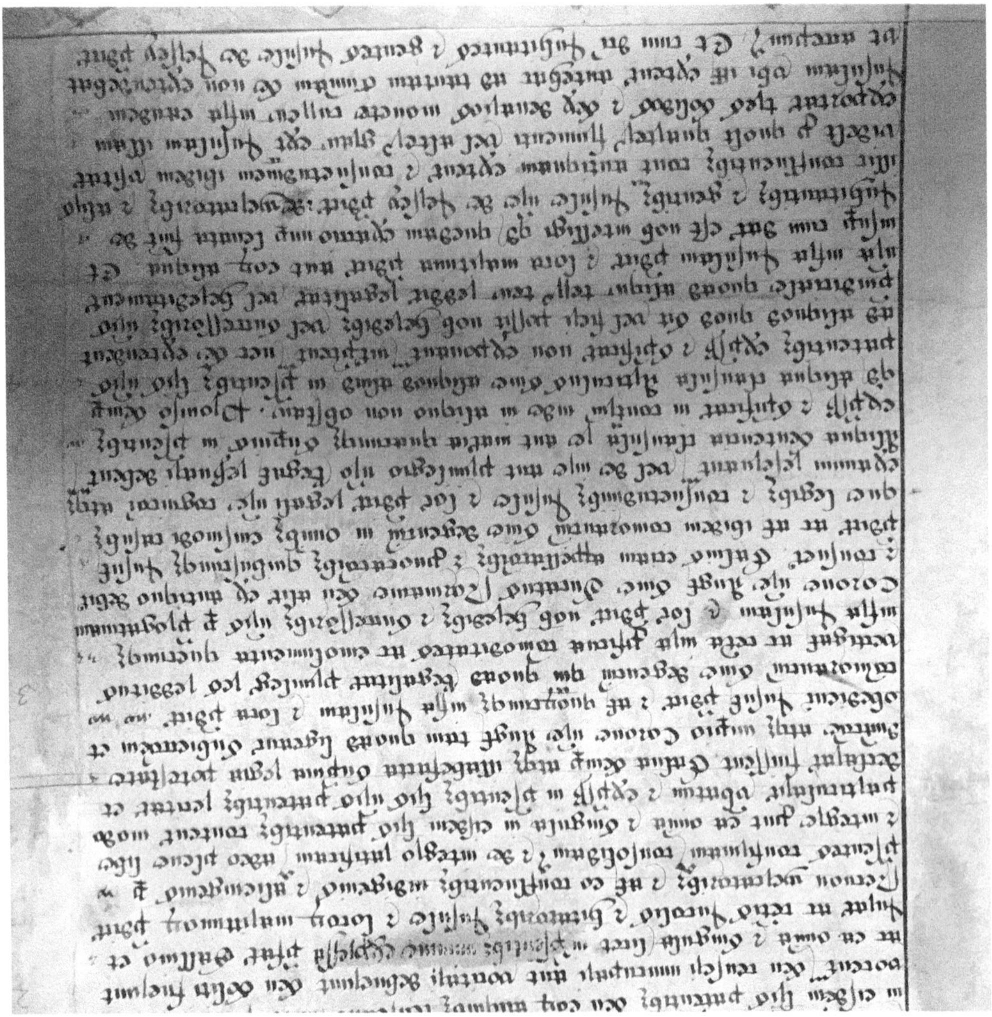

Plate 13 (v): The Royal Charter granted by James I in 1604.

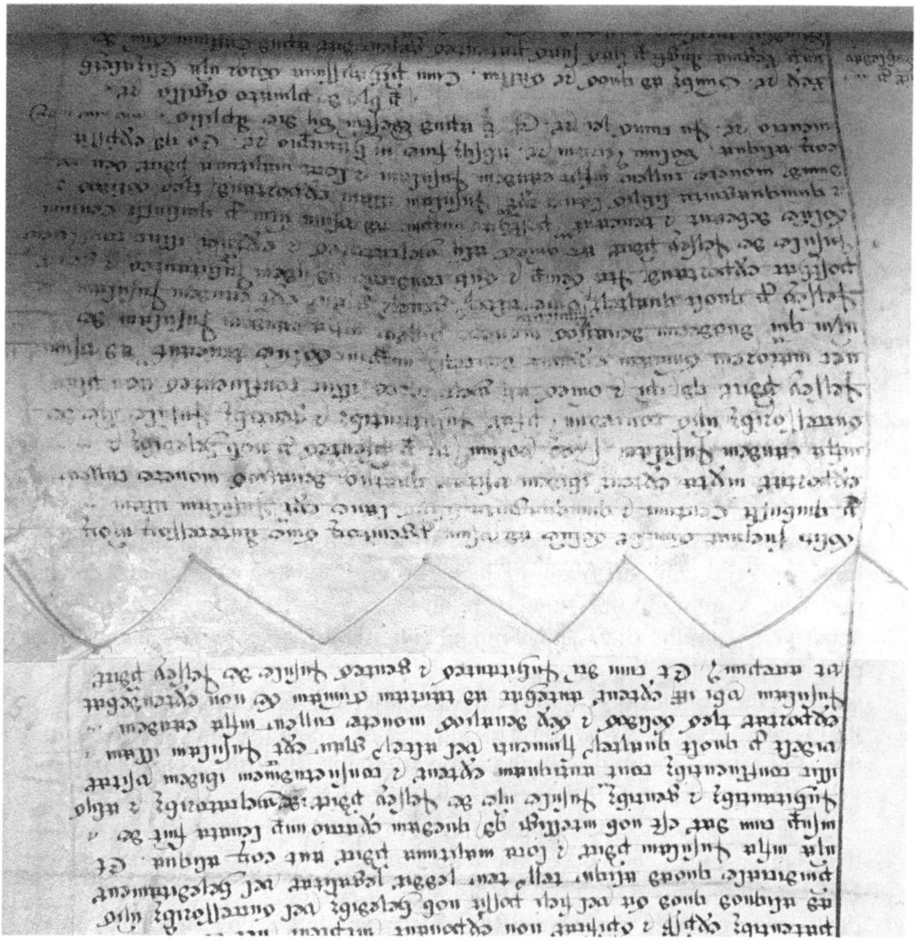

Plate 13 (vi): The Royal Charter granted by James I in 1604.

confirmed to them, the right to administer the weights and measures in the bailiwick, and the profits arising from this, in return for an annual payment of 20s.. Therefore, although the 1605 Guernsey charter in particular has the appearance of a marker of new beginnings in the island's history, in reality there was a strong underlying continuity at work.[3]

In Guernsey, this continuity included a very long tenure of the governorship: Sir Thomas Leighton had been appointed as long ago as 1570 and served until his death in 1610. Leighton was firmly committed to the cause of radical Protestantism and well connected both to its aristocratic and ministerial leaders, perhaps most obviously in his patronage of Thomas Cartwright. His support over the decades helped ensure that, even after his death, the Guernsey community's commitment to Presbyterianism in all its forms was not seriously threatened when in 1613–16 James seems to have sanctioned a challenge.[4]

Jersey's 1604 charter[5] followed closely the model of its predecessor of 1562, and hence the 1560 grant to Guernsey on which that Elizabethan grant to Jersey was modelled. It first restated the privileges granted in previous royal charters, then more precisely specified the right to exercise judicial power locally. It went on to confirm exemptions from duties, tolls and the like, and free commerce in time of war. Local laws and customs were confirmed, as was the power to try and determine pleas; no writ from England was to have the power to bring any inhabitant of Jersey to an English court. Inhabitants and merchants coming to the island were all to be included in this privilege. The departures from the Elizabethan model consisted of an extended statement of proviso, protecting the crown's position, and the charter also echoed closely some of the content of the Edward VI charter to both islands. It referred to the 'recent' levy of 3s. 6d. on each quarter of wheat or other grain, beyond the accustomed amount, with the same stipulation that they should pay just 12d. per quarter, but 3s. 6d. for each pound of wool.

Jersey's experience of the preceding few years had been more problematic than Guernsey's. The end of the long Paulet governorship, covering over half a century, ended with Sir Amias' son Sir Anthony (governor 1588 to his death in July 1600). Sir Walter Ralegh was appointed governor and captain

---

[3] Alderney also saw little disruption in this period: A. N. Symons (ed.), 'History of Alderney', *Report and Transactions of La Société Guernesiaise*, 13 (1937–45), 34–71, at pp. 42–3.

[4] Ogier, *Reformation and Society*, pp. 92–3; A. J. Eagleston, 'Guernsey under Sir Thomas Leighton (1570–1610)', *Report and Transactions of La Société Guernesiaise*, 13 (1937–45), 72–108.

[5] TNA, C 66/1654 (Patent Roll, 2 James I), part 24, printed in *Prison Board*, pp. 276–81.

of Jersey and Mont Orgueil on 26 August 1600.[6] Some of the issues Ralegh faced in Jersey in the last years of Elizabeth's reign were the perennial ones of a hostile France and Spain, as seen in June 1602 when the islands faced the threat of Spanish galleys at Le Conquet.[7] Ralegh's failure to cultivate James in Scotland, and James' reliance on Ralegh's enemy Lord Henry Howard, meant that Elizabeth's death in March 1603 was bound to undermine his position in the island. In May 1603, Ralegh lost his post as captain of the guard and on 15 July he was arrested for his alleged role in the so-called 'Main' plot, the scheme of George Brooke and his brother Henry Lord Cobham to displace James in favour of Arbella Stuart. On 30 July 1603, Sir John Peyton, who by chance was Ralegh's gaoler as lieutenant of the Tower, was appointed to succeed him as governor of Jersey.[8]

Later events have tended to obscure the limited challenge to Jersey's Presbyterian establishment in the early days of Peyton's governorship. There was, nonetheless, very soon a clear indication of his personal hostility to presbytery and his willingness to challenge it. This was not yet widely shared: a commission appointed in 1607 did not respond to Peyton's complaints against a 'presbyterial or popular jurisdiction' in the church.[9]

There was, however, very soon in James' reign conflict over the rights of the lieutenant and bailiff: Jean Hérault, who had been attached to the commission of 1607, and was emerging as an authority on the customs and laws of the island, urged greater power and independence for the States, while Peyton advocated the royal rights exercised by his predecessors as lieutenant. A challenge to the bailiff, George Paulet, by the law officers over the wardship of the seigneur of St Ouen, his grandson, brought the tension into the open. In 1605, the Council decided to send a commission, and when, finally, in 1607

---

[6] Thomas Rymer (ed.), *Foedera, conventiones, litterae, et cujuscunque generis acta publica*, rev. George Holmes, 3rd edn (10 vols, The Hague, 1739–45), vol. 7ii, pp. 4–5.

[7] *CSPD, 1601–03, Addenda 1547–65*, pp. 206, 220. Ralegh seems to have been in Bath, ill, in September: *ibid.*, p. 238.

[8] *CSPD, 1603–10*, pp. 10, 26; R. R. Lemprière, 'Messire Walter Ralegh, gouverneur de Jersey, 1600–03', *ABSJ*, 9 (1919–22), 96–106, at pp. 102–6; G. R. Balleine, *History of Jersey*, rev. Marguerite Syvret and Joan Stevens (Chichester, 1981), p. 93; Philip Ahier, *The Governorship of Sir Walter Ralegh in Jersey, 1600–1603: Together with some Local Raleghana* (St Helier, 1971), 138–43; Charles Le Quesne, *A Constitutional History of Jersey* (London, 1856), p. 215.

[9] A. J. Eagleston, *The Channel Islands under Tudor Government, 1485–1642: A Study in Administrative History* (Cambridge, 1949), pp. 109–10, 112–13; Peter Heylyn, *A Full Relation of Two Journeys: The One into the Main-land of France. The Other into some of the Adjacent Ilands* (London, 1656), p. 381, merely says 'Whether that so it was, I cannot say', so the hint identified by Eagleston was not a strong one.

it was appointed, Hérault was allocated to support Sir Robert Gardiner and Dr James Hussey.[10]

As well as nascent religious and especially political tensions in Jersey, the context for the charter grant was a new commercial environment. Over the last decades of the sixteenth century, Jersey had benefitted from a significant expansion in stocking knitting, drawing on wool supplies from England and supplying markets mainly in France.[11] In the context of ongoing debate about Jersey's role as an entrepot for trade with France in times of peace, international tension and outright hostilities,[12] this meant that particular scrutiny began to be devoted to the rights of Jerseymen to export materials from England, import them into the island, and then re-export manufactured goods.[13] This helps explain the appearance of the stipulations on the movement of wool (and grain) from England into the island. Although the wording of the 1604 charter suggested the issue was recent, in fact the formulation echoed a clause of the 1549 charter of Edward VI to the islands.[14] The Jersey community was therefore successful in 1604 in reasserting a position originally negotiated more than half a century before, and that had been omitted from the intervening document of 1562. This success was the more pronounced given the inflation that had occurred since the mid-sixteenth century. It was, nonetheless, an issue that was to continue to test relationships in the coming decades.

---

[10] Eagleston, *Channel Islands*, pp. 110–11; Helen Mary Elizabeth Evans, 'The Religious History of Jersey, 1558–1640' (Unpublished Ph.D. thesis, University of Cambridge, 1991), pp. 150–3.

[11] J. C. Appleby, 'Neutrality, Trade and Privateering 1500–1689', in A. G. Jamieson (ed.), *A People of the Sea: The Maritime History of the Channel Islands* (London, 1986), pp. 59–105, at pp.75–7; Joan Thirsk, 'The Fantastical Folly of Fashion: The English Stocking Knitting Industry, 1500–1700', in N. B. Harte and K. G. Ponting (eds), *Textile History and Economic History* (Manchester, 1973), pp. 50–73, esp. pp. 56–9, 69–70.

[12] *CSPD, 1581–90*, p. 402 (7 April 1587); John Roche Dasent (ed.), *Acts of the Privy Council of England*, vol. 15, *1587–1588* (London, 1897), pp. 128–9; W. S. Holdsworth, *A History of English Law*, vol. 5, *The Common Law and its Rivals* (Boston, 1924), p. 48; Balleine, *History of Jersey*, rev. Syvret and Stevens, p. 91.

[13] Appleby, 'Neutrality, Trade and Privateering', pp. 72–3: there was concern expressed in parliament in 1621 (Wallace Notestein, Frances Helen Relf, and Hartley Simpson (eds), *Commons Debates, 1621* (7 vols, New Haven CT, 1935), vol. 7, pp. 250, 253, 255).

[14] See above, pp. 87–8, 94, 98–9.

Text

James I confirmed the contents of Elizabeth's extensive grant of 1562, without mentioning that grant specifically but in very similar wording. James added a strengthened proviso protecting the crown's rights and a clause rehearsing the fixing of customs for wool and grain, in practice another restatement of earlier concessions. Specific to Jersey, but consistent with the Guernsey charter of 1604 through to the end of [8]; from the enrolment in The National Archives, C 66/1654, mm. 5–6, with reference to the edition presented in Prison Board, to which page references are provided, as [277] (etc.).

JACOBUS Dei gratia Anglie Scocie Francie et Hibernie Rex fidei defensor etc Omnibus ad quos presentes litere peruenerint salutem.

[1] Cum dilecti et fideles ligei et subditi nostri Balliuus et Jurati Insule nostre de Jersey ac ceteri Incole et habitatores ipsius Insule infra Ducatum nostrum Normanie et predecessores eorum a tempore cuius contrarii memoria hominum non existit per seperales cartas concessiones confirmationes et amplissima diplomata illustrium progenitorum et Antecessorum nostrorum tam Regum et Reginarum Anglie quam Ducum Normanie et aliorum quamplurima Jura iurisdiccionibus priuilegiis immunitatibus libertatibus exemptionibus et franchesiis libere quiete et inuiolabiliter vsi freti et gauisi fuerunt tam infra regnum nostrum Anglie quam alibi infra Dominia et loca ditioni nostre subiecta vltra citraque mare Quorum ope et beneficio Insula prenominata ac loca maritima in fide obediencia et seruicio tam nostris quam eorundem Progenitorum nostrorum constanter fideliter et inculpate perstiterunt ac perseuerauerunt liberaque commercia cum Mercatoribus ac aliis indigenis et alienigenis tam pacis quam belli temporibus habuerunt et exercuerunt Judicia eciam et cogniciones omnium et omnimodo causarum et querelarum accionum placitorum tam ciuilium quam criminalium et capitalium ac iudicialem potestatem ea omnia tractandi decidendi discutiendi audiendi et terminandi atque in eisdem procedendi et in Acta redigendi secundum leges et consuetudines Insule et locorum predictorum ex antiquo receptas et approbatas (preterquam in certis casubus cognitioni nostre Regie reseruatis de tempore in tempus exercuerunt executi Sunt et peregerunt.

[2] Que omnia et singula cuius et quanti momenti sunt et fuerunt ad tutelam et conseruationem Insule et locorum maritimorum predictorum in fide et obediencia Corone nostre Anglie Nos (ut equum est) perpendentes neque non immemores quam fortiter et fideliter Insulani predicti ac ceteri Incole et habitatores ibidem nobis et progenitoribus nostris inseruierunt quantaque detrimenta dampna et pericula tam pro assidua tuicione eiusdem Insule et locorum quam pro recuperacione et defensione Castri nostri de Mounte Orguill infra predictam Insulam nostram de Jersey sustinuerunt indiesque sustinent non

solum vt Regia nostra beneuolencia fauor et affectus erga prefatos Insulanos illustri aliquo nostre beneficencie testimonio ac certis iudiciis [sic – prefer previous reading of Indiciis] comprobetur verum eciam vt ipsi et eorum posteri deinceps imperpetuum prout antea solitam et debitam obedienciam erga nos heredes et successores nostros teneant et inuiolabiliter obseruent has literas nostras patentes magno sigillo nostro Anglie roboratas in forma qua sequitur illis concedere dignati sumus.

[3] Sciatis quod nos de gracia nostra speciali ac ex certa sciencia et mero motu nostris Dedimus et concessimus ac pro nobis heredibus et successoribus nostris per presentes Damus et concedimus prefatis Balliuo et Juratis Insule nostre de Jersey predicte ac ceteris Incolis et habitatoribus dicte Insule quod ipsi et eorum quilibet licet in presentibus non recitati seu cogniti per seperalia nomina sint et erunt semper infuturum ita liberi quieti et immunes in omnibus Ciuitatibus Burgis emptoriis et Nundinis mercatis villis mercatoriis et aliis locis ac portubus infra Regnum nostrum Anglie ac infra omnes prouincias dominia territoria et loca dicioni nostre subiecta tam citra quam vltra mare de et ab omnibus vectigalibus theoloneis custumiis subsidiis hidagiis tallagiis pontagiis pannagiis muragiis fossagiis operibus expeditionibus bellicis nisi in casu vbi corpus nostri heredum vel successorum nostrorum (quod absit) in prisona detineatur et de et ab omnibus aliis contribucionibus oneribus et exaccionibus quibuscunque nobis heredibus et successoribus nostris quouismodo debitis reddendis seu soluendis prout prefata Insula virtute aliquarum Cartarum Concessionum Confirmacionum siue diplomatum per predictos progenitores siue Antecessores [278] nostros quondam Reges Anglie et Duces Normanie siue alios seu virtute et vigore alicuius racionabilis et legalis vsus prescripcionis seu consuetudinis vnquam aliquando fuerunt aut esse debuerunt vel potuerunt debuit vel quouismodo potuit.

[4] Cumque nonnulla alia priuilegia iurisdicciones immunitates libertates et franchesie per predictos progenitores et predecessores nostros quondam Reges Anglie et Duces Normannie ac alios prefatis Insulanis indulta donata concessa et confirmata fuerunt ac a tempore cuius contrarii memoria hominum non existit infra Insulam et loca maritimos prenominatos inuiolabiliter vsitata et obseruata fuerunt de quibus vnum est quod tempore belli omnium nacionum Mercatores et alii tam alienigene quam indigene tam hostes quam amici libere licite et impune queant et possint dicte Insule et locis maritimis cum nauibus mercibus et bonis suis tam pro euitandis tempestatibus quam pro aliis licitis suis negociis inibi peragendis adire accidere commeare et frequentare ac libera commercia negociacionis ac rem mercatoriam ibidem exercere ac tuto et secure commorari indeque commeare et redire toties quoties absque damno molestia seu hostilitate quacunque in rebus mercibus bonis aut corporibus suis idque non solum infra Insulam et locos maritimos predictos ac procinctum earum

verumeciam infra spacia vndique ab eisdem distantia vsque ad visum hominis id est quatenus visus oculi posset assequi Nos eandem immunitatem impunitatem libertatem et priuilegia ac cetera omnia premissa vltime recitata rata grataque habentes ea pro nobis heredibus et successoribus nostris quantum in nobis est prefatis Balliuo et Juratis ac ceteris incolis habitatoribus Mercatoribus et aliis tam hostibus quam amicis et eorum cuilibet per presentes indulgemus ac elargimur authoritateque nostra regia renouamus reiteramus et confirmamus in tam amplis modo et forma prout incole et habitatores Insule predicte ac predicti indigene et alienigene Mercatores et alii preantea vsi vel gauisi fuerunt vel vti et gaudere debuerunt. Vniuersis igitur et singulis magistratibus Ministris et subditis nostris per vniuersum Regnum nostrum Anglie ac cetera Dominia et loca ditioni nostre subiecta vbilibet constitutis per presentes denunciamus et firmiter Iniungendo praecipimus ne hanc nostram donacionem concessionem et confirmacionem seu aliquid in eisdem expressum aut contentum temerarie aut aliter infringere seu quouismodo inuiolare presumant Et si quis ausu temerario contra fecerit seu attemptauerit volumus et decernimus quantum in nobis est quod restituat non solum ablata aut erepta sed quod eciam pro damno interesse et expensis ad plenariam recompensacionem et satisfaccionem compellatur per quecunque iuris nostri remedia seuereque puniatur vt regie nostre potestatis ac legum nostrarum contemptor temerarius.

[5] Preterea ex vberiori gracia nostra pro nobis heredibus et successoribus nostris per presentes ratificamus approbamus stabilimus et confirmamus omnes et singulas leges et consuetudines infra Insulam et locos maritimos predictos rite et legitime vsitatas et ex antiquo receptas et approbatas Dantes et tribuentes prefatis Balliuo et Juratis ac omnibus aliis Magistratibus Ministris et ceteris quibuscunque ibidem in Officio et funccione aliquo constitutis plenam integram et absolutam authoritatem potestatem et facultatem ordinandi cognoscendi iurisdicendi et iudicandi de se et super omnibus et omnimodis placitis processibus litibus accionibus querelis et causis quibuscunque [279] infra Insulam et loca predicta emergentibus tam personalibus realibus et mixtis quam criminalibus et capitalibus eaque omnia et singula ibidem et non alibi placitandi et peragendi prosequendi et defendendi atque in eisdem vel prosequendi vel supersedendi examinandi audiendi terminandi absoluendi condemnandi decidandi atque execucioni mandandi secundum leges et consuetudines Insule et locorum maritimorum predictorum preantea vsitatas et approbatas absque prouocacione seu appellacione quacunque preterquam in casibus qui cognicioni nostre regali ex antiqua consuetudine Insule et locorum predictorum reseruantur vel de iure aut priuilegio nostro regali reseruari debentur. Quamquidem authoritatem potestatem et facultatem preterquam in eisdem casibus reseruatis nos pro nobis heredibus et successoribus nostris prefatis Balliuo et Juratis ac aliis Damus comittimus concedimus et confirmamus per presentes adeo plene libere et integre prout prefati Balliuus et Jurati ac alii

vel eorum aliquis vnquam antehac eisdem rite et legitime vsi functi aut gauisi sunt vel vti fungi et gaudere debuerunt aut licite potuerunt debuit aut potuit.

[6] Volumus preterea ac pro nobis heredibus et successoribus nostris per presentes concedimus prefatis Balliuo et Juratis ac aliis Incolis et habitatoribus infra Insulam et locos maritimos predicta quod nullus eorum de cetero per aliqua breuia seu processus ex aliquibus Curiis nostris seu aliorum infra Regnum nostrum Anglie emergencia siue earum aliqua citetur apprehendatur euocetur in placita trahatur siue quouismodo aliter comparere aut respondere cogatur extra Insulam et locos maritimos predictos coram quibuscunque Judicibus Justiciariis Magistratibus aut Officiariis nostris aut aliis de aut super aliqua re lite materia seu causa quacunque infra Insulam predictam emanente Sed quod Insulani predicti et eorum quilibet huiusmodi citationibus apprehensionibus breuibus et processubus non obstantibus licite et impune valeant et possint infra Insulam et loca predicta residere commorari quiescere et Justiciam ibidem expectare absque aliqua pena corporali seu pecuniario fine redempcione aut mulcta proinde incurrenda forisfacienda Necnon absque aliqua offensione vel causa contemptus seu contumacie per nos heredes et successores nostros illis seu eorum alicui aut aliquibus proinde infligendi irrogandi vel aliter adiudicandi (exceptis tantummodo huiusmodi casubus qui per leges Insule et locorum predictorum Regali nostre cognicioni atque examini reseruentur vel de Jure vel priuilegio nostro Regali reseruari debentur.

[7] Et Vlterius de ampliori gratia nostra ac ex certa sciencia et mero motu nostris Dedimus concessimus et confirmauimus ac per presentes pro nobis heredibus et successoribus nostris (quantum in nobis est) Damus concedimus et confirmamus prefatis Balliuo et Juratis ceterisque Incolisque et habitatoribus Insule et locorum maritimorum predictorum Necnon Mercatoribus et aliis eo confluentibus tot tanta talia huiusmodi et Consimilia iura iurisdicciones immunitates impunitates indempnitates exempciones libertates franchesias et libertates [sic – repeats] quecunque quot quanta qualia et que prefati Balliuus et Jurati ac ceteri Incole et habitatores Mercatores et alii aut eorum aliquis antehac legitime et rite vsi freti seu gauisi fuerunt vsus fretus seu gauisus fuit ac omnia et singula quecunque alia in aliquibus cartis ordinacionibus aut literis patentibus nostris seu progenitorum seu Antecessorum nostrorum quondam Regum et Reginarum Anglie seu Ducum Normanie aut aliorum eis seu eorum predecessoribus antehac data concessa vel confirmata et non reuocata seu abolita quocunque nomine seu quibuscunque nominibus iidem Balliuus Jurati et ceteri Incole et habitatores eiusdem Insule et locorum maritimorum predictorum aut eorum predecessores seu eorum aliqui vel aliquis in eisdem literis patentibus seu eorum aliquibus censeantur nuncupentur aut vocentur seu censeri nuncupari aut vocitari debuerunt seu soliti fuerunt ac ea omnia et singula licet in presentibus minime expressa prefatis Balliuo

et Juratis ac ceteris Incolis et habitatoribus Insule et locorum maritimorum predictorum Necnon Mercatoribus et aliis eo confluentibus indigenis et alienigenis per presentes confirmamus consolidamus et de integro ratificamus adeo plene libere et integre prout ea omnia et singula in eisdem literis patentibus contenta modo particulariter verbatim et expresse in presentibus literis nostris patentibus recitata et declarata fuissent.

[8] Salua Semper atque illabefacta suprema regia potestate dominacione atque imperio Corone nostre Anglie tam quoad ligeanciam subieccionem et obedienciam Insulanorum predictorum et aliorum quorumcunque [sic] infra Insulam et loca predicta commorancium siue degencium quam quoad Regalitatem priuilegia res redditus vectigalia ac cetera iura proficua commoditates ac emolumenta quecunque infra Insulam et loca predicta nobis et heredibus et successoribus nostris per prerogatiuam Corone nostre Anglie siue Ducatus Normanie seu aliter ex antiquo debita et consueta. Saluis eciam appellacionibus et prouocacionibus quibuscunque Insulanorum predictorum ac aliorum ibidem comorancium siue degencium in omnibus eiusmodi casubus que legibus et consuetudinibus Insule et locorum predictorum regali nostre cognitioni atque examini reseruantur vel de iure aut priuilegio nostro Regali reseruari debentur Aliqua sentencia clausula re aut materia quacunque superius in presentibus expressa et specificata in contrarium inde in aliquo non obstantibus.

[9] Prouiso semper quod aliqua Clausula Articulus siue aliquod aliud in presentibus Literis nostris Patentibus expresum et specificatum non exponantur interpretentur nec se extendent ad aliquod quod sit vel fieri possit nobis heredibus vel successoribus nostris preiudiciale quoad aliqua terras tenementa redditus regalitates vel hereditamenta nostra infra Insulam predictam & loca maritima predicta aut eorum aliqua.

[10] Et insuper cum datum est nobis intelligi quod quedam exaccio nuper leuata fuerit de Inhabitantibus et gentibus Insule nostre de Jersey predicta et Mercatoribus et aliis illic confluentibus contra antiquam extentam et consuetudinem ibidem vsitatam videlicet pro quolibet quarterio frumenti vel alterius grani extra Insulam illam exportato tres solidos et sex denarios monete currentis infra eandem Insulam vbi illa Extenta antehac ad tantam summam se non extendebat vt accipimus Et cum dicti Inhabitantes et Gentes Insule de Jersey predicta soliti fuerunt similiter solvere ad vsum Progenitorum siue Antecessorum nostrorum pro quibuslibet Centum & quinquaginta libris lane extra Insulam illam exportatæ iuxta extentam ibidem vsitatam quatuor denarios monete currentis infra eandem Insulam Nos volumus ac per presentes pro nobis heredibus et successoribus nostris concedimus prefatis Inhabitantibus et gentibus Insule nostre de Jersey predicta quod ipsi et omnes alii Mercatores illuc confluentes non plus nec maiorem summam exnunc deinceps imperpetuum

soluere teneantur ad vsum nostrum quam duodecim denarios monete currentis infra eandem Insulam de Jersey pro quolibet quarterio frumenti siue alterius generis grani [281] extra eandem Insulam posthec exportandi. Ita semper et sub conditione quod iidem Inhabitantes et gens Insule de Jersey predicta ac omnes alii Mercatores et extranei illuc confluentes soluere debeant et teneantur posthac imperpetuum ad vsum nostrum pro quibuslibet Centum et quinquaginta libris lane extra Insulam illam exportandis tres solidos et dimidium monete currentis infra eandem Insulam et loca maritima predicta seu eorum aliqua.

[11] Volumus etiam etc. absque fine in Hanaperio etc. Eo quod expressa mencio etc. In cuius re etc. Teste Regis apud Westmonasterium vii die Aprilis

                                            Per breue de priuato sigillo etc.

Translation

James, by the grace of God, king of England, Scotland, France, and Ireland, Defender of the Faith, etc.

[1] To all to whom these present letters shall come, greeting. Whereas our beloved and faithful lieges and subjects, the bailiff and the jurats of our Island of Jersey, and the other sojourners in and inhabitants of the same island within our duchy of Normandy, and their predecessors, have from time beyond what the memory of men can reach, by virtue of several charters, grants, confirmations, and most ample writs, of our illustrious progenitors and ancestors, both kings and queens of England and dukes of Normandy, and others, used, enjoyed, and been in possession of very many rights, jurisdictions, privileges, immunities, liberties, and franchises, freely, quietly, and without any infringement of the same, both within the kingdom of England, and elsewhere within our dominions, and other places under our subjection on this side of, or beyond, the seas; by the aid and benefit of which grants, the aforesaid island and the maritime places have stood out and continued constantly, faithfully, and unblameably in faith, obedience, and service as well to us as to those same progenitors of ours, and have enjoyed and gone on in their commerce and trade with merchants, both natives and aliens, as well in time of peace, as in time of war, and exercised and executed their duties in giving their decrees, and taking cognisance of all and every cause, quarrel, action, both civil and criminal, and capital pleas; and the right of jurisdiction they were vested with, to take into their consideration, to take order, decide, discuss, hear, and determine, and to proceed in the premises, and keep records of their proceedings according to the laws and customs practised of old, and approved in the said island and other places aforesaid; except in certain cases reserved from time to time to our royal cognisance.

[2] And we considering of how great advantage and moment all and singular the premises are, and have been, toward the safe-keeping and conservation of the aforesaid island and maritime places in their fidelity and allegiance to our crown of England; and being always mindful (as is just) how courageously and loyally the said islanders and inhabitants have behaved themselves in our own and in our progenitors' service, and considering what great detriments, losses and dangers they have sustained and do daily sustain, both for the constant safeguarding of the said islands and places, and for the recovery and defence of our Castle of Mont Orgueil, in our aforesaid island of Jersey; to the end, not only to show some distinguished testimony and certain marks of our favour, affection, and royal beneficence towards the inhabitants aforesaid, but also to encourage them, and their posterity for ever, to persevere and continue inviolably in their accustomed and due obedience towards us, and our heirs and successors, we have thought proper to grant to them these our royal letters patent, confirmed under our great seal of England, in form following.

[3] Know ye, that we, of our special favour, certain knowledge, and mere motion, have given and granted, and for ourselves, our heirs and successors, we do by these present letters give and grant, to the said bailiff and jurats of our island of Jersey aforesaid, and to the other sojourners and inhabitants of the same island; that they themselves and every one of them (though not herein stated or declared by their particular names) have been and shall be, for the time to come, for ever free, exempted, and acquitted, in all our cities, boroughs, markets, and trading towns, and fairs, mart-towns, and other places and ports, within our kingdom of England, and within all our provinces, dominions, territories, and other places under our subjection, this side of, or beyond, the seas, from and of all tributes, tolls, customs, subsidies, hidage, taylage, pontage, panage, murage, fossage, works, and warlike expeditions (except in case our body, or that of our heirs and successors, should be held in prison (which God avert)), and of and from all other contributions, burdens, and exactions whatsoever, that may be due from, to be rendered by, or be payable by, and claimed from, the said islanders, to us, our heirs and successors, ever in any manner, by virtue of any charters, grants, confirmations, and writs of our said progenitors, formerly kings of England and dukes of Normandy, or others, or by virtue or reason of any reasonable and legal usage, prescription, or custom.

[4] And whereas some other privileges, jurisdictions, immunities, liberties, and franchises have been graciously given, granted, and confirmed by our progenitors and predecessors, formerly kings of England and dukes of Normandy, and others, to the aforesaid islanders, and have been used and observed constantly in the said islands and other maritime places, from the time whereof the memory of men reaches not to the contrary; one of which is, that in time of war merchants of all nations and others, both aliens and natives, both enemies

and friends, could and might freely, lawfully, without danger or punishment, come to, resort to, go to and fro, and frequent the said islands, and other aforesaid maritime places, with their ships, merchandise, and goods; both to avoid storms, and to conduct their other lawful business there, and to exercise there free commerce, business and trade, and securely, and without danger, remain there, and depart from thence, and return to the same, as often as they think fit, without any harm, molestation, or hostility whatsoever, in their goods, merchandise, or persons; and this not only within the said islands and maritime places, and all around the same, but likewise at such spaces and distances from the islands as the sight of man goes to, that is as far as the eye of man can reach: We, by virtue of our royal authority, do, for ourselves, our heirs and successors, indulge and enlarge, and renew, reiterate, and confirm, by these present letters, as far as in us lies, the same immunities, impunities, liberties, and privileges, and all the other premisses last mentioned, finding them to be reasonable and seasonable, to the said bailiff and jurats, and the other sojourners, inhabitants and merchants, and others, whether enemies or friends, and to each of them, in as ample form and manner as heretofore they, the said sojournors and inhabitants of the aforesaid island and the aforesaid merchants whether alien or native, have used or enjoyed the same, or ought to have used an enjoyed them. In order therefore to prevent any violation or infraction of this our grant, concession, and confirmation, or any thing therein contained, in any manner whatsoever, we declare and give this warning by these present letters to all our magistrates, officers and subjects in all parts of our kingdom of England, and throughout all our lordships and places under our obedience, wheresoever they lie, or are situated. And if any one of our said officers and subjects shall rashly or otherwise presume or attempt to transgress these our strict orders and commands, we order and decree (as far as in us lies), that he shall not only restore what has been taken or seized, but shall also be compelled to make a fuller restitution and satisfaction of all costs, interests, and damages, by whatever legal remedy, and he shall be severely punished for his audacious contempt of our royal power, and of our laws.

[5] Further, we, of our more gracious favour, do, for ourselves and our heirs and successors, by these present letters, ratify, approve, establish, and confirm, all and every one of the laws and customs which have been duly and legally from ancient times used, received, and approved within the aforesaid islands and maritime places; giving and granting to the aforesaid bailiff and jurats, and all other magistrates and officers of justice, and others who are appointed for performing the functions and executing the duties of any office, full and absolute authority, power, and faculty to have the cognisance, jurisdiction, and judgment concerning and touching all and all sorts of pleas, processes, law-suits, actions, quarrels, and causes arising within the island and places aforesaid; both those actions which are personal, real, and mixed, and those

which are criminal and capital, and to proceed there and not elsewhere, in hearing the parties in their pleadings, and prosecutions of their processes, in their defence; and to hear, examine, and supersede the same, making decrees, determining, absolving, condemning, and putting their sentences in execution, according to the laws and customs previously practised and approved in the island and maritime places aforesaid; without admitting any challenge or appeal, except in such cases as are reserved to our royal cognisance by the ancient customs of the island and places aforesaid, or which by our right or royal privilege ought to be reserved. Which authority, power, and faculty (except in the cases reserved to us), we commit, give, grant, and confirm, for ourselves and our heirs and successors aforesaid, to the said bailiffs and jurats, and to the others, by these present letters, as freely, fully, and entirely, as the said bailiff and jurats, or others or any of them, heretofore have rightfully and lawfully used, practised, and enjoyed, or might legally have used and enjoyed.

[6] Moreover, our will and pleasure is, and we grant, for ourselves, our heirs, and successors by these present letters, to the said bailiff and jurats, and the other inhabitants and sojourners in the islands and maritime places aforesaid, that for the time to come, none of them be cited, apprehended, summoned, or drawn into any lawsuit, or forced in any manner by any writs or process, issued from any of our courts, or the courts of others, within our kingdom of England, to appear and answer before any judges, courts, or other officers of justice of ourselves or others, out of the island and maritime places aforesaid, touching or concerning any thing, dispute, causes, or matters in controversy whatsoever, arising in the aforesaid island, but that the aforesaid islanders, and each of them, may lawfully and with impunity, notwithstanding the said citations, warrants, writs and processes, remain, reside quietly, and abide in the aforesaid island and places, waiting for justice there; without incurring any punishment, corporal or pecuniary, by way of fine, mulct, ransom, or forfeiture, by reason of any offence, contempt, or contumacy, committed towards us, our heirs and successors, for which they might be sued, arraigned, or condemned; except only in the cases, which by the laws of the island and places aforesaid are reserved to our royal cognisance and determination, or which by our right or royal privilege ought to be reserved.

[7] And moreover, of our more gracious favour, certain knowledge, and mere motion, we have given, granted, and confirmed, and by our present letters, for ourselves, our heirs and successors (as far as in us lies), we do give, grant, and confirm to the aforesaid bailiff and jurats, and other sojourners in, and inhabitants of, the aforesaid islands and maritime places; as also to merchants and others meeting there, the like, and as great, and as ample rights, jurisdictions, immunities, impunities, indemnities, exemptions, liberties, franchises, and liberties [sic] whatsoever, as the aforesaid bailiff and jurats, and other

sojourners and inhabitants, and merchants and others, or any of them, have heretofore rightfully and legally used, practised, and enjoyed; and all and singular other things whatsoever that has been heretofore given, granted, and confirmed to them or to their predecessors, in any charters, ordinances, or letters patent, of us or our progenitors, formerly kings and queens of England, or dukes of Normandy, or others, and not revoked or abolished, by whatsoever name or names the same bailiff and jurats, and other sojourners in, or inhabitants of, the same islands and maritime places aforesaid, or their predecessors, or any of them, may be supposed to have been comprised, called, or named, or ought to have been called or named, in the said letters patent, and all and singular which things, though not herein expressly mentioned, we do by these present letters confirm, consolidate, and ratify anew to the aforesaid bailiff and jurats, and other sojourners, and inhabitants, of the islands and maritime places aforesaid, and also merchants and others coming together there, those born there, and those born elsewhere, as fully, freely, and entirely, as if all and singular the things particularly mentioned and declared in the same letters patent were particularly and expressly recited and declared in these our present letters patent.

[8] Saving always entire and without detriment the regal and sovereign power, dominion, and empire of our crown of England, as to what may concern the allegiance, subjection, and obedience of the aforesaid islanders, and others, whoever they may be, dwelling for a shorter or longer time in the same island; and also as to what may concern the regality, privileges, incomes, revenues, tributes, and other rights, profits, commodities, and emoluments whatsoever, anciently due and accustomed to be paid to us, our heirs and successors, according to our royal prerogative as kings of England, or the prerogative of the duchy of Normandy, in the islands and places aforesaid; saving also to the aforesaid islanders, and others dwelling or being in the said islands, a right to appeal in all cases reserved to our cognisance and consideration by the laws and customs of the said island, or where by our right or royal privilege it ought to be reserved: notwithstanding any sentence, clause, thing, or matter whatsoever expressed above, or specially contained to the contrary in these present letters.

[9] Provided always that any clause, article, or any other thing expressed and specified in our present letters patent are not construed, interpreted nor extended to any thing that might be prejudicial to us, our heirs, or successors with regards to any of our lands, tenements, rents, regalities, or inheritances within the aforesaid island and maritime places or any of them.

[10] And in addition, since we are given to understand that an exaction has recently been levied upon the inhabitants and peoples of our island of Jersey

aforesaid, and on merchants and others gathering there against the ancient extent and custom there used, that is to say for each quarter of corn or other grain exported from the island three shillings and six pence in money current within the island, when that extent previously did not, as we understand, extend to so large a sum.

And since the said inhabitants and people of the aforesaid isle of Jersey were accustomed in the same way to pay to the use of our progenitors or ancestors for every one hundred and fifty pounds of wool exported from the island according to the extent there used four pence in the money current within the same island, we will, and by these present letters for us, our heirs, and successors do grant to the aforesaid inhabitants and peoples of our aforesaid island of Jersey, that they themselves, and all the other merchants gathering there from now henceforth for ever shall be bound to pay for our use a sum no more or greater than twelve pence in the money current within the same island of Jersey for each quarter of wheat or other type of grain hereafter exported from the same island. Thus, always, and on condition that the same inhabitants and peoples of the aforesaid island of Jersey and all other merchants and foreigners gathering there, owe and are bound to pay forever hereafter to our use for every one hundred and fifty pounds of wool exported from that island, three and a half shillings in the money current within the same island and aforesaid maritime places, or any of them.

[11] Furthermore, we wish etc. without fine in the Hanaper etc. [And that although] express mention etc.. In witness whereof etc.. Witness the king at Westminster the seventh day of April.

By writ of privy seal etc.

Charles I: 1627

Commentary

On 6 July 1627 Charles I confirmed the grant to Jersey made by his father James I. This action to continue the formulation of Jersey's rights, which sprang directly from the grant by Elizabeth I in 1562, was a natural response to the island's situation. Conflict with France was once more an important context for the royal grant, but it is equally significant set against another trend in Charles' policies, in the assertion of his personal authority.

Guernsey's charter, also issued in 1627, differed not only in confirming both the 1604 and 1605 charters for Guernsey, but also in additions relating

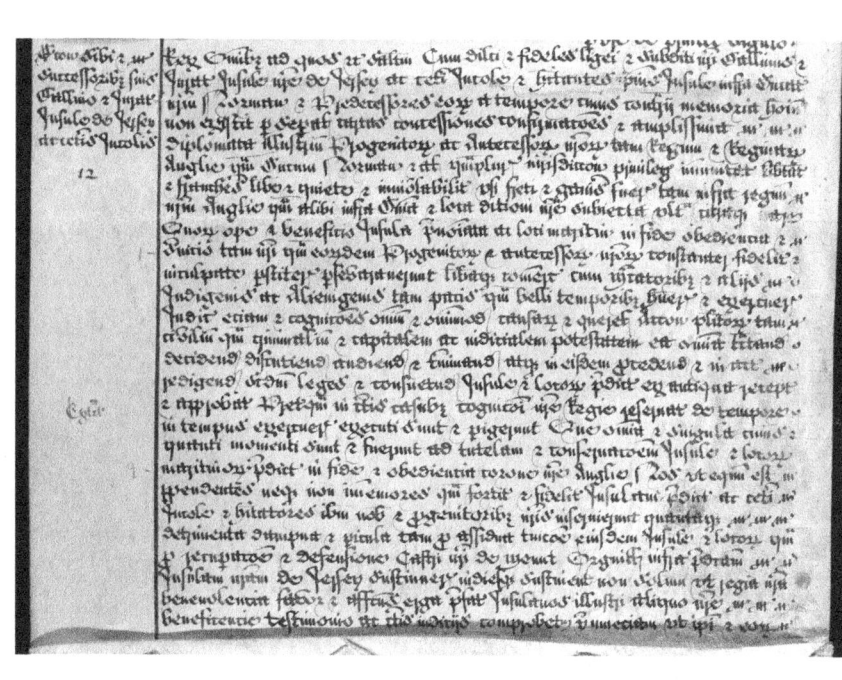

Plate 14 (i): The Royal Charter granted by Charles I in 1627.
Credit: The National Archives, ref. C 66/2431 (*continued overleaf*).

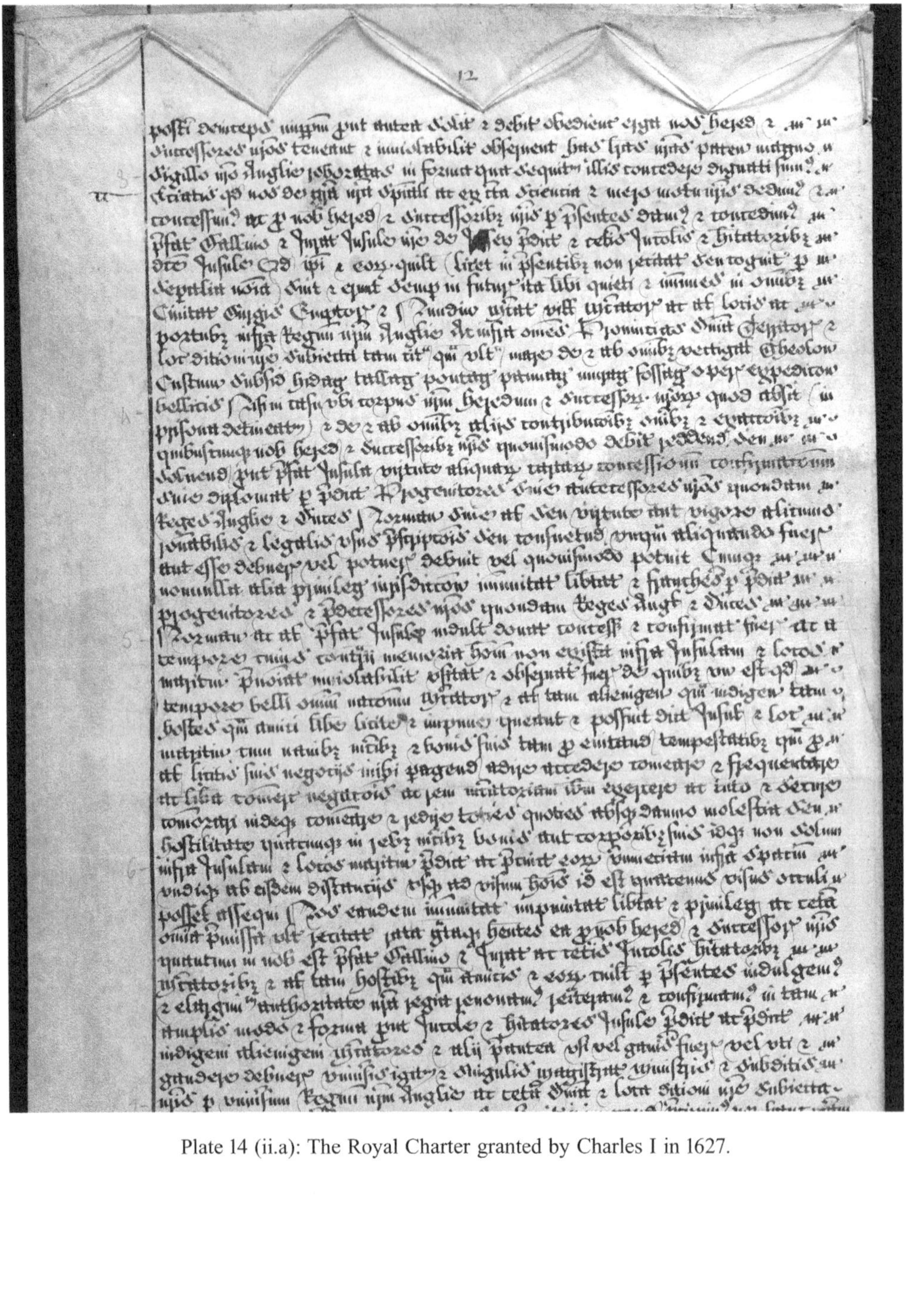

Plate 14 (ii.a): The Royal Charter granted by Charles I in 1627.

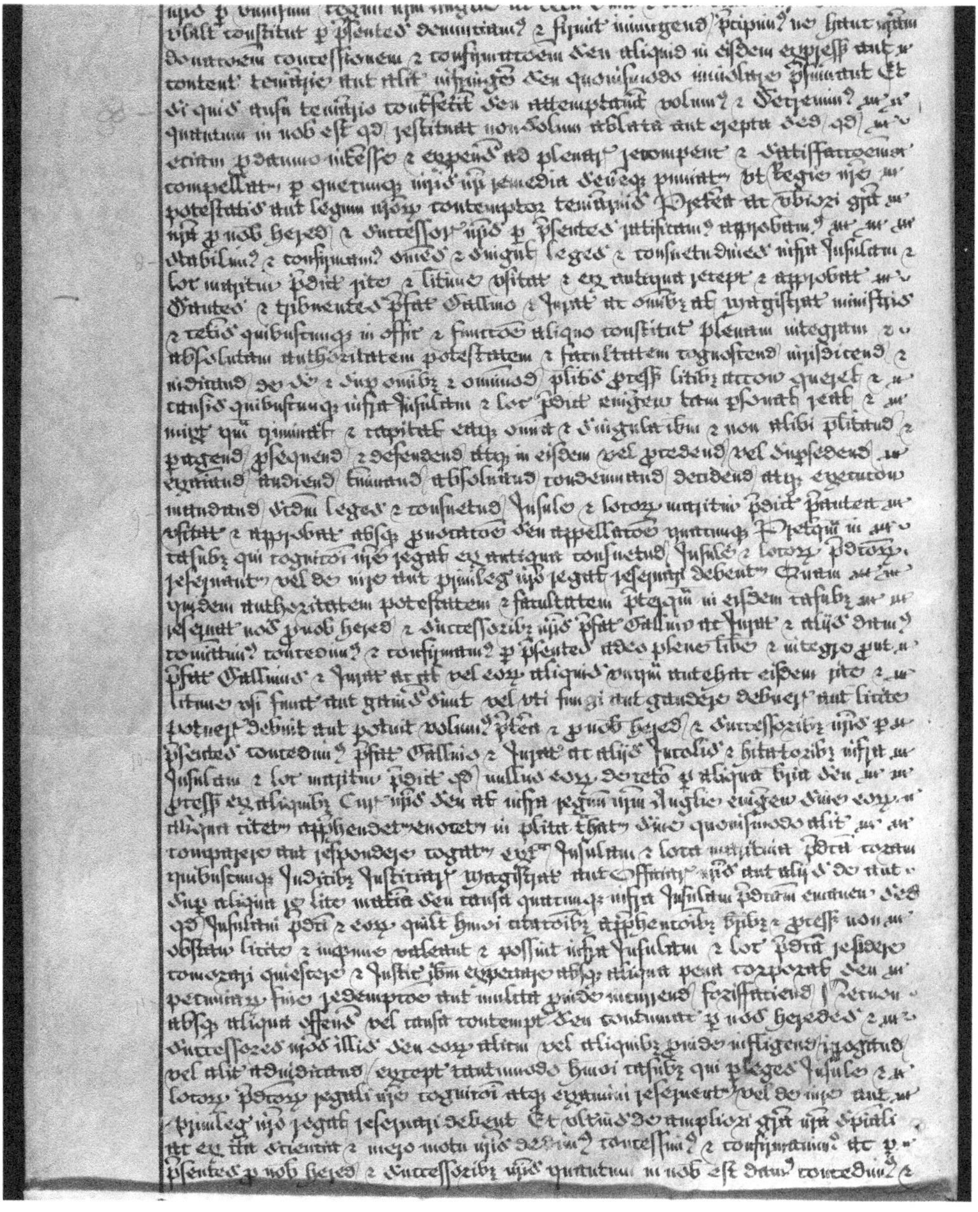

Plate 14 (ii.b): The Royal Charter granted by Charles I in 1627.

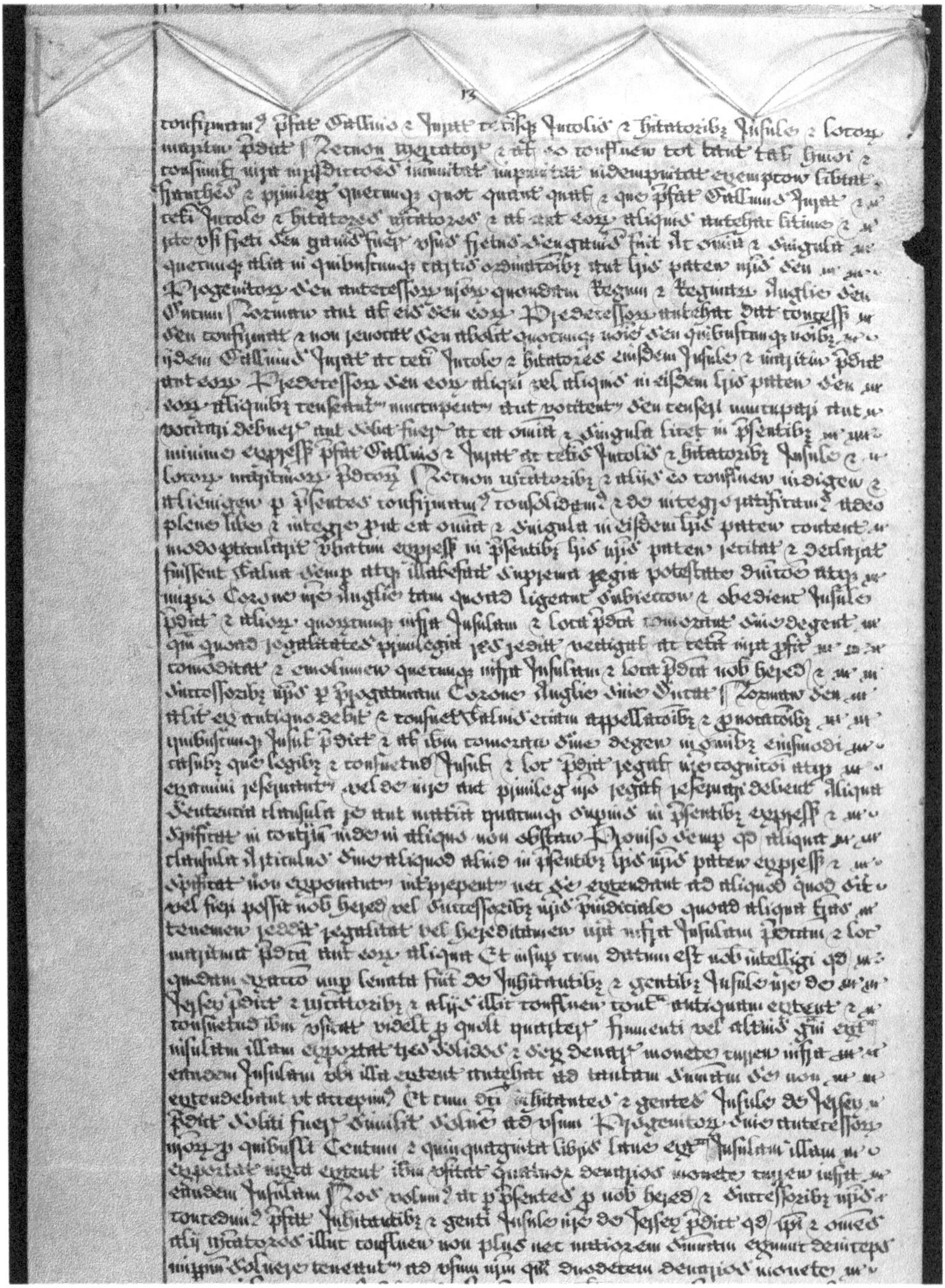

Plate 14 (iii.a): The Royal Charter granted by Charles I in 1627.

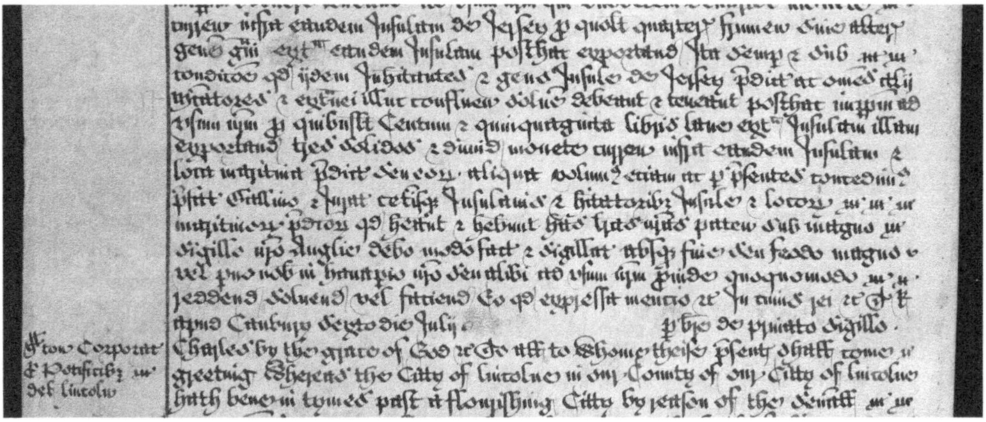

Plate 14 (iii.b): The Royal Charter granted by Charles I in 1627.

to the secularised properties associated with churches, chapels, hospitals and schools, which were safeguarded in the custody of the bailiff and jurats, and also a specific allowance of commodities to be exported without custom or other charges for the security of Castle Cornet and the island itself.[1]

During these years there were repeated rumours of a French threat to the islands, for example in 1626 when a pinnace was detailed to lie off Jersey to protect it, and in the summer of 1627 the defence of the islands was the one issue for which the recruitment of troops was maintained, albeit in the face of considerable logistical difficulties.[2] The English had been effectively at war with the French since the previous year. Hostilities were to worsen, and the islands' position was too vulnerable, and their communities' assistance too valuable, for there to be any incentive for major interference; further, the Huguenots, who might identify so closely with their co-religionists in the islands, were an ally of the English.[3] The English regime had suffered the

---

[1] Tim Thornton, *The Charters of Guernsey* (Bognor Regis, 2004), pp. 116–43. In Guernsey's case, we can trace the decision in 1626 to request the confirmation in *Actes des États de l'île de Guernesey* (8 vols, Guernsey, 1851–1938), vol. 1, pp. 70–2.

[2] *CSPD, 1625–26*, pp. 322, 336; *CSPD, 1627–28*, pp. 209, 227, 229, 234, 248, 253, 262, 264, 269, 274–6, 288, 296–7, 300, 306, 311, 313, 316–17, 347, 356, 361, 481; *CSP Venice, 1626–28*, p. 321, item 399; Royal Commission on Historical Manuscripts, *The Manuscripts of His Grace the Duke of Buccleuch and Queensberry K.G., K.T., preserved at Drumlanrig Castle* (3 vols, London, 1897–1926), vol. 3, pp. 318–19.

[3] For the general context of war and policy in these years, see Thomas Cogswell, *The Blessed Revolution: English Politics and the Coming of War, 1621–1624* (Cambridge, 1989); idem, 'Prelude to Ré: The Anglo-French Struggle over La Rochelle, 1624–1627', *History*, 71 (1986), 1–21.

acute embarrassment in 1625 of the ships it had loaned Louis XIII's chief minister Cardinal Richelieu being used to suppress an expected Huguenot uprising, making any chance of a French military alliance now impossible. Charles' marriage in 1625 to Louis' sister Henrietta Maria had not secured the amity of the kings, and the pressures on Charles at home had meant that he had not honoured most of the terms of the marriage treaty, while for their part the French did not lift the siege of La Rochelle as they had promised. Prohibitions on trade with Spain resulted in the seizure of many French ships by English captains in 1626. By the early part of 1627, when the concessions in the charters were made, the two nations' ships were clashing, and Charles was preparing an expedition to support the Huguenots in La Rochelle – which was to end in ruinous defeat on the Île de Ré.

Charles' well-known interest in reducing jurisdictional and especially religious autonomy across his realms and dominions prompts a comment on the way the 1627 charter continued so many of Jersey's liberties.[4] In the case of the Guernsey charter, although the specific reference to Nicholas Baudouin seen in the 1605 charter does not recur (unsurprisingly given his death on 16 April 1613), there is still the confirmation of the grant of 60 quarters of wheat for the minister of St Peter Port. In Jersey's case the grant made on 6 July very closely followed the example of James' reign in 1604.[5] Perhaps because of the challenging naval and military situation, in 1627 Charles and his ministers were happy to allow the islands' position to continue largely undisturbed.

Some of the first challenges to the status quo came in religious policy.[6] In Guernsey, Charles and his minister Archbishop Laud, in spite of the views of their governor, the earl of Danby, looked to challenge the Presbyterianism of the islanders, endowing scholarships in Oxford to train ministers committed to their form of Anglicanism, and even considering at one point removing all the children from the island to an education elsewhere as the only way of breaking the religious commitment of the islanders.[7] There are, in fact, hints in Guernsey's charter, if not in Jersey's, of what lay in store. Rights of free movement of goods were protected, but the charter's new clauses were the most restrictive of the sequence thus far. Quantities of goods were strictly limited, and customs officials were required to take sureties and keep records

---

[4] E.g. Conrad Russell, *The Causes of the English Civil War* (Oxford, 1990); idem, *The Fall of the British Monarchies, 1637–1642* (Oxford, 1991).

[5] TNA, C 66/2431, m. 12.

[6] Russell, *Causes of the English Civil War*, pp. 112–13.

[7] A. J. Eagleston, *The Channel Islands under Tudor Government, 1485–1642: A Study in Administrative History* (Cambridge, 1949), pp. 141–2; L. James Marr, *A History of the Bailiwick of Guernsey: The Islanders' Story* (Chichester, 1982), p. 20.

to ensure these limits were not exceeded. A growing challenge to the islands' position was beginning to make itself felt.[8]

In Jersey, the process of granting a straightforward confirmation of the island's rights was eased by the resolution of many of the previous reign's conflicts over civil and ecclesiastical authority. The contest between bailiff and governor came before the Council in the autumn of 1616, with a commission being appointed in March 1617 consisting of Sir Edward Conway, who, having been among other things governor of Brill in the Netherlands, brought to the role considerable military expertise and fervent Protestant commitment, and Sir William Bird, master in Chancery.[9] In their report of July of that year, they indicated that there had been no recent dramatic deterioration in the defensive readiness of the island, although the islanders' level of training and armaments left something to be desired. They therefore ordered an intensification of the manning of the castles and a twice-yearly review of the militia. On the question of the governor's position, however, they confirmed his overarching supremacy as having been given responsibility by the king for 'the charge and government of the Island'. That said, the settlement allowed for some aspects of the bailiff's case and petitions from the States, including the tax on wine for arms and the pier, the opening of records relating to revenue to scrutiny by jurats through their deposit in the Greffe, the confirmation of Elias de Carteret (Sir Philippe de Carteret's brother) as procureur (and hence of the governor's loss of that right over the law officers), and precedence for the bailiff over the governor, if only in the Royal Court and States.[10] The petitions also resulted in some other important changes, such as scholarships at English universities for islanders and the same rights in regard to wardship as had recently been agreed in England. As in Guernsey, this left a clear signal that the potential in civil matters for the local community to appeal to the support of the crown for the protection and even extension of its autonomy was significant.

The military threat to Jersey continued through the remaining years of the decade. In mid-March 1628 there were again rumours of an intended attack from France,[11] and the seriousness of the threat was evident when Sir Philippe de Carteret, governor of Jersey, was captured by five Dunkirker privateers off

---

[8] Thornton, *Charters of Guernsey*, p. 140. For Charles and the customs, and the difficulties of interpretation for those at the time, see for example, Pauline Croft, 'Fresh Light on Bate's Case', *Historical Journal*, 30 (1987), 523–39.

[9] TNA, SP 14/110/117, /122 (*CSPD, 1611–18*, pp. 445, 446–7). The king seems to have taken a personal interest, in January 1618, in Conway and Bird's views on Jersey: TNA, SP 14/95/4 (*CSPD, 1611–18*, p. 511).

[10] Toulmin Nicolle, 'Report of the Royal Commissioners sent to Jersey in 1617', *ABSJ*, 5 (1902–05), 386–96; Charles le Quesne, *Constitutional History of Jersey* (London, 1856), pp. 270–81.

[11] *CSPD, 1627–28*, p. 582; *CSP Venice, 1628–29*, p. 21, item 26.

the Isle of Wight on 20 March 1628.[12] Fears of French mustering in preparation for an attack on the islands grew in December 1628. The Venetian ambassador had heard through another source that the inhabitants were dissatisfied with the king of England.[13] The fears were, however, short-lived, having faded by the early part of January 1629.[14] Peace was to come, but in the meantime events continued to bear out the value of the island community's loyalty in a situation when control of the Channel was at stake.

Text

Charles I confirmed the 1604 charter of James I, itself a reiteration of the extensive grant of privileges made by Elizabeth in 1562. Specific to Jersey; from the enrolment in The National Archives, C 66/2431, m. 12, with reference to the edition presented in Prison Board, to which page references are provided, as [356] (etc.).

[1] Rex Omnibus ad quos etc salutem. Cum dilecti et fideles ligei et subditi nostri Balliuus et Jurati Insule nostre de Jersey ac ceteri Incole et habitantes ipsius Insule infra Ducatum nostrum Normanie et predecessores eorum a tempore cuius contrarii memoria hominum non existit per seperales cartas concessiones confirmaciones et amplissima diplomata illustrium Progenitorum ac antecessorum nostrorum tam Regum et Reginarum Anglie quam Ducum Normanie et aliorum quamplurima iurisdiccionibus priuilegiis immunitatibus libertatibus et franchesiis libere et quiete et inuiolabiliter vsi freti et gauisi fuerunt tam infra regnum nostrum Anglie quam alibi infra Dominia et loca ditioni nostre subiecta vltra citraque mare Quorum ope et beneficio Insula prenominata ac loci marittima in fide obediencia et seruicio tam nostri quam eorundem Progenitorum et antecessorum nostrorum constanter fideliter et inculpate perstiterunt perseuerauerunt liberaque commercia cum mercatoribus ac aliis indigenis et alienigenis tam pacis quam belli temporibus habuerunt et exercuerunt Judicia eciam et cogniciones omnium et omnimodo causarum et querelarum accionum placitorum tam ciuilium quam criminalium et capitalium ac iudicialem potestatem [Prison Board text here reads protestatem] ea omnia tractandi decidendi discutiendi audiendi et terminandi atque in eisdem procedendi et in acta redigendi secundum leges et consuetudines Insule et locorum predictorum ex antiquo receptas et approbatas Preterquam

---

[12] *CSPD, 1628–29*, pp. 41, 79; *CSP Venice, 1628–29*, p. 49, item 60 (5 April 1628); *CSPD 1628–29*, pp. 41, 79.
[13] *CSP Venice, 1628–29*, p. 438, item 628; pp. 457–58, item 655; p. 465, item 664; *CSPD 1628–29*, pp. 197, 409–11, 416, 419, 446, 450, 454, 484; *CSPD Addenda 1625–49*, p. 303.
[14] *CSP Venice, 1628–29*, p. 465, item 664 (5 January 1629).

in certis casubus cognitioni nostre Regie reseruatis de tempore in tempus exercuerunt executi sunt et perigerunt.

[2] Que omnia et singula cuius et quanti momenti sunt et fuerunt ad tutelam et conseruacionem Insule et locorum maritinorum predictorum in fide et obediencia corone nostre Anglie Nos vt equum est perpendentes neque non immemores quam fortiter et fideliter Insulani predicti ac ceteri incole et habitatores ibidem nobis et progenitoribus nostris inseruierunt quantaque detrimenta dampna et pericula tam pro assidua tuicione eiusdem Insule et locorum quam pro recuperacione et defensione Castri nostri de Mount Orguill infra predictam Insulam nostram de Jersey sustinuerunt indiesque sustinent non solum vt regia nostra beneuolencia [357] fauor et affectus erga prefatos Insulanos illustri aliquo nostre beneficencie testimonio ac ceteris iudiciis comprobetur verum eciam vt ipsi et eorum posteri deinceps imperpetuum prout antea solitam et debitam obedienciam erga nos heredes et successores nostros teneant et inuiolabiliter obseruent has literas nostras patentes magno sigillo nostro Anglie roboratas in forma qua sequitur illis concedere dignati sumus.

[3] Sciatis quod nos de gracia nostra speciali ac ex certa sciencia et mero motu nostris dedimus et concessimus ac pro nobis heredibus et successoribus nostris per presentes damus et concedimus prefatis Balliuo et Juratis Insule nostre de Jersey predicte ac ceteris incolis et habitatoribus dicte Insule Quod ipsi et eorum quilibet (licet in presentibus non recitati seu cogniti per seperalia nomina) sint et erunt semper in futurum ita liberi quieti et immunes in omnibus Ciuitatibus Burgis Emptoriis et Nundinis mercatis villis mercatoriis et aliis locis ac portubus infra Regnum nostrum Anglie ac infra omnes Prouincias Dominia Territoria et loca dicioni nostre subiecta tam citra quam vltra mare de et ab omnibus vectigalibus theoloneis custumiis subsidiis hidagiis tallagiis pontagiis pannagiis muragiis fossagiis operibus expeditionibus bellicis Nisi in casu vbi corpus nostrum heredum vel successorum nostrorum quod absit (in prisona detineatur) et de et ab omnibus aliis contribucionibus oneribus et exaccionibus quibuscunque nobis heredibus et successoribus nostris quouismodo debitis reddendis seu soluendis prout prefata Insula virtute aliquarum cartarum concessionum confirmacionum siue diplomatum per predictos progenitores siue antecessores nostros quondam Reges Anglie et Duces Normanie siue alios seu virtute et vigore alicuius racionabilis et legalis vsus prescripcionis seu consuetudinis vnquam aliquando fuerunt aut esse debuerunt vel potuerunt debuit vel quouismodo potuit.

[4] Cumque nonnulla alia priuilegia iurisdicciones immunitates libertates et franchesie per predictos progenitores et predecessores nostros quondam Reges Anglie et Duces Normannie ac alios prefate Insule indulta donata concessa et confirmata fuerunt ac a tempore cuius contrarii memoria hominum non

existit infra Insulam et locos maritimos prenominatos inuiolabiliter vsitata et obseruata fuerunt de quibus vnum est quod tempore belli omnium nacionum mercatores et alii tam alienigene quam indigene tam hostes quam amici libere licite et impune queant et possint dicte Insule et locis maritimis cum nauibus et bonis suis tam pro euitandis tempestatibus quam pro aliis licitis suis negociis inibi peragendis adire accedere commeare et frequentare ac Iibera commercia negociacionis ac rem mercatoriam ibidem exercere ac tuto et secure commorari indeque commeare et redire toties quoties absque damno molestia seu hostilitate quacunque in rebus mercibus bonis aut corporibus suis idque non solum infra Insulam et locos maritimos predictos ac procinctum eorum verum eciam infra spacium vndique ab eisdem distanciis vsque ad visum hominis id est quatenus visus occuli posset assequi Nos eandem immunitatem impunitatem libertatem et priuilegia ac cetera omnia premissa vltime recitata rata grataque habentes ea pro nobis heredibus et successoribus nostris quantum in nobis est prefatis Balliuo et Juratis ac ceteris Incolis habitatoribus mercatoribus et aliis tam hostibus quam amicis et eorum cuilibet per presentes indulgemus ac elargimur authoritata nostra regia renouamus reiteramus et confirmamus in tam amplis modo et forma prout Incole et habitatores Insule predicte ac predicti [358] indigeni alienigeni mercatores et alii preantea vsi vel gauisi fuerunt vel vti et gaudere debuerunt vniuersis igitur et singulis magistratus ministris et subditis nostris per vniuersum Regnum nostrum Anglie ac cetera Dominia et loca ditioni nostre subiecta vbilibet constitutis per presentes denunciamus et firmiter iniungendo praecipimus ne hanc nostram donaccionem concessionem et confirmacionem seu aliquid in eisdem expressum aut contentum temerarie aut aliter infringere seu quouismodo inuiolare presumant Et si quis ausu temerario contrafecerit seu attemptauerit volumus et decernimus quantum in nobis est quod restituat non solum ablata aut erepta sed quod eciam pro damno interesse et expensis ad plenariam recompensacionem et satisfaccionem compellatur per quecunque iuris nostri remedia seuereque puniatur vt Regie nostre potestatis aut legum nostrorum contemptor temerarius.

[5] Preterea ac [de] vberiori gracia nostra pro nobis heredibus et successoribus nostris per presentes ratificamus approbamus stabilimus et confirmamus omnes et singulas leges et consuetudines infra Insulam et locos maritimos predictos rite et legitime vsitatas et ex antiquo receptas et approbatas Dantes et tribuentes prefatis Balliuo et Juratis ac omnibus aliis Magistratibus Ministris et ceteris quibuscunque ibidem in officio et funccione aliquo constitutis plenam integram et absolutam authoritatem potestatem et facultatem cognoscendi iurisdicendi et iudicandi de se et super omnibus et omnimodis placitis processibus litibus accionibus querelis et causis quibuscunque infra Insulam et loca predicta emergentibus tam personalibus realibus et mixtis quam criminalibus et capitalibus eaque omnia et singula ibidem et non alibi placitandi peragendi prosequendi et defendendi atque in eisdem vel prosequendi vel supersedendi

examinandi audiendi terminandi absoluendi condemnandi decidandi atque execucioni mandandi secundum leges et consuetudines Insule et locorum maritimorum predictorum preantea vsitatas et approbatas absque prouocacione seu appellacione quacunque Preterquam in casubus qui cognicioni nostre regali ex antiqua consuetudine Insule et locorum predictorum reseruantur vel de iure aut priuilegio nostro regali reseruari debentur. Quam quidem authoritatem potestatem et facultatem preterquam in eisdem casubus reseruatis nos pro nobis heredibus et successoribus nostris prefatis Balliuo ac Juratis et aliis damus comittimus concedimus et confirmamus per presentes adeo plene libere et integre prout prefati Balliuus et Jurati ac alii vel eorum aliquis vnquam antehac eisdem rite et legitime vsi functi aut gauisi sunt vel vti fungi et gaudere debuerunt aut licite potuerunt debuit aut potuit.

[6] Volumus preterea ac pro nobis heredibus et successoribus nostris per presentes concedimus prefatis Balliuo et Juratis ac aliis Incolis et habitatoribus infra Insulam et locos maritimos predicta quod nullus eorum de cetero per aliqua breuia seu processus ex aliquibus Curiis nostris seu aliorum infra regnum nostrum Anglie emergencia siue eorum aliqua citetur apprehendetur euocetur in placita trahatur siue quouismodo aliter comparere aut respondere cogatur extra Insulam et loca maritina predicta coram quibuscunque Judicibus Justiciariis Magistratibus aut Officiariis nostris aut aliis de aut super aliqua re lite materia seu causa quacunque infra Insulam predictam emanente sed quod Insulani predicti et eorum quilibet huiusmodi citationibus apprehensionibus breuibus et processubus non obstantibus licite et impune valeant et possint infra Insulam et loca predicta residere commorari quiescere et Justiciam ibidem expectare absque aliqua pena corporali seu pecuniario fine redempcione aut mulcta proinde incurrenda [359] forisfacienda Necnon absque aliqua offensione vel causa contemptus seu contumacie [Prison Board here has continuac, almost certainly in error] per nos heredes et successores nostros illis seu eorum alicui vel aliquibus proinde infligendi irrogandi vel aliter adiudicandi exceptis tantummodo huiusmodi casubus qui per leges Insule et locorum predictorum regali nostre cognicioni atque examini reseruentur vel de iure aut priuilegio nostro regali reseruari debentur.

[7] Et vlterius de ampliori gratia nostra ac ex certa sciencia et mero motu nostris dedimus concessimus et confirmauimus ac per presentes pro nobis heredibus et successoribus nostris quantum in nobis est damus concedimus et confirmamus prefatis Balliuo et Juratis ceterisque Incolisque et habitatoribus Insule et locorum maritinorum predictorum Necnon mercatoribus et aliis eo confluentibus tot tanta talia huiusmodi et consimilia iura iurisdicciones immunitates impunitates indempnitates exempciones libertates franchesias et priuilegia quecunque quot quanta qualia et que prefati Balliuus Jurati ac ceteri Incole et habitatores mercatores et alii aut eorum aliquis antehac legitime et

rite vsi freti seu gauisi fuerunt vsus fretus seu gauisus fuit Ac omnia et singula quecunque alia in quibuscuque cartis ordinacionibus aut literis patentibus nostris seu progenitorum seu antecessorum nostrorum quondam Regum et Reginarum Anglie seu Ducum Normanie aut aliorum eis seu eorum predecessoribus antehac data concessa seu confirmata et non reuocata seu abolita quocunque nomine seu quibuscunque nominibus iidem Balliuus Jurati et ceteri Incole et habitatores eiusdem Insule et [locorum – missing word] maritinorum predictorum aut eorum predecessores seu eorum aliqui vel aliquis in eisdem literis patentibus seu eorum aliquibus censeantur nuncupentur aut vocitentur seu censeri nuncupari aut vocitari debuerunt aut soliti fuerunt ac ea omnia et singula licet in presentibus minime expressa prefatis Balliuo et Juratis ac ceteris Incolis et habitatoribus Insule et locorum maritinorum predictorum [Jersey Archive, D/AP/Z/5 survives from here:] Necnon mercatoribus et aliis eo confluentibus indigenis et alienigenis per presentes confirmamus consolidamus et de integro ratificamus adeo plene libere et integre prout ea omnia et singula in eisdem literis patentibus contenta modo particulariter verbatim et expresse in presentibus literis nostris patentibus recitata et declarata fuissent.

[8] Salua Semper atque illabefacta suprema regia potestate dominacione atque imperio Corone nostre Anglie tam quoad ligeanciam subieccionem et obedienciam Insule predicte et aliorum quorumcunque [sic] infra Insulam et loca predicta commorantium siue degentium quam quoad regalitates priuilegia res redditus vectigalia ac cetera iura proficua commoditates ac emolumenta quecunque infra Insulam et loca predicta nobis et heredibus et successoribus nostris per prerogatiuam Corone nostre Anglie siue Ducatus Normanie seu aliter ex antiquo debita et consueta. Saluis eciam appellacionibus et prouocacionibus quibuscunque Insulanorum predictorum ac aliorum ibidem comorancium siue degencium in omnibus eiusmodi casubus que legibus et consuetudinibus Insule et locorum predictorum regali nostre cognicioni atque examini reseruantur vel de iure aut priuilegio nostro regali reseruari debent aliqua sentencia clausula re aut materia quacunque superius in presentibus expressa et specificata in contrarium inde in aliquo non obstantibus.

[9] Prouiso semper quod aliqua clausula articulus siue aliquod aliud in presentibus literis nostris patentibus expressum et specificatum non exponantur interpretentur nec se exendant ad aliquod quod sit vel fieri possit nobis heredibus vel successoribus nostris preiudiciale quoad aliqua terras tenementa [360] redditus regalitates vel hereditamenta nostra infra Insulam predictam & loca maritina predicta aut eorum aliqua.

[10] Et insuper cum datum est nobis intelligi quod quedam exaccio nuper leuata fuerit de inhabitantibus et gentibus Insule nostre de Jersey predicta et mercatoribus et aliis illic confluentibus contra antiquam extentam et consuetudinem

ibidem vsitatam videlicet pro quolibet quarterio frumenti vel alterius grani extra Insulam illam exportato tres solidos et sex denarios monete currentis infra eandem Insulam vbi illa extenta antehac ad tantam summam se non extendebant vt accepimus. Et cum dicti inhabitantes et gentes Insule de Jersey predicta soliti fuerunt similiter soluere ad vsum progenitorum siue antecessorum nostrorum pro quibuslibet centum & quinquaginta libris lane extra Insulam illam exportatæ iuxta extentam ibidem vsitatam quatuor denarios monete currentis infra eandem Insulam Nos volumus ac per presentes pro nobis heredibus et successoribus nostris concedimus prefatis Inhabitantibus et gentibus Insule nostre de Jersey predicta quod ipsi et omnes alii mercatores illuc confluentes non plus nec maiorem summam exnunc deinceps imperpetuum soluere teneantur ad vsum nostrum quam duodecim denarios monete currentis infra eandem Insulam de Jersey pro quolibet quarterio frumenti siue alterius generis grani extra eandem Insulam posthac exportandi Ita semper et sub condicione quod iidem inhabitantes et gens Insule de Jersey predicta ac omnes alii mercatores et extranei illuc confluentes soluere debeant et teneantur posthac imperpetuum ad vsum nostrum pro quibuslibet centum et quinquaginta libris lane extra Insulam illam exportandis tres solidos et dimidium monete currentis infra eandem Insulam et loca maritima predicta seu eorum aliqua.

[11] Volumus etiam ac per presentes concedimus prefatis Balliuo et Juratis ceterisque Insulanis et habitatoribus Insule et locorum maritinorum predictorum quod habant et habebunt has litteras nostras absque fine seu feodo magno vel paruo nobis in Hanaperio nostro seu alibi ad vsum nostrum proinde quoquomodo redend soluend vel faciend. Eo quod expressa mencio [etc.] [de vero valore annuo aut de certitudine premissorum vel eorum alicuius aut – de aliis Donis siue Concessionibus per nos seu per aliquem Predecessorum nostrorum prefatis Balliuo et Juratis Insule nostre de Jersey predicte antehec tempora factis in presentibus minime fact' existit Aut aliquo Statuto Actu Ordinacione prouisione Proclamacione siue Restriccione antehac habitis factis editis ordinatis siue prouisis, aut aliqua alia re causa vel materia quacunque in contrarium inde in aliquo non obstante In cuius rei testimonium has literas nostras fieri fecimus patentes] In cuius re etc. Teste Regis [Teste me ipso] apud Canbury sexto die Julii [Anno Regnum nostri tercio]

[Wolseley]

per breue de priuato sigillo

Translation

[1] The King to all to whom etc., greeting. Whereas our beloved and faithful lieges and subjects, the bailiff and the jurats of our Island of Jersey, and the other sojourners in and inhabitants of the same island within our duchy of

Normandy, and their predecessors, have from time beyond what the memory of men can reach, by virtue of several charters, grants, confirmations, and most ample writs, of our illustrious progenitors and ancestors, both kings of England and dukes of Normandy, and others, used, enjoyed, and been in possession of very many jurisdictions, privileges, immunities, liberties, and franchises, freely and quietly, and without any infringement of the same, both within the kingdom of England, and elsewhere within our dominions, and other places under our subjection on this side of, or beyond, the seas; by the aid and benefit of which grants, the aforesaid island and maritime places have stood out and continued constantly, faithfully, and unblameably in faith, obedience, and service, as well to us as to those same progenitors and ancestors of ours, and have enjoyed and gone on in their commerce and trade with merchants, both natives and aliens, as well in time of peace, as in time of war, and exercised and executed their duties in giving their decrees, and taking cognisance of all and every cause, quarrel, action, both civil and criminal, and capital and judicial pleas; and the right of jurisdiction they were vested with, to take into their consideration, to take order, decide, discuss, hear, and determine, and to proceed in the premises, and keep records of their proceedings according to the laws and customs practised of old, and approved in the said island and other places aforesaid; except in certain cases reserved from time to time to our royal cognisance.

[2] And we considering of how great advantage and moment all and singular the premises are, and have been, toward the safe-keeping and conservation of the said aforesaid island and maritime places in their fidelity and allegiance to our crown of England; and being always mindful, as is just, how courageously and loyally the said islanders and inhabitants have behaved themselves in our own and in our progenitors' service, and considering what great detriments, losses and dangers they have sustained and do daily sustain, both for the constant safeguarding of the said island and places, and for the recovery and defence of our Castle of Mont Orgueil, in our aforesaid island of Jersey; to the end, not only to show some distinguished testimony and certain marks of our favour, affection, and royal beneficence towards the inhabitants aforesaid, but also to encourage them, and their posterity for ever, to persevere and continue inviolably in their accustomed and due obedience towards us, and our heirs and successors, we have thought proper to grant to them these our royal letters patent, confirmed under our great seal of England, in form following.

[3] Know ye, that we, of our special favour, certain knowledge, and mere motion, have given and granted, and for ourselves, our heirs and successors, we do by these present letters give and grant, to the said bailiff and jurats of our island of Jersey aforesaid, and to the other sojourners and inhabitants of the same island; that they themselves and every one of them (though not herein

stated or declared by their particular names) were and shall, for the time to come, be for ever free, exempted, and acquitted, in all our cities, boroughs, markets, and trading towns, fairs, mart-towns, and other places and ports, within our kingdom of England, and within all our provinces, dominions, territories, and other places under our subjection, this side of, or beyond, the seas, from and of all tributes, tolls, customs, subsidies, hidage, taylage, pontage, panage, murage, fossage, works, and warlike expeditions (except in case our body, or that of our heirs and successors, should be (held in prison) which God avert), and of and from all other contributions and exactions whatsoever, that may be due from, to be rendered by, or be payable by, and claimed from, the said islanders, or any of them, to us, our heirs and successors, ever in any manner, by virtue of any charters, grants, confirmations, and writs of our said progenitors, formerly kings of England and dukes of Normandy, or others, or by virtue or reason of any reasonable and legal usage, prescriptions, or custom.

[4] And whereas some other privileges, jurisdictions, immunities, liberties, and franchises have been graciously given, granted, and confirmed by our progenitors and predecessors, formerly kings of England and dukes of Normandy, and others, to the aforesaid islanders, and have been used and observed constantly in the said island and other maritime places, from the time whereof the memory of men reaches not to the contrary; one of which is, that in time of war merchants of all nations and others, both aliens and natives, both enemies and friends, could and might freely, lawfully, without danger or punishment, come to, resort to, go to and fro, and frequent the said island, and other aforesaid maritime places, with their ships and goods; both to avoid storms, and to conduct their other lawful business there, and to exercise there free commerce, business and trade, and securely, and without danger, remain there, and depart from thence, and return to the same, as often as they think fit, without any harm, molestation, or hostility whatsoever, in their goods, merchandise, or persons; and this not only within the said island and maritime places, and all around the same, but likewise at such spaces and distances from the island as the sight of man goes to, that is as far as the eye of man can reach: We, by virtue of our royal authority, do, for ourselves, our heirs and successors, indulge and enlarge, and renew, reiterate, and confirm, by these present letters, as far as in us lies, the same immunities, impunities, liberties, and privileges, and all the other premisses last mentioned, finding them to be reasonable and seasonable, to the said bailiff and jurats, and the other sojourners, inhabitants and merchants, and others, whether enemies or friends, and to each of them, in as ample form and manner as heretofore they have used and enjoyed the same, or should have used and enjoyed the same. In order therefore to prevent any violation or infraction, reckless or otherwise, of this our grant, concession, and confirmation, or any thing therein contained, in any manner whatsoever, we declare and give this warning by these present

letters to all our magistrates, officers and subjects in all parts of our kingdom of England, and throughout all our lordships and places under our obedience, wheresoever they lie, or are situated. And if any one of our said officers and subjects shall be so rash as to presume or attempt to transgress these our strict orders and commands, we order and decree (as far as in us lies), that he shall not only restore what has been taken or seized, but shall also be compelled to make a fuller restitution and satisfaction of all costs, interests, and damages, by whatever legal remedy, and he shall be severely punished for his audacious contempt of our royal power, or of our laws.

[5] Further, we, of our more gracious favour, for ourselves, our heirs and successors, do, by these present letters, ratify, approve, establish, and confirm, all and every one of the laws and customs which have been duly and legally used and from ancient times received and approved within the aforesaid island and maritime places; giving and granting to the aforesaid bailiff and jurats, and all other magistrates and officers of justice, and others who are appointed for performing the functions and executing the duties of any office, full and absolute authority, power, and faculty to have the cognisance, jurisdiction, and judgment concerning and touching all and all sorts of pleas, processes, law-suits, actions, quarrels, and causes arising within the island and maritime places aforesaid; both those actions which are personal, real, and mixed, and those which are criminal and capital, and to proceed in the said island, and not elsewhere, in hearing the parties in their pleadings, in prosecutions of their processes, and in their defence; and to hear, examine, and supersede the same, making decrees, determining, absolving, condemning, and putting their sentences in execution, according to the laws and customs previously practised and approved in the island and maritime places aforesaid; without admitting any challenge or appeal, except in such cases as are reserved to our royal cognisance by the ancient custom of the island and places aforesaid, or by our right and privilege ought so to be reserved. Which authority, power, and faculty (except in the cases reserved to us), we commit, give, grant, and confirm, for ourselves and our heirs and successors aforesaid, to the said bailiffs and jurats, and to the others, by these present letters, as freely, fully, and entirely, as the said bailiff and jurats, or others or any of them, heretofore have rightfully and lawfully used, practised, and enjoyed, or might legally have used and enjoyed.

[6] Moreover, our will and pleasure is, and we grant, for ourselves, our heirs, and successors by these present letters, to the said bailiff and jurats, and the other inhabitants and sojourners in the island and maritime places aforesaid, that for the time to come, none of them be cited, arrested, or summoned, or drawn into any lawsuit, or forced in any manner by any writs or process, issued from any of our courts or others of the kingdom of England, to appear

and answer before any of our judges, courts, or other officers of justice, or others, out of the island and maritime places aforesaid, touching or concerning any thing, dispute, causes, or matters in controversy whatsoever, arising in the aforesaid island, but that the aforesaid islanders, and each of them, may lawfully and without restraint, notwithstanding the said summons, warrants, writs and processes, remain, reside quietly, and abide in the aforesaid island and places, waiting for justice there; without incurring any punishment, corporal or pecuniary, by way of fine, mulct, ransom, or forfeiture, by reason of any offence, contempt, or contumacy, committed towards us, our heirs and successors, for which they might be sued, arraigned, or condemned; except only in the cases, which by the laws and customs of the island and places aforesaid are reserved to our royal cognisance and determination, or by our right and privilege ought to be so reserved.

[7] And moreover, of our more gracious favour, certain knowledge, and mere motion, we have given, granted, and confirmed, and by our present letters, for ourselves, our heirs and successors as far as in us lies, we do give, grant, and confirm to the aforesaid bailiff and jurats, and other sojourners in, and inhabitants of, the aforesaid island and maritime places; as also to merchants and others meeting there, the like, and as great, and as ample rights, jurisdictions, immunities, impunities, indemnities, exemptions, liberties, franchises, and privileges whatsoever, as the aforesaid bailiff, jurats, and other sojourners and inhabitants, and merchants and others, or any of them, have heretofore rightfully and legally used, practised, and enjoyed; and all and singular other things whatsoever that has been heretofore given, granted, and confirmed to them or to their predecessors, in any charters, orders, or letters patent, of us or our progenitors, formerly kings and queens of England, or dukes of Normandy, or others, and not revoked or abolished, by whatsoever name or names the same bailiff and jurats, and other sojourners in, or inhabitants of, the same island and maritime places aforesaid, or their predecessors, or any of them, may be supposed to have been comprised, called, or named, or ought to have been called or named, in the said letters patent, and all and singular which things, though not herein expressly mentioned, we do by these present letters confirm, consolidate, and ratify anew to the aforesaid bailiff and jurats, and other sojourners, and inhabitants, of the island and maritime places aforesaid, and also merchants and others coming together there, those born there, and those born elsewhere, as fully, freely, and entirely, as if all and singular the things particularly mentioned and declared in the same letters patent were particularly and expressly recited and declared in these our present letters patent.

[8] Saving always entire and without detriment the regal and sovereign power, dominion, and empire of our crown of England, as to what may concern the

allegiance, subjection, and obedience of the aforesaid islanders, and others, whoever they may be, dwelling for a shorter or longer time in the same island; and also as to what may concern the regality, privileges, incomes, revenues, tributes, and other rights, profits, commodities, and emoluments whatsoever, anciently due and accustomed to be paid to us, our heirs and successors, according to our royal prerogative as kings of England, or the prerogative of the duchy of Normandy, in the island and places aforesaid; saving also to the aforesaid islanders, and others dwelling or being there, a right to appeal in all cases reserved to our cognisance and consideration by the laws and customs of the said island, or which by our royal right or privilege ought to be so reserved. Notwithstanding any sentence, clause, thing, or matter whatsoever expressed above, or specially contained to the contrary in these present letters.

[9] Provided always that any clause, article, or any other thing expressed and specified in our present letters patent are not construed, interpreted nor extended to any thing that might be prejudicial to us, our heirs, or successors with regards to any of our lands, tenements, rents, regalities, or inheritances within the aforesaid island and maritime places or any of them.

[10] And in addition, since we are given to understand that an exaction has recently been levied upon the inhabitants and peoples of our island of Jersey aforesaid, and on merchants and others gathering there against the ancient extent and custom there used, that is to say for each quarter of corn or other grain exported from the island three shillings and six pence in money current within the island, when that extent previously did not, as we understand, extend to so large a sum. And since the said inhabitants and people of the aforesaid isle of Jersey were accustomed in the same way to pay to the use of our progenitors or ancestors for every one hundred and fifty pounds of wool exported from the island according to the extent there used four pence in the money current within the same island, we will, and by these present letters for us, our heirs, and successors do grant to the aforesaid inhabitants and peoples of our aforesaid island of Jersey, that they themselves, and all the other merchants gathering there from now henceforth for ever shall be bound to pay for our use a sum no more or greater than twelve pence in the money current within the same island of Jersey for each quarter of wheat or other type of grain hereafter exported from the same island. Thus, always, and on condition that the same inhabitants and peoples of the aforesaid island of Jersey and all other merchants and foreigners gathering there, owe and are bound to pay forever hereafter to our use for every one hundred and fifty pounds of wool exported from that island, three and a half shillings in the money current within the same island and aforesaid maritime places, or any of them.

[11] Furthermore, we wish and by these present letters we grant, that the said bailiff and jurats and other islanders and inhabitants of the aforesaid island and maritime places should and will have these our letters without fine or fee, great or small, rendered, made or paid to us in our Hanaper or elsewhere to our use for the same. And that although express mention etc. In testimony whereof etc. Witness the king at Canbury the sixth day of July.

[Wolseley]

By writ of privy seal

Charles II: 1662

Commentary

The Channel Islands had experienced the civil wars of the 1640s and 1650s in a particularly dramatic way. While Guernsey, with the exception of Castle Cornet, had been true to the parliamentarian cause, Jersey served as a refuge for Charles, prince of Wales, in 1646, and again in 1649. Jersey had finally succumbed after parliamentarian forces landed in October 1651, Castle Cornet shortly after in the same year, on 19 December. Once the monarchy was restored in 1660, the grant of a royal charter to Jersey in 1662 illustrates the impact of that struggle, both in the respect for the Jersey community and its leaders that it had engendered in the new king, and the way a period of rule by the Commonwealth and then Lords Protector had in the meanwhile affected local privileges.[1]

Charles left his exile in the Netherlands and reached London on 29 May 1660, following the invitation issued by the Convention Parliament that had assembled in April. The restoration of royal authority proceeded, and it was not without challenge for the islands. Discussion in the Jersey States on 9 May 1661 saw recognition of the need for a confirmation of their charter, particularly given the English government's intention to levy an impost of 1 ecu on all foreign ships arriving in their harbours – to 'la ruine manifeste de ce pais'. Philippe de Carteret of St Ouen, Edouard de Carteret, and Jean Nicolle, or two of them, were appointed to go to the king and Privy Council to seek an exemption and for confirmation of the island's privileges; a levy on the parishes was agreed and organised to provide for their expenses.[2]

---

[1] General accounts of this period are to be found in G. R. Balleine, *History of Jersey*, rev. Marguerite Syvret and Joan Stevens (Chichester, 1981), pp. 147–56; L. James Marr, *A History of the Bailiwick of Guernsey: The Islanders' Story* (Chichester, 1982), pp. 147–50.

[2] *Actes des états de l'île de Jersey, 1660–1675*, 15e publication de la Société Jersiaise (Jersey, 1900), pp. 8–9, 19–20.

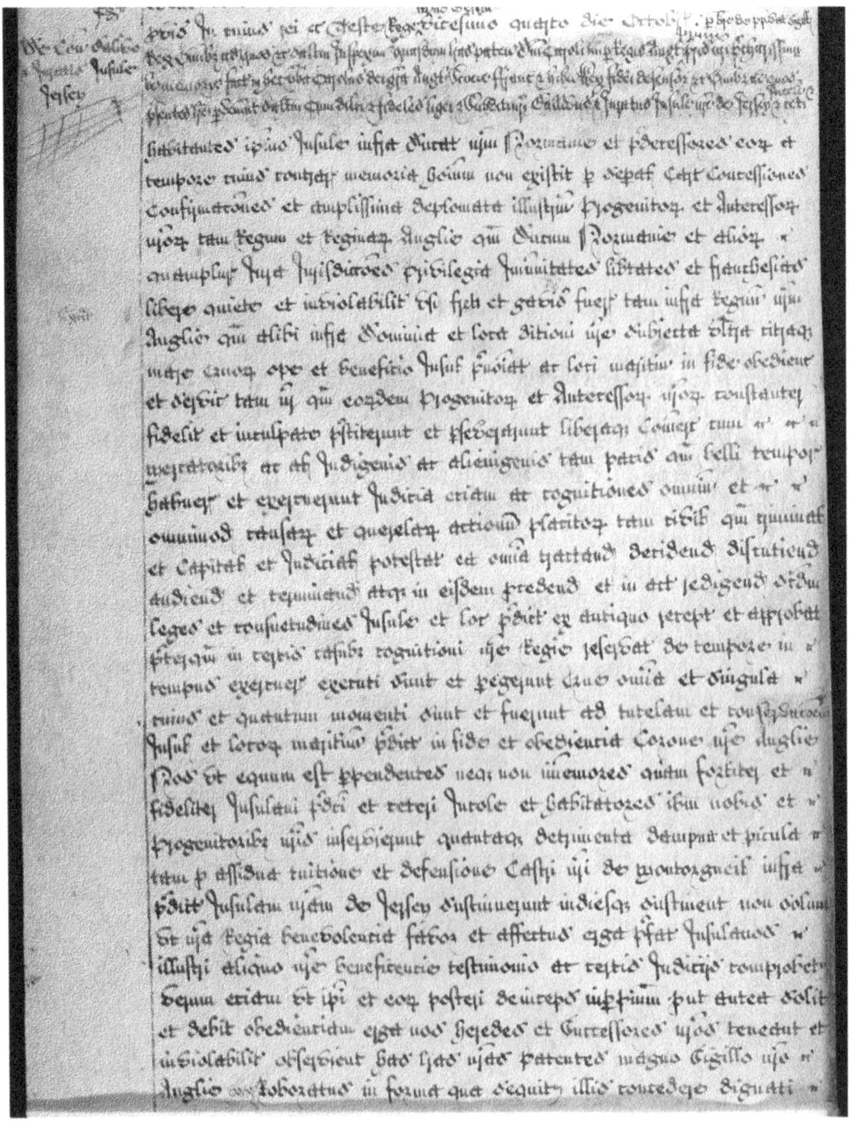

Plate 15 (i): The Royal Charter granted by Charles II in 1662.
Credit: The National Archives, ref. C 66/3005.

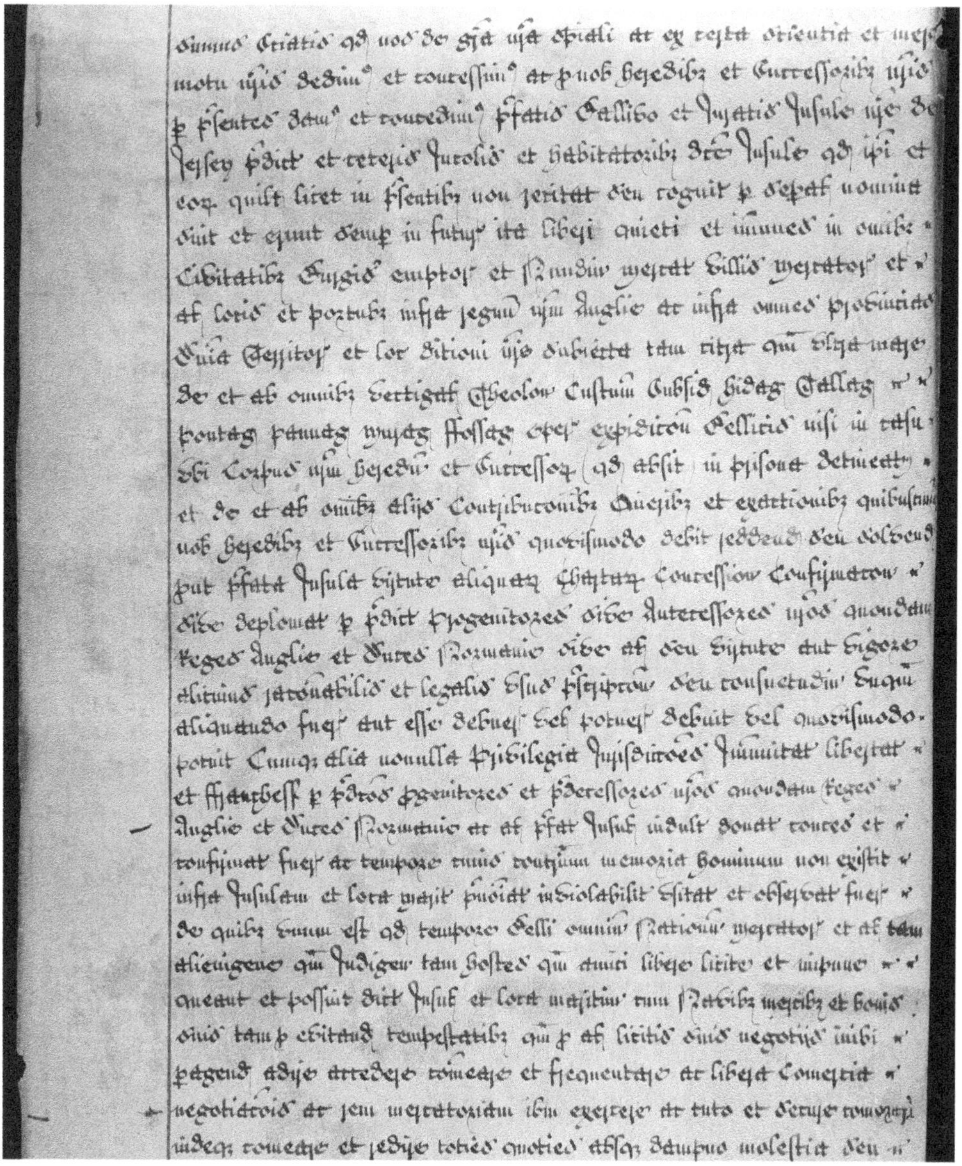

Plate 15 (ii.a): The Royal Charter granted by Charles II in 1662.

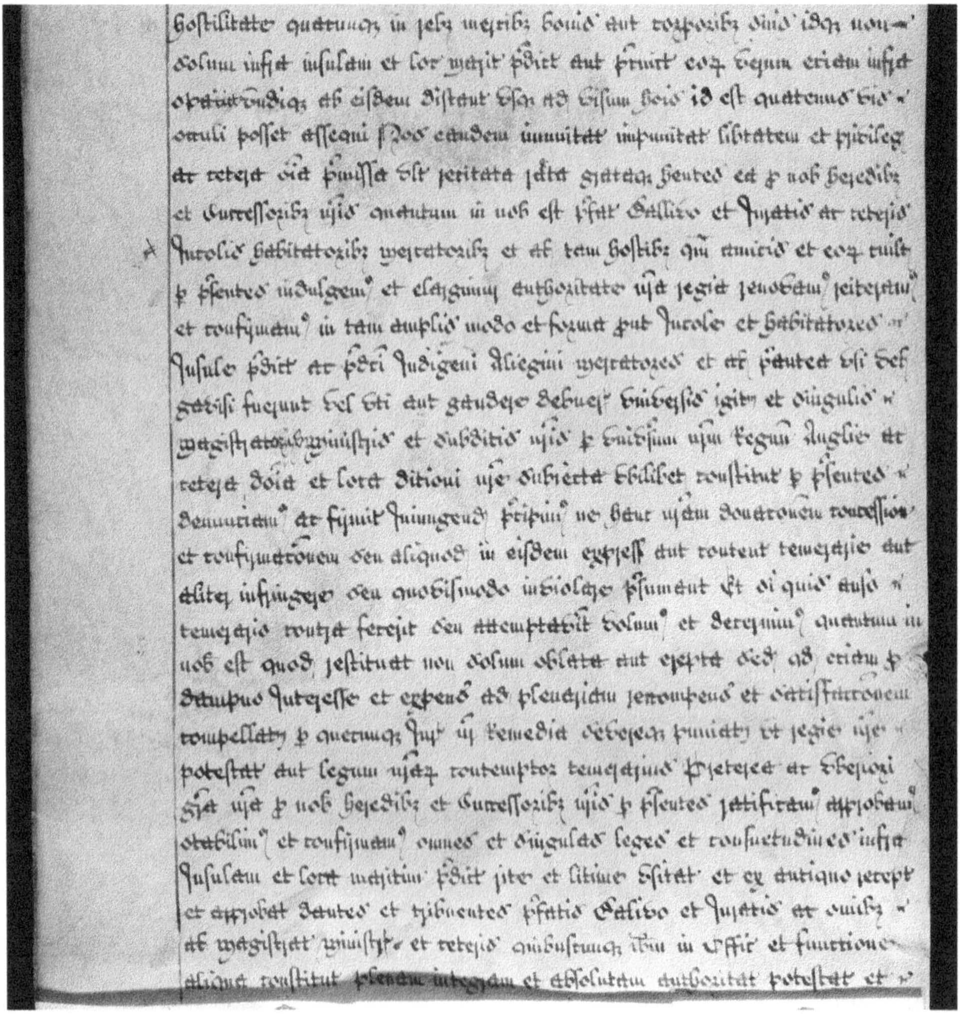

Plate 15 (ii.b): The Royal Charter granted by Charles II in 1662.

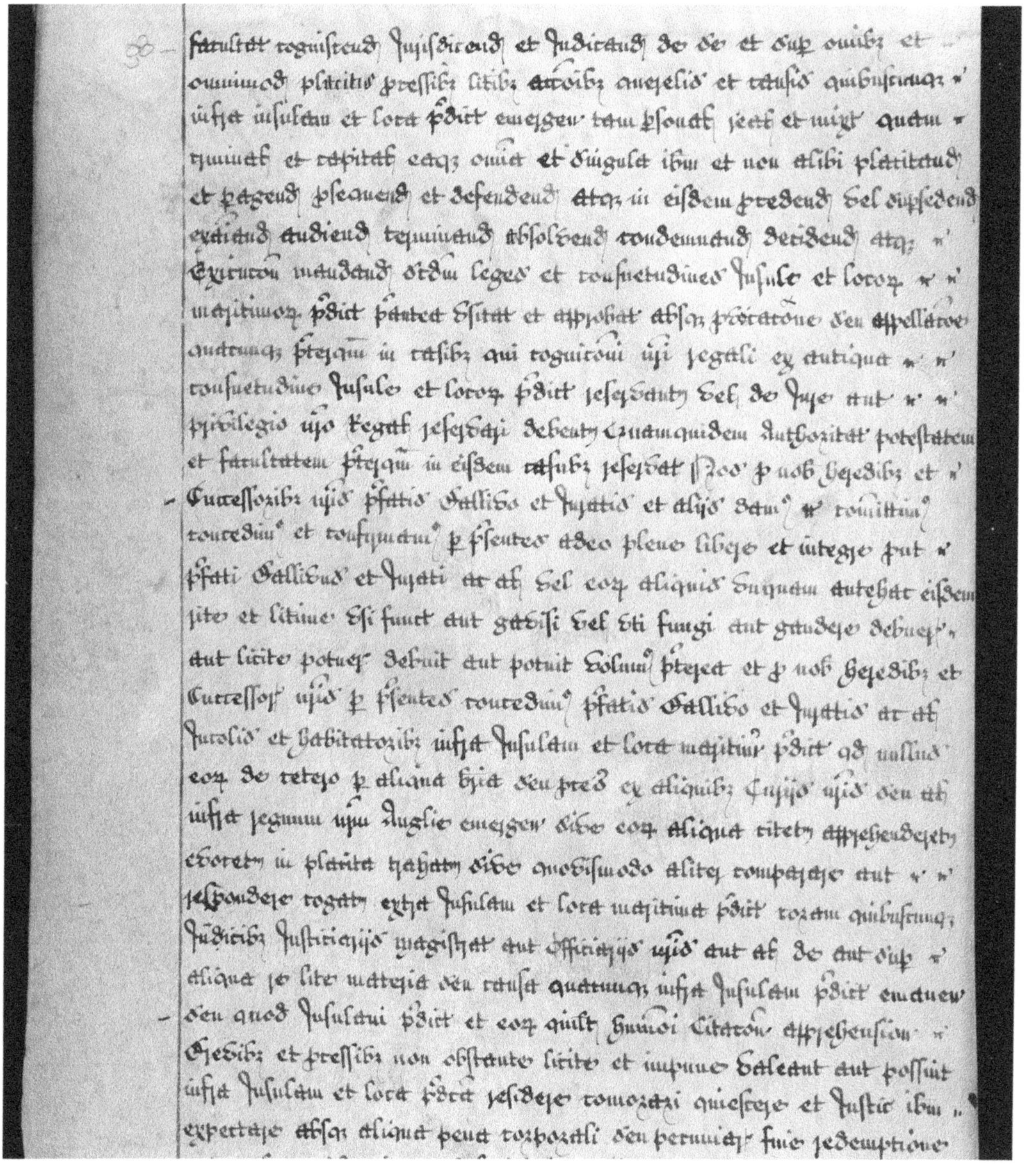

facultat cognoscend' jurisdicend' et judicand' de et sup omnibz et
omnimod' placitis processibz litibz accoibz querelis et causis quibuscumqz
infra insulam et loca p'dict emergen tam personal' real' et mixt' quam
criminal' et capital' eaqz omnia et singula ibm et non alibi placitand'
et pagend' prosequend' et defendend' atqz in eisdem procedend' vel supsedend'
examinand' audiend' terminand' absolvend' condemnand' decidend' atqz
Executon mandand' s'c'dm leges et consuetudines Insule et locor
maritimor p'dict p'ut eadem exigit et approbat absqz provocatione seu appellatoe
quacumqz p'terqm in casibz qui cognicon nre regali ex antiqua
consuetudine Insule et locor p'dict reservantur vel de jure aut
privilegio nro Regali reservari debent Quamquidem Authoritat' potestatem
et facultatem p'terqm in eisdem casibz reservat' p'dco p nob heredibz et
Successoribz nris p'fatis Ballivo et Juratis et aliis deinc' comittim'
concedim' et confirmam' p p'sentes adeo plene libere et integre p'ut
p'fati Ballivus et Jurati ac alii vel eor aliquis unquam antehac eisdem
jure et legitime usi fuerunt aut gavisi vel uti frui aut gaudere debuer'
aut licite potuer' debuit aut potuit Volum' p'terea et p nob heredibz et
Successor' nris p p'sentes concedim' p'fatis Ballivo et Juratis ac al'
Incolis et habitatoribz infra Insulam et loca maritima p'dict qd nullus
eor de cetero p aliqua bria seu proc' ex aliquibz Curiis nris seu al'
infra Regnum nrm Anglie emergen sive eor aliqua citet' apprehenderet'
evocet' in placitu trahat' sive quovismodo aliter compareret aut
respondere cogat' extra Insulam et loca maritima p'dict coram quibuscumqz
Judicibz Justiciariis magistrat aut officiariis nris aut al' de aut sup
aliqua re lite materia seu causa quacumqz infra Insulam p'dict emanen
seu quod Insulani p'dict et eor quilt huiuoi Citacon apprehension
breuibz et processibz non obstante licite et impune valeant aut possint
infra Insulam et loca p'dca residere comorari quiescere et Justic ibm
expectare absqz aliqua pena corporali seu pecuniar' sine redemptione

Plate 15 (iii.a): The Royal Charter granted by Charles II in 1662.

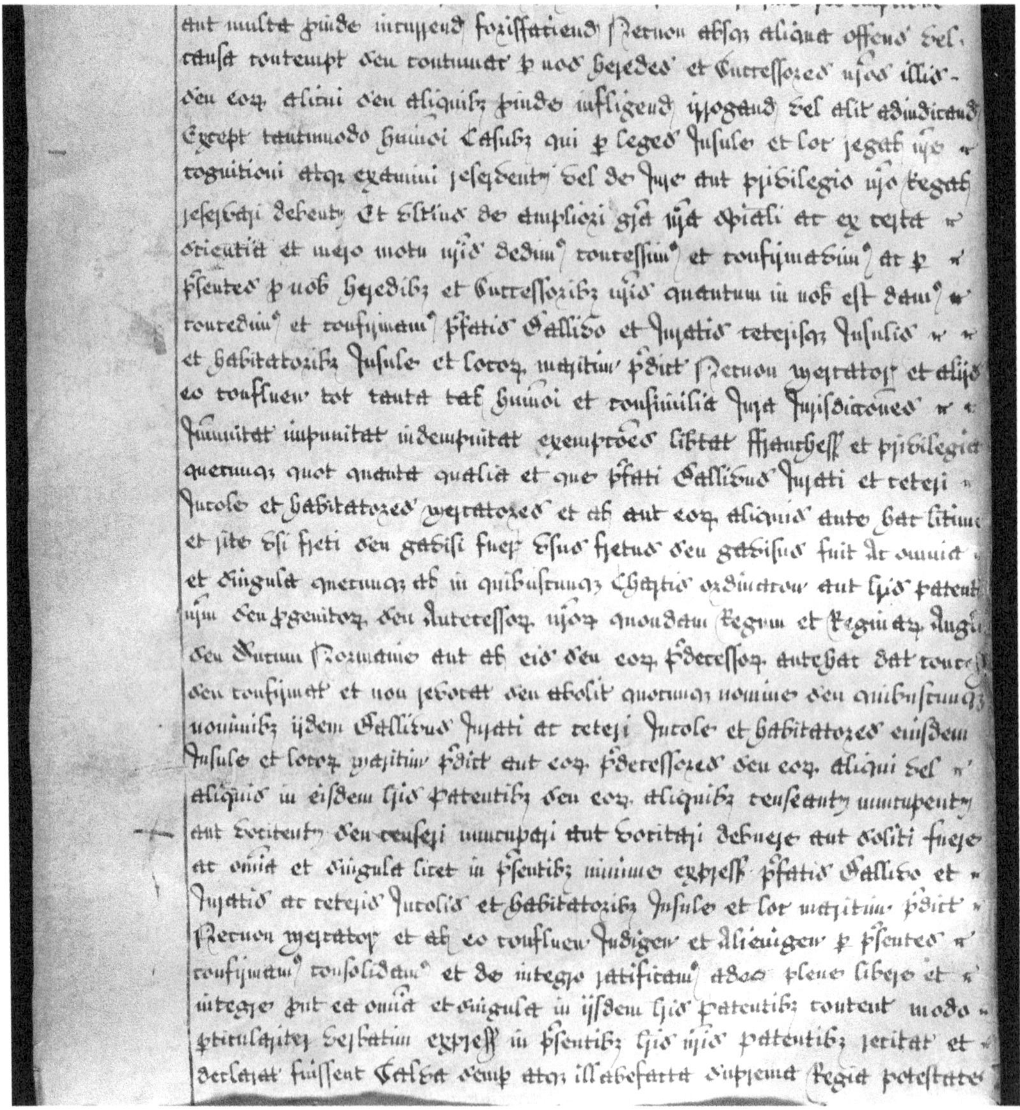

Plate 15 (iii.b): The Royal Charter granted by Charles II in 1662.

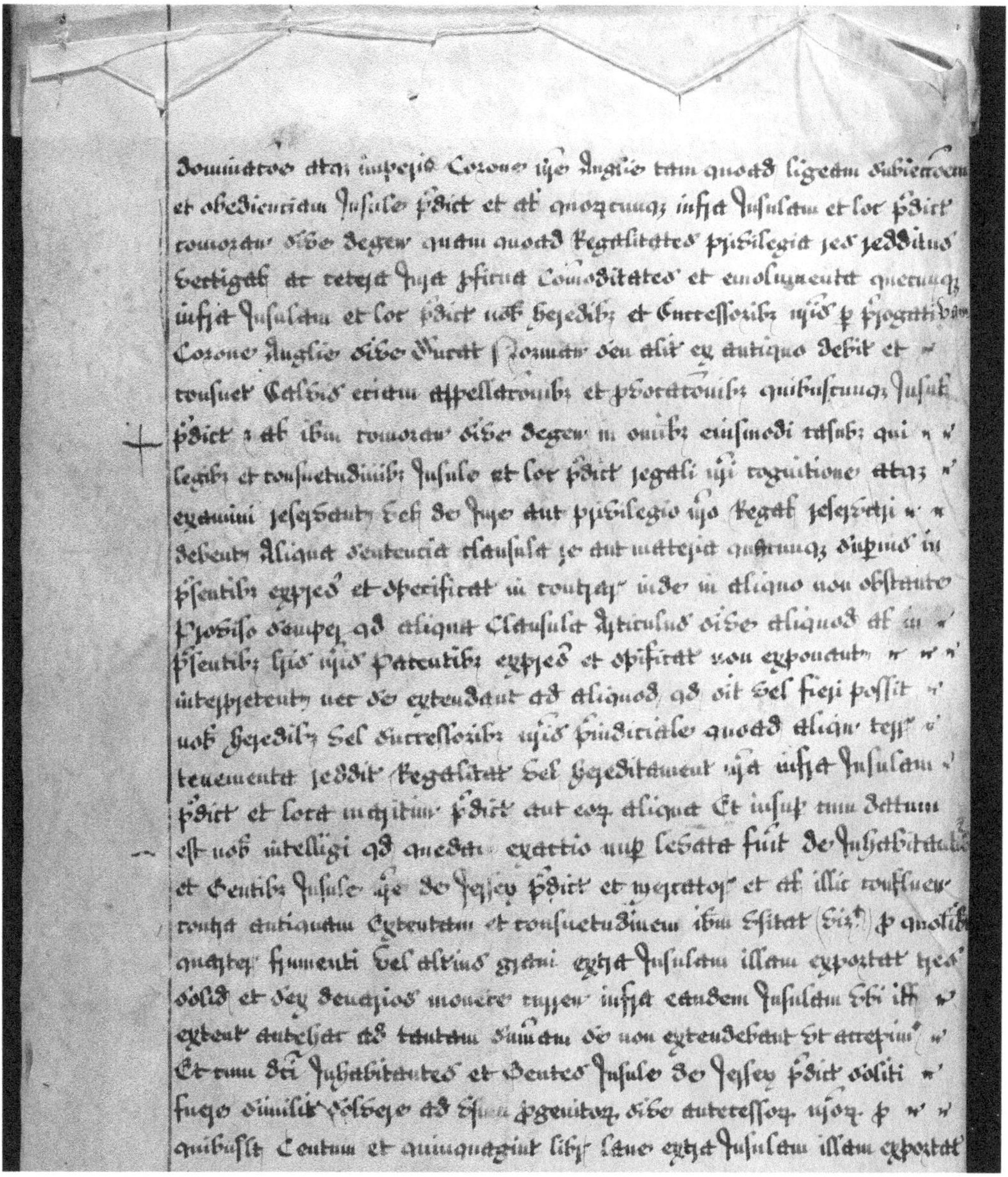

Plate 15 (iv.a): The Royal Charter granted by Charles II in 1662.

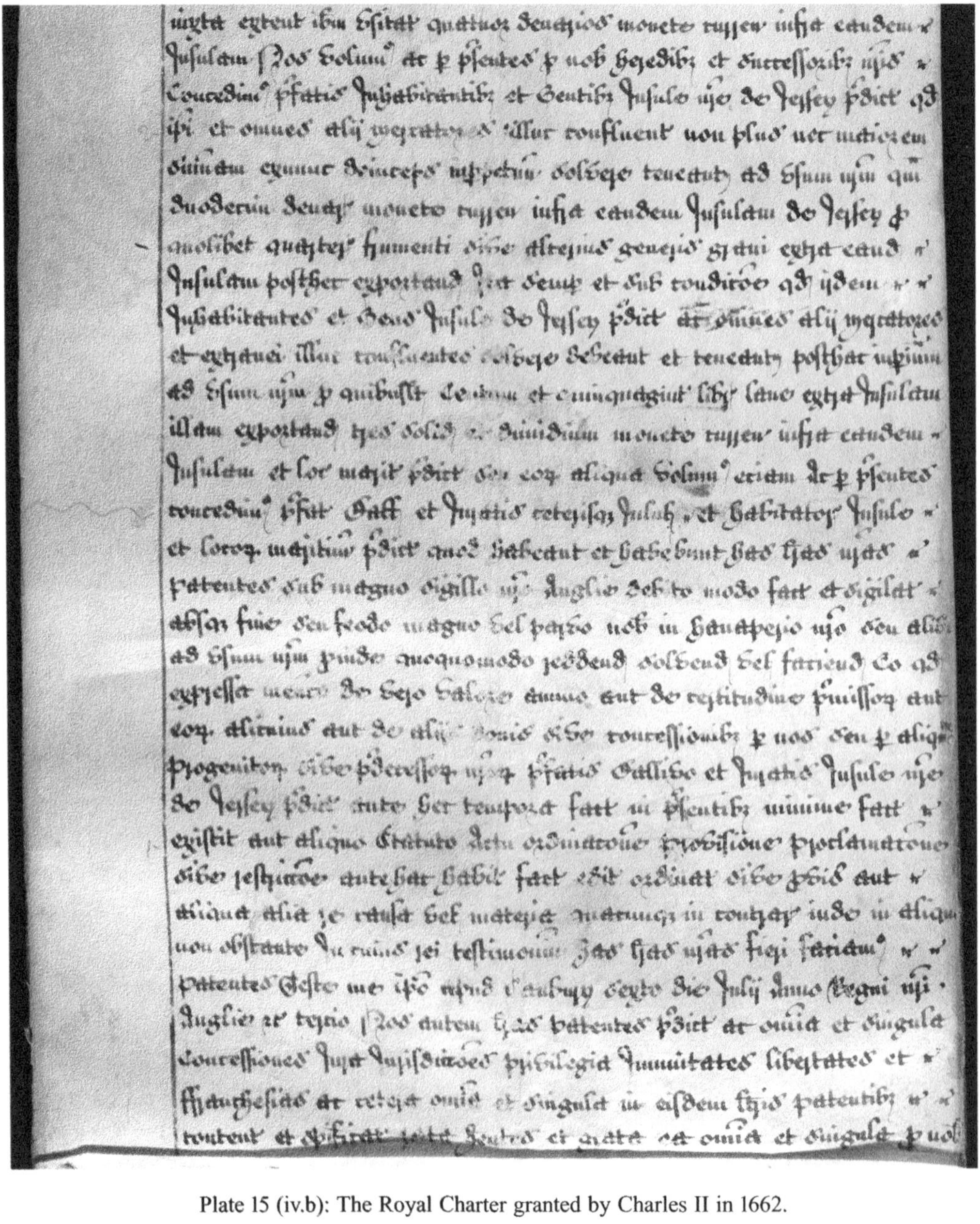

Plate 15 (iv.b): The Royal Charter granted by Charles II in 1662.

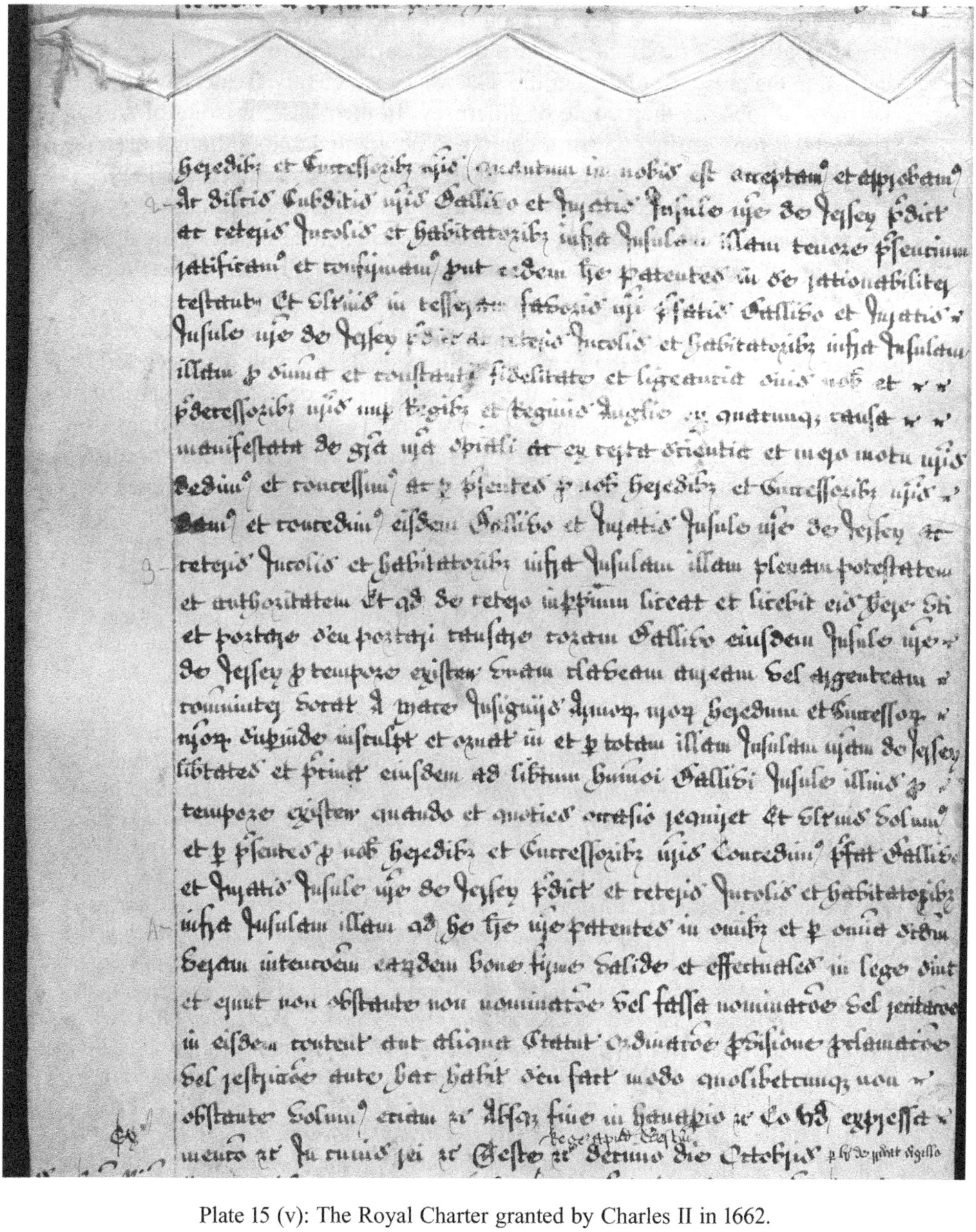

Plate 15 (v): The Royal Charter granted by Charles II in 1662.

On 10 October 1662 Charles II duly confirmed his father's grants to Jersey. The document was cast in the form of a traditional inspeximus, reciting and confirming specifically the charter of 6 July 1627. Notably, Charles also took the opportunity to show special favour to the people of Jersey. As a mark of his special favour he granted that a mace bearing the royal arms could be carried in the presence of the bailiff.[3] This was distinctively greater favour than he showed towards the people of Guernsey. In their case, in spite of earlier requests, it took until 1668 for a charter to be granted and, although nothing was taken from the preceding grant of 1627, neither was anything added.[4]

The charters reflected directly on the king's own personal experiences over the previous decades of conflict. Charles had spent some time in Jersey during the 1640s while the island, almost alone among the English king's territories, remained loyal to the royalist cause.[5] Charles was able to do so thanks to the successful effort of the de Carteret family, especially Sir George Carteret, to overcome a rebellion in the name of parliament. This revolt had been led by a disparate group of jurats and others opposed to the de Carterets, spanning, for example, the dean of Jersey David Bandinel (who had led the imposition of Anglicanism in the island) and the Huguenot Pierre d'Assigny, minister of the Town Church.[6] The de Carterets were soon triumphant, however, and George, who succeeded to their leadership on the death in 1643 of his uncle,

---

[3] TNA, C 66/3005, no. 3; Ralph Mollet, 'The Royal Mace of the Bailiff of Jersey', *ABSJ*, 12 (1932–35), 152–5.

[4] Tim Thornton, *The Charters of Guernsey* (Bognor Regis, 2004), pp. 144–70; Richard Hocart, *Guernsey in the Reign of Charles II* ([Guernsey], 2020), pp. 4–5, 49–50, 124–6.

[5] See in general S. Elliott Hoskins, *Charles the Second in the Channel Islands: A Contribution to his Biography and to the History of his Age* (2 vols, London, 1854); Balleine, *History of Jersey*, rev. Syvret and Stevens, pp. 122–6, 131–4; Ronald Hutton, *Charles the Second, King of England, Scotland, and Ireland* (Oxford, 1989), pp. 15–19, 42–5. Some fears creep in: Clarendon ??, xii. 75–7. Strikingly, some of Charles' biographers pay little attention to these visits: e.g. Arthur Bryant, *King Charles II* (London, 1931); J. R. Jones, *Charles II: Royal Politician* (London, 1987). Although the possibility that Charles fathered a child while in Jersey is remote, the early history of the story suggests an understanding of the importance of the visit to Jersey: A. Lang, 'The Master Hoaxer: James de la Cloche', *Fortnightly Review*, September 1909; Arthur Irwin Dasent, *The Private Life of Charles the Second* (London, 1927), pp. 18–27; G. Tarantino, 'Jacques de la Cloche: A Stuart Pretender in the Seventeenth Century', *Archivum Historicum Societatis Iesu*, 146 (2004), 425–41.

[6] *Articles Exhibited against Sir Philipp Carteret, Governour of the Isle of Jersy; Or, An Humble Information of the Estate of his Majesties Isle of Iersey, with Part of the Grievances of the Inhabitants, which was Presented by Divers Gentlemen of that Isle, to many Members of both the Honourable Houses in Parliament Assembled* (London: s.n., 1642).

the governor and bailiff Sir Philippe, was particularly prominent in the new regime. Charles' first visit took place from April to June 1646, as prince of Wales, and another, now as king, from September 1649 to February 1650. The second visit was far from insignificant in the eyes of his opponents, who were concerned by the fact of Charles' arrival in the island.[7] Both visits seem to have been enjoyed by Charles and others in his party, and the Jersey community impressed on him their loyalty. Ann, Lady Fanshawe, having arrived in Jersey a royalist refugee in a desperate state and heavily pregnant, observed: 'They are a cheerfull, good natur'd people and truly subject to the present Governour [Sir George Carteret, who] indeavoured with all his power to entertaine His Highness and court with all plenty and kindness possible, both which the iland afforded, and what was wanting he sent for out of France.'[8] Edward Hyde, earl of Clarendon, who played such an important role in creating the royalist narrative of the 'great rebellion' recalled that he enjoyed 'the greatest tranquillity of mind imaginable' living in Jersey with Lord Capel and Lord Hopton and later moved to join Sir George Carteret in Elizabeth Castle, to Hyde's 'wonderful contentment'.[9] During those months spent in Jersey, it would have been very clear that, with the exception of Castle Cornet, Guernsey's position was different, committing to the king's enemies.[10]

Jersey's resistance to the forces of the parliament, which had been so ably led by George Carteret, was consciously framed as a defence of its constitutional position based on the royal charters of liberties. Carteret's manifesto of 1646 emphasised Jersey was not part of England but of Normandy, with no business with the English parliament except in gaining permission to export wool into the island.[11] While it might have been that staking Jersey's resistance so clearly to the autonomy enshrined in the charter tradition was dangerous to it when the island eventually fell, in the event there is little sign of a serious threat to the island's liberties. The immediate actions of the victorious invading force led by Colonel James Heane in 1651 were focused on reinstating the

---

[7] Royal Commission on Historical Manuscripts, *Report on the Manuscripts of F. W. Leyborne-Popham, Esq. of Littlecote, co. Wilts.* (London, 1899), pp. 29–30.

[8] John Loftis (ed.), *The Memoirs of Anne, Lady Halkett, and Ann, Lady Fanshawe* (Oxford, 1979), pp. 118–19.

[9] Edward Hyde, *The Life of Edward Earl of Clarendon: In which is Included, A Continuation of his History of the Grand Rebellion, Written by Himself* (3 vols, Oxford, 1857), vol. 1, pp. 205–8, esp. 205, 208.

[10] See the many petitions to the crown on the restoration recalling service at Jersey: e.g. *CSPD, 1661–62*, pp. 26, 228, 626; and the diary of Jean Chevalier, from which extracts are printed in 'Extraits du journal de Jean Chevallier', *ABSJ*, 1 (1875–84), 260–4, at p. 261.

[11] A. C. Saunders, *Jean Chevalier and his Times: A Story of Sir George Carteret, Baronet, and the Great Rebellion* (Jersey, 1937), p. 159ff.

traditional structures of government, but populated with men who he believed would be true to the Commonwealth.[12] In December of the year, the Council of State restated former rights in the movement of wool from England to the island for the stocking trade, and later (in November 1652) decreed free movement of corn, and of 1,000 tods of wool, 400 dickers of leather, and 60 firkins of butter annually.[13] The reinstatement of the bailiff, Michael Lemprière, provided a figurehead for the defence of the island's constitution, and he sent the speaker of the Commons an 'account of the civil government of this island'. This was carried by his nephew James (or Jacques) Stocall, who very effectively translated it into an accessible account for a wider readership in England of *Freedome. Or, The Description of the Excellent Civill Government of the Island of Jersey*.[14]

The Council had ordered a review of the island's system of government soon after it was captured, and indicated that no new jurats should be appointed until this was complete. In 1652, the Commons also requested review by the Council.[15] The outcome, in October 1652, was a recommendation that the island's ancient constitution be restored, and that five local men should be appointed to a commission to establish the island's laws, with a change to annual election of office-holders.[16] This was not progressed, and a new parliament in 1653 (colloquially known as Barebones' Parliament) recommended an election for ten new jurats, to hold office for two years only.[17] But once again this was not taken forward. The potential for the island to be drawn into English governmental structures was apparent in 1652 with the appointment of a county committee on the same model as was being done for English counties. And the Instrument of Government, the constitution which established Oliver Cromwell as protector in 1653, included a provision for Jersey to be represented in the House of Commons of the English

---

[12] Balleine, *History of Jersey*, rev. Syvret and Stevens, p. 140. For a wider context to this failure of the Commonwealth regime to challenge local constitutional arrangements, see Tim Thornton, 'Nationhood at the Margin: Identity, Regionality and the English Crown in the Seventeenth Century', in Len Scales and Oliver Zimmer (eds), *Power and the Nation in European History* (Cambridge, 2005), pp. 232–47, esp. pp. 236–43.

[13] *CSPD, 1651–52*, pp. 53, 491; Balleine, *History of Jersey*, rev. Syvret and Stevens, p. 140.

[14] Hoskins, *Charles the Second in the Channel Islands*, vol. 2, pp. 395–400; James Stocall, *Freedome. Or, The Description of the Excellent Civill Government of the Island of Jersey* (London: printed for Robert Ibbitson, 1652); *CSPD, 1651–52*, p. 502 (22 November 1652); Balleine, *History of Jersey*, rev. Syvret and Stevens, p. 141.

[15] *Journals of the House of Commons* (51 vols, London, 1803), vol. 7, *1651–60*, pp. 124, 127, 193–4, 309.

[16] Balleine, *History of Jersey*, rev. Syvret and Stevens, p. 141.

[17] Balleine, *History of Jersey*, rev. Syvret and Stevens, p. 141.

parliament. It was, however, significant that 1652 saw the outbreak of war with the Dutch, and the potential for radical reform more generally across England and other territories unleashed by the eclipse of the royalist cause was refocused. Neither the appointment of a committee, nor the institution of English parliamentary representation, seem to have taken effect: for example, although the Instrument indicated that 'the Persons to be elected, to sit in Parliament from Time to Time, for the several Counties of England, Wales, the Isles of Jersey and Guernsey, and the Town of Berwick upon Tweed, and all Places within the same respectively, shall be according to the Proportions and Numbers hereafter express'd', it specified individual numbers for constituencies in England, Wales and Berwick, but for neither Jersey nor Guernsey.[18] In reality, the most likely cause of any such alignment with English practice was the simple failure of elements of Jersey's constitution to function, as with the shortage of jurats resulting from this sequence of abortive reforms and the failure of the States to meet. Soon, however, it became clear that the initiative of the English regime was aligned with the maintenance of the status quo, and in 1655 Cromwell nominated 11 jurats and the bailiff's position was confirmed by patent.[19]

If the Commonwealth and Protectorate turned out to be not unsympathetic to the traditional governance and rights of the island, by contrast they also initiated the effort to control trade via the Navigation Acts, which was to have a growing impact on Jersey, as well as Guernsey and the Isle of Man. Faced by powerful competition from the Dutch in particular, the principle that was laid out was that English trade, including trade with its colonies, should be handled in English vessels. This issue was already a cause for concern in the years of the Commonwealth and Protectorate, as the first of the Acts was passed in 1651.[20] The clearest impacts of that growing regime of control and restriction were not to be felt until the second half of Charles' reign, but their growth was starting to become apparent for Jersey in the years soon after his grant of a charter to the island.

---

[18] C. H. Firth and R. S. Rait (ed.), *Acts and Ordinances of the Interregnum, 1642–1660* (London, 1911), pp. 813–22, at pp. 814–16; Balleine, *History of Jersey*, rev. Syvret and Stevens, pp. 141–2; Blair Worden, *The Rump Parliament, 1648–1653* (Cambridge, 1974), pp. 292–313.

[19] *Ordres du Conseil et pièces analogues enregistrés à Jersey* (6 vols, Jersey, 1897–1906), vol. 2, 27 September 1655; 28 February 1654/5 (printed in Charles Le Quesne, *A Constitutional History of Jersey* (London, 1856), p. 342).

[20] J. I. Israel, 'England's Mercantilist Response to Dutch World Trade Primacy, 1647–74', in his *Conflicts of Empires: Spain, the Low Countries and the Struggle for World Supremacy, 1585–1713* (London, 1997), pp. 305–18; James E. Farnell, 'The Navigation Act of 1651, the First Dutch War and the London Merchant Community', *Economic History Review*, 2nd ser., 16 (1963–64), 439–54.

In Guernsey on the restoration of Charles as king, the local regime was displaced, and Amias Andros was installed as bailiff, in May 1661.[21] Andros had held out in Castle Cornet during the long years of siege before its fall in 1651, but his experience of those years and of the society to which he returned at the restoration was very different from Sir George Carteret's. Among other things, the Stuart regime Andros led went about imposing Anglican conformity in the previously stalwartly Presbyterian island, as well as in Alderney and Sark.[22] Meanwhile in Jersey, it was the de Carteret family that was triumphant. Sir George's position as vice-chamberlain of the Royal Household was confirmed, and in July he became treasurer of the navy; he could rely on the support, too, of his friend and former house-guest Edward Hyde, now the king's chief minister.[23] While there is no question that Carteret's acute political skills and (perhaps less refined) accounting technique were employed primarily to enhance his own position, he was an asset both to the navy in the years of war with the Dutch and to his island of origin. The ongoing tensions around restrictions on island shipping and efforts to impose a customs regime were undeniable, but the crown's willingness rapidly to recognise the core elements of Jersey's liberties was significantly attributable to the success of Carteret's personal leadership during the war years and after.[24]

Text

Charles II confirmed his father's charter for Jersey. Charles II added, as a mark of special favour, permission for a mace bearing the royal arms to be carried in the presence of the bailiff. Specific to Jersey; from the enrolment in The National Archives, C 66/3005, with reference to the edition presented in Prison Board, to which page references are provided, as [369] (etc.), and Jersey Archive D/AP/Z/8, an original charter version, which I have tended to prefer here.

[1] Carolus Secundus Dei Gratia Anglie Scotie Francie et Hibernie Rex fidei defensor &c Omnibus ad quos presentes Littere pervenerint salutem. Inspeximus quasdam literas Patentes Domini Caroli nuper Regis Anglie primi Patris Nostri precharissimi beate memorie factas in hec verba. Carolus Dei gratia Anglie Scotie Francie et Hibernie Rex fidei defensor &c Omnibus ad quos presentes litere pervenerint salute Cum dilecti et fideles Ligei et Subditi

---

[21] Marr, *History of the Bailiwick of Guernsey*, p. 91.

[22] Marr, *History of the Bailiwick of Guernsey*, p. 20.

[23] G. R. Balleine, *All for the King: The Life Story of Sir George Carteret* (St Helier, 1976).

[24] Sir Henry De Vic in Guernsey observed that Jersey had received its charter before Guernsey, and that they had got it without dispute through favour of their friends: Hocart, *Guernsey in the Reign of Charles II*, p. 126.

nostri Ballivus et Jurati Insule nostre de Jersey ac ceteri Incole et Habitantes ipsius Insule infra Ducatum nostrum Normanie et Predecessores eorum a tempore cuius contrarii memoria hominum non existit per seperales Cartas Concessiones Confirmationes et amplissima diplomata illustrium Progenitorum et Antecessorum nostrorum tam Regum et Reginarum Anglie quam Ducum Normanie et aliorum quamplurium Jura Jurisdicciones Privilegia Immunitates Libertates et Franchesias libere quiete et inviolabiliter vsi freti et gavisi fuerunt tam infra Regnum nostrum Anglie quam alibi infra Dominia et loca ditioni nostre Subiecta vltra citraque mare Quorum [370] ope et beneficio predicte Insule et loca maritima predicta in fide obediencia et servicio tam nostri quam eorundem Progenitorum et Antecessorum nostrorum constanter fideliter et inculpate perstiterunt ac perseverarunt liberaque Commercia cum Mercatoribus ac aliis Indigenis et Alienigenis tam pacis quam belli temporibus habuerunt et exercuerunt Judicia etiam et cognitiones omnium et omnimodo Causarum et querelarum actionum placitorum tam civilium quam criminalium et Capitalium et Judicialem potestatem ea omnia tractandi decidendi discutiendi audiendi et terminandi atque in eisdem procedendi et in acta redigendi secundum Leges et Consuetudines Insule et locorum predictorum ex antiquo receptas et approbatas preterquam in certis Casubus cognitioni nostre Regie reservatis de tempore in tempus exercuerunt executi sunt et peregerunt.

[2] Que omnia et singula cuius et quanti momenti sunt et fuerunt ad tutelam et conservacionem Insule et locorum maritimorum predictorum in fide et obediencia Corone nostre Anglie Nos vt equum est perpendentes neque non immemores quam fortiter et fideliter Insulani predicti ac ceteri Incole et Habitatores ibidem Nobis et Progenitoribus nostris inservierunt Quantaque detrimenta dampna et pericula tam pro assidua tuitione et defensione Castri nostri de Montorgueil infra predictam Insulam nostram de Jersey sustinuerunt indiesque sustinent non solum vt nostra Regia benevolentia favor et affectus erga prefatos Insulanos illustri aliquo nostre beneficencie testimonio ac certis Indiciis comprobetur. Verum etiam vt ipsi et eorum Posteri deinceps inperpetuum prout antea solitam et debitam obedientiam erga nos heredes et Successores nostros teneant et inviolabiliter observent has literas nostras Patentes magno Sigillo Anglie roboratas in forma qua sequitur illis concedere dignati sumus.

[3] Sciatis quod nos de gratia nostra speciali ac ex certa scientia et mero motu nostris Dedimus et Concessimus ac pro Nobis heredibus et Successoribus nostris per presentes Damus et Concedimus prefatis Ballivo et Juratis Insule nostre de Jersey predicte et ceteris Incolis et Habitatoribus dicte Insule quod ipsi et eorum quilibet licet in presentibus non recitati seu cogniti per seperalia nomina sint et erunt semper in futuro ita liberi quieti et immunes in omnibus Civitatibus Burgis Emptoriis & Nundiniis Mercatis Villis Mercatoriis et aliis

locis et Portubus infra Regnum nostrum Anglie ac infra omnes Provincias Dominia Territoria et loca ditioni nostra Subiecta tam citra quam vltra mare de et ab omnibus Vectigalibus Theoloniis Custumiis Subsidiis Hidagiis Tallagiis Pontagiis Pannagiis Muragiis Fossagiis operibus Expedicionibus Bellicis nisi in casu vbi Corpus nostrum heredum et Successorum (quod absit) in Prisona detineatur et de et ab omnibus aliis Contribucionibus Oneribus et Exaccionibus quibuscunque Nobis heredibus et Successoribus nostris quovismodo debitis reddendis seu solvendis prout prefata Insula virtute aliquarum Chartarum Concessionum Confirmacionum sive diplomatum per predictos Progenitores sive Antecessores nostros quondam Reges Anglie et Duces Normanie sive alios seu virtute aut vigore alicuius racionabilis et legalis vsus prescripcionis seu consuetudinis vnquam aliquando fuerunt aut esse debuerunt vel potuerunt debuit vel quovismodo potuit.

[4] Cumque alia nonulla Privilegia Jurisdicciones Immunitates libertates et Franchesias per predictos Progenitores et Predecessores nostros quondam Reges Anglie et [371] Duces Normanie ac aliis prefate Insule indulta donata concessa et confirmata fuere ac a tempore cuius contrarium memoria hominum non existit infra Insulam et loca Maritima prenominata inviolabiliter vsitata et observata fuere de quibus vnum est quod tempore Belli omnium Nationum Mercatores et alii tam Alienigeni quam Indigeni tam hostes quam Amici libere licite et impune queant et possint dictam Insulam et loca Maritima cum Navibus mercibus et bonis suis tam pro evitandis tempestatibus quam pro aliis licitis suis negotiis inibi peragendis adire accedere commeare et frequentare ac liberá Commercia negotiacionis et Rem Mercatoriam ibidem exercere ac tuto et secure commorari indeque commeare et redire toties quoties absque dampno Molestia seu hostilitate quacunque in rebus Mercibus bonis aut Corporibus suis, idque non solum infra Insulam et loca Maritima predicta aut Precinctum eorundem, verum etiam infra spatia vndique ab eisdem distantia vsque ad visum hominis id est quatenus visus oculi possit assequi Nos eandem Immunitates Impunitates libertatem et privilegia ac cetera omnia premissa vltima recitata rata gratáque habentes, Ea pro nobis heredibus et Successoribus nostris quantum in Nobis est prefatis Ballivo et Juratis ac ceteris Incolis Habitatoribus Mercatoribus et aliis tam hostibus quam Amicis et eorum cuilibet per presentes indulgemus et elargimur authoritateque nostra Regia renovamus reiteramus et Confirmamus in tam amplis modo et forma prout Incoli et Habitatores Insule predicte ac predicti Indigeni Alienigeni Mercatores et alii preantea vsi vel gavisi fuerunt vel vti aut gaudere debuerunt. vniversis igitur et singulis Magistratoribus Ministris et Subditis nostris per vniversum Regnum nostrum Anglie ac cetera Dominia et loca ditioni nostre Subiecta vbilibet constitutis per presentes denunciamus et firmiter iniungendo precipimus ne hanc nostram Donacionem Concessionem et Confirmacionem seu aliquid in eisdem expressum aut contentum temerarie aut aliter infringere

seu quovismodo inviolare presumant Et si quis ausu temerario contra fecerit seu attemptaverit Volumus et decernimus quantum in nobis est quod restituat non solum ablata aut erepta sed quod etiam pro dampno interesse et Expensis ad plenarium recompensam et satisfaccionem compellatur per quecunque iuris nostri Remedia severeque puniatur vt regie nostre potestatis ac Legum nostrarum Contemptor temerarius.

[5] Preterea ex vberiori gratia nostra pro nobis heredibus et Successoribus nostris per presentes Ratificamus approbamus stabilimus et Confirmamus omnes et singulas Leges et consuetudines infra Insulam et loca Maritima predicta rite et legitime vsitata et ex antiquo recepta et approbata Dantes et tribuentes prefatis Ballivo et Juratis ac omnibus aliis Magistratibus Ministris et ceteris quibuscunque ibidem in Officio et Functione aliqua constitutis plenam integram et absolutam authoritatem potestatem et facultatem cognoscendi iurisdicendi et iudicandi de se et super omnibus et omnimodis placitis processibus litibus Accionibus querelis et Causis quibuscunque infra Insulam et loca predicta emergentibus tam personalibus realibus et mixtis quam criminalibus et Capitalibus. Eaque omnia et singula ibidem et non alibi placitandi et peragendi prosequendi et defendendi atque in eisdem procedendi vel supersedendi examinandi audiendi terminandi absolvendi condemnandi decidendi atque Execucioni Mandandi secundum Leges et Consuetudines Insule et locorum maritimorum predictorum [372] preantea vsitatas et approbatas absque provocacione seu appellacione quacunque preterquam in Casubus qui Cognitioni nostre Regali ex antiqua consuetudine Insule et locorum predictorum reservantur vel de Jure aut privilegio nostro Regali reservari debentur Quamquidem authoritatem potestatem et facultatem preterquam in eisdem Casubus reservatas Nos pro nobis heredibus et Successoribus nostris prefatis Ballivo et Juratis et aliis Damus Comittimus Concedimus et Confirmamus per presentes adeo plene libere et integre prout prefati Ballivus et Jurati ac alii vel eorum aliquis vnquam antehac eisdem rite et legitime vsi functi aut gavisi vel vti fungi aut gaudere debuerunt aut licite potuerunt debuit aut potuit.

[6] Volumus preterea ac pro nobis heredibus et Successoribus nostris per presentes Concedimus prefatis Ballivo et Juratis ac aliis Incolis et Habitatoribus infra Insulam et loca maritima predicta quod nullus eorum de cetero per aliqua Brevia seu processus ex aliquibus Curiis nostris seu alibi infra Regnum nostrum Anglie emergencia sive eorum aliqui citetur apprehendetur evocetur in placita trahatur sive quovismodo aliter comparare aut respondere cogatur extra Insulam et loca maritima predicta coram quibuscunque Judicibus Justiciariis Magistratibus aut Officiariis nostris aut aliis de aut super aliqua re lite materia seu Causa quacunque infra Insulam predictam emanente seu quod Insulani predicti et eorum quilibet huiusmodi Citationibus apprehensionibus Brevibus et processibus non obstantibus licite et impune valeant aut possint infra

Insulam et loca predicta residere commorari quiescere et Justiciam ibidem expectare absque aliqua pena corporali seu pecuniario fine redempcione aut Mulcta proinde incurrenda forisfacienda Necnon absque aliqua Offensione vel causa contemptus Seu contumacie per nos heredes et Successores nostros illis seu eorum alicui aut aliquibus pro inde infligenda irroganda vel aliter adiudicanda (exceptis tantumodo huiusmodi Casubus qui per leges Insule et locorum predictorum Regali nostre Cognitioni atque examini reserventur vel de iure aut privilegio nostro Regali reservari debentur.

[7] Et vlterius de ampliori gratia nostra ac ex certa scientia et mero motu nostris Dedimus Concessimus et Confirmamus Ac per presentes pro nobis heredibus et Successoribus nostris quantum in nobis est Damus Concedimus et Confirmamus prefatis Ballivo et Juratis ceterisque Incolisque et Habitatoribus Insule et locorum Maritimorum predictorum Necnon Mercatoribus et aliis eo confluentibus tot tanta talia huiusmodi et consimilia Jura Jurisdicciones impunitates indempnitates exempciones libertates Franchesias et privilegia quecunque quot quanta qualia et que prefati Ballivus Jurati ac ceteri Incole et Habitatores Mercatores et alii aut eorum aliquis antehac legitime et rite vsi freti seu gavisi fuerunt vsus fretus seu gavisus fuit Ac omnia et singula quecunque alia in aliquibus Cartis Ordinacionibus aut Literis Patentibus nostrum seu Progenitorum seu Antecessorum nostrorum quondam Regum et Reginarum Angli seu Ducum Normanie aut aliorum eis seu eorum Predecessoribus antehac data concessa seu confirmata et non revocata seu abolita quocunque nomine aut quibuscunque nominibus iidem Ballivus Jurati et ceteri Incole et Habitatores eiusdem Insule et locorum Maritimorum predictorum aut eorum Predecessores seu eorum aliqui vel aliquis in eisdem Literis Patentibus seu eorum aliquibus censeantur nuncupentur [373] aut vocitentur seu censeri nuncupari aut vocitari debuere aut soliti fuere ac omnia et singula licet in presentibus minime expressa prefatis Ballivo et Juratis ac ceteris Incolis et Habitatoribus Insule et locorum Maritimorum predictorum Necnon Mercatoribus et aliis eo confluentibus Indigenis et Alienigenis per presentes Confirmamus consolidamus et de integro Ratificamus adeo plene libere et integre prout ea omnia et singula in eisdem Literis Patentibus contenta modo perticulariter verbatim expresse in presentibus Literis nostris Patentibus recitata et declarata fuissent.

[8] Salva semper atque illabefacta suprema Regia potestate Dominatione atque Imperio Corone nostre Anglie tam quoad Ligeam subieccionem et obediamenciam Insule predicte ac aliorum quorumcunque [sic] infra Insulam et loca predicta commorancium Sive degencium quam quoad Regalitatem Privilegia Res Redditus Vectigalia ac cetera Iura proficua Commoditates et Emolumenta quecunque infra Insulas et loca predicta nobis et heredibus et Successoribus nostris per prerogativam Corone nostre Anglie sive Ducatus Normannie seu aliter ex antiquo debita et Consueta. Salvis etiam appellacionibus et

provocacionibus quibuscunque Insulanorum predictorum ac aliorum ibidem comorancium sive degencium in omnibus eiusmodi Casibus et non aliis que legibus et consuetudinibus Insule et locorum predictorum Regali nostre cognitioni atque Examini reservantur vel de iure aut privilegio nostro Regali reservari debentur. Aliqua sentencia Clausula re aut materia quacunque superius in presentibus expressa sive specificata in contrarium inde in aliquo non obstantibus.

[9] Proviso semper quod aliqua Clausula Articulus sive aliquod aliud in presentibus Literis nostris Patentibus expresum et specificatum non exponantur interpretentur nec se extendant ad aliquod quod sit vel fieri possit Nobis heredibus vel Successoribus nostris preiudiciale quoad aliqua Terras Tenementa redditus Regalitates vel hereditamenta nostra infra Insulam predictam & loca maritima predicta aut eorum aliqua.

[10] Et insuper cum datum est nobis intelligi quod quedam Exactio nuper levata fuerit de Inhabitantibus et Gentibus Insule nostre de Jersey predicta et Mercatoribus et illis illic confluentibus contra antiquam Extentam et consuetudinem ibidem vsitatam (vizt) pro quolibet quarterio frumenti vel alterius grani extra Insulam illam exportato tres solidos et sex denarios monete currentis infra eandem Insulam vbi illa Extenta antehac ad tantam summam se non extendebat vt accipimus Et cum dicti Inhabitantes et Gentes Insule de Jersey predicta soliti fuere similiter solvere ad vsum Progenitorum sive Antecessorum nostrorum pro quibuslibet Centum & quinquaginta libris Lane extra Insulam illam exportatæ iuxta Extentam ibidem vsitatam quatuor denarios monete currentis infra eandem Insulam Nos volumus Ac per presentes pro nobis heredibus et Successoribus nostris Concedimus prefatis prefatis Inhabitantibus et Gentibus Insule nostre de Jersey predicta quod ipsi et omnes alii Mercatores illuc confluentes non plus nec maiorem summam exnunc deinceps inperpetuum solvere teneantur ad vsum nostrum quam duodecim denarios monete currentis infra eandem Insulam de Jersey pro quolibet quarterio frumenti sive alterius generis grani extra eandem Insulam posthec exportandi. Ita semper et sub conditione quod iidem Inhabitantes et Gens Insule de Jersey predicta ac omnes alii Mercatores et extranei illuc confluentes solvere debeant et teneantur posthac inperpetuum [374] ad vsum nostrum pro quibuslibet Centum et Quinquaginta Libris Lane extra Insulam illam exportandis tres solidos et dimidium monete currentis infra eandem Insulam & loca maritima predicta seu eorum aliqua.

[11] Volumus etiam Ac per presentes Concedimus prefatis Ballivo et Juratis ceterisque Insulanis et Habitatoribus Insule et locorum Maritimorum predictorum quod habeant et habebunt has literas nostras Patentes sub magno Sigillo nostro Anglie debito modo factas et Sigillatas absque fine seu feodo magno vel parvo nobis in Hanaperio nostro seu alibi ad vsum nostrum proinde

quoquomodo reddendis solvendis vel faciendis Eo quod expressa mencio de vero valore annuo aut de certitudine premissorum aut eorum alicuius aut de aliis donis sive Concessionibus per nos seu per aliquem Progenitorum sive Predecessorum nostrorum prefatis Ballivo et Juratis Insule nostre de Jersey predicta ante hec tempora factis in presentibus minime factis existit aut aliquo Statuto Actu Ordinacione provisione Proclamacione sive restriccione antehac habitis factis editis Ordinatis sive provisis aut aliqua alia re Causa vel materia quacunque in contrarium inde in aliquo non obstante In cuius rei testimonium has literas nostras fieri fecimus Patentes Teste me ipso apud Canbury sexto die Julii Anno Regni nostri Anglie &c Tertio.

[12] Nos autem literas Patentes predictas ac omnia & singula Concessiones Jura Jurisdicciones privilegia Immunitates libertates et franchesias ac cetera omnia et singula in eisdem literis Patentibus contenta et specificata rata habentes et grata. Ea omnia et singula pro nobis heredibus Successoribus nostris quantum in nobis est acceptamus et approbamus Ac dilectis Subditis nostris Ballivo et Juratis Insule nostre de Jersey predicta ac ceteris Incolis et Habitatoribus infra Insulam illam tenore presentium ratificamus et Confirmamus prout eedem Litere Patentes in se rationabiliter testantur Et vlterius in tesseram favoris nostri prefatis Ballivo et Juratis Insule nostre de Jersey predicta ac ceteris Incolis et Habitatoribus infra Insulam illam pro summa et constanti fidelitate et Ligeantia suis Nobis et Predecessoribus nostris nuper Regibus et Reginis Anglie ex quacunque Causa manisfestata De gratia nostra speciali ac ex certa scientia et mero motu nostris Dedimus et Concessimus Ac per presentes pro nobis heredibus et Successoribus nostris Damus et Concedimus eisdem Ballivo et Juratis Insule nostre de Jersey ac ceteris Incolis et Habitatoribus infra Insulam illam plenam potestatem et authoritatem Eo quod de cetero imperpetuum liceat et licebit eis habere vti et portare seu portari causare coram Ballivo eiusdem Insule nostre de Jersey pro tempore existente vnam Claveam Auream vel Argenteam communiter vocatam a Mace Insigniis Armorum nostrorum heredum et Successorum nostrorum super inde insculptam et ornatam in et per totam illam Insulam nostram de Jersey libertates et Precincta eiusdem ad libitum huiusmodi Ballivi Insule illius pro tempore existente quando et quoties occasio requiret.

[13] Et vlterius volumus et per presentes pro nobis heredibus et Successoribus nostris Concedimus prefatis Ballivo et Juratis Insule nostre de Jersey predicta et ceteris Incolis et Habitatoribus infra Insulam illam quod he litere nostre Patentes in omnibus et per omnia secundum veram intencionem earundem bone firme valide et effectuales in Lege sint et erunt Non obstante non nominacione vel falsa nominacione vel recitacione [375] in eisdem contentis aut aliquot Statuto Ordinacione Provisione Proclamacione vel restriccione antehac habitis seu factis modo quolibetcunque non obstante.

[14] Volumus etiam Ac per presentes Concedimus prefatis Ballivo et Juratis Insule nostre de Jersey predicta quod habeant et habebunt has Literas nostras Patentes sub magno Sigillo nostro Anglie debito modo factas et sigillatas absque ffine seu feodo magno vel parvo Nobis in Hanaperio nostro seu alibi ad vsum nostrum proinde quoquomodo reddendis solvendis vel faciendis. Eo quod expressa mencio de vero valore annuo aut de certitudine premissorum aut eorum alicuius aut de aliis donis sive Concessionibus per nos seu per aliquem Progenitorum sive Predecessorum nostrorum prefatis Ballivo et Juratis Insule nostre de Jersey predicta ante hec tempora factis in presentibus minime factis existit aut aliquo Statuto Actu Ordinacione Provisione Proclamacione sive restriccione antehac habitis factis editis Ordinatis sive provisis aut aliqua alia re causa vel materia quacunque in contrarium inde in aliquo non obstante In cuius rei testimonium has Literas nostras fieri fecimus Patentes Teste me ipso apud Westmonasterium Decimo die Octobris Anno Regni nostri Decimo quarto.

Howard

Per Breve de privato Sigillo

Translation

[1] Charles the Second, by the grace of God king of England, Scotland, France and Ireland, Defender of the Faith &c. To all to whom these present letters come, greeting. We have inspected certain letters patent of the Lord Charles formerly king of England our most dearly beloved father, of blessed memory, made in these words. Charles, by the grace of God king of England, Scotland, France and Ireland, Defender of the Faith &c. To all to whom the present letters come, greeting. Whereas our beloved and faithful lieges and subjects, the bailiff and the jurats of our Island of Jersey, and the other sojourners in and inhabitants of the same island within our duchy of Normandy, and their predecessors, have from time beyond what the memory of men can reach, by virtue of several charters, grants, confirmations, and most ample writs, of our illustrious progenitors and ancestors, both kings and queens of England and dukes of Normandy, and others, used, enjoyed, and been in possession of very many rights, jurisdictions, privileges, immunities, liberties, and franchises, freely and quietly, and without any infringement of the same, both within the kingdom of England, and elsewhere within our dominions, and other places under our subjection on this side of, or beyond, the seas; by the aid and benefit of which grants, the aforenamed island and maritime places have stood out and continued constantly, faithfully, and unblameably in our faith, obedience, and service, and that of our progenitors and predecessors, and have enjoyed and gone on in their commerce and trade with merchants, both natives and aliens, as well in time of peace, as in time of war, and exercised and executed their duties in giving their decrees, and taking cognisance of all and every cause,

quarrel, action, both civil and criminal, and capital and judicial pleas; and the right of jurisdiction they were vested with, to take into their consideration, decide, discuss, hear, and determine, and to proceed in the premises, and keep records of their proceedings according to the laws and customs practised of old, and approved in the said island and other places aforesaid; except in certain cases reserved from time to time to our royal cognisance.

[2] And we considering of how great advantage and moment all and singular the premises are, and have been, toward the safe-keeping and conservation of the aforesaid island and maritime places in their fidelity and allegiance to our crown of England; and being always mindful, as is just, how courageously and loyally the said islanders and inhabitants have behaved themselves in our own and in our progenitors' service, and considering what great detriments, losses and dangers they have sustained and do daily sustain, both for the constant safeguarding and defence of our Castle of Mont Orgueil, in our aforesaid island of Jersey; to the end, not only to show some distinguished testimony and certain marks of our favour, affection, and royal beneficence towards the inhabitants aforesaid, but also to encourage them, and their posterity for ever, to persevere and continue inviolably in their accustomed and due obedience towards us, and our heirs and successors; we have thought proper to grant to them these our royal letters patent, confirmed under our great seal of England, in form following.

[3] Know ye, that we, of our special favour, certain knowledge, and mere motion, have given and granted, and for ourselves, our heirs and successors, we do by these present letters give and grant, to the said bailiff and jurats of our island of Jersey aforesaid, and to the other sojourners and inhabitants of the same island; that they themselves and every one of them (though not herein stated or declared by their particular names) were and shall, for the time to come, be for ever free, exempted, and acquitted, in all our cities, boroughs, markets, and trading towns, fairs, mart-towns, and other places and ports, within our kingdom of England, and within all our provinces, dominions, territories, and other places under our subjection, this side of, or beyond, the seas, from and of all tributes, tolls, customs, subsidies, hidage, taylage, pontage, panage, murage, fossage, works, and warlike expeditions (except in case our body, or that of heirs and successors, should be held in prison (which God avert)), and of and from all other contributions, duties, and exactions whatsoever, that may be due from, to be rendered by, or be payable by, and claimed from, the said islanders, to us, our heirs and successors, ever in any manner, by virtue of any charters, grants, confirmations, and writs of our said progenitors, formerly kings of England and dukes of Normandy, or others, or by virtue or reason of any reasonable and legal usage, prescription, or custom.

[4] And whereas some other privileges, jurisdictions, immunities, liberties, and franchises have been graciously given, granted, and confirmed by our progenitors and predecessors, formerly kings of England and dukes of Normandy, and others, to the aforesaid islanders, and have been used and observed constantly in the said island and other maritime places, from the time whereof the memory of men reaches not to the contrary; one of which is, that in time of war merchants of all nations and others, both aliens and native, both enemies and friends, could and might freely, lawfully, without danger or punishment, come to, resort to, go to and fro, and frequent the said island, and other maritime places, with their ships and goods; both to avoid storms, and to conduct their other lawful business there, and to exercise there free commerce, business and trade, and securely, and without danger, remain there, and depart from thence, and return to the same, as often as they think fit, without any harm, molestation, or hostility whatsoever, in their goods, merchandise, or persons; and this not only within the said island and maritime places, and all around the same, but likewise at such spaces and distances from the island as the sight of man goes to, that is as far as the eye of man can reach: We, by virtue of our royal authority, do, for ourselves, our heirs and successors, indulge and enlarge, and renew, reiterate, and confirm, by these present letters, as far as in us lies, the same immunities, impunities, liberty, and privileges, and all the other premises last mentioned, finding them to be reasonable and seasonable, to the said bailiff and jurats, and the other sojourners, inhabitants and merchants, and others, whether enemies or friends, and to each of them, in as ample form and manner as heretofore they have used or enjoyed the same, or should have used or enjoyed the same. In order therefore to prevent any violation or infraction, reckless or otherwise, of this our grant, concession, and confirmation, or any thing therein contained, in any manner whatsoever, we declare and give this warning by these present letters to all our magistrates, officers and subjects in all parts of our kingdom of England, and throughout all our lordships and places under our obedience, wheresoever they lie, or are situated. And if any one of our said officers and subjects shall be so rash as to presume or attempt to transgress these our strict orders and commands, we order and decree (as far as in us lies), that he shall not only restore what has been taken or seized, but shall also be compelled to make a fuller restitution and satisfaction of all costs, interests, and damages, by whatever legal remedy, and he shall be severely punished for his audacious contempt of our royal power, or of our laws.

[5] Further, we, of our more gracious favour, for ourselves, our heirs and successors, do, by these present letters, ratify, approve, establish, and confirm, all and every one of the laws and customs which have been duly and legally used and from ancient times received and approved within the aforesaid island and maritime places; giving and granting to the aforesaid bailiff and jurats,

and all other magistrates and officers of justice, and others who are appointed for performing the functions and executing the duties of any office, full and absolute authority, power, and faculty to have the cognisance, jurisdiction, and judgment concerning and touching all and all sorts of pleas, processes, law-suits, actions, quarrels, and causes arising within the island and maritime places aforesaid; both those actions which are personal, real, and mixed, and those which are criminal and capital, and to proceed in the said island, and not elsewhere, in hearing the parties in their pleadings, in prosecutions of their processes, and in their defence; and to supersede, examine, and hear the same, determining, absolving, condemning, making decrees, and putting their sentences in execution, according to the laws and customs previously practised and approved in the island and maritime places aforesaid; without admitting any challenge or appeal, except in such cases as are reserved to our royal cognisance by the ancient custom of the island and places aforesaid, or by our royal right and privilege ought so to be reserved. Which authority, power, and faculty, except in the cases reserved to us, we give, commit, grant, and confirm, for ourselves and our heirs and successors aforesaid, to the said bailiffs and jurats, and to the others, by these present letters, as freely, fully, and entirely, as the said bailiff and jurats, or others or any of them, heretofore have rightfully and lawfully used, practised, and enjoyed, or might legally have used and enjoyed.

[6] Moreover, our will and pleasure is, and we grant, for ourselves, our heirs, and successors by these present letters, to the said bailiff and jurats, and the other inhabitants and sojourners in the island and maritime places aforesaid, that for the time to come, none of them be cited, arrested, or summoned, or drawn into any lawsuit, or forced in any manner by any writs or process, issued from any of our courts or others of the kingdom of England, to appear and answer before any of our judges, justices, magistrates, or officers, or others, out of the island and maritime places aforesaid, touching or concerning any thing, dispute, causes, or matters in controversy whatsoever, arising in the aforesaid island, but that the aforesaid islanders, and each of them, may lawfully and without restraint, notwithstanding the said summons, warrants, writs and processes, remain, reside quietly, and abide in the aforesaid island and places, waiting for justice there; without incurring any punishment, corporal or pecuniary, by way of fine, mulct, ransom, or forfeiture, by reason of any offence, contempt, or contumacy, committed towards us, our heirs and successors, for which they might be sued, arraigned, or condemned (except only in the cases, which by the laws of the island and places aforesaid are reserved to our royal cognisance and determination, or by our royal right and privilege ought to be so reserved.

[7] And moreover, of our more gracious favour, certain knowledge, and mere motion, we have given, granted, and confirmed, and by our present letters, for ourselves, our heirs and successors as far as in us lies, we do give, grant, and confirm to the aforesaid bailiff and jurats, and other sojourners in, and inhabitants of, the aforesaid island and maritime places; as also to merchants and others meeting there, the like, and as great, and as ample rights, jurisdictions, impunities, indemnities, exemptions, liberties, franchises, and privileges whatsoever, as the aforesaid bailiff, jurats, and other sojourners and inhabitants, and merchants and others, or any of them, have heretofore rightfully and legally used, practised, and enjoyed; and all and singular other things whatsoever that has been heretofore given, granted, and confirmed to them or to their predecessors, in any charters, orders, or letters patent, of us or our progenitors or predecessors, formerly kings and queens of England, or dukes of Normandy, or others, and not revoked or abolished, by whatsoever name or names the same bailiff and jurats, and other sojourners in, or inhabitants of, the same island and maritime places aforesaid, or their predecessors, or any of them, may be supposed to have been comprised, called, or named, or ought to have been called or named, in the said letters patent, and all and singular which things, though not herein expressly mentioned, we do by these present letters confirm, consolidate, and ratify anew to the aforesaid bailiff and jurats, and other sojourners, and inhabitants, of the island and maritime places aforesaid, and also merchants and others coming together there, those born there, and those born elsewhere, as fully, freely, and entirely, as if all and singular the things particularly mentioned and declared in the same letters patent were particularly in words expressly recited and declared in these our present letters patent.

[8] Saving always entire and without detriment the regal and sovereign power, dominion, and empire of our crown of England, as to what may concern the allegiance, subjection, and obedience of the aforesaid islanders, and others, whoever they may be, dwelling for a shorter or longer time in the same island; and also as to what may concern the regality, privileges, incomes, revenues, tributes, and other rights, profits, commodities, and emoluments whatsoever, anciently due and accustomed to be paid to us, our heirs and successors, according to our royal prerogative as kings of England, or the prerogative of the duchy of Normandy, in the island and places aforesaid; saving also to the aforesaid islanders, and others dwelling or being in the said island, a right to appeal in all cases reserved to our cognisance and consideration by the laws and customs of the said island, or which by our royal right or privilege ought to be so reserved. Notwithstanding any sentence, clause, thing, or matter whatsoever expressed above, or specially contained to the contrary in these present letters.

[9] Provided always that any clause, article, or any other thing expressed and specified in our present letters patent are not construed, interpreted nor extended to any thing that might be prejudicial to us, our heirs, or successors with regards to any of our lands, tenements, rents, regalities, or inheritances within the aforesaid island and maritime places or any of them.

[10] And in addition, since we are given to understand that an exaction has recently been levied upon the inhabitants and peoples of our island of Jersey aforesaid, and on merchants and others gathering there against the ancient extent and custom there used, that is to say for each quarter of corn or other grain exported from the island three shillings and six pence in money current within the island, when that extent previously did not, as we understand, extend to so large a sum. And since the said inhabitants and people of the aforesaid isle of Jersey were accustomed in the same way to pay to the use of our progenitors or ancestors for every one hundred and fifty pounds of wool exported from the island according to the extent there used four pence in the money current within the same island, we will, and by these present letters for us, our heirs, and successors do grant to the aforesaid inhabitants and peoples of our aforesaid island of Jersey, that they themselves, and all the other merchants gathering there from now henceforth for ever shall be bound to pay for our use a sum no more or greater than twelve pence in the money current within the same island of Jersey for each quarter of wheat or other type of grain hereafter exported from the same island. Thus, always, and on condition that the same inhabitants and peoples of the aforesaid island of Jersey and all other merchants and foreigners gathering there, owe and are bound to pay forever hereafter to our use for every one hundred and fifty pounds of wool exported from that island, three and a half shillings in the money current within the same island and aforesaid maritime places, or any of them.

[11] Furthermore, we wish and by these present letters we grant, that the said bailiff and jurats and other islanders and inhabitants of the aforesaid island and maritime places should and will have these our letters patent made in the proper way and sealed under our great seal of England without fine or fee, great or small, rendered, made or paid to us in our Hanaper or elsewhere to our use for the same. The fact that express mention of the true annual value, or of the certainty of the premises, or of any one or of other gifts or grants made by us or by any of our progenitors or predecessors, to the aforesaid bailiff and jurats of our aforesaid island of Jersey before these times is not made in these present letters, or in any statute, act, ordinance, proviso, proclamation, or restriction to the contrary thereof heretofore had, made, published, setting there in order, or provided to, or in any other thing, cause or matter whatsoever in any way notwithstanding; in witness whereof we caused these our letters

to be made patent; witness myself, at Canbury the sixth day of July in the year of our reign in England etc. the third.

[12] We moreover finding the aforesaid Letters Patent and all and singular concessions, rights, jurisdictions, privileges, immunities, liberties, and franchises, and all and singular other things contained and specified in the same Letters Patent to be reasonable and acceptable, for ourselves, our heirs and successors, as far as in us lies, accept and approve, and to our beloved subjects the bailiff and jurats of our aforesaid island of Jersey and the other sojourners in and inhabitants of that island, for their great and constant faith and allegiance shown to us and our predecessors formerly kings and queens of England, for whatever cause, of our special favour and certain knowledge, and mere motion we have given and granted and by these present letters for ourself, our heirs and successors we give and grant to the same bailiff and jurats of our island of Jersey and other sojourners in and inhabitants of that island full power and authority that finally in perpetuity it is and will be permitted to them to have, use, and carry, or cause to be carried in the presence of the bailiff of our same island of Jersey for the time being what is commonly called a 'Mace' of gold or silver sculpted and garnished with the our arms and the arms of our heirs and successors upon it, in and through the whole of that island of Jersey, its liberties and precincts at the will of bailiff of that island for the time being, when and as often as the occasion requires.

[13] And further we wish and by these present letters for ourselves, our heirs and successors, we grant to the said bailiff and jurats of our aforesaid island of Jersey, and the other soujourners and inhabitants within that island, that these our letters patent, in and through all matters, will be good, firm, valid and effectual in law according to the true intention of the same. Notwithstanding failure to identify, or the false identification or recitation contained in the same or notwithstanding any statute, ordinance, provision, proclamation, or restriction of whatsoever kind heretofore had or made.

[14] Furthermore, we wish and by these present letters we grant, that the said bailiff and jurats and other islanders and inhabitants of the aforesaid island and maritime places should and will have these our letters patent made in the proper way and sealed under our great seal of England without fine or fee, great or small, rendered, made, or paid to us in our Hanaper or elsewhere to our use for the same. And that although express mention of the true annual value, or of the certainty of the premises, or any one or of other gifts or grants made by us or by any of our progenitors or predecessors, to the aforesaid bailiff and jurats of our aforesaid island of Jersey before these times is not made in these present letters, or in any statute, act, ordinance, proviso, proclamation, or restriction to the contrary thereof observed, made, published, ordained,

or provided, or any other thing, cause, or matter whatsoever in any way notwithstanding. In testimony whereof we have caused these our Letters to be made Patent. Witness myself, at Westminster on the tenth day of October in the fourth year of our reign.

Howard

By writ of privy seal

James II: 1687

Commentary

While the reign of James II soon saw escalating concern from many of his subjects about his religious policies, in Jersey there was more reason to be optimistic. James knew Jersey well from his time there during the civil wars, and his accession was initially welcomed by many islanders. Increasing crisis in England, however, began to have an effect in the islands. Now there was pressure arising from fear of the island's potentially disruptive role in what was an increasingly restrictive English trade policy, combining with worry that Jersey might form part of James' plan to subvert the Protestant establishment and eventually that it might be a route for his escape and a resource in continued resistance by his supporters. The charter granted on 15 April 1687 reflected these pressures.

Very soon after the news of James' accession, the Jersey community had begun preparations to petition for a confirmation of privileges and for redress of its concerns about trade supporting the stocking-knitting industry. On 12 March 1685, the States agreed to raise £1,200 as part of this effort, and on 21 April good wishes were extended to the governor on his departure for England on this mission.[1] Nothing was achieved in the following months, and by November 1686 the negotiation, now led by the bailiff, Philip de Carteret, had folded concerns about the role of customs officers in with the more general request for a confirmation of the island's privileges.[2]

Success was eventually achieved, and the warrant for the grant of a charter was issued on 19 March 1687, with the charter itself bearing the date 15 April 1687. The charter was read in the States on 2 February 1688 and it was ordered to be enrolled, with thanks being offered to the bailiff for his role in the successful effort.[3]

---

[1] *Actes des états de l'île de Jersey, 1676–1688*, 16e publication de la Société Jersiaise (Jersey, 1899), pp. 86–92.

[2] *Actes des états de l'île de Jersey, 1676–1688*, pp. 101–2.

[3] TNA, C 66/3293, no. 10, mm. 33–7; *Actes des états de l'île de Jersey, 1676–1688*, pp. 104–5; *London Gazette*, 5 March 1685, p. 3.

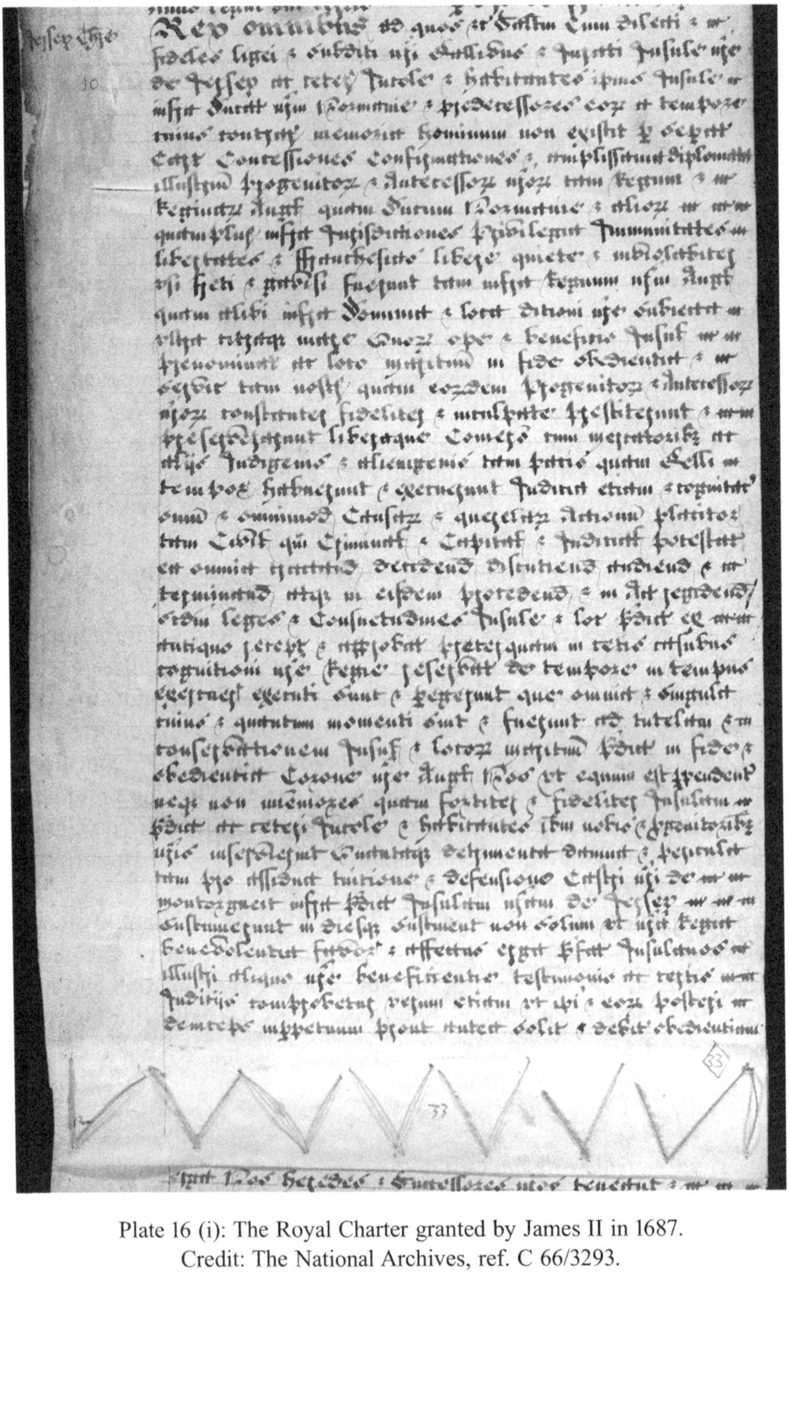

Plate 16 (i): The Royal Charter granted by James II in 1687.
Credit: The National Archives, ref. C 66/3293.

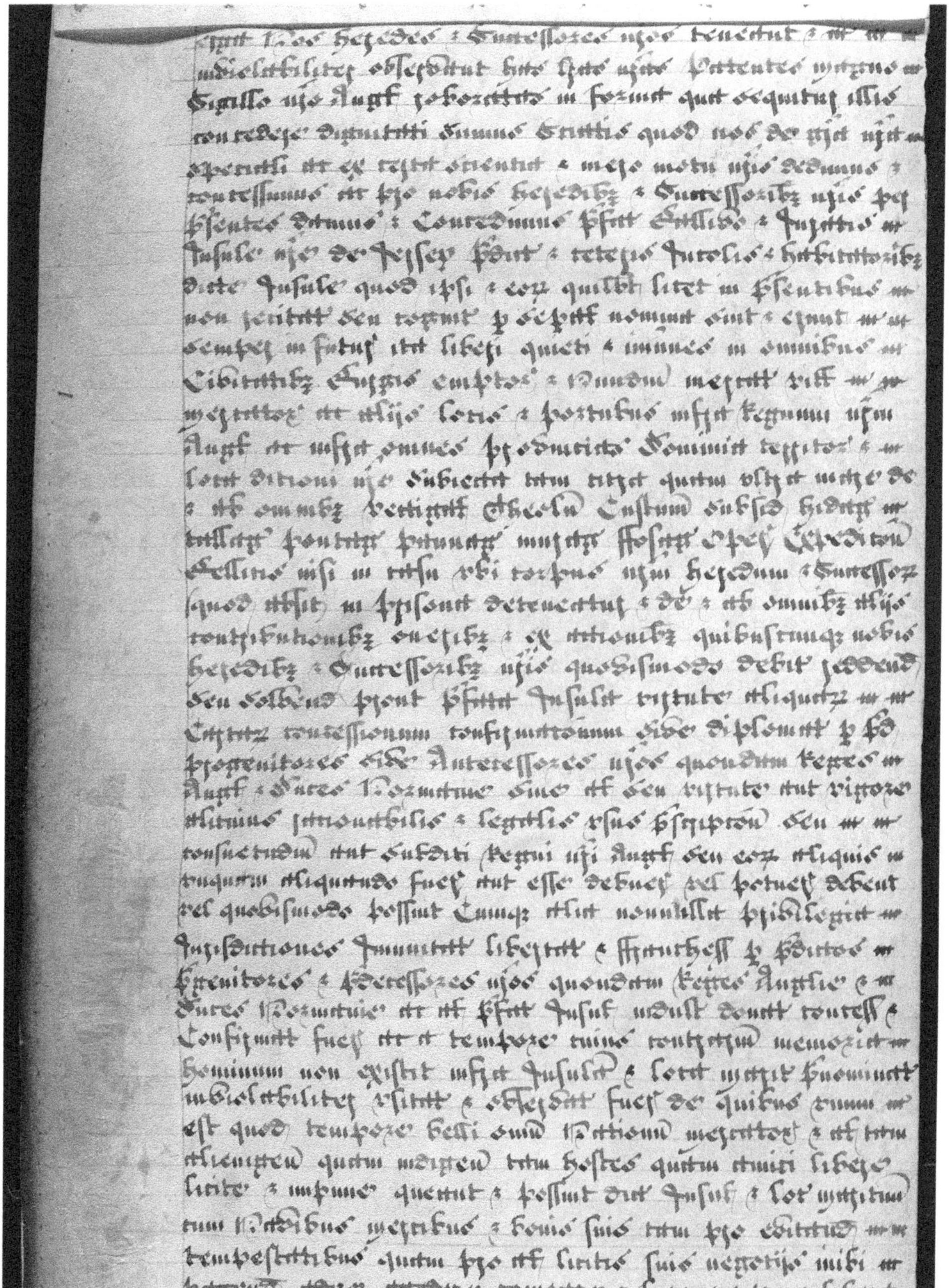

Plate 16 (ii.a): The Royal Charter granted by James II in 1687.

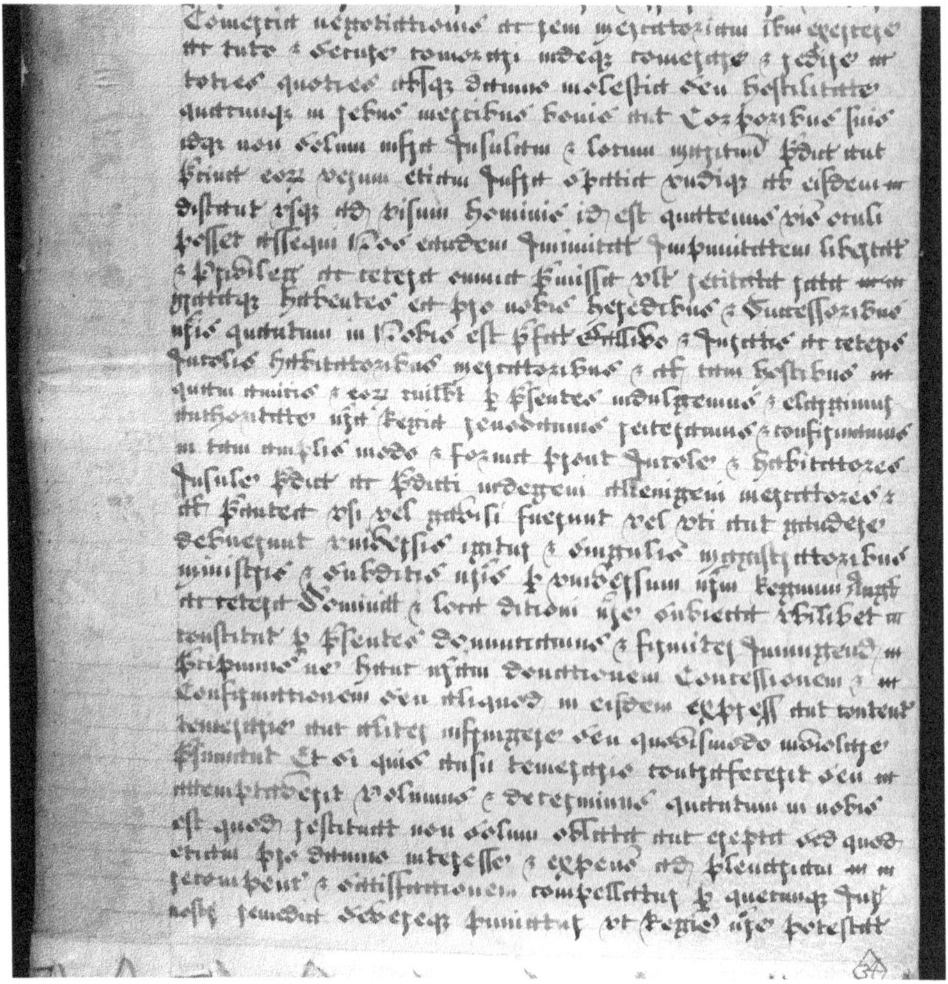

Plate 16 (ii.b): The Royal Charter granted by James II in 1687.

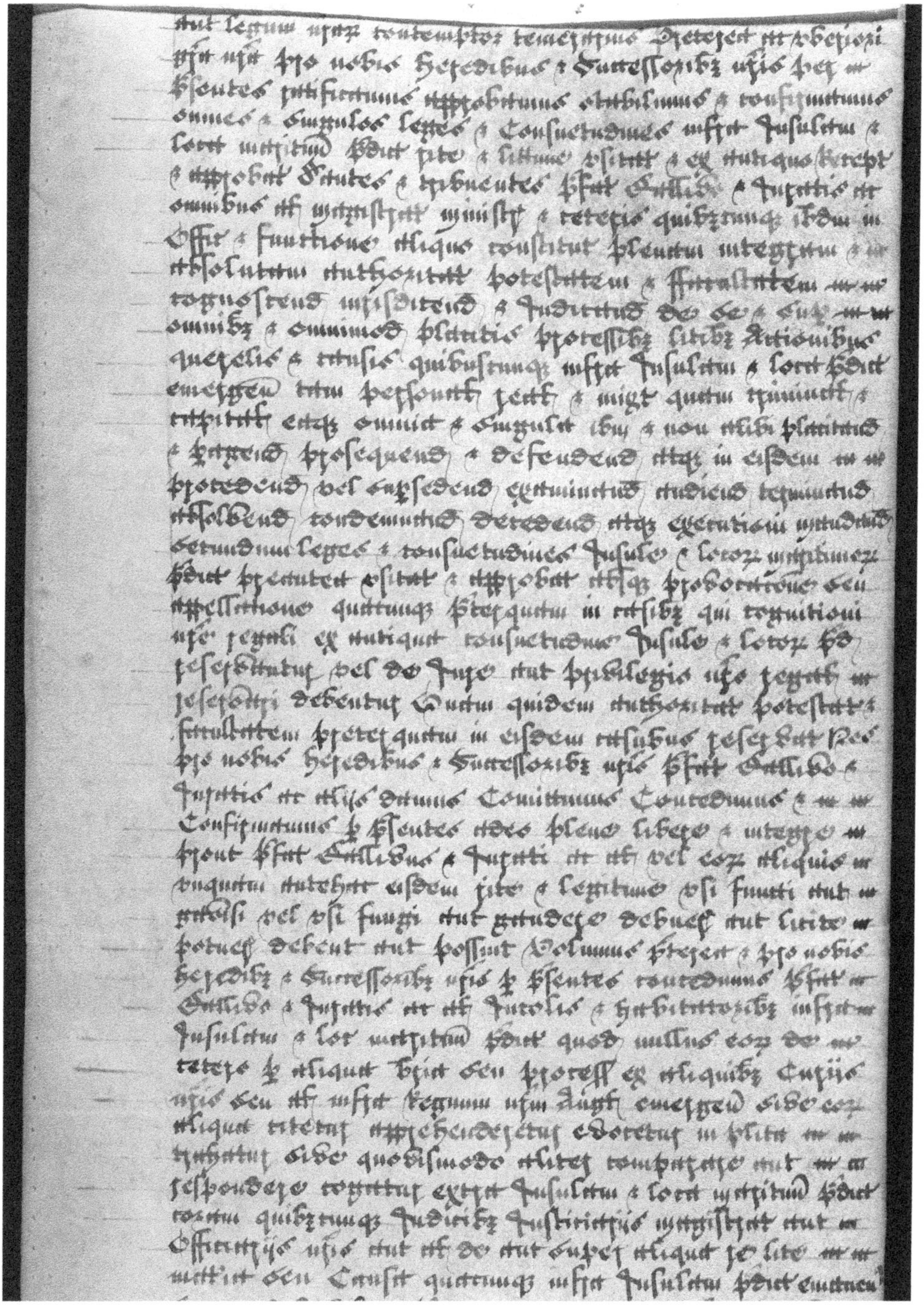

Plate 16 (iii.a): The Royal Charter granted by James II in 1687.

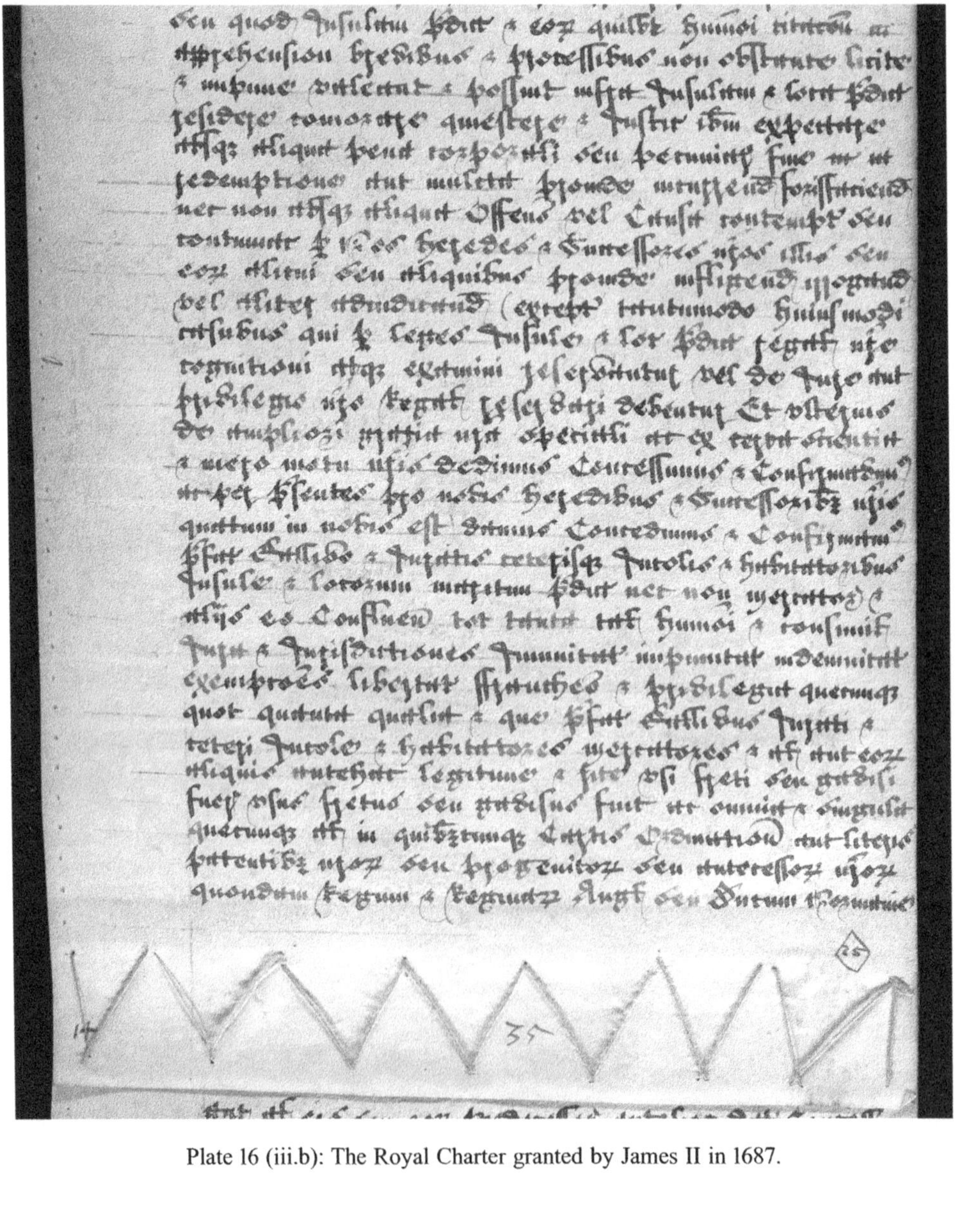

Plate 16 (iii.b): The Royal Charter granted by James II in 1687.

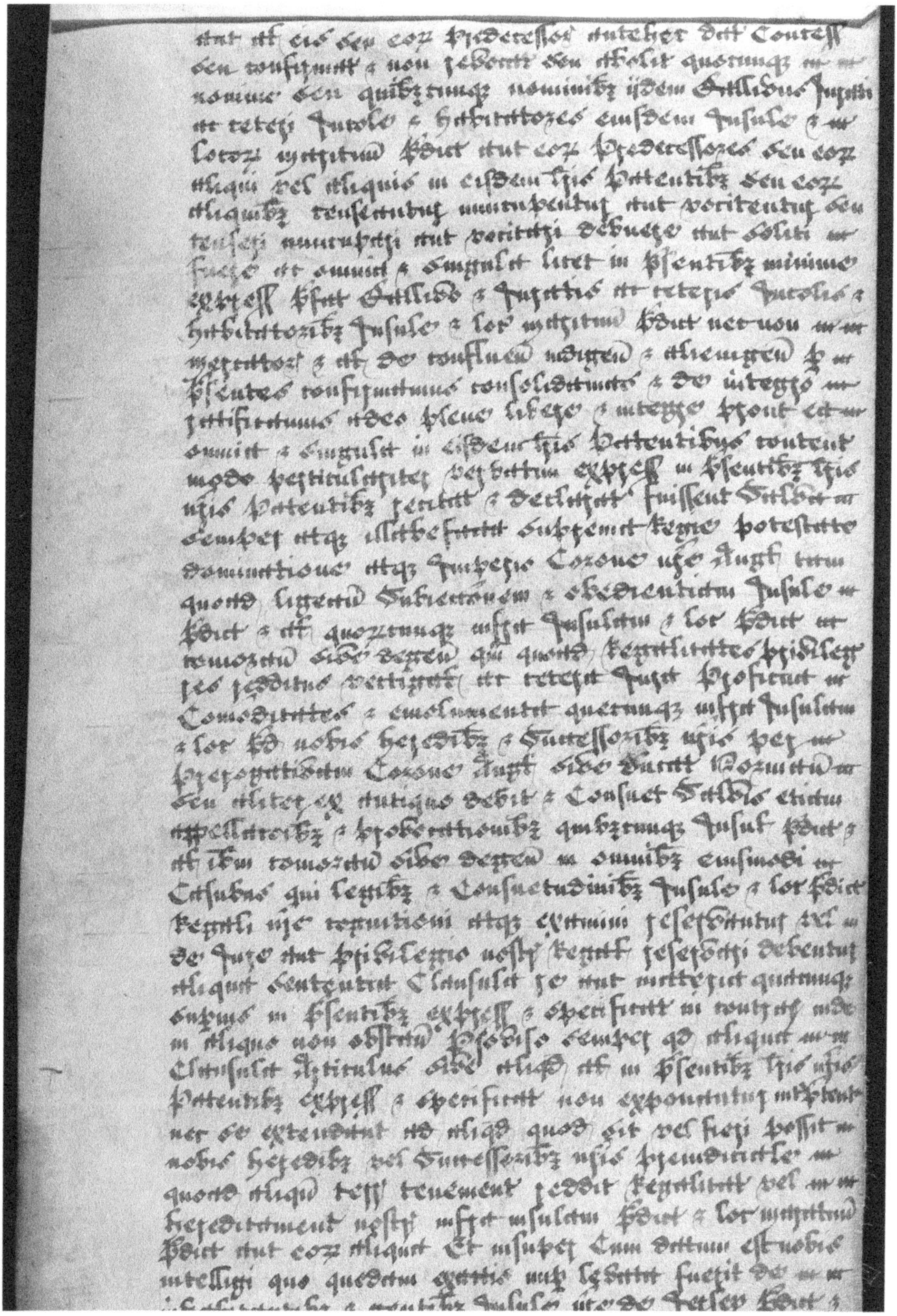

Plate 16 (iv.a): The Royal Charter granted by James II in 1687.

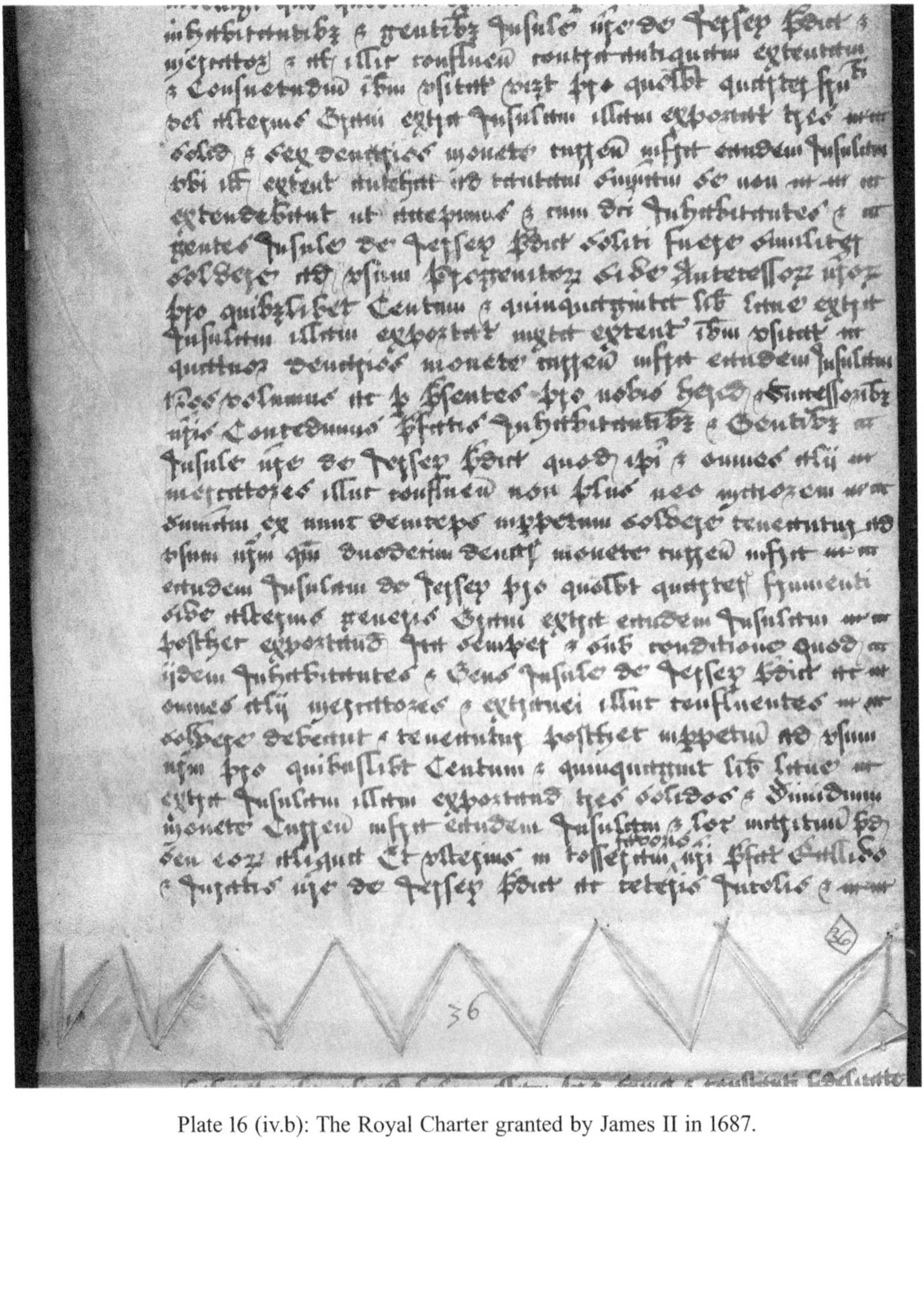

Plate 16 (iv.b): The Royal Charter granted by James II in 1687.

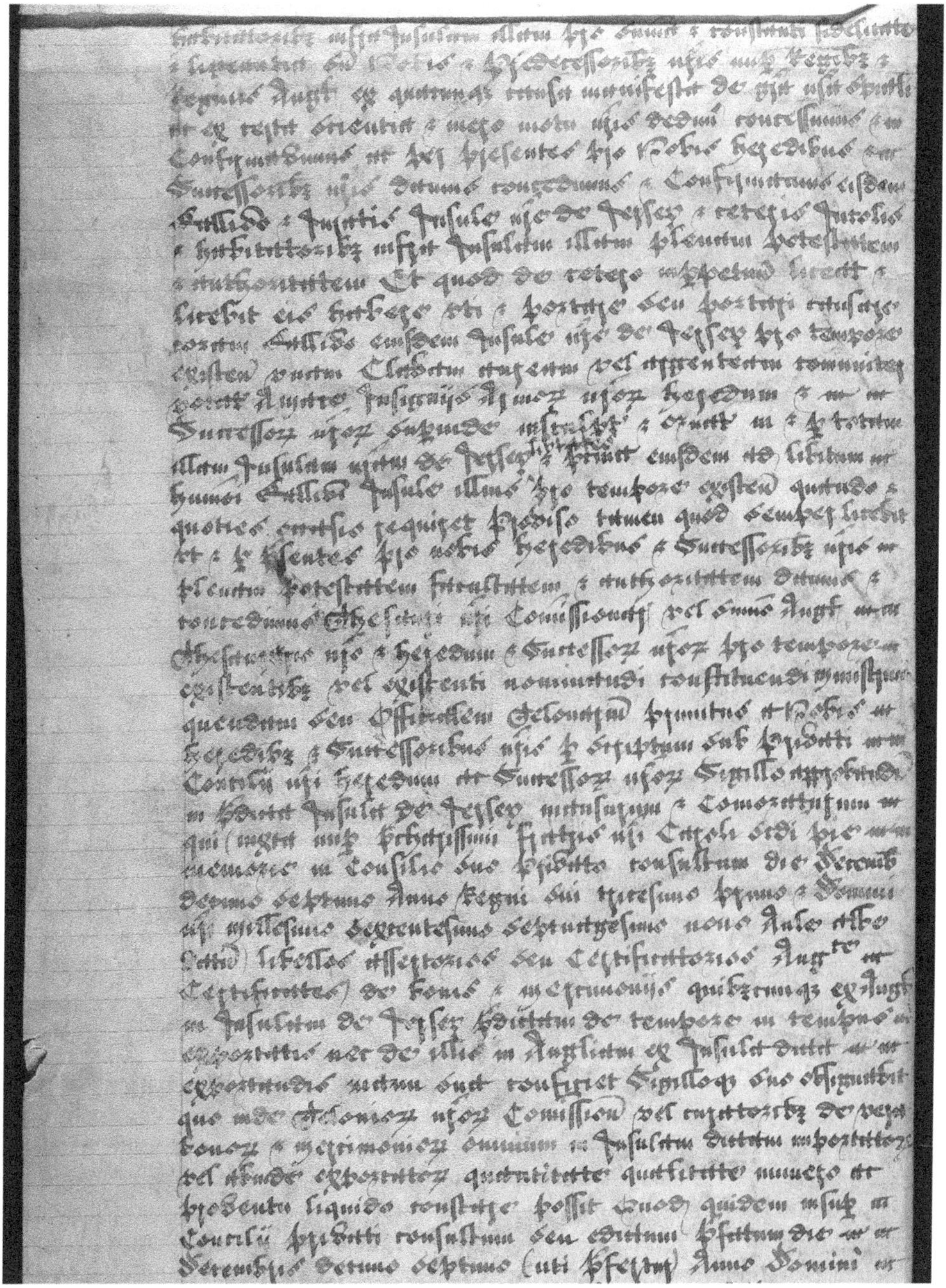

Plate 16 (v.a): The Royal Charter granted by James II in 1687.

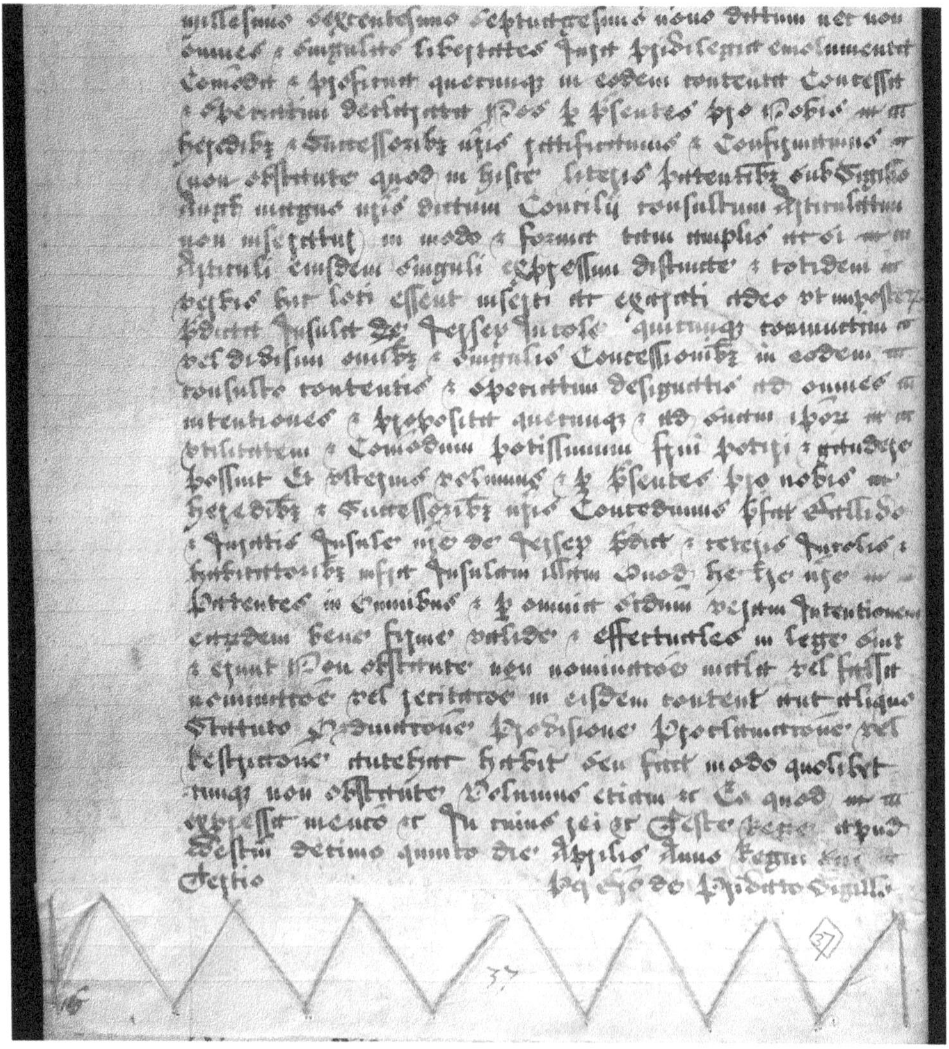

Plate 16 (v.b): The Royal Charter granted by James II in 1687.

This success, albeit one that took longer than originally anticipated to achieve, was a result in part of the close relationship the island community had forged with the new king. In Jersey, islanders were familiar with James as duke of York, and he with the island. When Charles II had visited Jersey for the second time, in 1649, he brought James with him, and when Charles departed for the Netherlands early in 1650, James was left as governor of the island. While the deputy governor, Sir George Carteret, exercised effective control, James was nonetheless able to become familiar with the island through the months until September 1650, when he in turn left for the Netherlands. James seems to have impressed the islanders; James in turn initially enjoyed his time in Jersey, although the limited opportunities for military action once Charles had left meant his frustrations grew. This relationship was recognised in the positive responses from Jersey to James' accession in 1685, which included Philippe Dumaresq's presentation to the new monarch of his *Survey of ye Island of Jersey*, and a congratulatory letter from the States to the new king noted in the *London Gazette* on 5 March 1685.[4] On the island itself it was reported that James' proclamation as king had been greeted 'with a great demonstration of joy and allegiance'.[5]

Jersey's positive relationship with the new regime is well set in context when contrasted with the situation in Guernsey. There, Captain Edward Scot, the commander-in-chief on the island, pursued complaints of treasonous speech against islanders including a jurat, Elizée de Saumares, and this reflected a wider tension between him and the lieutenant-bailiff and jurats.[6] Guernsey also experienced higher levels of tension associated with James' favour for Roman Catholicism, for example in the determined resistance of the bailiff and jurats to the grant to a Roman Catholic priest of a place to celebrate mass in the churchyard. It was no surprise, therefore, that Guernsey was not to receive a charter of confirmation under James.

Unlike Guernsey, Jersey also benefitted from a set of close personal relationships between the island and the new regime, reinforced in the tenure of Thomas Jermyn as governor of Jersey from 1684. He was the grandson of Sir Thomas Jermyn, the leading courtier who had been made governor of Jersey in December 1631. When Sir Thomas died around the turn of 1645, he was

---

[4] John Miller, *James II* (New Haven CT, 2000), p. 13; John Callow, *The Making of King James II* (Stroud, 2000), p. 58; Edward Hyde, *The History of the Rebellion and Civil Wars in England*, ed. W. Dunn Macray (6 vols, Oxford, 1888), vol. 6, pp. 354, 377, 398–9; idem, *The Life of Edward Earl of Clarendon: In which is Included, A Continuation of his History of the Grand Rebellion, Written by Himself* (2 vols, Oxford, 1857), vol. 2, pp. 205–10, 224; Maurice Ashley, *James II* (London, 1977), pp. 26–7; BL, Lansdowne MS 657; Julia M. Marett, 'Philip Dumaresq', *ABSJ*, 12 (1932–35), 413–14; 'A Survey of ye Island of Jersey', *ABSJ*, 12 (1932–35), 415–46; G. R. Balleine, *A Biographical Dictionary of Jersey* (London, 1948), pp. 245–8, esp. pp. 247–8; London Gazette, 5 March 1685, p. 3; JA, D/Y/F1/67 1684–6, fols 82–3; A. C. Saunders, *Jersey in the 17th Century, Containing a History of the Island before and during the Rebellion of 1642–60 and after the Restoration, 1660–1700* (Jersey, 1932), pp. 209–10, 216–17; A. C. Saunders, *Jean Chevalier and his Times: A Story of Sir George Carteret, Baronet, and the Great Rebellion* (Jersey, 1937), pp. 160–74; O. Ogle, W. H. Bliss, W. Dunn Macray and F. J. Routledge (eds), *Calendar of the Clarendon State Papers* (5 vols, Oxford, 1869–1932), vol. 2, pp. 50–1.

[5] *CSPD Feb.–Dec. 1685*, no. 186.

[6] *CSPD June 1687–Feb. 1689*, nos 992, 998.

succeeded in Jersey by his son Henry. Henry Jermyn was very influential in the royalist cause and was created Baron Jermyn of St Edmundsbury in 1643 and earl of St Albans in 1660 on the basis of his close association with Queen Henrietta Maria.[7] The power Henry wielded is evidenced by his overruling of Sir Edward Hyde when Jermyn brought the prince of Wales from Jersey to Paris in June 1646. Henry exercised great influence after the restoration; Thomas, his nephew, was given a commission in the Jersey garrison, which he held until 1679. Thomas therefore knew the island very well, and the return of a Jermyn to the governorship of Jersey in 1684 seems to have been welcomed by all concerned. In turn, Thomas Jermyn valued the abilities of the Jerseyman Philip Falle, then rector of Trinity, sufficiently for him to employ him from 1687 as tutor to his only son in England.[8] This continuity of interest and authority in the Jermyn family helped to reinforce positive relationships between the island and the court.

By contrast, the increasing impact on Jersey of the English Navigation Acts and of concerns about the customs regime meant that there had already been growing tension between the States and successive governors, and beyond them the Privy Council. The case of Philip English (born Philippe Langlois in Trinity, one of the most successful merchants in New England) in 1676, accused of importing tobacco from New Jersey, led to customs officers being sent to Jersey. A petition of the States resulted on 1 May 1679 in the Privy Council accepting there should be no levying of tunnage on trade to and from the island.[9] A newly appointed governor, Sir John Lanier, pursued the issue, however, and on 17 December 1679 the Privy Council reversed its previous

---

[7] G. E. C[ockayne], *The Complete Peerage of England, Scotland, Ireland, Great Britain and the United Kingdom, Extant, Extinct and Dormant*, rev. Vicary Gibbs, ed. H. A. Doubleday, D. Warrand, and Lord Howard de Walden, new edn (13 vols in 14, London, 1910–59), vol. 7, pp. 85–7; Andrew Thrush and John P. Ferris (eds), *The History of Parliament: The House of Commons, 1604–1629* (6 vols, Cambridge, 2010), vol. 4, pp. 894–901; Basil Duke Henning (ed.), *The History of Parliament: The House of Commons, 1660–1690* (3 vols, London, 1983), vol. 2, p. 651; S. H. A. H[ervey] (ed.), *Rushbrook Parish Registers, 1567 to 1850: With Jermyn and Davers Annals* (Woodbridge, 1903), pp. 248–97, esp. pp. 250–1, 258, 261–2; J. A. Messervy, 'Liste des gouverneurs, lieut.-gouverneurs et deputes-gouverneurs de l'île de Jersey', *ABSJ*, 4 (1897–1901), 373–94, at pp. 380–9.

[8] *Rushbrook Parish Registers*, pp. 303–8; Edward Durell, 'Sketch of the Life of the Rev. Philip Falle', in Philip Falle, *An Account of the Island of Jersey*, new edn (Jersey, 1837), pp. xiii–xx, at pp. xvi, xviii; William Burns, 'Falle, Philip (1656–1742), Historian and Church of England Clergyman', *ODNB*, vol. 18, pp. 992–3, at p. 992.

[9] *Ordres du Conseil et pièces analogues enregistrés à Jersey* (6 vols, Jersey, 1897–1906), vol. 2, p. 24; Balleine, *Biographical Dictionary of Jersey*, p. 353; Philip Ahier, 'The "Customer" of Jersey and the "Register" of Certificates', *ABSJ*, 19 (1965–68), 61–70, at pp. 62–3.

decision.[10] The States resisted firmly: Laurence Cole was appointed to collect on 4 August 1680, but this was not registered by the States until 19 March 1681, and then only under protest.[11] Cole refused to take an oath as required by the States until 19 May 1681.[12] Early in James' reign, on 4 October 1685, Cole was succeeded by William Hely, but no action was taken when the letter of appointment was read to the States on 12 January 1686.[13] Therefore another royal letter, dated 24 February 1686, received on 15 April, reinforced the order.[14] The States responded by registering the order without prejudice, and Hely was finally sworn.[15]

The grant of the charter in April 1687 did not resolve these issues with customs, although at paragraph 12 provision was made for the appointment of customs officers by the crown in line with the Privy Council decision of 17 December 1679. On 8 September 1687 a royal letter pointed out that one officer was not enough to stop smuggling; and orders in council directed the States to give assistance to any auxiliary officer appointed.[16] On 4 November 1687 the registrar of certificates was authorised to ask for the assistance of the connétable or others in searching for contraband material, especially tobacco.[17]

The Privy Council must have been informed about the practice of transporting English wool into France, for on 15 June 1688 Thomas Jermyn received a letter from the Privy Council talking of the common practice in Jersey of 'transporting wool of the growth of that place into France and that upon a late trial in the Royal Court there, the same had been justified on pretence of the privileges granted to the said Island'.[18]

By this point, James' authority was beginning to crumble, following the reissuing of the Declaration of Indulgence, which gave freedom of worship to Roman Catholics and Protestant dissenters, and the stubborn resistance to his religious policy from the Seven Bishops. The birth of James' son on 10 June 1688 catalysed the resistance of many leading noblemen, and an invitation was issued to William of Orange, husband of James' daughter Mary, to invade.

---

[10] *Ordres du Conseil*, vol. 2, p. 34; Ahier, '"Customer" of Jersey', p. 63.

[11] *Ordres du Conseil*, vol. 2, p. 44, footnote; *Calendar of Treasury Books, 1679–80* (London, 1913), pp. 674, 690, 712–13; Ahier, '"Customer" of Jersey', pp. 63–4.

[12] *Actes des états de l'île de Jersey, 1676–1688*, 19 Mar. 1681; Ahier, '"Customer" of Jersey', p. 64.

[13] *Ordres du Conseil*, vol. 2, p. 90; reinforced by Royal Letter; *Actes des États de l'île de Jersey, 1676–1688*, pp. 94–5; Ahier, '"Customer" of Jersey', p. 64. NB Samedi Court records show it was 16 January, not 12 January.

[14] *Ordres du Conseil*, vol. 2, p. 100; Ahier, '"Customer" of Jersey', p. 65.

[15] *Ordres du Conseil*, vol. 2, p. 99; *Actes des états de l'île de Jersey, 1676–1688*, pp. 96–7; Ahier '"Customer" of Jersey', p. 65.

[16] *Ordres du Conseil*, vol. 2, p. 142; Ahier, '"Customer" of Jersey', p. 65.

[17] *Ordres du Conseil*, vol. 2, p. 147; Ahier, '"Customer" of Jersey', p. 65.

[18] *Ordres du Conseil*, vol. 2, pp. 151–2.

James' fall and continued Jacobite resistance proved disruptive of the crown's efforts to tighten control of trade though the islands. William Hely remained loyal to the Jacobite cause and was a traitor to William and Mary in the ensuing war. His smuggling activity is recounted in the 'Narration' of 1693, which referred to him as 'probably one of the greatest traitors in the kingdom'.[19] The tradition of Jersey's charter was not to be developed further in the form considered in this volume, but it remained a powerful influence on the rights and position of Jersey and its neighbours.

Text

James II confirmed the grant made by Charles II, adding a clause [12] on the role of a customs official. Specific to Jersey; from the enrolment in The National Archives, C 66/3293, mm. 33–37, with reference to the edition presented in Prison Board in incomplete form.

[1] Rex Omnibus ad quos etc Salutem Cum dilecti et fideles ligei et subditi nostri Ballivus et Jurati Insule nostre de Jersey ac ceteri Incole et habitantes ipsius Insule infra Ducatum nostrum Normanie et predecessores eorum a tempore cujus contrarii memoria hominum non existit per seperales Cartas Concessiones Confirmationes et amplissima diplomata illustrium progenitorum et Antecessorum nostrorum tam Regum et Reginarum Anglie quam Ducum Normanie et aliorum quamplurium infra [error for Jura] Jurisdictiones Privilegia Immunitates libertates et Franchesias libere quiete et inviolabiter [sic] usi freti et gavisi fuerunt tam infra Regnum nostrum Anglie quam alibi infra Dominia et loca ditioni nostre subjecta ultra citraque mare Quorum ope et beneficio Insule prenominate ac loco maritim' in fide obedientia et servicio tam nostri quam eorundem Progenitorum et Antecessorum nostrorum constanter fideliter et inculpate prestiterunt ac preserverarunt liberaque Commersia cum Mercatoribus ac aliis Indigenis et alienigenis tam pacis quam Belli temporibus habuerunt et execuerunt [sic] Judicia etiam et cognitaciones [sic] omnium et omnimodo Causarum et querelarum Actionum placitorum tam Civilium quam Criminalium et Capitalium et Judicialem potestatem ea omnia tractandi decidendi discutiendi audiendi et terminandi atque in eisdem procedendi et in Acta regidendi secundum leges et Consuetudines Insule et locorum predictorum ex [448] antiquo receptas et approbatas preterquam in cetis [sic] casubus cognitioni nostre Regie reservatis de tempore in tempus exercuerunt executi sunt et peregerunt.

---

[19] *CSPD 1693*, pp. 446–7; Ahier, '"Customer" of Jersey', pp. 65–6.

JAMES II: 1687 201

[2] que omnia et singula cujus et quantum momenti sint et fuerunt ad tutelam et conservationem Insule et locorum maritimorum predictorum in fide et obediencia Corone nostre Anglie Nos vt equum est perpendentes neque non immemores quam fortiter et fideliter Insulani predicti ac ceteri Incole et habitantes ibidem nobis et progenitoribus nostris inservierint Quantaque detrimenta damna et pericula tam pro assidua tuitione et defensione Castri nostri de Montorgueit [sic] infra predictam Insulam nostram de Jersey sustinuerunt indiesque sustinent non solum ut nostra Regia benevolentia favor et affectus erga prefatos Insulanos illustri aliquo nostre beneficentie testimonio ac certis Judiciis comprobetur verum etiam ut ipsi et eorum posteri deinceps inperpetuum prout antea solitam et debitam obedientiam erga Nos heredes et Successores nostros teneant et inviolabiliter observent has literas nostras Patentes magno Sigillo nostro Anglie roboratas in forma qua sequitur illis concedere dignitati sumus.

[3] Sciatis quod nos de gratia nostra speciali ac ex certa scientia et mero motu nostris dedimus et concessimus ac pro nobis heredibus et Successoribus nostris per presentes damus et Concedimus prefatis Ballivo et Juratis Insule nostre de Jersey predicte et ceteris Incolis et habitatoribus dicte Insule quod ipsi et eorum quilibet licet in presentibus non recitati seu cogniti per seperalia nomina sint et erunt semper in futuro ita liberi quieti et immunes in omnibus Civitatibus Burgis emptoriis & Nundiniis mercatis villis Mercatoriis et aliis locis et portubus infra Regnum nostrum Anglie ac infra omnes provincias Dominia territoria et loca ditioni nostra subjecta tam citra quam ultra mare de et ab omnibus vectigalibus Theoloniis Custumiis subsidiis hidagiis tallagiis pontagiis pannagiis muragiis Fossagiis Operibus Expedicionibus Bellicis nisi in casu ubi corpus nostrum heredum et Successorum (quod absit) in prisona detineatur et de et ab omnibus aliis contribucionibus oneribus et exationibus quibuscunque nobis heredibus et Successoribus nostris quovismodo debitis reddendis seu solvendis prout prefata Insula virtute aliquarum Cartarum concessionum confirmacionum sive diplomatum per predictos progenitores sive Antecessores nostros quondam Reges Anglie et Duces Normanie sive alios seu virtute aut vigore alicujus racionabilis et legalis usus prescripcionis seu consuetudinis aut subditi Regni nostri Anglie seu eorum aliquis unquam aliquando fuerunt aut esse debuerunt vel potuerunt debent vel quouismodo possint.

[4] Cumque alia nonnulla privilegia Jurisdictiones Immunitates libertates et Franchesias per predictos progenitores et predecessores nostros quondam Reges Anglie et Duces Normanie ac aliis prefate Insule indulta donata concessa et Confirmata fuere ac a tempore cujus contrarium memoria hominum non existit infra Insulam et loca Maritima prenominata inviolabiliter usitata et observata fuere de quibus unum est quod tempore belli omnium Nationum Mercatores et

alii tam alienigeni quam indigeni tam hostes quam amici libere licite et impune queant et possint dictam Insulam et loca maritima cum Navibus mercibus et bonis suis tam pro evitandis tempestatibus quam pro aliis licitis suis negociis inibi peragendis adire accedere commeare et frequentare et [449] Iibera Comercia negotiationis ac rem mercatoriam ibidem exercere ac tuto et secure commorari indeque comerare et redire toties quoties absque damno molestia seu hostilitate quacunque in rebus mercibus bonis aut Corporibus suis idque non solum infra Insulam et loca maritima predicta aut precinctum eorundem verum etiam infra spatia undique ab eisdem distantia usque ad visum hominis id est quatenus vis oculi posset assequi. Nos eandem Immunitates Impunitatem libertatem et Privilegia ac cetera omnia premissa ultima recitata rata grataque habentes ea pro nobis heredibus et Successoribus nostris quantum in Nobis est prefatis Ballivo et Juratis ac ceteris Incolis habitatoribus mercatoribus et aliis tam hostibus quam amicis et eorum cuilibet per presentes indulgemus et elargimur authoritate nostra Regia renovamus reiteramus et confirmamus in tam amplis modo et forma prout Incole et Habitatores Insule predicte ac predicti indigeni alienigeni Mercatores et alii preantea usi vel gavisi fuerunt vel uti aut gaudere debuerunt universis igitur et singulis Magistratoribus Ministris et subditis nostris per uniuersum nostrum Regnum Anglie ac cetera Dominia et loca ditioni nostre subjecta ubilibet constitutis per presentes denunciamus et firmiter injungendo precipimus ne hanc nostram donacionem Concessionem et Confirmacionem seu aliquod in eisdem expressum aut contentum temerarie aut aliter infringere seu quovismodo inviolare presumant Et si quis ausu temerario contrafecerit seu attemptaverit volumus et decernimus quantum in nobis est quod restituat non solum oblate [sic] aut erepta sed quod etiam pro damno interesse et expensis ad plenariam recompencam et satisfactionem compellatur per quecunque Juris nostri remedia severeque puniatur ut Regie nostre potestatis ac legum nostrarum contemptor temerarius.

[5] Preterea ex uberiori gratia nostra pro nobis heredibus et successoribus nostris per presentes ratificamus approbamus stabilimus et confirmamus omnes et singulos leges et Consuetudines infra Insulam et loca Maritima predicta rite et legittime usitata et ex antiquo Recepta et approbata Dantes et tribuentes prefatis Ballivo et Juratis ac omnibus aliis Magistratibus Ministris et ceteris quibuscunque ibidem in Officio et functione aliquot constitutis plenam integram et absolutam authoritatem potestatem et Facultatem cognoscendi jurisdicendi et Judicandi de et super omnibus et omnimodis placitis processibus litibus Actionibus querelis et causis quibuscunque infra Insulam et loca predicta emergentibus tam personalibus realibus et mixtis quam criminalibus et capitalibus. Eaque omnia et singula ibidem et non alibi placitandi et peragendi prosequendi et defendendi atque in eisdem procedendi vel supersedendi examinandi audiendi terminandi absolvendi condemnandi decidendi atque executioni mandandi secundum leges et consuetudines Insule et locorum

maritimorum predictorum preantea usitatas et approbatas absque provocacione seu appellacione quacunque preterquam in casibus qui cognitioni nostre regali ex antiqua consuetudine Insule et locorum predictorum reservantur vel de Jure aut Privilegio nostro regali reservari debentur. Quam quidem authoritatem potestatem et facultatem preterquam in eisdem casubus reservatas Nos pro nobis heredibus et successoribus nostris prefatis Ballivo et Juratis et aliis Damus Comittimus Concedimus [450] et Confirmamus per presentes adeo plene libere et integre prout prefati Ballivus et Jurati ac alii vel eorum aliquis unquam antehac eisdem rite et legitime usi functi aut gavisi vel uti fungi aut gaudere debuerunt aut licite potuerunt debuit aut potuit.

[6] Volumus preterea ac pro nobis heredibus et successoribus nostris per presentes concedimus prefatis Ballivo et Juratis ac aliis Incolis et habitatoribus infra Insulam et loca maritima predicta quod nullus eorum de cetero per aliqua brevia seu processus ex aliquibus Curiis nostris seu alibi infra Regnum nostrum Anglie emergencia sive eorum aliqua citetur apprehendetur evocetur in placita trahatur sive quovismodo aliter comparare aut respondere cogatur extra Insulam et loca maritima predicta coram quibuscunque Judicibus Justiciariis Magistratibus aut Officiariis nostris aut aliis de aut super aliqua re lite materia seu Causa quacunque infra Insulam predictam emanente seu quod Insulani predicti et eorum quilibet huiusmodi citacionibus apprehensionibus brevibus et processibus non obstante licite et impune valeant et possint infra Insulam et loca predicta residere commorari quiescere et Justiciam ibidem expectare absque aliqua pena corporali seu pecuniario fine redemptione aut mulcta proinde incurrenda forisfacienda nec non absque aliqua Offensione vel Causa contemptus seu contumacie per Nos heredes et Successores nostros illis seu eorum alicui aut aliquibus pro inde infligenda irroganda vel aliter adjudicanda exceptis tantumodo hujusmodi casubus qui per leges Insule et locorum predictorum regali nostre cognitioni atque examini reserventur vel de Jure aut privilegio nostro Regali reservari debentur.

[7] Et ulterius de ampliori gratia nostra speciali ac ex certa scientia et mero motu nostris dedimus Concessimus et Confirmamus ac per presentes pro nobis heredibus et Successoribus nostris quantum in nobis est Damus Concedimus et Confirmamus prefatis Ballivo et Juratis ceterisque Incolis et habitatoribus Insule et locorum maritimorum predictorum nec non mercatoribus et aliis eo Confluentibus tot tanta talia huiusmodi et consimilia Jura et Jurisdictiones Imunitates impunitates indemnitates exempciones libertates Franchesias et privilegia quecunque quot quanta qualia et que prefati Ballivus Jurati ac ceteri Incole et habitatores mercatores et alii aut eorum aliquis antehac legitime et rite usi freti seu gavisi fuerunt usus fretus seu gavisus fuit ac omnia et singula quecunque alia in quibuscunque Cartis Ordinationibus aut literis patentibus nostrum seu progenitorum seu antecessorum nostrorum quondam

Regum et Reginarum Angli seu Ducum Normanie aut aliorum eis seu eorum Predecessoribus antehac data Concessa seu confirmata et non revocata seu abolita quocunque nomine seu quibuscunque nominibus iidem Ballivus Jurati ac ceteri Incole et habitatores ejusdem Insule et locorum maritimorum predictorum aut eorum predecessores seu eorum aliqui vel aliquis in eisdem literis Patentibus seu eorum aliquibus censeantur nuncupentur aut vocitentur seu censeri nuncupari aut vocitari debuere aut soliti fuere ac omnia et singula licet in presentibus minime expressa prefatis Ballivo et Juratis ac ceteris Incolis et habitatoribus Insule et locorum maritimorum predictorum necnon mercatoribus et aliis eo confluentibus indigenis et alienigenis per presentes confirmamus consolidamus et de integro ratificamus adeo plene [451] libere et integre prout ea omnia et singula in eisdem literis Patentibus contenta modo particulariter verbatim expresse in presentibus literis nostris Patentibus recitata et declarata fuissent.

[8] Salua semper atque illabefacta suprema Regie potestate dominatione atque Imperio Corone nostre Anglie tam quoad ligeanciam Subjeccionem et obedientiam Insule predicte ac aliorum quorumcunque [sic] infra Insulam et loca predicta comorancium sive degencium quam quoad Regalitatem privilegia res redditus vectigalia ac cetera Jura Proficua Commoditates et emolumenta quecunque infra Insulam et loca predicta nobis heredibus et successoribus nostris per Prerogativam Corone Anglie sive Ducatus Normannie seu aliter ex antiquo debita et Consueta. Salvis etiam appellacionibus et provocationibus quibuscunque Insulanorum predictorum et aliorum ibidem comorancium sive degencium in omnibus ejusmodi Casubus qui legibus et Consuetudinibus Insule et locorum predictorum Regali nostre cognitioni atque examini reservantur vel de Jure aut privilegio nostro Regali reservari debentur aliqua sententia Clausula re aut materia quacunque superius in presentibus expressa sive specificata in contrarium inde in aliquo non obstantibus.

[9] Proviso semper quod aliqua Clausula Articulus sive aliquod aliud in presentibus literis nostris Patentibus expressum et specificatum non exponantur interpretentur nec se extendant ad aliquod quod sit vel fieri possit nobis heredibus vel Successoribus nostris prejudiciale quoad aliqua terras tenementa redditus Regalitates vel hereditamenta nostra infra insulam predictam & loca maritima predicta aut eorum aliqua.

[10] Et insuper cum datum est nobis intelligi quo [sic] quedam exactio nuper levata fuerit de inhabitantibus et gentibus Insule nostre de Jersey predicta mercatoribus et aliis illic confluentibus contra antiquam extentam et Consuetudinem ibidem usitatam vizt pro quolibet quarterio frumenti vel alterius Grani extra Insulam illam exportato tres solidos et sex denarios monete currentis infra eandem Insulam ubi illa extenta antehac ad tantam summam

se non extendebant ut accepimus et cum dicti Inhabitantes et gentes Insule de Jersey predicta soliti fuere similiter solvere ad usum Progenitorum sive Antecessorum nostrorum pro quibuslibet Centum & quinquaginta libris lane extra Insulam illam exportatæ juxta Extentam ibidem usitatam quatuor denarios monete currentis infra eandem Insulam Nos volumus ac per presentes pro nobis heredibus et Successoribus nostris Concedimus prefatis prefatis Inhabitantibus et Gentibus Insule nostre de Jersey predicta quod ipsi et omnes alii mercatores illuc confluentes non plus nec majorem summam exnunc deinceps inperpetum [sic] solvere teneantur ad usum nostrum quam duodecim denarios monete currentis infra eandem Insulam de Jersey pro quolibet quarterio frumenti sive alterius generis Grani extra eandem Insulam posthec exportandi Ita semper et sub conditione quod iidem Inhabitantes et Gens Insule de Jersey predicta ac omnes alii mercatores et extranei illuc confluentes solvere debeant et teneantur posthec inperpetuum ad usum nostrum pro quibuslibet Centum et quinquaginta libris lane extra Insulam illam exportandis tres solidos et Dimidium monete Currentis infra eandem Insulam & loca maritima predicta seu eorum aliqua [452].

[11] Et ulterius in tosseram [for tesseram] favoris nostri prefatis Ballivo et Juratis nostre de Jersey predicta ac ceteris Incolis et habitatoribus infra Insulam illam pro summa et constanti fidelitate et ligeantia suis Nobis et Predecessoribus nostris nuper Regibus et Reginis Anglie ex quacunque causa manifesta de gratia nostra speciali ac ex certa scientia et mero motu nostris dedimus concessimus et Confirmavimus ac per presentes pro Nobis heredibus et Successoribus nostris damus concedimus et Confirmamus eisdem Ballivo et Juratis Insule nostre de Jersey ac ceteris Incolis et habitatoribus infra Insulam illam plenam potestatem et authoritatem Et quod de cetero imperpetuum liceat et licebit eis habere uti et portare seu portari causare coram Ballivo ejusdem Insule nostre de Jersey pro tempore existente unam Clavam auream vel argenteam comuniter vocatam a Mace Insigniis Armorum nostrorum heredum et Successorum nostrorum superinde insculptam et ornatam in et per totam illam Insulam nostram de Jersey libertates et precincta ejusdem ad libitum huiusmodi Ballivi Insule illius pro tempore existente quando et quoties occasio requiret.

[12] Proviso tamen quod semper licebit ut et per presentes pro nobis heredibus et Successoribus nostrorum pro tempore existentibus vel existenti nominandi constituendi Ministrum quendam seu Officialem Telonarium primitus a Nobis heredibus et Successoribus nostris per scriptum sub Privati Concilii nostri heredum ac Successorum nostrorum Sigillo approbandum in predicta Insula de Jersey mansurum et Comoraturum qui (juxta nuper precharissimi fratris nostri Caroli secundi pie memorie in Consilio sub Privato consultum die Decemb' decimo septimo Anno Regni sui tricesimo primo et Domini nostri millesimo

sexcentesimo septuagesimo nono Aule albe datum) libellos assertorios seu Certificatorios Ang'ce Certificates de bonis et mercimoniis quibuscunque ex Anglia in Insulam de Jersey predictam de tempore in tempus exportatis nec de illis in Angliam ex Insula dicta exportandis manu sua conficiet Sigilloque suo obsignabit quo inde Teloniorum nostrorum Commissionum vel curatoribus de vera bonorum et mercimoniorum omnium in Insulam dictam importatorum vel abinde exportatorum quantitate qualitate numero ac proventu liquido constare possit Quod quidem insuper Concilii Privati consultum seu edictum prefatum die Decembris decimo septimo (uti prefertur) Anno Domini millesimo sexcentesimo septuagesimo nono datum nec non omnes et singulas libertates Jura privilegia emolumenta Commoda et proficua quecunque in eodem contenta Concessa et speciatim declarata Nos per presentes pro Nobis heredibus et Successoribus nostris ratificamus et Confirmamus (non obstante quod in hisce Literis Patentibus sub Sigillo Anglie magno nostris dictum Concilii consultum Articulatim non inseratur) in modo et forma tam amplis ac si Articuli eiusdem Singuli expressim distincte et totidem verbis hic loci essent inserti ac exarati adeo vt imposter' predicta Insula de Jersey Incole quicunque coniunctim vel divisim omnibus et singulis Concessionibus in eodem consulto contentis et speciatim designatis ad omnes intentiones et proposita quecunque suam iporum vtilitatem et Commodum potissimum frui potiri et gaudere possint.

[13] Et vlterius volumus et per presentes pro nobis heredibus et Successoribus nostris Concedimus prefatis Ballivo et Juratis Insule nostre de Jersey predicta et ceteris Incolis et habitatoribus infra Insulam illam quod he litere nostre Patentes in Omnibus et per omnia secundum veram Intencionem earundem bene firme valide et effectuales in Lege sint et erunt Non obstante non nominacione mala vel falsa nominacione vel recitacione in eisdem contentis aut aliquo Statuto Ordinacione Provisione Proclamacione vel Restriccione antehac habitis seu factis modo quolibetcunque non obstante.

[14] Volumus etiam etc. Eo quod expressa mencio etc. In cuius rei etc. Teste Regis apud Westmonasterium decimo quinto die Aprilis Anno Regni nostri Tertio.

Per breve de de Privato Sigillo

Translation

[1] The King to all those to whom etc., greeting. Whereas our beloved and faithful lieges and subjects, the bailiff and the jurats of our Island of Jersey, and the other sojourners in and inhabitants of the same island within our duchy of Normandy, and their predecessors, have from time beyond what the memory of men can reach, by virtue of several charters, grants, confirmations, and most

ample writs, of our illustrious progenitors and ancestors, both kings and queens of England and dukes of Normandy, and others, used, enjoyed, and been in possession of very many rights, jurisdictions, privileges, immunities, liberties, and franchises, freely and quietly, and without any infringement of the same, both within the kingdom of England, and elsewhere within our dominions, and other places under our subjection on this side of, or beyond, the seas; by the aid and benefit of which grants, the aforenamed island and maritime places have stood out and continued constantly, faithfully, and unblameably in our faith, obedience, and service, and that of our progenitors and predecessors, and have enjoyed and gone on in their commerce and trade with merchants, both natives and aliens, as well in time of peace, as in time of war, and exercised and executed their duties in giving their decrees, and taking cognisance of all and every cause, quarrel, action, both civil and criminal, and capital and judicial pleas; and the right of jurisdiction they were vested with, to take into their consideration, decide, discuss, hear, and determine, and to proceed in the premises, and keep records of their proceedings according to the laws and customs practised of old, and approved in the said island and other places aforesaid; except in certain cases reserved from time to time to our royal cognisance.

[2] And we considering of how great advantage and moment all and singular the premises are, and have been, toward the safe-keeping and conservation of the aforesaid island and maritime places in their fidelity and allegiance to our crown of England; and being always mindful, as is just, how courageously and loyally the said islanders and inhabitants have behaved themselves in our own and in our progenitors' service, and considering what great detriments, losses and dangers they have sustained and do daily sustain, both for the constant safeguarding and defence of our Castle of Mont Orgueil, in our aforesaid island of Jersey; to the end, not only to show some distinguished testimony and certain marks of our favour, affection, and royal beneficence towards the inhabitants aforesaid, but also to encourage them, and their posterity for ever, to persevere and continue inviolably in their accustomed and due obedience towards us, and our heirs and successors; we have thought proper to grant to them these our royal letters patent, confirmed under our great seal of England, in form following.

[3] Know ye, that we, of our special favour, certain knowledge, and mere motion, have given and granted, and for ourselves, our heirs and successors, we do by these present letters give and grant, to the said bailiff and jurats of our island of Jersey aforesaid, and to the other sojourners and inhabitants of the same island; that they themselves and every one of them (though not herein stated or declared by their particular names) were and shall, for the time to come, be for ever free, exempted, and acquitted, in all our cities, boroughs,

markets, and trading towns, fairs, mart-towns, and other places and ports, within our kingdom of England, and within all our provinces, dominions, territories, and other places under our subjection, this side of, or beyond, the seas, from and of all tributes, tolls, customs, subsidies, hidage, taylage, pontage, panage, murage, fossage, works, and warlike expeditions (except in case our body, or that of heirs and successors, should be held in prison (which God avert)), and of and from all other contributions, duties, and exactions whatsoever, that may be due from, to be rendered by, or be payable by, and claimed from, the said islanders, to us, our heirs and successors, ever in any manner, by virtue of any charters, grants, confirmations, and writs of our said progenitors, formerly kings of England and dukes of Normandy, or others, or by virtue or reason of any reasonable and legal usage, prescription, or custom, of a subject of our kingdom of England or of any of them.

[4] And whereas some other privileges, jurisdictions, immunities, liberties, and franchises have been graciously given, granted, and confirmed by our progenitors and predecessors, formerly kings of England and dukes of Normandy, and others, to the aforesaid islanders, and have been used and observed constantly in the said island and other maritime places, from the time whereof the memory of men reaches not to the contrary; one of which is, that in time of war merchants of all nations and others, both aliens and native, both enemies and friends, could and might freely, lawfully, without danger or punishment, come to, resort to, go to and fro, and frequent the said island, and other maritime places, with their ships and goods; both to avoid storms, and to conduct their other lawful business there, and to exercise there free commerce, business and trade, and securely, and without danger, remain there, and depart from thence, and return to the same, as often as they think fit, without any harm, molestation, or hostility whatsoever, in their goods, merchandise, or persons; and this not only within the said island and maritime places, and all around the same, but likewise at such spaces and distances from the island as the sight of man goes to, that is as far as the eye of man can reach: We, by virtue of our royal authority, do, for ourselves, our heirs and successors, indulge and enlarge, and renew, reiterate, and confirm, by these present letters, as far as in us lies, the same immunities, impunity, liberty, and privileges, and all the other premises last mentioned, finding them to be reasonable and seasonable, to the said bailiff and jurats, and the other sojourners, inhabitants and merchants, and others, whether enemies or friends, and to each of them, in as ample form and manner as heretofore they have used or enjoyed the same, or should have used and enjoyed the same. In order therefore to prevent any violation or infraction, reckless or otherwise, of this our grant, concession, and confirmation, or any thing therein contained, in any manner whatsoever, we declare and give this warning by these present letters to all our magistrates, officers and subjects in all parts of our kingdom of England, and throughout

all our lordships and places under our obedience, wheresoever they lie, or are situated. And if any one of our said officers and subjects shall be so rash as to presume or attempt to transgress these our strict orders and commands, we order and decree (as far as in us lies), that he shall not only restore what has been taken or seized, but shall also be compelled to make a fuller restitution and satisfaction of all costs, interests, and damages, by whatever legal remedy, and he shall be severely punished for his audacious contempt of our royal power, or of our laws.

[5] Further, we, of our more gracious favour, for ourselves, our heirs and successors, do, by these present letters, ratify, approve, establish, and confirm, all and every one of the laws and customs which have been duly and legally used and from ancient times received and approved within the aforesaid island and maritime places; giving and granting to the aforesaid bailiff and jurats, and all other magistrates and officers of justice, and others who are appointed for performing the functions and executing the duties of any office, full and absolute authority, power, and faculty to have the cognisance, jurisdiction, and judgment concerning and touching all and all sorts of pleas, processes, law-suits, actions, quarrels, and causes arising within the island and maritime places aforesaid; both those actions which are personal, real, and mixed, and those which are criminal and capital, and to proceed in the said island, and not elsewhere, in hearing the parties in their pleadings, in prosecutions of their processes, and in their defence; and to supersede, examine, and hear the same, determining, absolving, condemning, making decrees, and putting their sentences in execution, according to the laws and customs previously practised and approved in the island and maritime places aforesaid; without admitting any challenge or appeal, except in such cases as are reserved to our royal cognisance by the ancient custom of the island and places aforesaid, or by our royal right and privilege ought so to be reserved. Which authority, power, and faculty, except in the cases reserved to us, we give, commit, grant, and confirm, for ourselves and our heirs and successors aforesaid, to the said bailiffs and jurats, and to the others, by these present letters, as freely, fully, and entirely, as the said bailiff and jurats, or others or any of them, heretofore have rightfully and lawfully used, practised, and enjoyed, or might legally have used and enjoyed.

[6] Moreover, our will and pleasure is, and we grant, for ourselves, our heirs, and successors by these present letters, to the said bailiff and jurats, and the other inhabitants and sojourners in the island and maritime places aforesaid, that for the time to come, none of them be cited, arrested, or summoned, or drawn into any lawsuit, or forced in any manner by any writs or process, issued from any of our courts or others of the kingdom of England, to appear and answer before any of our judges, justices, magistrates, or officers, or

others, out of the island and maritime places aforesaid, touching or concerning any thing, dispute, causes, or matters in controversy whatsoever, arising in the aforesaid island, but that the aforesaid islanders, and each of them, may lawfully and without restraint, notwithstanding the said summons, warrants, writs and processes, remain, reside quietly, and abide in the aforesaid island and places, waiting for justice there; without incurring any punishment, corporal or pecuniary, by way of fine, mulct, ransom, or forfeiture, by reason of any offence, contempt, or contumacy, committed towards us, our heirs and successors, for which they might be sued, arraigned, or condemned (except only in the cases, which by the laws of the island and places aforesaid are reserved to our royal cognisance and determination, or by our royal right and privilege ought to be so reserved.

[7] And moreover, of our more gracious special favour, certain knowledge, and mere motion, we have given, granted, and confirmed, and by our present letters, for ourselves, our heirs and successors as far as in us lies, we do give, grant, and confirm to the aforesaid bailiff and jurats, and other sojourners in, and inhabitants of, the aforesaid island and maritime places; as also to merchants and others meeting there, the like, and as great, and as ample rights and jurisdictions, immunities, impunities, indemnities, exemptions, liberties, franchises, and privileges whatsoever, as the aforesaid bailiff, jurats, and other sojourners and inhabitants, and merchants and others, or any of them, have heretofore rightfully and legally used, practised, and enjoyed; and all and singular other things whatsoever that has been heretofore given, granted, and confirmed to them or to their predecessors, in whatsoever charters, orders or letters patent, of us or our progenitors or predecessors, formerly kings and of England, or dukes of Normandy, or others, and not revoked or abolished, by whatsoever name or names the same bailiff and jurats, and other sojourners in, or inhabitants of, the same island and maritime places aforesaid, or their predecessors, or any of them, may be supposed to have been comprised, called, or named, or ought to have been called or named, in the said letters patent, and all and singular which things, though not herein expressly mentioned, we do by these present letters confirm, consolidate, and ratify anew to the aforesaid bailiff and jurats, and other sojourners, and inhabitants, of the island and maritime places aforesaid, and also merchants and others coming together there, those born there, and those born elsewhere, as fully, freely, and entirely, as if all and singular the things particularly mentioned and declared in the same letters patent were particularly in words expressly recited and declared in these our present letters patent.

[8] Saving always entire and without detriment the regal and sovereign power, dominion, and empire of our crown of England, as to what may concern the allegiance, subjection, and obedience of the aforesaid islanders, and others,

whoever they may be, dwelling for a shorter or longer time in the same island; and also as to what may concern the regality, privileges, incomes, revenues, tributes, and other rights, profits, commodities, and emoluments whatsoever, anciently due and accustomed to be paid to us, our heirs and successors, according to our royal prerogative as kings of England, or the prerogative of the duchy of Normandy, in the island and places aforesaid; saving also to the aforesaid islanders, and others dwelling or being in the said island, a right to appeal in all cases reserved to our cognisance and consideration by the laws and customs of the said island, or which by our royal right or privilege ought to be so reserved. Notwithstanding any sentence, clause, thing, or matter whatsoever expressed above, or specially contained to the contrary in these present letters.

[9] Provided always that any clause, article, or any other thing expressed and specified in our present letters patent are not construed, interpreted nor extended to any thing that might be prejudicial to us, our heirs, or successors with regards to any of our lands, tenements, rents, regalities, or inheritances within the aforesaid island and maritime places or any of them.

[10] And in addition, since we are given to understand that an exaction has recently been levied upon the inhabitants and peoples of our island of Jersey aforesaid, and on merchants and others gathering there against the ancient extent and custom there used, that is to say for each quarter of corn or other grain exported from the island three shillings and six pence in money current within the island, when that extent previously did not, as we understand, extend to so large a sum. And since the said inhabitants and people of the aforesaid isle of Jersey were accustomed in the same way to pay to the use of our progenitors or ancestors for every one hundred and fifty pounds of wool exported from the island according to the extent there used four pence in the money current within the same island, we will, and by these present letters for us, our heirs, and successors do grant to the aforesaid inhabitants and peoples of our aforesaid island of Jersey, that they themselves, and all the other merchants gathering there from now henceforth for ever shall be bound to pay for our use a sum no more or greater than twelve pence in the money current within the same island of Jersey for each quarter of wheat or other type of grain hereafter exported from the same island. Thus, always, and on condition that the same inhabitants and peoples of the aforesaid island of Jersey and all other merchants and foreigners gathering there, owe and are bound to pay forever hereafter to our use for every one hundred and fifty pounds of wool exported from that island, three and a half shillings in the money current within the same island and aforesaid maritime places, or any of them.

[11] And further, in a token of our favour to the aforesaid bailiff and jurats of our [island of] Jersey aforesaid and the other sojourners in and inhabitants of that island, for their great and constant faith and allegiance shown to us and our predecessors formerly kings and queens of England, for whatever cause, of our special faviour and certain knowledge, and mere motion we have given, granted and by these present letters for ourself, our heirs and successors we give, grant, concede and confirm to the same bailiff and jurats of our island of Jersey and other sojourners in and inhabitants of that island full power and authority that finally in perpetuity it is and will be permitted to them to have, use and carry, or cause to be carried in the presence of the bailiff of our same island of Jersey for the time being what is commonly called a 'Mace' of gold or silver sculpted and garnished with the our arms and the arms of our heirs and successors on it, in and through the whole of that island of Jersey, its liberties and precincts at the will of bailiff of island for the time being when and as often as the occasion requires.

[12] Provided, however, that it will always be permitted and by these present letters for ourselves, our heirs and successors for the time being or to be, to nominate or constitute a certain minister or official of the customs for the first time by us, our heirs and successors, confirmed under the seal of our Privy Council and that of our heirs and successors, to stay and abide in the aforesaid island of Jersey who (according to our former most beloved brother Charles the Second of pious memory in Privy Council on the seventeenth of December in the thirty first year of his reign and AD 1679 given at Whitehall) will write up with his own hand, and seal with his own seal, the books declaratory and certificatory referred to in English as 'Certificates' of whatsoever goods and merchandise are from time to time exported from England into the said island of Jersey, and not of those things which have to be exported into England from the said island; by which the Commissioners of our Customs can establish the true quantity, quality, number and clear profits of all the good and merchandise imported into the island or exported from there. Which aforesaid Privy Council decree or edict given on the seventeenth of December AD 1679 (as aforementioned) all and singular liberties, rights, privileges, emoluments, advantages, and profits whatsoever contained, granted and in particular declared in the same, we by these present letter for ourselves, our heirs and successors ratify and confirm (not withstanding that in the Letters Patent under our great seal of England the aforesaid decree of our Council might not be specifically articulated) as if the articles were inserted and noted down as clearly, distinctly and in as many words as previously, the aforesaid island of Jersey and the inhabitants and whosoever of them, jointly or separately, by all and singular grants contained in the same resolution, above all should be able to enjoy, possess and benefit from their use and benefit, as fully as was intended and purposed in any manner whatsoever.

[13] And further we wish and by these present letters for ourselves, our heirs and successors, we grant to the said bailiff and jurats of our aforesaid island of Jersey, and the other soujourners and inhabitants within that island, that these our letters patent, in and through all matters, will be good, firm, valid and effectual in law according to the true intention of the same. Notwithstanding failure to identify, or the false identification or recitation contained in the same or notwithstanding any statute, ordinance, provision, proclamation, or restriction of whatsoever kind heretofore had or made.

[14] Furthermore, we wish, etc. And that although express mention, etc. In testimony whereof, etc. Witness the King, at Westminster on the twenty-fifth day of April in the third year of our reign.

By writ of Privy Seal

Postscript

Although there were no further confirmations of Jersey's royal charters, it is possible to trace their influence through succeeding decades. Litigation in the early years of the eighteenth century tested the regime of customs imposed on goods from and passing through the islands. This affected the allegedly unlawful export of wool and the attempts to set up customs administration in the island.[1] There were petitions from the island raising concerns at the negative impacts of a more restrictive regime on the local stocking-knitting industry.[2] The three decades after the grant of James II's charter saw the inheritance of that charter and its predecessors translated into statute.

In the period 1700–17, it was the British government's imposition of duties on cider and perry from the islands that was successfully challenged before the Privy Council. The later years of this litigation were notable for increasingly clear and wide-ranging assertions of the islands' rights. In 1714–15, it was argued on behalf of the inhabitants of Jersey, Guernsey, Sark and Alderney that, as dominions, they were exempt from tonnage, and that 'their Charters and Privileges confirm'd to them by 11 or 12 of His Majestyes most Noble Predecessors ... expresses [sic] their Exemptions to be, Pro Nobis hæredibus et Successoribus nostris' (i.e. granted for those monarchs and for their heirs and successors).[3] Further, on 4 May 1716 a petition from the deputies of Jersey, Guernsey, Alderney and Sark to the House of Commons complained of the threat to the islands represented by a Bill on woollen manufactures that had just been read for the second time. The deputies' petition reminded the House of the constant commitment the islands had shown to the Protestant succession.[4] As so often before, the circumstances of a potentially contested succession, and in the summer of

---

[1] TNA, PC 1/3314; /3461.

[2] TNA, PC 1/2/127.

[3] 'The Case of the Inhabitants of the Islands of Jersey, Guernsey, Sark and Alderney', *ABSJ*, 4 (1897–1901), 49–60.

[4] *Journals of the House of Commons: From August the 1st 1714, in the First Year of the Reign of King George the First, to September the 15th 1718, in the Fourth Year of the Reign of King George the First*, reprinted (London, 1803), p. 437.

1714 one that had weighty religious implications, created controversy. The debates of the spring of 1716 in George I's first parliament occurred against the background of the Jacobite rebellion of 1715, which had only in the early months of 1716 finally run its course.

In 1716 the British parliament passed an Act that was intended, among other things, 'to obviate a Doubt concerning Goods imported from the Islands of Jersey, Guernsey, Sark and Alderney'. This Act incorporated the rights of Channel Islanders to export goods free of tariffs as confirmed in the charters, referring to the fact that,

> the inhabitants of the islands of Jersey, Guernsey, Sark, and Alderney, have always been permitted and allowed to import into England, any goods, wares, and merchandizes of the growth, produce, or manufacture of those respective isles, upon certificates from the respective governors, lieutenant or deputy governors, or commanders in chief, for the time being, and oaths before the magistrates of the said islands

although it did not refer to any of the other charter rights.[5] This exemption, conferred in 1716, has survived in essentially the same form, through various enactments, right up to the present day, via section 5 of the Customs and Excise Duties (General Reliefs) Act 1979, for example.[6] The legislative history is complex, but essentially the provision remained unchanged throughout the intervening period. It might therefore be said that the 1716 Act and subsequent Acts reflect the charter rights crystallised with the final charter of James II.

---

[5] George I, c. 4, #5; Parliamentary Archives, HL/PO/PU/1/1716/3G1n6; Danby Pickering (ed.), *The Statutes at Large*, vol. 13, *From the Twelfth Year of Queen Anne, to the Fifth Year of King George I.*, ed. (Cambridge, 1764), pp. 324–8, at pp. 325–6. The bill was discussed May–June 1715: *Journals of the House of Commons 1 August 1714 to 15 September 1718*, pp. 116, 119, 122, 126, 139, 142, 147, 161, 163. Predecessor legislation on duties on cider, perry etc, to which the island clause was added, includes 12 Anne, c. 2; 12 Anne 2, c. 3; 1 George I, c. 2.

[6] Customs and Excise Duties (General Reliefs) Act 1979, c. 3. Section 5 of the 1979 Act has been repealed entirely by the UK government as part of its reforms to its customs legislation following Brexit. However, its effect was saved by regulation 5 of the Finance Act 2016, section 126 (Appointed Day), the Taxation (Cross-border Trade) Act 2018 (Appointed Day No. 8, Transition and Saving Provisions), and the Taxation (Post-transition Period) Act 2020 (Appointed Day No. 1) (EU Exit) Regulations 2020 (legislation.gov.uk). The effect of regulation 5 is that section 5 of the 1979 Act 'shall continue to have effect ... in relation to goods removed to Great Britain from the Channel Islands.' Jersey's post-Brexit customs relationship with the UK is now implemented in UK and Jersey law by further agreements and enactments, but the continuing application of section 5 of the 1979 Act arguably reflects the underlying charter rights. I am grateful to Adv. Matt Berry of the Jersey Law Officers' Department for advice on this point.

These Acts simply sought to ensure those established rights, to the extent they needed to be, were implemented in the legislation of the British parliament. On 11 April 1717 a petition to the Commons asserted the importance of the islands' privilege to be able to import into England products of the islands free of any custom.[7] In evidence submitted to the Royal Commission on the Criminal Law of Jersey of 1846–47 it was stated that the Act of 1716 explicitly confirmed Jersey's rights in the charters subsequent to the final charter of James II. In a very positive summary, it was stated that the evidence indicated the Act '*removes all doubts,* and encourages the people to continue that firm and steady loyalty and fidelity to the Crown of Great Britain, &c., and confirms the previous Charters'.[8]

Charter rights were also confirmed, for example, in the order of king and council of 21 May 1679 (registered by the States on 3 July)[9] which indicated the priority of charter privileges; and the order's confirmation in the code of 1771 referred to:

> The Laws and Privileges of the Island are confirmed as of old, and no Orders, Warrants, or Letters of whatsoever nature they may be, shall be executed in the Island, but that they have been presented to the Royal Court, in order there to be registered and published: and in case such Orders, Warrants or Letters shall be found to be contrary to the Charters and Privileges, and onerous to the said Island, the registration, execution, and publication thereof may be suspended by the Court, until the case has been represented to His Majesty, and until His good pleasure has been signified thereon: and as for Acts of Parliament in which reference is made to the Island, and in which it has an interest, such Acts must be exemplified in form, under the Great Seal, and sent to the said Island, there to be registered, and published, in order that the inhabitants may have knowledge thereof, and avoid the penalties of transgressing the same.

Over the course of the eighteenth century, the medium of political exchange had changed. The importance of the ministers of the crown in the English

---

[7] Successor bills were debated in March–May 1716: *Journals of the House of Commons 1 August 1714 to 15 September 1718*, pp. 397, 398, 404, 410, 416, 419, 433, 438. In March–June 1717: *ibid.*, pp. 509, 510, 513, 515, 520, 522, 524, 530, 532, 536, 540, 547, 560, 562, 566, 570, 571, 576, 578, 580, 581, 601–2; *Journals of the House of Lords*, xx: *1714–1717* (London, 1774), pp. 488, 504, 506–7. In January 1718: *Journals of the House of Commons 1 August 1714 to 15 September 1718*, pp. 669, 671–2, 675, 684, 688, 689, 692, 693, 701, 707, 716, 724, 725, 743, 769. NB Petitions on cider trade from Gloucester and Worcester: pp. 694 (28 January 1718), 713 (5 February 1718).

[8] *First Report of the Commissioners Appointed to Inquire into the State of the Criminal Law in the Channel Islands* (London, 1847) (italic in the source).

[9] *Actes des Etats de l'île de Jersey, 1676–1688*, pp. 26–34, esp. p. 29.

House of Commons and its interest in taxation, the regulation of trade, and customs revenues now led the debate. The charter tradition, nonetheless, remained clearly present and influential, for many islanders still a point of orientation and an ultimate source of authority.

BIBLIOGRAPHY

Primary Sources: Manuscript

Kew, The National Archives of the United Kingdom

C 66 Chancery and Supreme Court of Judicature: Patent Rolls
C 76 Chancery: Treaty Rolls
C 81 Chancery: Warrants for the Great Seal, Series I
E 30 Exchequer: Treasury of Receipt: Diplomatic Documents
E 101 Exchequer: King's Remembrancer: Accounts Various
E 159 Exchequer: King's Remembrancer: Memoranda Rolls and Enrolment Books
E 404 Exchequer: Warrants for Issues
PC 1 Privy Council and Privy Council Office: Miscellaneous Unbound Papers
SC 8 Special Collections: Ancient Petitions
SP 1 State Papers, Henry VIII: General Series
SP 14 Secretaries of State: State Papers Domestic, James I
SP 15 Secretaries of State: State Papers Domestic, Edward VI – James I

London, British Library

Lansdowne MS 657 Collections relating to the islands of Guernsey and Jersey … (1685–1758)
Stowe MS 146 Royal Orders and Warrants, 1512–15

Northampton, Northamptonshire Record Office

Finch Hatton 312

St Helier, Jersey, Lord Coutanche Library, Société Jersiaise

de St Martin Contrat, unnumbered: 12 Aug 1514
'I 1500 to 1560 Soc. Jers.': contrat, 16 Sept 1514.

St Helier, Jersey, Jersey Archive

D/Y/F1 Judicial Greffe, Samedi Court, Samedi Division Registers
G/C/09/A St Saviour's Church Records: St Saviour's Church – Registers

Westminster, Parliamentary Archives

HL/PO/PU/1/1716/3G1n6 3 George I, c. 4

Primary Sources: Printed

Actes des États de l'île de Guernesey (8 vols, Guernsey, 1851–1938).
Actes des Etats de l'Ile de Jersey 1524–1596, 12e publication de la Société Jersiaise (St Helier, 1897).
Actes des états de l'île de Jersey, 1660–1675, 15e publication de la Société Jersiaise (Jersey, 1900).
Actes des états de l'île de Jersey, 1676–1688, 16e publication de la Société Jersiaise (Jersey, 1899).
'*Ancient Petitions of the Chancery and the Exchequer*': *ayant trait aux îles de la Manche, conservées au 'Public Record Office' à Londres*, Société Jersiaise, publication spéciale (St Helier, 1902).
Articles Exhibited against Sir Philipp Carteret, Governour of the Isle of Jersy; Or, An Humble Information of the Estate of his Majesties Isle of Iersey, with Part of the Grievances of the Inhabitants, which was Presented by Divers Gentlemen of that Isle, to many Members of both the Honourable Houses in Parliament Assembled (London, 1642).
Basin, Thomas, *Histoire des règnes de Charles VII et de Louis XI*, ed. J. Quicherat (4 vols, Paris, 1855–59).
Bisson, S. W., *The Jersey Chantry Certificate of 1550* (St Helier, 1975).
Brewer, J. S., Gairdner, J., and Brodie, R. H. (eds), *Letters and Papers, Foreign and Domestic, of the Reign of Henry VIII* (21 vols in 37, London, 1864–1932).
Calendar of the Close Rolls Preserved in the Public Record Office (London, 1892–).
Calendar of the Fine Rolls Preserved in the Public Record Office (London, 1911–).
'Calendar of French Rolls, Henry VI', in *Forty-Eighth Annual Report of the Deputy Keeper of the Public Records* (London, 1887), appendix, 2.
Calendar of the Patent Rolls Preserved in the Public Record Office (London, 1891–).
Calendar of State Papers, Domestic Series, ed. Mary Anne Everett Green [et al.] (London, 1856–).
Calendar of State Papers: Domestic Series, February – December 1685 (London, 1960).
Calendar of State Papers: Domestic Series, June 1687 – February 1689 (London, 1972).
Calendar of State Papers: Domestic Series, 1693 (London, 1903).
Calendar of Treasury Books, 1679–80 (London, 1913).
Campbell, William (ed.), *Materials for a History of the Reign of Henry VII. from Original Documents preserved in the Public Record Office*, Rolls Ser., 60 (2 vols, London, 1873–75).
Carriazo, Juan de Mata (ed.), *El Victorial: crónica de Don Pero Niño, Conde de Buelna* (Madrid, 1940).

Carte, Thomas, *Catalogue des rolles gascons, normans et françois conservés dans les archives de la Tour de Londres: et contenant le précis & le sommaire de tous les titres qui s'y trouvent concernant la Guienne, la Normandie & les autres provinces de la France sujettes autrefois aux rois d'Angleterre* (2 vols, Paris, 1743).
'The Case of the Inhabitants of the Islands of Jersey, Guernsey, Sark and Alderney', *ABSJ*, 4 (1897–1901), 49–60.
The Chronicle and Political Papers of King Edward VI, ed. W. K. Jordan (London, 1966).
Chronique des quatre premiers Valois (1327–1393), ed. Siméon Luce (Paris, 1862).
Les Chroniques de Jersey, ed. Bronwyn Matthews (St Helier, 2017).
Coke, Edward, *The Fourth Part of the Institutes of the Laws of England: Concerning the Jurisdiction of Courts* (London, 1648).
Commynes, Philippe de, *Memoirs: The Reign of Louis XI, 1461–83*, trans. Michael Jones (Harmondsworth, 1972).
'Contrat de 1513', *ABSJ*, 6 (1906–09), 210–11.
Dasent, John Roche (ed.), *Acts of the Privy Council of England*, new series, vol. 2, *1547–1550* (London, 1890).
Dasent, John Roche (ed.), *Acts of the Privy Council of England*, new series, vol. 15, *1587–1588* (London, 1897).
[de Gruchy, G. F. B., R. R. Marett, and E. T. Nicolle (eds)], *Cartulaire des îles Normandes: recueil de documents concernant l'histoire de ces îles, conservés aux archives du département de la Manche et du Calvados, de la Bibliothèque nationale, du Bureau des rôles, du château de Warwick, etc* ([St Helier], 1924 [i.e. 1918–24]).
'Documents Concerning the Proceedings of the Royal Commissioners of 1531', *ABSJ*, 6 (1906–09), 87–110.
d'Orronville dit Cabaret, Jean, *La chronique du bon duc Loys de Bourbon*, ed. A.-M. Chazaud (Paris, 1876).
Extente de l'Ile de Jersey (St Helier, 1876).
The Extentes of Guernsey 1248 and 1331, and Other Documents Relating to Ancient Usages and Customs in that Island, ed. Havilland de Sausmarez (Guernsey, 1934).
'Extraits du journal de Jean Chevallier', *ABSJ*, 1 (1875–84), 260–4.
First Report of the Commissioners Appointed to Inquire into the State of the Criminal Law in the Channel Islands (London, 1847).
Firth, C. H., and R. S. Rait (eds), *Acts and Ordinances of the Interregnum, 1642–1660* (London, 1911).
Froissart, Jean, *Oeuvres: Chroniques*, ed. baron Kervyn de Lettenhove (25 vols in 26, Brussels, 1867–77).
Gairdner, James (ed.), *Letters and Papers Illustrative of the Reigns of Richard III and Henry VII*, ed., Rolls Ser., 24 (2 vols, London, 1861–63).
Gairdner, James (ed.), *The Paston Letters* (6 vols in 1; reprinted Gloucester, 1983, from the Library Edition of 1904).
Gilliodts-Van Severen, M. L. (ed.), *Le Cotton manuscrit Galba B.I.*, transcribed Edward Scott (Bruxelles, 1896).

Given-Wilson, C. et al. (eds), *The Parliament Rolls of Medieval England, 1275–1504* (16 vols, Woodbridge and London, 2005).
Green, Mary Anne Everett (ed.), *Calendar of State Papers: Domestic Series, of the Reign of Elizabeth, 1601–1603, with Addenda 1547–1565* (London, 1870).
The Guernsey and Jersey Magazine, 2 (1836).
H[ervey], S. H. A. (ed.), *Rushbrook Parish Registers, 1567 to 1850: With Jermyn and Davers Annals* (Woodbridge, 1903).
Heylyn, Peter, *A Full Relation of Two Journeys: The One into the Main-land of France. The Other into some of the Adjacent Ilands* (London, 1656).
Hinds, Allen B. (ed.), *Calendar of State Papers and Manuscripts, Relating to English Affairs, Existing in the Archives and Collections of Venice, and in Other Libraries of Northern Italy*, vol. 20, *1626–1628* (London, 1914).
Horrox, Rosemary, and P. W. Hammond (eds), *British Library Harleian Manuscript 433* (4 vols, Upminster and Gloucester, 1979–83).
'How the Duke of Bourbon, the Constable and the Marshal took the Islands of Jersey and Guernsey which face Brittany', *ABSJ*, 16 (1953–56), 281–3.
Hughes, Paul L., and James F. Larkin (eds), *Tudor Royal Proclamations* (3 vols, New Haven CT, 1964–69).
Hunter, J., and J. Caley (ed.), *Valor Ecclesiasticus* (6 vols, London, 1810–34).
Hyde, Edward, *The Life of Edward Earl of Clarendon: In which is Included, A Continuation of his History of the Grand Rebellion, Written by Himself* (2 vols, Oxford, 1857).
Hyde, Edward, *The History of the Rebellion and Civil Wars in England*, ed. W. Dunn Macray (6 vols, Oxford, 1888).
Journals of the House of Commons (51 vols, London, 1803).
Journals of the House of Lords, vol. 20, *1714–1717* (London, 1774).
Kirby, Joan (ed.), *The Plumpton Letters and Papers*, Camden Soc., 5th ser., 8 (1996).
Le Patourel, John, D. H. Gifford, and R. H. Videlo (eds), *List of Records in the Greffe, Guernsey*, vol. 1, *Jugements, Ordonnances et Ordres de Conseil*, List and Index Society, special ser., 2 (London, 1969).
Lenfestey, J. H. (ed.), *List of Records in the Greffe, Guernsey*, vol. 2, *Documents under Bailiwick Seal*, List and Index Society, special ser., 11 (London, 1978).
Letters and Papers relating to the War with France, 1512–1513, ed. Alfred Spont, Publications of the Navy Records Society, 10 (London, 1897).
Loftis, John (ed.), *The Memoirs of Anne, Lady Halkett, and Ann, Lady Fanshawe* (Oxford, 1979).
London Gazette, 5 March 1685.
Lyon, Mary (ed.), *The Wardrobe Book of William de Norwell, 12 July 1338 to 26 May 1340* (Bruxelles, 1983).
Marret-Godfray, M. H., 'Documents relatifs aux attaques sur les îles de la Manche, 1338–1345', *ABSJ*, 3 (1891–96), 11–53.
Merlin-Chazelas, Anne (ed.), *Documents relatifs au clos des galées de Rouen et aux armées de mer du Roi de France de 1293 a 1418* (2 vols, Paris, 1978).
Nicolas, Harris (ed.), *Proceedings and Ordinances of the Privy Council of England* (7 vols, London, 1834–37).

Nicolas, Nicholas Harris (ed.), *Wardrobe Accounts of Edward the Fourth: With a Memoir of Elizabeth of York* (London, 1830).
Nicolle, Toulmin (ed.), 'Report of the Royal Commissioners sent to Jersey in 1617', *ABSJ*, 5 (1902–05), 386–96.
Notestein, Wallace, Frances Helen Relf, and Hartley Simpson (eds), *Commons Debates, 1621* (7 vols, New Haven CT, 1935).
Ogier, D. M. (ed.), 'Guernsey's *précepte d'assize* of 1441: Translation and Notes', *Jersey and Guernsey Law Review*, 12 (2008), 207–19.
Ogle, O., W. H. Bliss, W. Dunn Macray, and F. J. Routledge (eds), *Calendar of the Clarendon State Papers* (5 vols, Oxford, 1869–1932).
Oppenheim, M. (ed.), *Naval Accounts and Inventories of the Reign of Henry VII, 1485–8 and 1495–7*, Navy Records Society, 8 (London, 1896).
'Ordonnance de 1462 pour la garde du château de Montorgueil et la police de l'île de Jersey', *ABSJ*, 7 (1910–14), 187–92.
Ordres du Conseil et pièces analogues enregistrés à Jersey (6 vols, Jersey, 1897–1906).
Papers Connected with the Privy Council's Consideration of the Jersey Prison Board Case (3 vols, printed but not published; [London], 1891–94).
Pickering, Danby (ed.), *The Statutes at Large*, vol. 13, *From the Twelfth Year of Queen Anne, to the Fifth Year of King George I.* (Cambridge, 1764).
Pintoin, Michel, *Chronique du religieux de Saint-Denys: contenant le règne de Charles VI, de 1380 à 1422*, ed. L. Bellaguet and Prosper Brugière baron de Barante (6 vols, Paris, 1839–52).
Riley, H. T. (ed.), 'Annales Ricardi Secundi et Henrici Quarti Regis Angliae', in *Chronica Monasterii S. Albani: Johannis de Trokelowe, et Henrici de Blaneforde ... Chronica et Annales*, Rolls Ser., 28iii (London, 1866), pp. 153–420.
Royal Commission on Historical Manuscripts, *Calendar of the Manuscripts of the Most Honourable the Marquess of Salisbury* (24 vols, London, 1883–1976).
Royal Commission on Historical Manuscripts, *Report on the Manuscripts of F. W. Leyborne-Popham, Esq. of Littlecote, co. Wilts.* (London, 1899).
Royal Commission on Historical Manuscripts, *The Manuscripts of His Grace the Duke of Buccleuch and Queensberry K.G., K.T., preserved at Drumlanrig Castle* (3 vols, London, 1897–1926).
Rymer, Thomas (ed.), *Foedera, conventiones, litterae, et cujuscunque generis acta publica*, rev. George Holmes, 3rd edn (10 vols, The Hague, 1739–45).
Rymer, Thomas, and Sanderson, Robert (eds), *Foedera, conventiones, litterae, et cujuscunque generis acta publica*, rev. John Caley and Frederick Holbrooke (4 vols in 7, London, 1816–69).
Stevenson, Joseph (ed.), *Letters and Papers Illustrative of the Wars of the English in France during the Reign of Henry the Sixth, King of England*, Rolls Ser., 22 (2 vols in 3, London, 1861–64).
Stocall, James, *Freedome. Or, The Description of the Excellent Civill Government of the Island of Jersey* (London, 1652).
Stow, George B., Jr (ed.), *Historia vitae et regni Ricardi Secundi* ([Philadelphia PA], 1977).
'A Survey of ye Island of Jersey', *ABSJ*, 12 (1932–35), 415–46.

Symons, A. N. (ed.), 'History of Alderney', *Report and Transactions of La Société Guernesiaise*, 13 (1937–45), 34–71.
Thornton, Tim, *The Charters of Guernsey* (Bognor Regis, 2004).
Twemlow, J. A. (ed.), *Calendar of Entries in the Papal Registers Relating to Great Britain and Ireland: Papal Letters*, vol. 13, *1471–84* (2 vols, London, 1955).
Waurin, Jehan de, *Recueil des Croniques et anchiennes istories de la Grant Bretaigne, a present nomme Engleterre*, ed. William Hardy & Edward L. C. P. Hardy, Rolls Ser., 39 (5 vols, London, 1864–91).
Webb, J. T., 'Translation of a French Metrical History of the Deposition of Richard II', *Archaeologia*, 20 (1824), 1–423.

Secondary Sources: Printed

Ahier, John Patriarche, *Tableaux historiques de la civilization à Jersey* (Jersey, 1852).
Ahier, Philip, 'The "Customer" of Jersey and the "Register" of Certificates', *ABSJ*, 19 (1965–68), 61–70.
Ahier, Philip, *The Governorship of Sir Walter Ralegh in Jersey, 1600–1603: Together with some Local Raleghana* (St Helier, 1971).
Allmand, Christopher, *Henry V*, new edn (New Haven CT, 1997).
Appleby, J. C., 'Neutrality, Trade and Privateering, 1500–1689', in A. G. Jamieson (ed.), *A People of the Sea: The Maritime History of the Channel Islands* (London, 1986), pp. 59–64.
Arthurson, I., and Kingwell, N., 'The Proclamation of Henry Tudor as King of England, 3 November 1483', *BIHR*, 63 (1990), 100–06.
Ashley, Maurice, *James II* (London, 1977).
Balleine, G. R., *A Biographical Dictionary of Jersey* (London, 1948).
Balleine, G. R., *All for the King: The Life Story of Sir George Carteret* (St Helier, 1976).
Balleine, G. R., *History of Jersey*, rev. Marguerite Syvret and Joan Stevens (Chichester, 1981).
Barton, Kenneth James, 'Excavations at the Vale Castle, Guernsey, C. I.', *Report and Transactions of La Société Guernesiaise*, 21 (1981–85), 485–538.
Bennett, Michael, *The Battle of Bosworth* (Gloucester, 1985).
Bennett, Michael J., 'Richard II and the Wider Realm', in Anthony Goodman and James L. Gillespie (eds), *Richard II: The Art of Kingship* (Oxford, 1999), pp. 187–204.
Bindoff, S. T. (ed.), *The House of Commons, 1509–1558* (3 vols, London, 1982).
Bisson, Peter, 'The Fief and Seigneurs of Samarès in the Middle Ages', *ABSJ*, 24 (1985–88), 339–53.
Bisson, Peter, 'Philippe de Barentin and the Payns of Samarès', *ABSJ*, 26 (1993–96), 537–52.
Bryant, Arthur, *King Charles II* (London, 1931).
Burns, William, 'Falle, Philip (1656–1742), historian and Church of England clergyman', *ODNB*, vol. 18, pp. 992–3.
Burton, John Richard, *A History of Bewdley; with Concise Accounts of Some Neighbouring Parishes* (London, 1883).

Bush, Michael L., *The Government Policy of Protector Somerset* (London, 1975).
Callow, John, *The Making of King James II* (Stroud, 2000).
Calmette, J., and Périnelle, G., *Louis XI et l'Angleterre, 1461–1483* (Paris, 1930).
Carr, A. D., *Owen of Wales: The End of the House of Gwynedd* (Cardiff, 1991).
Chrimes, S. B., *Henry VII*, corrected paperback edn (London, 1977).
Clowes, Wm. Laird, *The Royal Navy: A History, from the Earliest Times to the Present* (7 vols, London, 1897–1903).
C[ockayne], G. E., *The Complete Peerage of England, Scotland, Ireland, Great Britain and the United Kingdom, Extant, Extinct and Dormant*, rev. Vicary Gibbs, ed. H. A. Doubleday, D. Warrand, and Lord Howard de Walden, new edn (13 vols in 14, London, 1910–59).
Cogswell, Thomas, 'Prelude to Ré: The Anglo-French Struggle over La Rochelle, 1624–1627', *History*, 71 (1986), 1–21.
Cogswell, Thomas, *The Blessed Revolution: English Politics and the Coming of War, 1621–1624* (Cambridge, 1989).
Croft, Pauline, 'Fresh Light on Bate's Case', *Historical Journal*, 30 (1987), 523–39.
Cruickshank, C. G., *Army Royal: Henry VIII's Invasion of France, 1513* (Oxford, 1969).
Currin, John M., 'Henry VII and the Treaty of Redon (1489): Plantagenet Ambitions and Early Tudor Foreign Policy', *History*, 81 (1996), 343–58.
Curry, Anne, 'Lancastrian Normandy: The Jewel in the Crown?', in David Bates and Anne Curry (eds), *England and Normandy in the Middle Ages* (London and Rio Grande OH, 1994), pp. 235–52.
Dasent, Arthur Irwin, *The Private Life of Charles the Second* (London, 1927).
Davies, C. S. L., 'Richard III, Henry VII and the Island of Jersey', *The Ricardian*, 9 (1991–93), 334–42.
Davies, C. S. L., 'Richard III, Brittany and Henry Tudor', *Nottingham Mediaeval Studies*, 37 (1993), 110–26.
Davies, C. S. L., 'Tournai M.P.s at Westminster?' *Parliamentary History*, 20 (2001), 233–5.
Davies, R. R., *The First English Empire: Power and Identities in the British Isles 1093–1343* (Oxford, 2000).
de Guérin, T. M. W., 'An Account of the Families of de St Martin and de la Court (Seigneurs of Trinity)', *ABSJ*, 9 (1919–22), 54–95.
de la Croix, J., *Jersey: ses antiquités, ses institutions, son histoire* (3 vols, Jersey, 1859–61).
de La Grassière, Paul Bertrand, *Le Chevalier au Vert Lion: le maréchal de France Robert Bertrand, sire de Bricquebec (1273–1348) et l'intégration de la Normandie au royaume de France* (Paris, 1969).
des Longrais, F. Joüon, 'La lutte sur mer au xive siècle et la prise de Jersey en 1406 par Hector de Pontbriand', *Bulletin Archéologique de l'Association Bretonne*, 3rd ser., 10 (1891), 145–205.
Dupont, Gustave, *Histoire du Cotentin et de ses îles* (4 vols, Caen, 1870–85).
Durell, Edward, 'Sketch of the Life of the Rev. Philip Falle', in Philip Falle, *An Account of the Island of Jersey*, new edn (Jersey, 1837).
Eagleston, A. J., 'The Dismissal of the Seven Jurats in 1565', *Report and Transactions of La Société Guernesiaise*, 12 (1933–36), 508–16.

Eagleston, A. J., 'The Chroniques de Jersey in the Light of Contemporary Documents', *ABSJ*, 13 (1936–39), 37–62.

Eagleston, A. J., 'Guernsey under Sir Thomas Leighton (1570–1610)', *Report and Transactions of La Société Guernesiaise*, 13 (1937–45), 72–108.

Eagleston, A. J., *The Channel Islands under Tudor Government, 1485–1642: A Study in Administrative History* (Cambridge, 1949).

Emden, A. B., *A Biographical Register of the University of Oxford to 1540* (3 vols, Oxford, 1957–59).

Everard, J. A., and Holt, J. C., *Jersey 1204: The Forging of an Island Community* (London, 2004).

Faith, R. J., 'The "Great Rumour" of 1377 and Peasant Ideology', in R. H. Hilton and T. H. Aston (eds), *The English Rising of 1381* (Cambridge, 1984), pp. 43–73.

Farnell, James E., 'The Navigation Act of 1651, the First Dutch War and the London Merchant Community', *Economic History Review*, 2nd ser., 16 (1963–64), 439–54.

Fletcher, Christopher, *Richard II: Manhood, Youth, and Politics, 1377–1399* (Oxford, 2008).

Ford, C. J., 'Piracy or Policy: The Crisis in the Channel 1400–03', *Transactions of the Royal Historical Society*, 5th ser., 29 (1979), 63–77.

Frame, Robin, *The Political Development of the British Isles, 1100–1400*, new edn (Oxford, 1995).

Gibon, Paul de, *Un archipel Normand: les îles Chausey et leur histoire*, 2nd edn (Évreux, 1935).

Given-Wilson, Chris (ed.), *Chronicles of the Revolution, 1397–1400: The Reign of Richard II* (Manchester, 1993).

Given-Wilson, Chris, 'Richard II and the Higher Nobility', in Anthony Goodman and James L. Gillespie (eds), *Richard II: The Art of Kingship* (Oxford, 1999), pp. 107–28.

Given-Wilson, Chris, *Henry IV* (New Haven CT, 2016).

Goodman, Anthony, *The Wars of the Roses: Military Activity and English Society, 1452–97* (London, 1981).

Griffiths, Ralph A., *The Reign of Henry VI: The Exercise of Royal Authority, 1422–1461* (London, 1981).

Griffiths, R. A., 'The English Realm and Dominions and the King's Subjects in the Later Middle Ages', in J. G. Rowe (ed.), *Aspects of Late Medieval Government and Society: Essays Presented to J. R. Lander* (Toronto (Ont), 1986), pp. 83–105, reprinted in R. A. Griffiths, *King and Country: England and Wales in the Fifteenth Century* (London, 1991), pp. 33–54.

Griffiths, Ralph A., and Thomas, Roger S., *The Making of the Tudor Dynasty*, paperback edn (Stroud, 1993).

Grummitt, David, *The Calais Garrison: War and Military Service, 1436–1558* (Woodbridge, 2008).

Gunn, S. J., 'The Accession of Henry VIII', *Historical Research*, 64 (1991), 278–88.

Gunn, S. J., *Henry VII's New Men and the Making of Tudor England* (Oxford, 2016).

Harrison, Frederic, *Annals of an Old Manor-House: Sutton Place, Guildford* (London, 1899).

Havet, Julien, *Les cours royales des îles Normandes* (Paris, 1878).
Hawkyard, A. D. K., 'The Enfranchisement of Constituencies, 1504–1558', *Parliamentary History*, 10 (1991), 1–26.
Hay, Denys, *Polydore Vergil* (Oxford, 1952).
Hay, Paul, sieur du Chastelet, jr, *Histoire de Bertrand Du Guesclin, connétable de France et des royaumes de Léon, de Castille* (Paris, 1666).
Henderson, Virginia K., 'Rethinking Henry VII: The Man and his Piety in the Context of the Observant Franciscans', in Douglas Biggs, Sharon D. Michalove, and Compton Reeves (eds), *Reputation and Representation in Fifteenth-Century Europe* (Leiden, 2004), pp. 317–47.
Henning, Basil Duke (ed.), *The History of Parliament: The House of Commons, 1660–1690* (3 vols, London, 1983).
Hicks, Michael, *Warwick the Kingmaker* (Oxford, 1998).
Hicks, Michael, *Richard III: The Self-Made King* (New Haven CT, 2019).
Hocart, Richard, *Guernsey in the Reign of Charles II* ([Guernsey], 2020).
Holdsworth, W. S., *A History of English Law*, vol. 5, *The Common Law and its Rivals* (Boston MA, 1924).
Horrox, Rosemary, *Richard III: A Study in Service*, corrected paperback edn (Cambridge, 1991).
Hoskins, S. Elliott, *Charles the Second in the Channel Islands: A Contribution to his Biography and to the History of his Age* (2 vols, London, 1854).
Hoyt, Robert S., 'The Nature and Origins of the Ancient Demesne', *English Historical Review*, 65 (1950), 145–74.
Hutton, Ronald, *Charles the Second, King of England, Scotland, and Ireland* (Oxford, 1989).
Israel, J. I., 'England's Mercantilist Response to Dutch World Trade Primacy, 1647–74', in his *Conflicts of Empires: Spain, the Low Countries and the Struggle for World Supremacy, 1585–1713* (London, 1997), pp. 305–18.
Jacqueline, Bernard, 'Sixte IV et la piraterie dans les Iles Anglo-Normandes (1480)', *Revue du département de la Manche*, 20 (1978), 197–202.
Johnson, P. A., *Duke Richard of York 1411–1460*, corrected paperback reprint (Oxford, 1991).
Jones, J. R., *Charles II: Royal Politician* (London, 1987).
Jordan, W. K., *Edward VI – The Young King: The Protectorship of the Duke of Somerset* (London, 1968).
Kelleher, Alexander, 'Petitions from the Channel Islands in the Thirteenth and Fourteenth Centuries', *Jersey and Guernsey Law Review* (2021), 31–61.
Kendall, Paul Murray, *Louis XI: The Universal Spider*, paperback edn (London, 2001).
Kirby, J. L., *Henry IV of England* (London, 1970).
Lang, A., 'The Master Hoaxer: James de la Cloche', *Fortnightly Review*, September 1909.
Langton, C., 'The Seigneurs of Samarès', *ABSJ*, 11 (1928–31), 376–427.
Laynesmith, J. L., *Cecily, Duchess of York* (London, 2017).
Le Cornu, C.-P., 'Le chateau de Grosnez, *ABSJ*, 4 (1897–1901), 14–48.
Lehmberg, Stanford, 'Weston, Sir Richard (*c.* 1465–1541), Courtier', *ODNB*, vol. 58, pp. 295–6.

Lemoine, Jean, 'du Guesclin à Jersey (1373–1376)', *Revue Historique*, 61 (1896), 45–61.
Lemprière, R. R., 'Messire Walter Ralegh, gouverneur de Jersey, 1600–03', *ABSJ*, 9 (1919–22), 96–106.
Lemprière, R. R., 'L'occupation de Jersey par le comte de Maulevrier', *ABSJ*, 10 (1923–27), 102–55.
Lemprière, Raoul, *History of the Channel Islands* (London, 1974).
Le Patourel, John, *The Medieval Administration of the Channel Islands, 1199–1399* (London, 1937).
Le Quesne, Charles, *A Constitutional History of Jersey* (London, 1856).
Livius, Titus, *Vita Henrici Quinti* (Oxford, 1716).
MacCaffrey, Wallace T., 'The Newhaven Expedition, 1562–1563', *Historical Journal*, 40 (1997), 1–21.
Marett, Julia M., 'Philip Dumaresq', *ABSJ*, 12 (1932–35), 413–14.
Marr, L. James, *A History of the Bailiwick of Guernsey: The Islanders' Story* (Chichester, 1982).
McIntosh, Marjorie Keniston, 'The Privileged Villeins of the English Ancient Demesne', *Viator*, 7 (1976), 295–328.
McSheffrey, Shannon, *Seeking Sanctuary: Crime, Mercy, and Politics in English Courts, 1400–1550* (Oxford, 2017).
Messervy, J. A., 'Extraits des anciens roles de la cour royale', *ABSJ*, 4 (1897–1901), 294–314.
Messervy, J. A., 'Liste de jurés-justiciers de la cour royale de Jersey', *ABSJ*, 4 (1897–1901), 213–36.
Messervy, J. A., 'Liste des gouverneurs, lieut.-gouverneurs et deputes-gouverneurs de l'île de Jersey', *ABSJ*, 4 (1897–1901), 373–94.
Messervy, J. A., 'Listes des recteurs de l'Ile de Jersey: recteurs de Saint-Hélier', *ABSJ*, 7 (1910–14), 75–98.
Miller, John, *James II* (New Haven CT, 2000).
Minois, Georges, *Du Guesclin* (Paris, 1993).
Mollet, Ralph, 'The Royal Mace of the Bailiff of Jersey', *ABSJ*, 12 (1932–35), 152–5.
Mortimer, Ian, *The Fears of Henry IV: The Life of England's Self-Made King* (London, 2007).
Müller, Miriam, 'The Aims and Organisation of a Peasant Revolt in Early Fourteenth-century Wiltshire', *Rural History*, 14 (2003), 1–20.
Murphy, Neil, 'Henry VIII's First Invasion of France: The Gascon Expedition of 1512', *English Historical Review*, 130 (2015), 25–56.
Nicholls, David, 'Social Change and Early Protestantism in France: Normandy, 1520–62', *European Studies Review*, 10 (1980), 279–308.
Nicolle, Edmund Toulmin, *Mont Orgueil Castle: Its History and Description* (Jersey, 1921).
Nicolle, Ed. Toulmin, 'L'occupation de Jersey par les comtes de Maulevrier de 1461 à 1468', *ABSJ*, 9 (1919–22), 168–88.
Nicolle, E. T., '"Le Victorial" and the Attack on Jersey in 1406', *ABSJ*, 10 (1923–27), 32–46.

Nicolle, E. Toulmin, 'The Capture of Sark by the French in 1549 and its Re-capture in 1553 by a Flemish Corsair', *ABSJ*, x (1923–27), 157–73.
Ogier, D. M., *Reformation and Society in Guernsey* (Woodbridge, 1996).
Ormrod, W. M., *The Reign of Edward III: Crown and Political Society in England, 1327–1377* (New Haven CT, 1990).
Ormrod, W. Mark, *Edward III* (New Haven CT, 2012).
Ormrod, W. Mark, Lambert, Bart, and Mackman, Jonathan, *Immigrant England, 1300–1550* (Manchester, 2018).
Ormrod, W. Mark, and Mackman, Jonathan, 'Resident Aliens in Later Medieval England: Sources, Contexts, and Debates', in Mark Ormrod, Nicola McDonald, and Craig Taylor (eds), *Resident Aliens in Later Medieval England* (Turnhout, 2017), pp. 3–32.
Palmer, J. J. N., 'The Anglo-French Peace Negotiations, 1390–6', *Transactions of the Royal Historical Society*, 5th ser., 16 (1966), 81–94.
Palmer, J. J. N., 'The Background to Richard II's Marriage to Isabel of France (1396)', *Bulletin of the Institute of Historical Research*, 44 (1971), 1–17.
Penman, Michael A., *David II, 1329–71* (East Linton, 2004).
Philpotts, Christopher, 'The Fate of the Truce of Paris, 1396–1415', *Journal of Medieval History*, 24 (1998), 61–80.
Platt, Colin, *A Concise History of Jersey: A New Perspective* (St Helier, 2009).
Pocquet du Haut-Jussé, B.-A., *François II, Duc de Bretagne, et l'Angleterre (1458–1488)* (Paris, 1929).
Prestwich, Michael, *The Three Edwards: War and State in England, 1272–1377* (London: Weidenfeld and Nicolson, 1980).
Rodger, N. A. M., *The Safeguard of the Sea: A Naval History of Britain, 660–1649* (London, 1997).
Roskell, J. S., *The Impeachment of Michael de la Pole Earl of Suffolk in 1386 in the Context of the Reign of Richard II* (Manchester, 1984).
Ross, Charles, *Edward IV*, new edn (New Haven CT, 1997).
Ross, Charles, *Richard III*, new edn (New Haven CT, 1999).
Roth, Cecil, 'Perkin Warbeck and his Jewish Master', *Transactions of the Jewish Historical Society of England*, 9 (1918–20), 143–62.
Russell, Conrad, *The Causes of the English Civil War* (Oxford, 1990).
Russell, Conrad, *The Fall of the British Monarchies, 1637–1642* (Oxford, 1991).
Rybot, N. V. L., *Gorey Castle (Le Château Mont Orgueil): Official Guide Book* ([St Helier?], 1933).
Saul, N. E., 'The Fragments of the Golafre Brass in Westminster Abbey', *Transactions of the Monumental Brass Society*, 15i (1992), 19–32.
Saul, Nigel, *Richard II* (New Haven CT, 1997).
Saul, Nigel, *Death, Art, and Memory in Medieval England: The Cobham Family and their Monuments 1300–1500* (Oxford, 2001).
Saunders, A. C., *Jersey in the 17th Century, Containing a History of the Island before and during the Rebellion of 1642–60 and after the Restoration, 1660–1700* (Jersey, 1932).
Saunders, A. C., *Jersey in the 15th and 16th Centuries* (Jersey, 1933).
Saunders, A. C., *Jean Chevalier and his Times: A Story of Sir George Carteret, Baronet, and the Great Rebellion* (Jersey, 1937).

Scarisbrick, J. J., *Henry VIII* (London, 1968).
Schickler, Fernand de, *Les églises du refuge en Angleterre* (3 vols, Paris, 1892).
Scofield, Cora L., *The Life and Reign of Edward the Fourth. King of England and France and Lord of Ireland* (2 vols, London, 1923).
Strohm, Paul, *England's Empty Throne: Usurpation and the Language of Legitimation, 1399–1422* (New Haven CT, 1998).
Sumption, Jonathan, *The Hundred Years War* (5 vols, London, 1990–2023).
Sutherland, Donald W., *Quo Warranto Proceedings in the Reign of Edward I, 1278–1294* (Oxford, 1963).
Sutton, Anne F., 'England and Brittany 1482–86: Politics, Trade and War', *Nottingham Medieval Studies*, 62 (2018), 137–82.
Tarantino, G., 'Jacques de la Cloche: A Stuart Pretender in the Seventeenth Century', *Archivum Historicum Societatis Iesu*, 146 (2004), 425–41.
Thirsk, Joan, 'The Fantastical Folly of Fashion: The English Stocking Knitting Industry, 1500–1700', in N. B. Harte and K. G. Ponting (eds), *Textile History and Economic History* (Manchester, 1973), pp. 50–73.
Thornton, Tim, 'The English King's French Islands: Jersey and Guernsey in English Politics and Administration, 1485–1642', in George W. Bernard and Steven J. Gunn (eds), *Authority and Consent in Tudor England: Essays Presented to C. S. L. Davies* (Aldershot, 2002), pp. 197–217.
Thornton, Tim, 'Nationhood at the Margin: Identity, Regionality and the English Crown in the Seventeenth Century', in Len Scales and Oliver Zimmer (eds), *Power and the Nation in European History* (Cambridge, 2005), pp. 232–47.
Thornton, Tim, *The Channel Islands, 1370–1640: Between England and Normandy* (Woodbridge, 2012).
Thornton, Tim, 'Lordship and Sovereignty in the Territories of the English Crown: Sub-kingship and Its Implications, 1300–1600', *Journal of British Studies*, 60 (2021), 848–66.
Thrush, Andrew, and Ferris, John P. (eds), *The History of Parliament: The House of Commons, 1604–1629* (6 vols, Cambridge, 2010).
Tout, T. F., *Chapters in the Administrative History of Medieval England: The Wardrobe, the Chamber and the Small Seals* (6 vols, Manchester, 1920–33).
Tuck, Anthony, *Richard II and the English Nobility* (London, 1973).
Vernier, Richard, *The Flower of Chivalry: Bertrand Du Guesclin and the Hundred Years War* (Woodbridge, 2003).
Vickers, Kenneth Hotham, *Humphrey, Duke of Gloucester: A Biography* (London, 1907).
Watts, J. L., 'When did Henry VI's Minority End?' in Dorothy J. Clayton, Richard G. Davies, and Peter McNiven (eds), *Trade, Devotion and Governance: Papers in Later Medieval History* (Stroud, 1994), pp. 116–39.
Wernham, R. B., *Before the Armada: The Growth of English Foreign Policy 1485–1588* (London, 1966).
Wilkins, Christopher, *The Last Knight Errant: Edward Woodville and the Age of Chivalry* (London, 2009).
Williams, C. H., 'The Rebellion of Humphrey Stafford in 1486', *English Historical Review*, 63 (1928), 181–9.

Williams, Trevor, 'The Importance of the Channel Islands in British Relation [sic] with the Continent during the Thirteenth and Fourteenth Centuries: A Study in Historical Geography', *ABSJ*, 11 (1928–31), [xxxix–xl], 1–89.
Wolffe, B. P., *Henry VI* (London, 1981).
Worden, Blair, *The Rump Parliament, 1648–1653* (Cambridge, 1974).
Wylie, J. H., and Waugh, W. T., *The Reign of Henry V* (3 vols, Cambridge, 1914–29).

Unpublished dissertations

Evans, Helen Mary Elizabeth, 'The Religious History of Jersey, 1558–1640' (Unpublished Ph.D. thesis, University of Cambridge, 1991).
Lambe, Simon Edwardes John, 'The Paulet Family and the Gentry of Early Tudor Somerset, 1485–1547' (Unpublished Ph.D. thesis, University of Surrey, 2014).
Penman, Michael A., 'The Kingship of David II, 1329–71' (Unpublished Ph.D. thesis, University of St Andrews, 1999).

INDEX

Alderney   7, 11, 12, 13, 16, 21–2, 28, 43–4, 52–3, 64–5, 73–5, 79, 83, 96–8, 172
Aquitaine, duchy of   5, 14, 24
Arthur, prince of Wales   67, 77, 78
Asthorp, Sir William   14

bailiff of Jersey   111–16, 134–6, 154, 180–2, 209
Baker, Matthew   68, 69
Bandinel, David   168
Beauchamp, Anne   39
Beauchamp, Anne (Neville)   39
Beauchamp, Henry, earl of Warwick   39
Bedford, John, duke of   38
Béhuchet, Nicolas   7
Bertrand, Robert   7, 8
Bird, Sir William   145
Blount, Walter   51
Bouley Bay   90
Boulogne   90
Brampton, Sir Edward   59
Brétigny, treaty of   14, 31
Brittany   14, 16, 18, 25, 31, 59, 60, 61, 67, 68, 70, 78, 79, 222, 225, 230
Bruce, David (David II, king of Scotland)   7, 9
Bruges, treaty of   15

Calais   17, 18, 53, 77, 90, 101
Carbonnel, Jean   48
Castle Cornet   7, 8, 9, 10, 14, 143, 159, 169, 172
Catherine of Valois, queen consort of Henry V   31
Charles I, king of England, Scotland & Ireland   139–46, 151–7, 168
Charles II, king of England, Scotland & Ireland   159–72, 179–86
Charles IV, king of France   6
Charles VI, king of France   24, 25
Charles VII, king of France   49

Cherbourg   16, 38, 49 n.5
Cobham, John Lord   18, 19, 26
Cole, Laurence   199
Conway, Sir Edward   145
Cotentin   8, 10, 11, 16, 48
customs, *see* tolls, customs & other charges

d'Assigny, Pierre   168
David II, king of Scotland, *see* Bruce, David
de Brézé, Pierre   48, 49, 50
de Carbonnel, Jean   49, 50
de Calveley, Sir Hugh   15, 16, 18.
de Carteret family   48, 79, 168, 172
de Carteret, Edouard   67
de Carteret, Edouard   159
de Carteret, Elias   145
de Carteret, Sir George   168–9, 172, 196
de Carteret, Helier   79–80, 90
de Carteret, Sir Philippe (d. 1643)   145, 168–9
de Carteret, Sir Philippe (d. 1662)   159
de Carteret, Sir Philip (d. 1693)   187
de Carteret, Renaud   8, 10
de Ferrers, Thomas   8
de Golafre, Sir John   18
de Grandison, Otto   5, 6, 8
de Penhoët, Jean   25
de St Hilaire, Guillaume   8 n.9
de St Martin, Guillaume   48
de St Martin, Jean   14, 16
de St Martin, Richard   10
de St Martin, Thomas   67, 68, 69
de Rocquier, Peter   101
du Guesclin, Bertrand   14, 15
Dumaresq, Philippe   197

Edward I, king of England   5, 6
Edward II, king of England   6
Edward III, king of England   5–11, 12, 13, 14, 16, 17, 21–2, 24, 25, 28–9, 34–5, 43–4, 53, 64, 88

234 INDEX

Edward IV, king of England   47–54, 56–7, 61, 68, 69, 70, 73, 82, 84, 85, 88, 96, 97
Edward VI, king of England   85, 96–8, 124
Elizabeth I, queen regnant of England & Ireland   101–6, 111–16, 117, 139
Elizabeth of York, queen consort of Henry VII   78
Esplechin, truce of   9

Fanshawe, Lady Anne   169
fossage 54; *see also* tolls, customs & other charges
France   6, 7, 8, 10, 13, 14, 16, 24, 25, 31, 53, 59, 61, 67, 78, 80, 89–90, 101, 125, 126, 139, 143–4, 145–6
freedom of movement in time of war   99, 112, 113, 133–4, 153–4, 181, 208–9

Gardiner, Sir Robert   126
Gascony   7
Gloucester, Humphrey, duke of   38
Grosnez castle   14
Guernsey   6, 7, 8, 9, 10, 11, 12, 13, 14, 16, 17, 18, 19, 21–2, 25, 28, 31, 37, 38, 39, 43–4, 51, 52–3, 59, 61, 64–5, 68, 69, 73–5, 79, 83, 85, 90–1, 96–8, 104–5, 106, 117, 124, 139, 144, 145, 168, 169, 171–2, 197

Hampton, Thomas of   10
Harliston, Richard   50, 51–2, 60, 69, 70, 77, 85
Heane, Colonel James   169–70
Hely, William   199, 200
Henriettta Maria, queen consort of Charles I   144, 198
Henry IV, king of England   23–6, 28–9, 31, 32, 34–5, 37, 43–4, 53
Henry V, king of England   31–2, 34–5, 37, 43–4, 53
Henry VI, king of England   37–40, 43–4, 47, 53, 67, 85
Henry VII, king of England   59–60, 67, 68, 73–5, 77, 80, 82, 84, 85, 88, 96, 97
Henry VIII, king of England (& Ireland, from 1541)   77–80, 82–4, 85, 88, 89, 96, 98
Henry of Grosmont, duke of Lancaster   10

Hérault, Jean   125, 126
hidage, *see* tolls, customs & other charges
Huguenots   143–4, 168
Hussey, Dr James   126
Hutton, Thomas   60
Huwet, Walter   14
Hyde, Edward   169, 172, 198

Interregnum (Commonwealth & Protectorate, 1649–60)   159, 169–71
Isabella of France, queen consort of Edward II   6
Isabella of Valois, queen consort of Richard II   19

James I, king of England & Ireland (James VI, king of Scotland)   117–26, 132–7, 144
James II, king of England & Ireland (James VII, king of Scotland)   187–200, 206–12
Jermyn, Henry   197–8
Jermyn, Sir Thomas   197
Jermyn, Thomas   197–8, 199
jurats   111–16, 134–6, 154, 180–2, 209

Lanier, Sir John   198–9
le Cerf, Thomas   8
le Hardy, Clement   68
Lemprière, Michael   170
Lemprière, Raoul   10
Lemprière, Renaud   50, 77
Lemprière, Thomas   79, 80
Leulingham, truce of   18
Louis XI, king of France   48, 49, 50, 53, 60
Low Countries   9

mace   185, 212
Margaret of Anjou, queen consort of Henry VI   47, 48, 49, 52
Markele, Robert   18
Mary I, queen regnant of England   104
Maunsell, Thomas   61
Mont Orgueil Castle   7, 8, 14, 16, 49, 50, 51, 52, 53, 57, 61, 69, 70, 83, 85, 97, 98, 112, 125, 133, 152, 180, 207
Morise, Guillaume   106
murage 54; *see also* tolls, customs & other charges

Nanfan, John   47

Navigation Acts 171, 198
Neele, Jean 67–8
Nesfield, John 61
Neville, Richard, earl of Warwick 39, 47, 48, 51, 52, 61
Nicolle, Hostes 106
Nicolle, Jean 159
Normandy 5, 6, 8, 10, 18, 31, 32, 37, 38, 50, 79, 91, 101, 104, 105, 169
　duchy of 16, 50, 53, 79, 101, 106, 111, 115, 132, 151, 156, 179, 183, 206
　dukes of 111, 113, 115, 133, 152, 153, 155, 180, 207

Owain ap Thomas ap Rhodri (Owen of Wales) 14

pannage 54; *see also* tolls, customs & other charges
Paulet, Sir Amyas 106, 124
Paulet, Sir Anthony 124
Paulet, George 125
Paulet, Sir Hugh 105, 106
Payton, Sir John 125
Philip IV, king of France 5
Philip V, king of France 6
Philips, David 69
pontage 54; *see also* tolls, customs & other charges
Presbyterianism 124, 125, 144, 172
privileges & rights 12, 21–2, 28, 34–5, 43–5, 57, 64, 83, 96–7, 98, 112, 114, 132, 152, 154–5, 179–80, 182, 207, 209
Privy Council 212
Protestantism 90–1, 101, 104–6, 124, 172, 187

Ralegh, Sir Walter 124–5
Richard II, king of England 13–19, 20–1, 22, 23, 24, 26, 28–9, 32, 34–5, 37, 43–4, 53, 56, 61, 64, 73–5, 83, 85, 88
Richard III, king of England 58–61, 64–5, 68, 69, 70, 85
Rose, Sir Edmund 14
Rutland, Edward, earl of & duke of Aumale 18, 19, 24, 25, 26
Ryther, Henry 18

Sark 7, 11, 12, 16, 18, 21–2, 28, 43–4, 64–5, 73–5, 83, 90, 96–8, 172
Scotland 9, 89–90, 117, 125
Seymour, Edward, duke of Somerset 85, 88, 89, 98
Sluys 8, 9 n.14, 11
Stocall, Jacques 170
stocking industry 126, 170, 187

tallage 54
tolls, customs & other charges 22, 43–4, 56–7, 65, 73, 83, 97, 98, 99, 112–13, 133, 153, 180, 207–8, 212
trade 99; *see also* freedom of movement in time of war

Vaughan, Sir Hugh 77, 79

Warwick, Edward, earl of 69
Weston, Edmund 51, 68, 69, 77
Weston, Richard 77–8, 79
wheat 88, 99, 137, 144, 156, 184, 211
Woodville, Anthony 51, 61
wool 88, 99, 117, 124, 126, 137, 156, 169–70, 184, 199, 211